THIRD EDITION

Suzanne LoPorto

Student Success in College

Tom Peterson

DOING WHAT WORKS!

CHRISTINE HARRINGTON

Center for Student Success at the
New Jersey Council of County Colleges

Middlesex County College

Aknenaton Images/Shutterstock.com

CENGAGE

Australia • Brazil • Mexico • Singapore • United Kingdom • United States

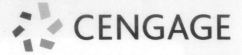

Student Success in College: Doing What Works!
Third Edition
Christine Harrington

Product Director: Lauren Murphy

Product Manager: Sarah Seymour

Content Developer: Courtney Triola

Product Assistant: Emily Wiener

Marketing Manager: Allison Moghaddasi

Senior Content Project Manager: Margaret Park Bridges

Manufacturing Planner: Beverly Breslin

IP Analyst: Ann Hoffman

Senior IP Project Manager: Kathryn Kucharek

Production Service: Lumina Datamatics

Compositor: Lumina Datamatics

Art Director: Diana Graham

Text Designer: Delgado and Company

Cover Designer: Diana Graham

Cover Image: Akhenaton Images/ Shutterstock.com, iStock.com/Rawpixel

For product information and technology assistance, contact us at
Cengage Customer & Sales Support, 1-800-354-9706.

For permission to use material from this text or product,
submit all requests online at **www.cengage.com/permissions.**
Further permissions questions can be emailed to
permissionrequest@cengage.com.

Library of Congress Control Number: 2017944246

Student Edition:
ISBN: 978-1-337-40613-0

Loose-leaf Edition:
ISBN: 978-1-337-40623-9

Cengage
20 Channel Center Street
Boston, MA 02210
USA

Cengage is a leading provider of customized learning solutions with employees residing in nearly 40 different countries and sales in more than 125 countries around the world. Find your local representative at **www.cengage.com.**

Cengage products are represented in Canada by Nelson Education, Ltd

To learn more about Cengage platforms and services, visit **www.cengage.com.**

Purchase any of our products at your local college store or at our preferred online store **www.cengagebrain.com.**

Printed in the United States of America
Print Number: 01   Print Year: 2017

Brief Contents

Contents

PART 2 | Strategies and Skills for Success   73

PART 3   Being Successful: Plans and Perseverance   165

Exploring the Research in Summary

Preface

What Makes Student Success in College: Doing What Works! Unique?

An Academically Rigorous, Research-Based Approach

- Research-Based Strategies
- Original Research Studies: Students Learn How to Read Scholarly Sources

Just Seven Chapters Allows for Meaningful Exploration of Success Strategies

- More Time to Dive Deep into the Content
- Build Essential Information Literacy and Critical Thinking Skills

A Guided Pathways Framework That Helps Students Choose a Career Pathway

- Extensive Coverage of Career Theories and Exploration Process
- Academic, Financial, and Career Planning

ABOUT THE AUTHOR

Dr. Christine Harrington is serving as the executive director of the New Jersey Center for Student Success at the New Jersey Council of County Colleges on a two-year term. In this position, she uses a guided pathways framework to increase successful experiences and outcomes at all 19 community colleges in New Jersey. Previously, Dr. Harrington has worked at Middlesex County College for 16 years as a professor of psychology, student success course coordinator, director of the Center for the Enrichment of Learning and Teaching, counselor, and disability service provider. Dr. Harrington was the 2016 recipient of the Excellence in Teaching First-Year Seminars award that was presented at the annual First-Year Experience conference. She also teaches graduate courses on teaching and learning at Rutgers University. Dr. Harrington frequently shares her expertise and passion about teaching, learning, and student success at national and local conferences as well as at colleges and universities across the United States. She is also the author of *Dynamic Lecturing: Research-based Strategies to Enhance Lecture Effectiveness.*

Tom Peterson

ACKNOWLEDGMENTS

I am beyond grateful to my family, colleagues, students, and my amazing team at Cengage. Writing this book would not be possible without the never-ending support and encouragement provided by my husband, Dan, and two sons, Ryan and David. I'd also like to thank my mom, dad, mother-in-law, and niece Ashley for always being there for me and supporting me every step of the way.

I would also like to thank my many FYE colleagues across the nation for sharing their endless passion and ideas about how to best help students achieve their goals. I am particularly thankful for the collaborative partnerships with my colleagues at the New Jersey Council of County Colleges and across the state, the New Jersey Department of Labor and Workforce Development, the Office of the Secretary of Higher Education, and the Department of Education. It is a true pleasure working with such wonderful colleagues across the state, my fellow executive directors in other states with Centers for Student Success, and national partners such as Jobs for the Future who are so committed to student success.

Thanks to Tom Peterson and Suzanne LoPorto for their incredible photographs in this text, and to the many students who appear in them. I would also like to thank Ryan Harrington and Aditya Shah for developing the index.

My students have always been, and will continue to be, a source of inspiration, but it is difficult to describe the positive feeling I experience when students share how this book has helped them achieve their goals. I am tremendously grateful for the positive feedback about the book as well as their suggestions about how to improve it. I am also thankful to the many reviewers whose feedback was incredibly valuable and helped strengthen this text.

Andrii Kondiuk/Shutterstock.com

An Academically Rigorous, Research-Based Approach

- **Research-Based Strategies**

  - Moving beyond advice, *Student Success in College: Doing What Works!* provides students with research-based strategies so that they can "Do What Works!" and successfully achieve their goals.

  - There are nearly 400 references, most from original research studies.

- **Exploring the Research in Summary**
  - Every chapter begins with a summary of a research study on a related chapter topic.
  - This research article serves as a visual reminder that the strategies shared are based on research.
  - Research article summaries can also be a great way to engage students with the chapter content.

- **Learning How to Read and Use Peer-Reviewed Research**
  - In Chapter 1, students will learn about peer-reviewed research, the different parts or elements of research studies, and how professionals read peer-reviewed research so that students feel confident in their ability to use and apply research.

- **Original Research Studies: Exploring the Research in Depth**

  In the appendix, students will find numerous original research studies. Prior to each study, students will be guided through a four-step process:
  - Engaging via prediction
  - Reading for key points
  - Critically thinking about the research
  - Building information literacy skills

Just Seven Chapters Allows for Meaningful Exploration of Success Strategies

- **No Need to Rush**
  - Instead of rushing through a chapter or more each week during a 15- to 16-week term, instructors can spend up to two weeks on each chapter.
  - In a seven- to eight-week term, instructors can still spend a full week on each chapter.
  - Research shows that learning is more likely when we really engage with the content, which is achievable with the seven-chapter approach used in *Student Success in College: Doing What Works!*

iStock.com/papparaffie

- **In-Depth Coverage of Content**
  - Rather than bringing just surface-level coverage of every possible success topic, the seven-chapter approach in *Student Success in College: Doing What Works!* allows instructors and students to deeply explore the most essential success strategies:
    - Chapter 1: Value of education, decision-making, information literacy, and critical thinking
    - Chapter 2: Goals and career exploration
    - Chapter 3: Academic skills: Memory, reading, note-taking, and study strategies
    - Chapter 4: Soft skills: Professionalism, time and project management, interpersonal skills, and leadership
    - Chapter 5: Academic integrity, papers, presentations, and tests
    - Chapter 6: Academic, career, and financial planning
    - Chapter 7: Reflecting on progress, staying motivated, managing stress, and being resilient and developing grit

- Flexibility
  - Having only seven chapters allows time for instructors and students to introduce other topics, especially institution-specific content, that are deemed important without sacrificing learning of key success strategies.

- Increased Opportunity for Critical Thinking and Information Literacy
  - There's more time to deeply explore the research on success strategies using the original studies provided at the end of the book or students can search the library databases for additional research on topics of interest.

A Guided Pathways Framework That Helps Students Choose a Career Pathway

Shutter_M/Shutterstock.com

- Setting Effective Career and Academic Goals Using the ABCS Goal-Setting Framework
  - A research-based alternative to SMART goals, the ABCS approach to goal setting helps students set and monitor progress toward goals.
    - Aim high
    - Believe in yourself
    - Care and commit
    - Specify and self-reflect

- Mapping Your Path to Success: Academic, Financial, and Career Plans
  - While engaging in self-assessment and finding career information are important parts of the career planning process, *Student Success in College: Doing What Works!* goes above and beyond, bringing theory and research related to the career exploration process into practice. For example, students also learn how to:
    - Expand and strengthen their network
    - Create a professional presence
    - Choose courses and academic experiences that help them achieve their goal in a timely fashion
    - Understand the long-term financial implications of their choices today
    - Develop the following soft skills that are needed in most, if not all, careers: professionalism, time and project management, interpersonal skills, and leadership skills

- Staying on Track
  - Recognizing that life can sometimes get us off track, *Student Success in College: Doing What Works!* focuses on how to reflect on progress and make changes as needed, stay motivated, manage stress, be resilient, and develop grit.

How This Text Benefits Students

Choose a career pathway and related major

- Learn about ways to set goals, drive decision-making, and choose a path.
- Create an academic and career plan and get on track to a successful future early.

Practice success strategies

- Discover and practice key strategies that will be useful to get a degree, land a position aligned to your interests, and advance in your career.
- Use the end-of-chapter note-taking methods to focus on most important concepts and learn success strategies.
- Hone numerous soft skills that transfer to work, school, and life.
- Test knowledge with Quick Quizzes as a powerful way to study and learn.
- Author and student videos in MindTap help improve reading comprehension.
- Build information literacy skills by learning how to read and analyze peer-reviewed research articles and determine credible sources.
- Build critical thinking skills to use in conversation, courses, and meetings.

Monitor your progress

- With MindTap, easily see grades and track progress over the term.
- Assignments and assessments build knowledge and help you determine how well you are learning the course content.

How This Text Benefits Instructors

Keep students engaged in class and online with author-created resources

- The Instructor Manual contains assignments, in-person activities, and online discussion boards that align to learning outcomes.
- Visually effective PowerPoint slides can be modified to fit your needs.
- Multimedia integration and customizability of MindTap offer endless possibilities for enriching learning with informative and engaging activities.

Test student knowledge

- A robust test bank of 100 questions for each chapter can be used within MindTap, your LMS, or be printed for in-class use.
- Quick Quizzes are placed throughout the text.

Track student progress

- The MindTap Progress App, or gradebook, offers tools to track student progress on assignments, grade activities, and map student engagement in the course.
- Offers individualized support to students based on their assessment results and engagement level.

Train faculty to achieve course learning outcomes

- Recognizing faculty development needs, Student Success in College: Doing What Works! comes with numerous teaching demonstration videos that can be used to train new faculty.
- Sample syllabi can be customized to match course goals.

What's New in the Third Edition?

- Improved organization and flow focuses first on helping students with determining their path to success, then building skills and strategies for success, and finally on developing plans and perseverance
- Revised organization aligned to guided pathways
- Increased career, academic, and financial planning coverage
- New chapter on soft skills
  - Professionalism
  - Time and project management
  - Interpersonal skills including communication, conflict management, emotional intelligence, teamwork and collaboration, and diversity and cultural competence
  - Leadership
- Increased focus on information literacy
- More Quick Quizzes to maximize student learning via the testing effect
- Updated research—Over 125 new references, mostly from original research studies
- Each chapter now begins with the Exploring the Research in Summary feature, keeping the research behind the strategies front and center for students
- Exploring the Research in Depth articles have been moved to an appendix, so they're centrally located and improve the flow within each chapter
- MindTap for *Student Success in College: Doing What Works!* has additional enhancements
  - Activities, known as Time for Actions in the previous edition, are now exclusively in MindTap to provide a consistent experience for students, who can then save and print their responses
  - Assessments have been digitized and moved exclusively into MindTap for ease of scoring and interpretation
  - An instructor resource center has been added, which includes content such as additional videos

Side-by-Side Comparison of Second and Third Editions

Second Edition	Third Edition
	Introduction: Getting Started • College Expectations: Getting a Strong Start (moved from Chapter 1 plus new content on campus and community resources) • Value of the First-Year Seminar Course (moved from Chapter 1; 7 Smart Success Strategies now called Success Strategies at a Glance)
Chapter 1: College Expectations: Being a Critical Thinker • You've Made the Right Decision (still in Chapter 1) • Faculty Expectations (moved to Introduction) • Critical Thinking (still in Chapter 1) • Active Reading (moved to Chapter 3) • Peer-Reviewed Journal Articles (still in Chapter 1)	Chapter 1: Discovering the Value of Education and Sharpening Key Thinking Skills • Value of College Education (new focus on purpose and societal value) • Decision-Making (moved from Chapter 7) • Information Literacy (new section with some content from Chapter 4; includes Peer-Reviewed Journal Articles) • Critical Thinking
Chapter 2: Skills You Need: Memory, Note-Taking, and Studying Techniques • How Memory Works (moved to Chapter 3) • Note-Taking: Our Only Hope (moved to Chapter 3) • Studying Approaches That Work (moved to Chapter 3)	Chapter 2: Setting Goals and Choosing a Career Path • Setting Goals (moved from Chapter 3) • Career Exploration and Decision-Making (moved from Chapter 7 with new content on career indecision and how we make career decisions)
Chapter 3: Setting Effective Goals and Making the Most of Your Time • Power of Long- and Short-Term Goals (moved to Chapter 2) • The ABCS of Setting and Implementing Effective Goals (moved to Chapter 2) • Celebrating Progress and Achievement (moved to Chapter 7) • Time Management (moved to Chapter 4) • Organizational Tools (moved to Chapter 4) • Avoid Multitasking: Single-Task It! (moved to Chapter 4)	Chapter 3: Building Academic Skills • How Memory Works (moved from Chapter 2) • Active Reading Strategies (moved from Chapter 1 plus new content on prior knowledge) • Note-Taking (moved from Chapter 2) • Study Strategies (moved from Chapter 2 plus an increased focus on teaching to learn)
Chapter 4: It's Show Time: Papers, Presentations, and Tests • Academic Integrity (moved to Chapter 5) • Papers and Presentations (moved to Chapter 5) • Test-Taking Strategies (moved to Chapter 5) • Group Projects (still in Chapter 4)	Chapter 4: Strengthening Soft Skills • New chapter • What Are Soft Skills? (new content) • Professionalism (new content) • Time and Project Management (moved from Chapter 3 plus new content) • Interpersonal Skills (moved from Chapter 4 plus new content on communication, conflict management, teamwork and collaboration, and diversity and cultural competence) • Leadership (new content)

Second Edition	Third Edition
Chapter 5: Motivation, Resilience, and Stress Management: Strategies for When College and Life Get Challenging • Motivation (moved to Chapter 7) • Resilience (moved to Chapter 7) • Stress Management (moved to Chapter 7)	**Chapter 5: Demonstrating Knowledge and Skills** • Purpose of Academic Tasks (new content) • Academic Integrity (moved from Chapters 1 and 4) • Papers and Presentations (moved from Chapter 4) • Tests (moved from Chapter 4)
Chapter 6: How Are You Doing? Maximizing Learning via Self-Reflection • The Academic Self-Regulation Process (moved to Chapter 7) • The Accuracy of Self-Assessments (moved to Chapter 7) • Making Mistakes: The Role of Attribution Theory (moved to Chapter 7) • Self-Reflection Techniques (moved to chapter 7)	**Chapter 6: Mapping Your Path to Success: Plans and Action Steps** • Creating an Academic Plan (moved from Chapter 7 plus new content on double majors and connecting with your advisor) • Career Planning: Discovering the Power of Networking (new content on networking, elevator speech, expanding and strengthening your network and job search tips; plus creating a professional presence content moved from Chapter 7) • Financial Planning (new content on financing your education, return on investment, and financial planning and budgeting; plus establishing good credit moved from Chapter 7)
Chapter 7: Making Good Academic, Career, and Financial Decisions • The Decision-Making Process (moved to Chapter 1) • Academic Options (moved to Chapter 6) • Career Decision-Making (moved to Chapter 2) • Financial Decisions (moved to Chapter 6)	**Chapter 7: Staying on Track and Celebrating Success** • Reflecting on Progress (moved from Chapter 6) • Staying Motivated (moved from Chapter 5) • Managing Stress (moved from Chapter 5) • Being Resilient and Developing Grit (moved from Chapter 5 plus new content on grit) • Celebrating Success (moved from Chapter 3)

	Research in Depth Appendix
	• Research in Depth articles moved to an appendix at the end of the text
	• New Research Articles:
	  • Travis, T. (2011). From the classroom to the boardroom: The impact of information literacy instruction on workplace research skills. *Education Libraries*, *34*(2), 19–31. Retrieved from ERIC database.
	  • Deepa, S., & Seth, M. (2013). Do soft skills matter? Implications for educators based on recruiters' perspective. *IUP Journal of Soft Skills*, *7*(1), 7–20. Retrieved from Business Source Elite.
	  • Oliver, J., & Kowalczyk, C. (2013). Improving student group marketing presentations: A modified Pecha Kucha approach. *Marketing Education Review*, *23*(1), 55–58. doi:10.2753/MER1052-8008230109

Tom Peterson

PART 1

DETERMINING YOUR PATH TO SUCCESS:

Introduction: Getting Started

1. What are some of the differences between high school and college?

2. Why is the syllabus so important?

3. How can you find out what resources are available to you as a college student?

4. What does the research say about the first-year seminar course?

5. Why is it important to learn about research-based success strategies?

College Expectations: Getting a Strong Start

Tom Peterson

Learning about what is expected of college students, the differences between high school and college, and the importance of resources such as the syllabus will help you get off to the right start in college. As you know, college is quite different than high school. For starters, the schedule is significantly different, with some courses meeting only once or twice per week and classes often being longer in duration. A typical full-time college student is in class only for approximately 15–20 hours per week. However, college students are expected to engage in significant learning outside of the classroom. Most student success professionals and faculty recommend spending approximately 2–3 hours outside of class learning and studying for every hour you spend in class. Thus, if you are a full-time college student, a general rule of thumb is to plan to spend at least 30 hours per week engaged in studying behaviors outside of class. Keep in mind that the actual time needed for studying may vary from student to student and perhaps even from semester to semester based on factors such as how much you already know about a subject, the difficulty of the subject, and the nature of the assignments and tasks.

In college, you will have the opportunity to deeply engage with the content and complete tasks that will help you further develop high-level skills such as critical thinking. Take full advantage of these learning opportunities by:

- Taking time to fully understand what is expected of you
- Using research-based success strategies
- Putting high levels of effort into these tasks
- Knowing what resources are available to you and using these resources as needed

The Syllabus

The syllabus is an important resource that will help you understand what is expected of you (see Sample Syllabus Figure). The syllabus is typically posted in the course's learning management system or distributed on the first day of class. It provides you with an overview of the course, including a course description, contact information for your professor, resources you'll need, and the course learning outcomes. Learning outcomes are what your professors expect you to be able to know, think, or do as a result of taking the course. The learning outcomes are incredibly important because they capture the purpose of the course. When you look at your course learning outcomes, you'll discover that your professors are going to expect you to do much more than just memorize information; you will also need to think critically about different disciplines and create a variety of high-level academic products. Focusing on what you will be learning will help you meet with success.

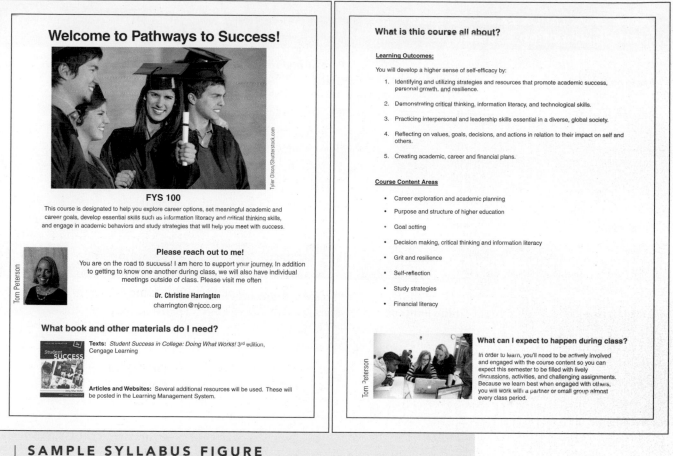

Welcome to Pathways to Success!

FYS 100

This course is designated to help you explore career options, set meaningful academic and career goals, develop essential skills such as information literacy and critical thinking skills, and engage in academic behaviors and study strategies that will help you meet with success.

Please reach out to me!

You are on the road to success! I am here to support your journey. In addition to getting to know one another during class, we will also have individual meetings outside of class. Please visit me often

Dr. Christine Harrington
charrington@njccc.org

What book and other materials do I need?

Texts: *Student Success in College: Doing What Works!* 3rd edition, Cengage Learning

Articles and Websites: Several additional resources will be used. These will be posted in the Learning Management System.

What is this course all about?

Learning Outcomes:

You will develop a higher sense of self-efficacy by:

1. Identifying and utilizing strategies and resources that promote academic success, personal growth, and resilience.

2. Demonstrating critical thinking, information literacy, and technological skills.

3. Practicing interpersonal and leadership skills essential in a diverse, global society.

4. Reflecting on values, goals, decisions, and actions in relation to their impact on self and others.

5. Creating academic, career and financial plans.

Course Content Areas

- Career exploration and academic planning
- Purpose and structure of higher education
- Goal setting
- Decision making, critical thinking and information literacy
- Grit and resilience
- Self-reflection
- Study strategies
- Financial literacy

What can I expect to happen during class?

In order to learn, you'll need to be actively involved and engaged with the course content so you can expect this semester to be filled with lively discussions, activities, and challenging assignments. Because we learn best when engaged with others, you will work with a partner or small group almost every class period.

Tyler Olson/Shutterstock.com

Tom Peterson

SAMPLE SYLLABUS FIGURE
EXAMPLE OF A COURSE SYLLABUS

The syllabus also contains information about assignments and learning activities. Completing these tasks will help you achieve the course learning goals. To help you better understand expectations for assignments, your professors will often include detailed information about the assignment or rubrics in the syllabus. Rubrics are tools used to provide students with specific information about expectations related to the assignment, showing what you will need to do in order to earn a high grade and successfully accomplish the task. Rubrics are also used by professors during the grading process.

The syllabus will also provide you with information about how much each assignment counts toward the final grade. This refers to weighting. Different assignments are often weighted differently. For example, exams are typically weighted more heavily than quizzes, meaning exams count more than quizzes toward your final grade. To calculate your final grade, you will need to know the weighting for each category of assignments (i.e., quizzes, lab reports, exams, etc.) and how many of each type of assignment you will need to do throughout the semester. Many learning management systems automatically calculate your grade, but if this is not the case, you can use a grade calculator app for this purpose. Take a look at Grade Calculation Examples Table to see how weighting can impact your final grade.

Another key feature of the syllabus is the course outline; the course outline will provide you with a calendar for the course. It will include information about when topics will be addressed and due dates for assignments. As soon as you get copies

GRADE CALCULATION EXAMPLES TABLE
Grade Calculation Example 1

Assignment	Grade Earned	Percentage toward Final Grade	
Research paper	90	60	
Quizzes	70 70 70 70	10	Final Grade in Course: 87% B+
Final exam	86	30	

Grade Calculation Example 2

Assignment	Grade Earned	Percentage toward Final Grade	
Research paper	90	15	
Quizzes	70 70 70 70	45	Final Grade in Course: 79% C+
Final exam	86	40	

This table provides two grade calculation examples, demonstrating how the weighting of different assignment types results in different final grades.

of all of your syllabi, transfer the course calendar information, especially due dates, into a master calendar that you will use throughout the semester. Having important due dates on your calendar will help you keep track of what you need to do each week. The next step is planning when you will work on the assignments. In other words, schedule time to work on these activities in your calendar. Planning will help you complete assignments on schedule. The importance of the syllabus cannot be overstated—be sure to keep your syllabi in a safe place and regularly refer to them to stay on top of course requirements.

THE SYLLABUS: INFORMATION YOU NEED

- Overview of the course—course description, professor contact information, resources needed
- Learning outcomes—what you will learn
- Assignment and grading information
- Course outline and due dates

Campus and Community Resources

As you begin your first semester, it is important to know about the resources that are available to you as a college student. Successful individuals reach out for help when needed and it will be easier for you to reach out for assistance if you know about the different types of support services available on your campus. Check out your college website or ask your professor to learn about the various offices and departments on campus that can support you during college. For example, most colleges and universities offer a variety of support with academic tasks. Professional or peer tutors are typically available as are librarians and your college professors when you need assistance with completing academic assignments. Academic advisors and career counselors are available to help you develop an academic and career plan and develop networking skills. If you are struggling with personal issues, many colleges and universities offer confidential counseling on campus or can refer you to services in the local community. There are also a variety of specialized services such as Disability Services, Veteran Services, and Minority Student Affairs Services. If you are living on campus, you will also have access to a resident advisor who can help you find the support you are looking for. If you are a first-generation college student, it may be particularly important for you to connect with campus supports. By doing so, you can more quickly learn about how to transition to college effectively and develop a support system that will help you with this process.

Tom Peterson

During the first few weeks of college, investigate what services exist on your campus or in your local community. In addition to learning about the services provided, it is helpful to know where the services are located and their hours of operation. Knowing this information early on in the semester will make it easier for you to take advantage of these resources when needed.

Value of the First-Year Seminar Course

Research has consistently indicated that first-year seminar courses contribute to student success in college (Boudreau & Kromrey, 1994; Derby & Smith, 2004; Potts & Shultz, 2008). Studies have shown that this course is beneficial for students of all ability levels (Howard, 2000; Miller, Janz, & Chen, 2007). For example, researchers have found that students who took a first-year seminar course had higher grades and earned more credits early on, as compared to those who did not take the first-year seminar course, and that these academic advantages were long-lasting (Karp, Raufman, Efthimiou, & Ritze, 2015). Based on a review of research studies investigating the effectiveness of first-year seminars, Jaijairam (2016) noted the following benefits of the course:

Tom Peterson

- Better grades
- More likely to graduate on schedule

- More likely to reflect on academic performance and progress
- More likely to think critically
- More likely to participate in class
- Increased self-confidence
- Better sense of career options

Given this long list of benefits, it is not surprising that most colleges offer this type of course and many even require it. In fact, in a national survey, approximately 90% of the colleges that responded indicated that they offered a first-year seminar course at their institutions (Young & Hopp, 2014). The first-year seminar course helps students transition successfully to college.

As you are getting ready to embark on this challenging, yet exciting, journey called college, think about the topic of this text for a moment: student success. You probably already have an opinion about why some students are successful in college while others are not. Others do, too. You could walk up to 10 different people on the street and ask them what it takes to be successful in college, and you'll probably get 10 different answers. Our views, and personal advice, are often based on individual experiences. Unfortunately, just because a technique worked for someone else doesn't mean it will work for you. Research, on the other hand, is more powerful than advice. Information gathered from thousands of students makes it more likely that the techniques shown to be effective will also work for you. In other words, findings from research are typically more accurate and meaningful than advice from one person.

This text takes you beyond advice and into the science of success. It is filled with research-based information to help you succeed. In addition to learning about topics such as time management, goal setting, motivation, and study strategies, you will also learn about how to read and extract key information from scholarly sources such as peer-reviewed journal articles. Although this activity can definitely be a challenging one for new students, learning this skill early will serve you well in college. College professors will expect you to be able to read and use scholarly sources in your work, but there is often not much, if any, class time devoted to teaching you how to read research articles and extract the key information. This text will teach you strategies for reading these challenging articles, give you practice at summarizing the key points, and prompt you to think critically about the findings and their value. You will also build your information literacy skills by searching library databases to find additional research on student success topics. After this course, you'll be ready to include information from these sources in your papers and presentations, which will help you create successful academic products for your other classes.

WHY LEARNING ABOUT RESEARCH-BASED SUCCESS STRATEGIES IS IMPORTANT

- Sometimes well-intentioned advice is not accurate and therefore won't support your success.
- Research findings are often based on hundreds or thousands of students, making it more likely that the results will apply to you.

- Because researchers often carefully control and assess for many factors, it is more likely that the results are accurate.

- As you are learning about strategies that work, you are also increasing your skills related to being able to read and use scholarly sources. You will be able to use this new skill set as you prepare for papers and presentations in your other classes.

- Research-based student success studies will help you build your reading, critical thinking, and information literacy skills.

- Using strategies that really work will help you achieve your academic goals.

Taking this course will give you the skills and confidence you need to reach your goal. Specifically, you will learn that a variety of factors, such as using supports and resources, being motivated, making good decisions, managing time well, setting goals, thinking positively, and using effective study strategies, have been found to be connected to academic success (DeBerard, Speilmans, & Julka, 2004; Johnson, 1997; Lammers, Onwuegbuzie, & State, 2001; Murray & Wren, 2003). More good news—these factors are within your control. Once you are armed with solid, accurate information about how these factors contribute to success, you will be able to use this information to achieve your goals. In essence, you will be ready to "Do What Works!" Let's start by checking your current knowledge about what works.

Student Success Myths or Facts? Test Your Knowledge!

Myth or Fact? Decide whether you believe the following statements are true or false.

1. Because the world is an ever-changing place, memorizing information is not that important.

2. Highlighting is one of the most effective reading strategies.

3. Reading skills are the best predictor of how well you will comprehend what you read.

4. Students who study alone are more productive and learn more than students who study with others.

5. The best way to study is to review and reread your notes.

6. Students today are much better at multitasking.

7. When taking a multiple-choice test, it is always best to "go with your gut" and stick with your first answer.

8. Professors expect you to use numerous quotations in your research papers.

9. Students are generally pretty accurate when predicting their grades in a course.

10. Being focused on grades will help you learn a lot and achieve at high levels.

Gordana Simic/Shutterstock.com

Some of the information you learn from this text and your course will not be new to you—you have after all been a student for a long time. However, you might be surprised to find that you are using strategies that are only minimally effective. In fact, all of the Myth or Fact statements are false. For a sneak peek at strategies that work, check out the Success Strategies at a Glance for each chapter.

Success Strategies at a Glance

There's something magical about the number seven. It's not just lucky; it's a number that researchers have found to be most productive in terms of memory. This is why there are seven chapters in this text. Findings from a famous psychological study tell us that seven chunks of information are what work best naturally within our memory systems (Miller, 1956). We've put this research into practice, using it to shape the organization of the text.

There's a lot to learn and do in this course. This introductory section is designed to get you on your way. It provides an overall organizational structure to guide you at the start of the semester and will continue to be a great reference tool throughout the entire semester. Before you start reading the first chapter, take a few moments to get familiar with this text to see how it can be helpful to you. This brief, powerful preview activity will familiarize you with the key concepts you need to know as you begin your college journey. Here's a great way to become familiar with the key success strategies:

- Flip through the Success Strategies at a Glance pages that highlight research-supported success strategies for each chapter.

- Write down strategies that you are already using. Think about how these strategies will help you in college.

- Identify at least three strategies you would like to learn more about. Go to their corresponding chapter, find the section that describes the strategy, and learn about the strategy.

- Choose at least one strategy that you can start using and try it out!

Success Strategies at a Glance

Chapter 1 • Discovering the Value of Education and Sharpening Key Thinking Skills

1 **Focus on the purpose and value of getting an education.**

Knowing why a college education matters can motivate you. Focus on the purpose and benefits of a college education. College is not just about preparing you for a career; college also prepares you for life and helps you become a productive, contributing member of society.

2 **Practice good decision-making skills.**

Good decisions don't happen by accident. Good decisions happen by engaging in a thoughtful process that includes keeping your goals visible, gathering important information, and exploring and evaluating your options. Assessing whether your decision resulted in a positive outcome is also important.

3 **Improve your information literacy skills.**

Being able to determine what information you need, how to find that information, and then evaluate information is an important skill in college and careers. In the academic world, information literacy skills will help you successfully complete assignments. In many careers, you will also need information in order to make good decisions and complete projects.

4 **Evaluate credibility of websites and other sources of information.**

One of the biggest information literacy challenges is being able to determine whether the information you find or come across has value. You can use the CRAAP test, which was developed by librarians, to help you determine if the information is credible. This involves evaluating currency, relevance, authority, accuracy, and purpose.

5 **Get confident reading and using scholarly sources.**

College-level work requires you to use more sophisticated information sources. Professors want you to back your opinion up with data and research. Learn how to access library databases, and understand and apply information you find in peer-reviewed journals. With the help of your professor, you will gain skills and confidence in this area by reading and using the research in this text.

6 **Build your foundational knowledge.**

Having a strong foundational knowledge base is important. As described in Bloom's taxonomy, remembering key information is a first and necessary step before being able to engage in high-level tasks. Learn research-based study strategies that will help you build foundational knowledge.

7 **Learn how to be a critical thinker.**

Your professors expect you to engage in high-level cognitive tasks. Discover what actions you can take to think critically. Learn about the importance of developing a strong knowledge base, believing in yourself, and being motivated. Embrace the challenges you'll encounter in college and use available support to help you succeed.

Chapter 2 • Setting Goals and Choosing a Career Path

1

Establish short- and long-term goals.

Students who set goals are more likely to succeed. Long-term goals are valuable because they help you focus on the big picture, emphasizing your values and priorities. Short-term goals pave the way for success because they make it easier for you to monitor your progress toward your long-term goals.

2

Challenge yourself by setting high goals.

Research has shown that we are most likely to achieve at high levels when we set high goals. Thus, it is important to challenge yourself and set goals that will help you to achieve at high levels.

3

Use the ABCS approach to goal setting.

Aim high—research shows that students who have challenging goals are more likely to succeed. Believe in yourself—if you believe you can successfully achieve your goal, you'll be more likely to continue working toward your goal even if you experience setbacks. Care and commit—students who care about their goals and are committed to achieving them are more likely to have successful outcomes. Specify and self-reflect—having specific goals makes it easier to monitor your progress and the self-reflection process allows you to make adjustments as needed so that you stay on track toward your goals.

4

Recognize the importance of engaging in active career exploration.

Deciding on a career path can be a challenging task. Unfortunately, many students choose a path without first engaging in significant exploration activities. Exploring before deciding will help you make a better decision.

5

Reach out for assistance with career decision-making as needed.

There are many resources available to students that are focused on helping them find and evaluate the information needed to make important career decisions. Seeking out guidance can be especially helpful if you are still exploring options, but it can also help you further explore your field of interest if you have selected a career pathway.

6

Engage in self-assessment activities to make better career decisions.

Reflecting on your values is an important first step in the career exploration process. Considering your skills, interests, and personality style will help you make good career decisions. Meeting with a career counselor is recommended.

7

Check out career websites and conduct informational interviews.

In addition to learning about yourself, learn about various careers. Informative websites, such as the Occupational Outlook Handbook, give you a good overview of many careers. Informational interviews allow you to get a more personal view of careers and can help you build your professional network.

Success Strategies at a Glance

Chapter 3 • Building Academic Skills

1 **Learn how memory works.**

Knowing how memory works helps you make the most out of your study time. The goal is getting the information you are learning into your long-term memory so that it is available when you need it. Elaboration or identifying examples are strategies you can use to strengthen memories.

2 **Actively read your textbook—try the 3R and SQ3R techniques.**

To make the most of your reading time, engage in the 3R (Read-Recite-Review) technique or the SQ3R (Survey-Question-Read-Recite-Review) technique. Both approaches focus on you using your own words to summarize what you've read and have you interact with the text several times (read, recite, review). The SQ3R technique adds two additional steps: surveying or previewing the chapter and developing questions to answer before reading. Taking notes while reading further increases learning.

3 **Be prepared so that you can actively participate.**

Completing reading and written assignments prior to class gives you the background information you need so that you can be an active participant. Being active and engaged in class not only assists you with learning the material but also sends the message that you are serious about being successful.

4 **Use a note-taking method that works.**

Taking notes ensures you will have the information you need when it is time to study. Explore the various note-taking methods, such as the Cornell Method, concept maps, outlines, matrixes, and digital notes. Choose a method that works for you during class and then be sure to use a method that focuses on organization of content such as the matrix or concept map after class. By using the organizing strategies within these methods, you will increase your understanding of the content.

5 **Use a multisensory approach.**

We are all multisensory learners, which means that we learn best when we use several senses to take in information. Visuals are particularly powerful, so pay attention to charts, graphs, and images.

6 **Test yourself regularly and chunk information when studying.**

Research has shown that recalling information helps us learn. Take advantage of practice tests in your texts or on the textbook publisher's website, or you can create your own. Practice tests allow you to learn from your mistakes while not negatively impacting your grade in the course. When studying, find connections between concepts to maximize learning. Research has consistently shown that students who use these strategies perform better than students who mostly focus on reviewing.

7 **Teach to learn and participate in study groups.**

One of the most powerful ways to learn is to teach someone else. Teaching can happen naturally in study groups. In a study group, you can teach your fellow study group members part of a chapter and then learn from others teaching you content from other sections of the chapter.

Chapter 4 • Strengthening Soft Skills

1 **Embrace opportunities to learn soft skills.**

Soft skills are skills that are needed in almost every career. Examples include communication, interpersonal or teamwork skills, and being responsible and a good time manager. Many of these skills will be developed in your courses, but you can further enhance these skills by participating in extracurricular activities. Seek out opportunities where you can strengthen your soft skills.

2 **Practice professionalism.**

Professionalism involves being honest, responsible, and hardworking. Always put forth high levels of effort and be respectful of others. Employers desire employees who act professionally and ethically.

3 **Balance life, school, and work obligations.**

Research has shown that working too much while going to school can be one of the biggest obstacles to success. However, working part-time may be associated with positive academic outcomes and can also help you learn new skills including learning how to manage your time. Find a balance between your many responsibilities and focus on what is most important to you.

4 **Break tasks down to avoid procrastination.**

Most students avoid tasks because they are difficult or not interesting. Breaking tasks down into manageable chunks can make it easier for you to start working on larger assignments. You are more likely to meet with success if you avoid procrastination and, instead, engage in spaced practice, working on parts of a project over time.

5 **Use to-do lists and planners to manage your time.**

The to-do list is a simple but effective tool to help you keep track of the tasks you need to complete. You can use a calendar to schedule blocks of time to accomplish these tasks.

6 **Focus on one task at a time.**

The research is clear: Multitasking does not work. When you are trying to complete two different tasks at the same time, it actually takes you longer. Instead "single-task it" and focus on one activity at a time. This allows you be more productive and less stressed.

7 **Develop interpersonal and leadership skills.**

College is a perfect opportunity to develop and further enhance interpersonal and leadership skills. Practice the 5R approach (establish rapport, determine rule and roles, get ready to work and support one another, and remember to evaluate) to increase productivity when working in a group.

Chapter 5 • Demonstrating Knowledge and Skills

1 Focus on why first.

Before you begin to work on an assignment, be sure you understand the purpose of the assignment. Knowing the why behind the assignment can motivate you and can also help you better understand the assignment expectations, so you can meet with success.

2 Engage in academically honest work.

Academic integrity is important. Familiarize yourself with the academic integrity policy on your campus. Learn about plagiarism and cheating so that you can avoid engaging in dishonest behaviors unintentionally.

3 Know when and how to cite sources.

Always cite sources unless you are presenting your own original idea or common knowledge. Learning how to cite appropriately helps you avoid unintentional plagiarism. Get familiar with APA and MLA citation styles. There are online tools that can help you with citing sources.

4 Plan, write, and then revise.

Before you write a paper, carefully review the assignment and plan by writing an outline. Begin with a clear, strong opening statement that communicates your topic. Address your key points, adding supporting details and examples as needed. Connect all concepts to one another. Summarize your key points at the end, bringing attention to what you want to emphasize. Revise your work after you've had a chance to take a break from it. Start the revision process by looking at the big picture and then considering the details.

5 Engage your audience when presenting.

The more prepared you are, the easier it is to engage your audience. Look at your audience and highlight important points by changing your voice pattern, sharing a related story, or repeating information. Adding brief, active learning opportunities, such as a written reflection or a Turn and Talk, can also increase audience engagement and learning.

6 Create effective visual aids.

According to research, images are better than words. Limit the use of words on your slides and draw attention to the most important points. Avoid adding extra information or using bells and whistles that may distract from your main points. Use simple, conversational language.

7 Use test-taking techniques that work.

Preparing well for an exam is the single best way to improve exam performance. However, there are also some strategies you can use when taking a test. When taking a multiple-choice test, predict the answer before reading the options, read all the options, and eliminate the incorrect responses. Skip difficult questions and change your answer if you have good reason for doing so. When taking an essay exam, address the question directly using a clear organizational structure.

7 Success Strategies at a Glance

Chapter 6 • Mapping Your Path to Success: Plans and Action Steps

1 **Meet with your advisor.**

Students who meet with their advisor are more successful than students who do not. Take advantage of the advising services offered at your college. Your advisor can help you map out an academic and career plan and serve as a mentor throughout your college experience.

2 **Understand curriculum and graduation requirements.**

Knowing what courses and experiences are required of graduates will help you plan effectively. Understanding the structure of a degree will be helpful to you as you map out an academic plan, making it more likely that you will be able to complete graduation requirements on schedule.

3 **Explore academic options, such as online courses.**

Meet with your academic advisor to learn about your academic options. Consider the advantages and disadvantages of different learning experiences. For example, online classes offer flexibility and convenience, but you may miss the traditional classroom experience. Gather relevant information before deciding whether online learning or other academic options will be a good fit for you.

4 **Embrace study abroad, service learning, and internship opportunities.**

There are many long-lasting benefits, such as increased independence, associated with studying abroad. Service learning can increase your learning while you make societal contributions. Internships not only enhance your skills and experiences but also give you a great opportunity to network with professionals in the field.

5 **Expand and strengthen your network.**

One of the most effective ways to discover career opportunities is through networking. Building your networking skills and your network early on in your college career will serve you well now and in the future. Find a mentor and discover ways to build your network. Because relationships take work, you'll also want to spend time strengthening relationships with current members of your network.

6 **Have a professional media presence.**

Employers look at social media sites, so be sure that your online presence is positive and professional in nature. Be careful about what you post online—it may have negative consequences later. Before you look for a new job, delete inappropriate photos or posts. Use social media to promote a professional image of yourself by sharing your accomplishments online.

7 **Make good financial decisions and establish a good credit score.**

Be careful about accumulating too much debt. Think about the financial choices you make each day and the long-term consequences of these decisions. Open one or two credit card accounts, but be sure to make payments on time. Don't charge more than 25% of your credit limit. These actions help you build a good credit score.

1 **Regularly engage in academic self-regulation.**

Academic self-regulation involves three main phases: setting a goal, using learning strategies to work toward the goal, and self-reflecting on whether or not you are making progress toward your goal. Successful students ask themselves, "How am I doing?" regularly.

2 **Interpret mistakes productively.**

We all make mistakes. How you interpret your mistakes can often make a huge difference in whether or not you achieve success. Successful students attribute their mistakes to internal, changeable factors. In other words, focus on factors, such as effort, that are within your control. This leads to more productive outcomes.

3 **Practice good stress management.**

Keeping stress at a moderate level is best. There are many effective ways to manage stress. Practice the basics—eating nutritiously, sleeping well, and exercising regularly. Avoid unhealthy options, such as drinking alcohol or using other substances. Instead, engage in effective strategies such as mindfulness and positive thinking.

4 **Stick with tasks.**

Individuals who see tasks through to completion are much more likely to meet with success. This concept of sticking with tasks and continuing to persevere is often referred to as grit. Care about what you do and do it well.

5 **Adopt an optimistic attitude and focus on what is within your control.**

Having an optimistic attitude is one of the most powerful resilient factors. Resilience is the ability to bounce back after negative experiences. Although you are not always able to control the events in your life, you are able to choose whether you will view the event from a positive or negative lens. Challenge yourself to view the situation from a more positive perspective. Focusing on what you can control is a productive strategy.

6 **Use your support system.**

Surrounding yourself with others who care about you and want you to be successful is what successful people do. Our support systems can provide us with encouragement, especially when we are facing challenging situations. You may need to expand your support system to get all of your needs met. If this is the case, there are many supports available to you on your college campus.

7 **Celebrate your accomplishments.**

Savor the moment and feel proud of your accomplishments. Success can lead to even more success. Research has found that achieving your goal can build your self-efficacy. Individuals with higher self-efficacy set higher goals and individuals with higher goals achieve more. Celebrating your accomplishments can positively influence this cycle.

Discovering the Value of Education and Sharpening Key Thinking Skills

> The value of a college education is not the learning of many facts but the training of the mind to think.
>
> —*Albert Einstein*

1. What is the purpose of higher education? How does getting a college education benefit you and society?

2. How do successful people make decisions?

3. When faced with a decision or project, how can you best determine what information is needed and where to find this information?

4. What strategies will assist you in evaluating information?

5. What is a peer-reviewed journal? Why will learning about this scholarly source be helpful to you?

6. What is Bloom's taxonomy and how does it relate to critical thinking?

7. How can you become a critical thinker?

Exploring the Research in Summary

Research Study Citation

Head, A. J. (2012). *Learning curve: How college graduates solve information problems once they join the workplace.* Project Information Literacy Research Report (ERIC Document Reproduction Service No. ED536470).

INTRODUCTION: THE RESEARCH QUESTION

What question did the researcher seek to answer?

Information literacy refers to the ability to find, evaluate, and use information. Recognizing the important role of information literacy skills in the workplace, Head (2012) investigated the following questions:

1. What do employers expect from college graduates in terms of information literacy skills?

2. What challenges, if any, do recent graduates face in terms of information literacy skills in the workplace?

METHOD: THE STUDY

Who participated in the study? What did the researchers ask the participants to do?

The researcher conducted interviews and focus groups with employers and recent college graduates. A total of 23 employer interviews were conducted. It is important to note that employers were from several different states and a variety of different career fields. Thirty-three recent graduates from four different public and private colleges and universities in the United States participated in one of five focus groups. During the interviews and focus groups, employers and students answered a series of questions related to information literacy. Specifically, the research investigated information problem-solving skills.

RESULTS: THE FINDINGS

What were the answers to the research questions?

Employers rated the "ability to obtain and process information" (Head, 2012, p. 9) as being an essential skill, noting that their employees need to be able to search online (going beyond information found via Google) and use databases and data files. Some of the other important skills desired by employers included ability to work in a team, excellent communication skills, and decision-making skills, and being able to prioritize and plan work. Employers noted that these skills are related to information problem-solving and that students need to be patient as this process takes time. Almost all of the recent graduates indicated that finding, evaluating, and using information were required skill sets in their job. Some of the challenges recent graduates identified related to information problem-solving, which included the quick turnaround time needed, not having much direction or structure with the task, and the social nature of the process (i.e., needing to talk with others to find information needed). However, recent graduates noted that their college experiences helped them become effective at critically evaluating information. Thus, graduates reported having a good foundation, but several indicated that further training, especially opportunities to practice finding information without much structure, would help them to be better prepared for the world of work.

DISCUSSION AND SO WHAT FACTOR

How can YOU use this information as a student?

This research provides evidence that information literacy is an essential skill that is developed in college. However, a gap between the skills of recent graduates and the needs of employers exists. In other words, although graduates come to employers with some information literacy skills, additional skills are needed. To help bridge this gap, professors can engage students in information problem-solving tasks that are more complex and less defined. Students can also approach information literacy tasks from a broader perspective, thinking about how to access and evaluate information from a variety of sources, including other credible people. Students can also seek out opportunities such as being a leader of a club where they will be able to practice information literacy skills. Finally, when students begin a new position as a recent college graduate, having a mentor can be quite helpful. Bouncing ideas off of another person who has strong information literacy skills can be helpful.

Value of a College Education

Going to college is one of the best decisions you can make! The knowledge, skills, and confidence you gain not only will increase your career opportunities but will also be beneficial to you and others in a multitude of ways. Many students view college as a means to an end, a necessary step to enter a desired career, and this is certainly one benefit of education. Many careers do require a college degree. However, career training was never the primary purpose of higher education. Early leaders in the field of education, such as John Dewey, focused on how education was a way to better society by creating citizens who were armed with the knowledge and skills needed to make a positive impact

Tyler Olson/shutterstock.com

on the world (Chan, 2016). In other words, it was hoped that college graduates would be more informed, engaged, and productive citizens. McArther (2011) noted, "It is the participation in higher education, the interactions with peers, teachers and diverse forms of knowledge that will enable people to live richer lives and contribute to greater social justice through work and other social activities" (p. 746). In other words, college graduates will use their knowledge and skills in a productive way to benefit their communities. College is so much more than career preparation.

Sanders (2012) encourages you to focus on who you will become as a result of your educational experiences, noting that "so much of what you do in college, such as doing research and taking general education classes, is designed to help you become a more intelligent, capable, understanding, aware, and competent person—regardless of your major" (p. 4). By fully engaging in the college experience, you will be able to use skills you have learned to make significant contributions in your communities. As a college graduate, you are more likely to be involved in your community and engaged in actions that have a positive impact on others. This is often referred to as civic engagement. Researchers have found that college graduates are more likely to participate in community service, give to charities, and vote, as compared to individuals who did not attend college (Chan, 2016; Ishitani, 2009). Baum, Ma, and Payea (2010) reported that 43% of adults with a bachelor's degree volunteered, compared to only 19% of adults with only a high school diploma. In addition to more graduates volunteering, it is also important to note that these individuals were more likely to volunteer more hours. Why might this be? For starters, college graduates often see getting involved as one of their civic duties. In other words, graduates often believe that all members of society need to make a contribution. College graduates will also have many talents to share and typically find it rewarding to make a difference. Thus, by getting a college education, you will be more likely to positively impact the lives of others.

As Sukkon (2016) points out, "The good news is that the skills—what many in the academy refer to as learning outcomes—valued by employers and critical for employment are the same as those needed for civic engagement. Critical thinking, problem-solving, working in diverse teams, ethical reasoning, communicating—these make both good employees and good citizens." Therefore, getting a college education and developing these essential skill sets will serve you and others well. As college is preparing you to be a productive citizen, you will most certainly learn skills needed in the world of work. Preparing you for a career is one of the goals of college, but by going to college, you're learning skills that far exceed that single goal.

Some countries focus almost exclusively on getting students prepared for the world of work by only requiring coursework that is directly connected to a student's selected major or career. This is not the case in the United States. As previously mentioned, the higher education system was built on the idea that education can prepare individuals to be productive, contributing members of society. It is believed that in order to accomplish this task, knowledge and skills beyond the specialty area—often called a major—are needed. While undergraduate programs in the United States value major- and career-specific coursework as an essential part of a degree program of study, if you look at your overall degree requirements, you'll quickly notice that courses in your selected major may only be approximately one-third of the required coursework. In addition to taking major-specific courses, you will also need to take general education courses and electives. In these courses, you will be exposed to a variety of perspectives and opportunities that set the foundation for the development of essential skills such as information literacy, critical thinking, and interpersonal skills needed to excel in various careers and as a citizen. Thus, as a college graduate, you walk away with not only a deep knowledge of the discipline you chose to major in but also a broad range of essential skills that will serve society well.

In addition to benefiting the larger community, getting a degree can also benefit your current or future family members. Baum, Ma, and Payea (2012) found that college graduates were more likely to exhibit better parenting behaviors, such as reading to their children and taking their children to community events. The education you receive will help you make better parenting choices in the future and these choices will have a long-lasting impact on your children and even your grandchildren. Your family will therefore benefit from you getting a college education.

Additionally, getting an education can be good for your overall well-being. A study conducted by Yakovlev and Leguizamon (2012) found that individuals with more education were happier than individuals with less education. Likewise, Sironi (2012) found that more education was associated with fewer depressive symptoms (see Mental Health Figure). Baum, Ma, and Payea (2010) also found that college graduates were more likely to be satisfied with their job and to report a sense of accomplishment with their work.

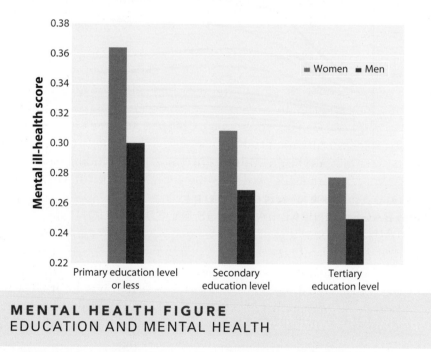

MENTAL HEALTH FIGURE
EDUCATION AND MENTAL HEALTH

Source: *International Journal of Mental Health* by M.E./SHARPE, INC. Reproduced with permission of M.E./SHARPE, INC. in the format republished in a book via Copyright Clearance Center.

Researchers have found that there are also physical benefits associated with being a college graduate. College graduates were less likely to have physical health problems later in life (Goesling, 2007; Zhang, Chen, McCubbin, McCubbin, & Foley, 2011). For example, college graduates were less likely to engage in unhealthy behaviors, such as smoking, and were more likely to engage in healthy behaviors, such as exercising regularly (Baum, Ma, and Payea, 2010). More specifically, the Washington Higher Education Board (2012) reported that college graduates are much less likely to smoke cigarettes (10%) as compared to those with a high school diploma (24%) or GED (45%). Getting an education helps you make better choices that will help you stay healthy and increases the likelihood that you will have access to health insurance benefits. Ninety-two percent of individuals with a bachelor's degree reported having health insurance as compared to only 69% of individuals with a high school diploma reporting that they have health insurance (Washington Higher Education Board, 2012).

As you probably know, earning a degree will also increase your earning potential. See Salary Table for a quick look at average salaries for full-time workers with varying levels of education (Julian & Kominski, 2011). As you can see, earning a bachelor's degree increases the average salary by almost $23,000 per year. This means individuals with bachelor's degrees make approximately a million dollars more than their peers with only a high school education throughout the course of a lifetime. This turns into approximately 2 million more dollars in your lifetime if you get a doctoral degree. The Annual Earnings Figure visually displays the positive financial consequences of higher education.

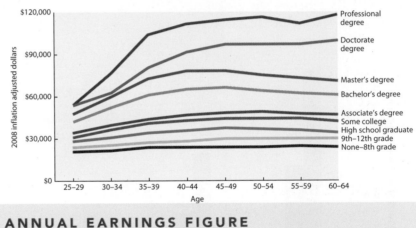

ANNUAL EARNINGS FIGURE
AVERAGE ANNUAL EARNINGS BY EDUCATION ATTAINMENT

SALARY TABLE
Average Annual Salaries Based on Education Level

Education Level	Average Salary ($)
High school	34,197
Associate's degree	44,086
Bachelor's degree	57,026
Master's degree	69,958
Professional or doctorate degree	88,867–103,411

Source: Adapted from: Julian, T. A. and Kominski, R. A. (2011). Education and synthetic work-life earnings estimates. American Community Survey Reports, ACS-14. U.S. Census Bureau, Washington, DC.

Although the cost of college has been increasing, research conducted by Abel and Deitz (2014) suggests that college is still a worthwhile investment. Over the past 40 years, the average wage has been consistently higher for those who had earned a bachelor's degree. Likewise, individuals with an associate's degree have been consistently earning higher salaries as compared to those with a high school diploma. Not surprisingly, there can be much variability in salary based on the career field (Oreopoulus & Petronijevic, 2013). Kim, Tamborini, and Sakamoto (2015) found that some career fields such as law, business, and medical had much higher salaries than other career fields. It is important to note that while the financial benefits of a college degree have a direct impact on that individual and his or her family, society also benefits. As Trostel (2010) points out, college graduates pay more in taxes because of their higher income levels, which benefits both the individual and society.

College graduates are also less likely to be unemployed (Gillie & Isenhour, 2003) and are more likely to work for companies that provide higher-level benefit packages such as healthcare, paid vacation, and sick time. For example, in a study conducted by the Washington Higher Education Board (2012), 90% of individuals with a bachelor's degree indicated receiving paid vacation or sick leave as compared to only 75% of individuals who had a high school diploma or less.

SUMMARY: BENEFITS OF HIGHER EDUCATION

- Civic engagement
  - More likely to vote
  - More likely to volunteer and engage in community service
  - More likely to make charitable donations
- Overall well-being
  - Happier, less likely to become depressed
  - More likely to engage in healthy behaviors such as exercising
  - Less likely to have physical health problems and engage in unhealthy behaviors such as smoking
- Future generations
  - More likely to use effective parenting strategies, such as reading to children
- Career satisfaction
  - Increased satisfaction and sense of accomplishment
- Salary and benefits
  - Higher salaries and more significant contributions to society via taxes
  - Less likely to be unemployed or need to rely on government support
  - More likely to have access to healthcare

VALUE OF COLLEGE EDUCATION QUICK QUIZ

1. How does society benefit from individuals getting a college education?
2. How does a college education impact your overall well-being?
3. What are the financial benefits of getting a college education? On average, how much more does a person with a bachelor's degree earn per year compared to someone with only a high school diploma?

Decision-Making

Lucky Business/Shutterstock.com

Life is full of decisions! In fact, one could argue that the most important life skill is being able to make good decisions. Decisions range from simple ones, such as what to eat for dinner, to very complex choices, such as which career pathway to pursue. Making decisions is a part of our daily life, and college demands that you make many. See Decision-Making Table for an overview of the decision-making process.

We are social beings; others affect our decision-making. When faced with challenging decisions, many of us seek guidance or support from friends, family, or other important people in our lives. What others think about the choices that we make often matters to us. Some cultures, such as those in Indonesia and Guatemala, emphasize social or group needs over individual ones. This collectivist value focuses, for instance, on how individuals need each other and places a higher value on the group versus the individual (Triandis & Suh, 2002). If this matches your value system, then your decision-making process will likely be inclusive, involving the important people in your life. Other cultures—ones that are more individualistic in nature, such as those in the United States and Australia—place a higher value on independence; if this sounds like your background, the other people in your life may only have a minimal or moderate impact on your choices.

Your decisions impact others. Sometimes the impact on others is very obvious. For example, if you start working more hours, you won't be able to spend as much time with your friends and family. Taking a job that requires your significant other to move to another state with you clearly impacts both of you, as well as your family and friends. Sometimes the impact on others may be less apparent. Perhaps you decided to post some pictures from a party on your Facebook (or other social media) page and your friend later has difficulty with his or her employer because of a picture that you posted. Sometimes your actions may seem insignificant to you but may really matter to someone else. Although it is difficult to foresee all the ways your actions may impact others, it is important that you step back and consider how your actions may affect other people.

DECISION-MAKING TABLE
Six Steps to Effective Decision-Making

Step 1: Keep Your Goal(s) Visible—Ask, "What Do I Want?"
Our goals should guide us as we make decisions. It is therefore critical that you keep your goal front and center as you move through the steps of effective decision-making. This makes it more likely that you will engage in actions that will assist you with reaching your goal.

Step 2: Gather Relevant Information—Ask, "What Do I Need to Know?"
Gathering information that is relevant to the decision you must make is important. Too often, we make decisions based on limited data (Crittenden & Woodside, 2007), and the more information you have, the better decision you will make. Ask yourself, "What do I need to know in order to make this decision?" Think about personal or situational factors in the present and future that may play a role in your decision. Good decisions are based on relevant information.

Step 3: Creatively Identify and Explore Possible Options—Ask, "What Are My Options?"
There are often many good choices or options available to you. In other words, most decisions don't have only a right and a wrong choice. During this stage, be open to many different possible options and avoid judging them—there will be time for this later. Judging your options at this stage limits your creativity, which can potentially result in fewer options to consider. Many find it helpful to seek input from others as they will often think of options you did not identify.

Step 4: Evaluate Options—Ask, "What Are the Pros and Cons?
After you've identified a list of options, the next step is to evaluate these options. Before you begin, you will want to make sure you are working with a reasonable list of options, which means you may need to narrow the list down to a manageable number of alternatives. Having too many or too few options can hinder the decision-making process (Kuksov & Villas-Boas, 2010). Once you have identified a reasonable number of options to explore, write down the pros and cons associated with each one.

Note that a longer list of positive or negative consequences alone should not determine the outcome. Some consequences may be more significant or meaningful and therefore would matter more than other, less meaningful consequences. In addition to thinking about immediate consequences, consider possible consequences that might occur in the future. Focusing on the long-term impact of your decisions is important. Asking for help from others, such as family, friends, or professionals, during this evaluation process is a great idea. Input from others who know you well will help you make a decision that matches your goals and values.

Step 5: Decide and Take Action—Ask "What Is My Decision?"
You've worked really hard to get to this step. Trust the process you've gone through to get here. Now it's time to make a decision and act on it. Remember, most of our decisions are not "forever" ones. In other words, if you make a decision that isn't the best fit, you will usually be able to make a different choice in the future.

Step 6: Assess Whether Your Choice Supported Your Goal and Was Effective—Ask "Was This Decision a Good One?"
Reflecting on whether you made a good decision or not can help you improve your decision-making skills. In this step, take a few moments to reflect on whether your decision helped you move toward or away from your goal. Taking some time to evaluate your decision helps you determine if you need to make a new choice and also assists you with making better decisions in the future.

DECISION-MAKING QUICK QUIZ

1. What are the six steps of the decision-making process?
2. What is the role of others in our decision-making?

Information Literacy

iStock.com/Ioan Florin Cnejevici

We live in a world full of information. As we just discovered, information plays an essential role in decision-making. It is therefore not surprising that information literacy is a primary goal at many colleges and universities. Learning how to navigate the endless amount of information available to find and use information for a task at hand is an important skill that will serve you well personally and professionally.

Information literacy skills are incredibly important and useful in all facets of life. Identifying, finding, and evaluating relevant and meaningful information will result in you making better academic and personal decisions. For example, being able to navigate all of the information presented to you will help you make good decisions about buying a car or home.

What Is Information Literacy?

Roman Motizov/Shutterstock.com

According to the Association of College and Research Libraries (2016), "Information literacy is the set of integrated abilities encompassing the reflective discovery of information, the understanding of how information is produced and valued, and the use of information in creating new knowledge and participating ethically in communities of learning" (p. 12). Simply put, learning to sift through what often seems like an endless amount of information, and find and evaluate information that will assist you with a task, is important.

The Association of College and Research Libraries recently adopted a framework for information literacy (ACRL, 2016). According to this framework, there are six essential components to information literacy that are described in the Information Literacy Table. You'll also find an academic and personal example in this table. It is important to note that the components outlined are not sequential. In other words, you don't need to consider each one in order, but rather together they will assist you in developing information literacy skills.

Information literacy is a skill that will serve you well in your personal, academic, and professional aspects of your life. Being able to find and evaluate information will undoubtedly help you make personal decisions such as what career to choose, where to live, and what car to drive. This skill will also help you tackle academic tasks in college. Samson (2010) points out that academic assignments such as research projects help you develop and enhance your information literacy skills. A research project requires you to determine what information is needed, locate and evaluate information, and then synthesize and organize the information into a meaningful product.

In addition, information literacy is a skill that you'll use regularly in your career. In a survey of college graduates, 78% indicated that learning how to find relevant information was an important work-related skill that was learned in college, and approximately 90% indicated that information literacy skills were being used at least monthly in their current job (Travis, 2011). As you can imagine,

INFORMATION LITERACY TABLE
Six Components of Information Literacy

Components of Information Literacy	Questions to Ask	Academic Example: Research Paper on Active Learning Teaching Strategies	Personal Example: Buying a Car
Authority is constructed and contextual *Authority typically relates to whether the person is recognized as an expert in the field.*	**Who might be an expert or credible source for this purpose? Why?**	• Educators' or teaching supervisors' personal experiences • Researchers with graduate degrees in field of education research studies • Authors of books on teaching strategies	• Consumer Reports or other independent researchers • Car sales person • Owners of different car models • Online reviews
Information creation as a process *Experts look not only at the product that was created but also how this product was developed.*	**What was the purpose of this information product and how did this influence its creation?**	• Who funded the research? Was it an independent source or was it funded by a business with an interest in selling a product? • What benefit, if any, would the author of the information receive based on the findings?	• Consumer Reports or other independent research reports are probably not biased • Car salesman will likely present only positive research • Difficult to know if an online reviewer has an agenda
Information has value *Information products have been created by an author. It is essential that we give proper credit to the author for his or her work.*	**Who deserves credit for the information? What is intellectual property?**	• Cite sources to give credit to author, researcher, or educator (important to also cite personal communications)	• Independent researcher • Anonymous reviewers online
Research as inquiry *Information allows us to explore answers to questions.*	**What questions can shape research and discovery? What conclusions can be drawn from research?**	• Do active learning and teaching strategies lead to increased learning? What other benefits might there be? • Need to evaluate the nature of the study to see the validity and generalizability of the information (i.e., studies with larger number of participants may have stronger and more meaningful results)	• Which car has the features I need? • What is the cost difference between different options? • Need to exercise caution when interpreting anonymous reviews or information provided by someone who has a vested interest in which car you choose

continued on following page

continued from previous page

Components of Information Literacy	Questions to Ask	Academic Example: Research Paper on Active Learning Teaching Strategies	Personal Example: Buying a Car
Scholarship as conversation *By exploring all of the research on a topic, we can understand information within a context. In other words, we can evaluate how new information fits into what is already known.*	**What are the various perspectives? What best represents the current knowledge or thinking in this area?**	• What do supporters of active learning say? What do nonsupporters say? What evidence do they present? • What finding seems to be consistent across studies?	• What are the pros and cons of different models? • Is there consistency between what reviewers say and what the salesperson says?
Searching as strategic exploration *It is important to determine what information is most relevant to the task at hand. Searching for information requires the use of strategies that are based on the reason for needing the information.*	**What information would be most useful to the task at hand? What search strategies will work best?**	• What research exists on this topic? What search terms might work best? How can I best narrow the results to find useful data? • What experiences have educators had with active learning strategies? What questions should I ask educators to get meaningful information?	• How can I find out the total cost including maintenance and gas? • What search terms can I use to find websites with the information I need?

(ACRL, 2016)

employers will value employees who can skillfully engage with and use information. This skill becomes even more important as the amount of information available increases. It can be quite a complicated task to sift through the endless amounts of information available and determine what information will best assist with the task at hand and guide our actions. According to Bruce (1999), there are seven key facets of information literacy that relate to the world of work:

1. Using information technology to learn and communicate with others
2. Being able to identify appropriate sources of information
3. Engaging in problem-solving to sort through information
4. Organizing and bringing meaning to information
5. Developing expertise in an area of interest
6. Adopting new perspectives or novel approaches or ideas
7. Using information to benefit others

INFORMATION LITERACY QUICK QUIZ

1. How would you define *information literacy*?
2. Why is information literacy important?

Websites and Evaluating Sources

Given the vast amount of information that exists in the world, it is important to consider where you can find the information you will need for the various decisions and tasks you face. Not surprisingly, Google is often the first place students go to find information (Salisbury & Karasmanis, 2011). Google and other search engines can help you get familiar with the vocabulary and concepts related to a topic and might even help you identify search terms that you can then use in the library databases. However, it is essential that you critically evaluate the information you find. As you know, anyone can post information on the Internet, so although finding the information may not take very long, evaluating it can be quite a time-consuming task.

iStock.com/vgajic

One primary consideration when evaluating sources will be whether or not the person or organization that provided the information is qualified to do so. For example, if you found information on a psychological disorder, you would expect that the person who provided the information has an advanced degree in psychology. Another important consideration is whether or not the information you found seems to be consistent with other information. In other words, are many different sources coming up with the same conclusions? These are only a few of the questions you'll need to ask. To assist students with evaluating sources, Meriam Library at California State University (2010) developed the CRAAP test (Currency, Relevance, Authority, Accuracy, Purpose). This test (see CRAAP Test Figure) provides you with a comprehensive list of questions to ask yourself when trying to decide whether or not a source is credible.

WEBSITES AND EVALUATING SOURCES QUICK QUIZ

1. Why is it important to evaluate websites?
2. What criteria should you use to determine if a website is a credible source?

Peer-Reviewed Journal Articles

Information from original research studies can be quite helpful in academic and professional work. You can find research studies in peer-reviewed journal articles. Professors prefer and expect students to use scholarly sources, such as peer-reviewed journals, from library databases when conducting research (Valentine, 2001). On a survey conducted by Travis (2011), almost half of the graduates indicated that empirical research was needed in their career. However, as we just discussed, most students over-rely on the Internet for information when the need for information arises. In fact, research conducted by OCLC (2005) found that 90% of students go to a search engine first, even though 72% of the students in the survey indicated that library databases are worthwhile sources (as cited in Jones, Johnson-Yale, Millermaier, & Perez, 2005). Unfortunately, only 14% of students surveyed indicated that they use the library database to find a scholarly journal article (Salisbury & Karasmanis, 2011). Part of the problem may be that students do not feel confident using databases and reading journal articles. Almost half

Amy Johansson/Shutterstock.com

Evaluating Information – Applying the CRAAP Test
Meriam Library 📖 California State University, Chico

When you search for information, you're going to find lots of it...but is it good information? You will have to determine that for yourself, and the **CRAAP** Test can help. The **CRAAP** Test is a list of questions to help you evaluate the information you find. Different criteria will be more or less important depending on your situation or need.

Key: ■ indicates criteria is for Web

Evaluation Criteria

Currency: *The timelines of the information...*
- When was the information published or posted?
- Has the information been revised or updated?
- Does your topic require current information, or will older sources work as well?
- Are the links functional?

Relevance: *The importance of the information for your needs.*
- Does the information relate to your topic or answer your question?
- Who is the intended audience?
- Is the information at an appropriate level (i.e. not too elementary or advanced for your needs)?
- Have you looked at a variety of sources before determining this is one you will use?
- Would you be comfortable citing this source in your research paper?

Authority: *The source of the information.*
- Who is the author/publisher/source/sponsor?
- What are the author's credentials or organizational affiliations?
- Is the author qualified to write on the topic?
- Is there contact information, such as a publisher or email address?
- Does the URL reveal anything about the author or source?
  examples: .com .edu .gov .org .net

Accuracy: *The reliability, truthfulness and correctness of the content.*
- Where does the information come from?
- Is the information supported by evidence?
- Has the information been reviewed or refereed?
- Can you verify any of the information in another source or from personal knowledge?
- Does the language or tone seem unbiased and free of emotion?
- Are there spelling, grammar or typographical errors?

Purpose: *The reason the information exists.*
- What is the purpose of the information? Is it to inform, teach, sell, entertain or persuade?
- Do the authors/ sponsors make their intentions or purpose clear?
- Is the information fact, opinion or propaganda?
- Does the point of view appear objective and impartial?
- Are there political, ideological, cultural, religious, institutional or personal biases?

| **CRAAP TEST FIGURE**
| EVALUATION CRITERIA

Source: Meriam Library—California State University, Chico, http://www.csuchico.edu/lins/handouts/eval_websites.pdf.

of the college students in a research study conducted by Burton and Chadwick (2000) indicated that they did not receive training on how to use the library databases, and many students (45.2%) said they didn't know the elements of a peer-reviewed article that qualified it for publication (Salisbury & Karasmanis, 2011).

The good news is that when students receive information literacy instruction during their first year, they do utilize a variety of sources beyond Google, including peer-reviewed research articles (Samson, 2010). As with most skills, learning is enhanced when you are challenged and supported. Research shows that information literacy skills significantly improve when students are given challenging, meaningful research assignments that require high levels of critical thinking and information literacy (Hayes-Bohanan & Spievak, 2008). As you would expect, students also report higher degrees of confidence in information literacy and critical thinking with increased academic experiences, meaning students reported higher levels of confidence in upper- versus lower-level courses (Henderson, Nunez-Rodriguez, & Casari, 2011). You'll find that college will offer you many challenging learning tasks such as papers, presentations, and projects that will help you develop these skills.

Students are often most successful with these high-level academic tasks when there is also a high level of support. Not surprisingly, Schroeter and Higgins (2015) found that students who were provided with guided instruction on information literacy skill development were more confident with their ability to determine what information is needed, find that information, and use the information in a meaningful way. In addition to being more confident, students who received guided instruction also demonstrated higher skill level in tasks requiring information literacy. As you are discovering, this challenge and support model is one of the basic premises of this text. You will be encouraged to use high-level sources such as research articles as a vehicle to help you develop and enhance information literacy and critical thinking skills.

What is a peer-reviewed journal article? One of the most scholarly sources is the peer-reviewed journal article, which can be defined as a theoretical or research-written work that has been deemed worthy of publication by experts in the field. These articles are published in journals that are monitored by professionals in that area of study. Most articles are based on original research.

To fully appreciate the value of peer-reviewed research, it is important to look at the process an author must undertake in order to get a work published (see Peer-Review Figure). It starts with the author submitting the work to the editor of a journal. If the article is considered appropriate for that particular journal, the work is then anonymously distributed to several professional experts (called the reviewers) in that field for their review and recommendation. Typically, the reviewers recommend numerous revisions before the work is published, and many times works are not accepted for publication. In fact, some journals have rejection rates as high as 90% (American Psychological Association, 2008). This means that 90% of the articles submitted are denied, and only 10% are published. The reviewers carefully attend to the research to be sure it is of high caliber, in keeping with the professional standards of the field, and that it adds a significant contribution to the current literature in that area. In a nutshell, an author must go through a rigorous peer-review process before the work ever makes it to print.

Why is this important for you to know? Basically, it means that someone else has done the groundwork for you. You don't need to spend your time trying to figure out if it is a good source. This, of course, does not prevent you from doing your own analysis and critical thinking about the material. Rather, it frees you to focus on how the information from the article helps you with the task at hand. If, on the other hand, you go to a website, you have to spend a significant amount of time first determining if the information is credible.

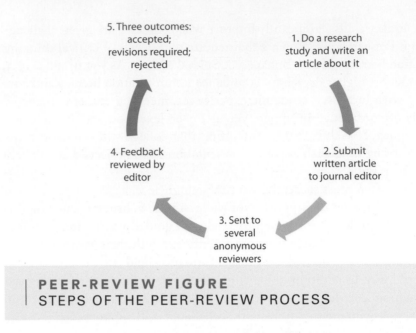

5. Three outcomes:
accepted;
revisions required;
rejected

1. Do a research
study and write an
article about it

4. Feedback
reviewed by
editor

2. Submit
written article
to journal editor

3. Sent to
several
anonymous
reviewers

PEER-REVIEW FIGURE
STEPS OF THE PEER-REVIEW PROCESS

The parts or elements of research articles. Research articles can be broken down into parts. Each research article has the following elements: abstract, introduction, method (subjects and procedure), results, and discussion.

Abstract and Introduction. Abstract is another word for summary. In the abstract, the author(s) briefly describes the nature of the study and the key findings. Since the abstract contains the purpose and main findings, reading this paragraph several times will help you understand the rest of the article. You can also return to the abstract whenever you find that you are struggling to understand the study as the abstract provides a basic overview of the reason for and results of the study.

Introduction is the first official section after the abstract (see Abstract and Introduction Figure). Sometimes it is labeled "Introduction," while other times the text simply begins without a heading. In the introduction, the author sets the stage for why this research was conducted, discusses why the topic is important, and describes research that has already been done in that area. You will notice that the author cites the sources within the body of the text according to APA (American Psychological Association) or MLA (Modern Language Association) style. The source citations clearly indicate where the information came from so that the reader could go directly to that source if a deeper understanding of the topic is desired (Raimes & Jersky, 2011). If you find these source citations distracting you as you read, block them out using a pencil or other method. Just be sure that you will be able to read them later if necessary. As you become more comfortable reading journal articles, you will naturally skip or jump over the citations.

The author then talks about how this study adds to what we know about the topic. The research question or hypothesis (educated guess about the relationship between the variables), which is the key purpose of the study, is also identified. Keep this purpose front and center in your mind as you read the rest of the article. Think of yourself as the detective seeking an answer to the question. This helps you stay focused on the key point and not get distracted by the other content.

Research Study | **Howard, H. E., & Jones, W. P. (2000). Effectiveness of a Freshman Seminar in an Urban University: Measurement of Selected Indicators**

This study investigated the effectiveness of a freshman seminar in enhancing the students' overall perception of: (a) being prepared for the university experience, (b) satisfactory selection of a college major, (c) general confidence as a student, (d) knowledge of campus resources, and (e) study skills competence. One-hundred eighteen students responded to pre-and post-test questionnaires. Results indicated a significant gain on four of the five with no evident positive impact on the selection of a major. On the other four questions, positive change was evident independent of entering ability levels with the exception of study skills where the greater gain was obtained by students with low high school grade point averages.

This is the abstract or summary of the article.

The introduction starts immediately after the abstract. In this section, the researchers describe the purpose of the study.

A common concern among institutions of higher education in the United States is retention. Schaeffer (1999) reports a national attrition rate of 25 percent and notes that the costs are more than just loss of funds to the institution. There is a significant negative personal impact on many of the students.

Historically (Beal & Noel, 1980), the period between freshman and sophomore years has been the time of greatest attrition. Tinto (1987) found that of the students who leave, 75% do so during or immediately after the first semester. Liu and Liu (1999) confirm a continuing problem with freshmen retention, noting that transfer students tend to continue enrollment at a higher rate than do entering freshmen.

Students enter the college and university setting from a myriad of diverse backgrounds, including various levels of academic preparation, ages, socioeconomic backgrounds, and reasons for enrolling in college. There are, of course, many reasons for leaving, not all of which are within the scope of responsibility of the institution. It is, however, reasonable to assume that in many instances the decision to leave rests simply on the student's lack of success in the setting. This appears particularly evident for freshman who enter the setting unprepared personally and academically for the difficult transition from secondary to post-secondary education. Kendall (1999) found, for example, that in one state system, one-half of the system's entering freshmen are required to take remedial classes in math and English.

Colleges and universities often consider offering a freshman course or seminar focused on content and experiences to facilitate the transition between secondary and post-secondary education. Fidler and Hunter (1989) report that of the various interventions used to enhance freshman success, the freshman seminar is typically the most effective. With samples obtained over a period of fourteen years, they found that students at the University of South Carolina who took the freshman seminar course had a higher sophomore retention rate and found similar findings of positive relationships between retention and participation in freshman seminar courses at a variety of other institutions as well.

Shanley and Witten (1990) and Cone (1991) also report that dropout rates for freshman seminar participants were significantly lower than non-participants. Participation in such seminars results in increased knowledge about campus services and activities (Fidler & Hunter, 1989), and this may be one of the features which enhances the retention rate.

Studies also suggest a link between participation in a freshman seminar and higher eventual grade point averages. For example, Maisto and Tammi (1991) found that students enrolled in a freshman seminar course earn significantly higher grade point averages than do non participants and also report more out of class contact with faculty. In a study at a small liberal arts college, Hyers and Joslin (1998) found that grades earned in a required freshman year seminar were better predictors of academic achievement and persistence than high school rank and S.A.T. scores.

Wilkie and Kuckuck (1989) report that freshman seminar courses result in many positive developments

ABSTRACT AND INTRODUCTION FIGURE
ABSTRACT AND INTRODUCTION SECTIONS OF A RESEARCH ARTICLE

Method. The next section is called method, which generally has two subheadings: subjects or participants and procedure (see Method Figure). In the subject/participants section, the author describes the people who participated in the research study. One reason why it is important for the author to do this is because it helps the reader understand how easily the results will generalize or apply to other populations. For example, if you are a college student and read an article that found pure memorization was the most effective study strategy, you might want to focus your energy on memorization. However, what if you discovered that the subjects in this study were second graders? Would you still want to use this information as a college student? Similarly, if the research study only used male students, would you be as interested in the results as a female? The size of the sample (how many subjects were in the study) is also important. If only five people participated, would you feel as confident with the findings as compared to a study that had 500 participants?

The procedure section outlines exactly how the study was conducted. It should provide you with enough detail that if you wanted to replicate it (do the same study), you would be able to do so. This is where the author tells you about the variables (concepts or factors of interest) that are being investigated. The author also tells you when and how these variables are measured. In many cases, a questionnaire or test will be given to measure the variables. This information allows a reader to critically evaluate the meaningfulness of the results. For example, you may get more excited about a research study that used official grades as compared to one where they simply asked students to provide their grade, because students may not provide information accurately.

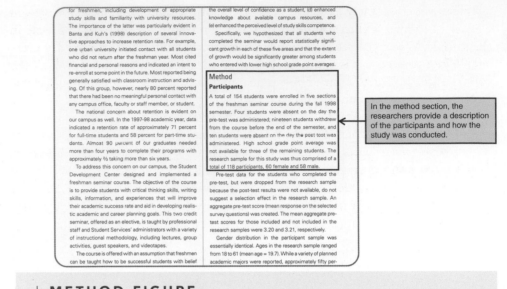

for freshmen, including development of appropriate study skills and familiarity with university resources. The importance of the latter was particularly evident in Banta and Kuh's (1998) description of several innovative approaches to increase retention rate. For example, one urban university initiated contact with all students who did not return after the freshman year. Most cited financial and personal reasons and indicated an intent to re-enroll at some point in the future. Most reported being generally satisfied with classroom instruction and advising. Of this group, however, nearly 80 percent reported that there had been no meaningful personal contact with any campus office, faculty or staff member, or student.

The national concern about retention is evident on our campus as well. In the 1997-98 academic year, data indicated a retention rate of approximately 71 percent for full-time students and 58 percent for part-time students. Almost 90 percent of our graduates needed more than four years to complete their programs with approximately ⅔ taking more than six years.

To address this concern on our campus, the Student Development Center designed and implemented a freshman seminar course. The objective of the course is to provide students with critical thinking skills, writing skills, information, and experiences that will improve their academic success rate and aid in developing realistic academic and career planning goals. This two credit seminar, offered as an elective, is taught by professional staff and Student Services' administrators with a variety of instructional methodology, including lectures, group activities, guest speakers, and videotapes.

The course is offered with an assumption that freshmen can be taught how to be successful students with belief the overall level of confidence as a student, (d) enhanced knowledge about available campus resources, and (e) enhanced the perceived level of study skills competence.

Specifically, we hypothesized that all students who completed the seminar would report statistically significant growth in each of these five areas and that the extent of growth would be significantly greater among students who entered with lower high school grade point averages.

Method
Participants

A total of 154 students were enrolled in five sections of the freshman seminar course during the fall 1998 semester. Four students were absent on the day the pre-test was administered; nineteen students withdrew from the course before the end of the semester, and ten students were absent on the day the post test was administered. High school grade point average was not available for three of the remaining students. The research sample for this study was thus comprised of a total of 118 participants, 60 female and 58 male.

Pre-test data for the students who completed the pre-test, but were dropped from the research sample because the post-test results were not available, do not suggest a selection effect in the research sample. An aggregate pre-test score (mean response on the selected survey questions) was created. The mean aggregate pre-test scores for those included and not included in the research samples were 3.20 and 3.21, respectively.

Gender distribution in the participant sample was essentially identical. Ages in the research sample ranged from 18 to 61 (mean age = 19.7). While a variety of planned academic majors were reported, approximately fifty per-

> In the method section, the researchers provide a description of the participants and how the study was conducted.

METHOD FIGURE
METHOD SECTION OF A RESEARCH ARTICLE

Results. The most challenging section of peer-reviewed journal articles is the next section, results, which tells you about the findings of the research study (see Results Figure). This section is often filled with statistics and numbers; however, you don't need to understand all of the statistical information in order to walk away with the key findings. Your mathematical skills will increase as you take more courses, so this section will become easier to understand with time. The good news is that the authors also have to use words to describe all of the results. As you become more advanced in math, you'll be able to appreciate and value the results section, but as a beginner, it is fine to focus on the words. However, having a basic understanding of some of the key statistics will help you understand the findings.

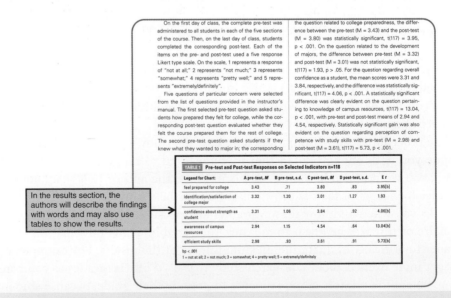

On the first day of class, the complete pre-test was administered to all students in each of the five sections of the course. Then, on the last day of class, students completed the corresponding post-test. Each of the items on the pre- and post-test used a five response Likert type scale. On the scale, 1 represents a response of "not at all;" 2 represents "not much;" 3 represents "somewhat;" 4 represents "pretty well;" and 5 represents "extremely/definitely".

Five questions of particular concern were selected from the list of questions provided in the instructor's manual. The first selected pre-test question asked students how prepared they felt for college, while the corresponding post-test question evaluated whether they felt the course prepared them for the rest of college. The second pre-test question asked students if they knew what they wanted to major in; the corresponding the question related to college preparedness, the difference between the pre-test (M = 3.43) and the post-test (M = 3.80) was statistically significant, t(117) = 3.95, p < .001. On the question related to the development of majors, the difference between pre-test (M = 3.32) and post-test (M = 3.01) was not statistically significant, t(117) = 1.93, p > .05. For the question regarding overall confidence as a student, the mean scores were 3.31 and 3.84, respectively, and the difference was statistically significant, t(117) = 4.06, p < .001. A statistically significant difference was clearly evident on the question pertaining to knowledge of campus resources, t(117) = 13.04, p < .001, with pre-test and post-test means of 2.94 and 4.54, respectively. Statistically significant gain was also evident on the question regarding perception of competence with study skills with pre-test (M = 2.98) and post-test (M = 3.61), t(117) = 5.73, p < .001.

> In the results section, the authors will describe the findings with words and may also use tables to show the results.

TABLE 1 Pre-test and Post-test Responses on Selected Indicators n=118

Legend for Chart:	A pre-test, *M*	B pre-test, s.d.	C post-test, *M*	D post-test, s.d.	E *t*
feel prepared for college	3.43	.71	3.80	.83	3.95[b]
identification/satisfaction of college major	3.32	1.20	3.01	1.27	1.93
confidence about strength as student	3.31	1.06	3.84	.92	4.06[b]
awareness of campus resources	2.94	1.15	4.54	.64	13.04[b]
efficient study skills	2.98	.93	3.61	.91	5.73[b]

bp < .001
1 = not at all; 2 = not much; 3 = somewhat; 4 = pretty well; 5 = extremely/definitely

---

RESULTS FIGURE
RESULTS SECTION OF A RESEARCH ARTICLE

Here is an extremely basic overview of statistical language that will serve you well as a beginner. When you see n, it typically refers to the number of people in the sample. When you see X, it stands for mean, which is another word for average. When you see r, it is telling you about a correlation or relationship between variables (see Statistics Table). Note that a relationship does not mean one variable caused the other. The numbers do however tell you about the size or strength of the finding, which is important. The larger the correlation, the stronger the relationship between the variables. The difference between means or averages of different groups is also meaningful. Let's say that a researcher found a significant difference in the grade point average between students who used electronic textbooks and students who used traditional textbooks. If the average GPAs were 3.1 and 3.2 for the two groups, you may not care as much as you would if the GPAs for the groups were 2.5 and 3.0. The larger difference would be of more interest and value.

STATISTICS TABLE Very Basic Statistics	
n	Number of people
X	Mean or average
r	Correlation (numbers closest to 1 or −1 indicate stronger relationships)

Discussion.   The last section is called the discussion (see Discussion Figure). In this section, the researchers put the key findings into more everyday language without the numbers, making it easier for everyone to understand. Here, the researchers go back to their original research question or hypothesis that was discussed in the introduction and then answer the question or tell the reader whether the hypothesis was in fact supported. The researchers go beyond just reporting the findings and also explain the findings. The findings are usually explained in the context of what is already known, so you will likely see the researcher reference other similar studies and their findings. Then, there is a discussion of the study limitations, cautioning the reader to interpret the results carefully. Finally, in this section, the value of these findings will be highlighted. When reading this section, think about how you can use the results and apply them to your life as a college student.

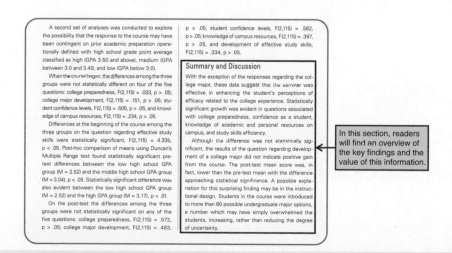

DISCUSSION FIGURE
DISCUSSION SECTION OF A RESEARCH ARTICLE

PARTS OF A PEER-REVIEWED RESEARCH ARTICLE

- Abstract—Summary of the study
- Introduction—Review of past research and current research question (why current study is being conducted)
- Method—How the study is conducted; the number of participants and what they were asked to do
- Results—Answers the research question; the findings; detailed statistics
- Discussion—Summary of key findings; cautions about interpreting results accurately; the value of the research findings

Reading journal articles. As you know, reading is an essential skill in college. Although general reading strategies are important for all of the reading you do, there will be times when applying different strategies or techniques will be advantageous. Reading a journal article is different than reading a textbook. Most professionals do not read journal articles in order. Instead, professionals bounce around from section to section, taking in the key points and exploring details as needed. Check out Reading Journal Articles Figure for tips on how to read journal articles.

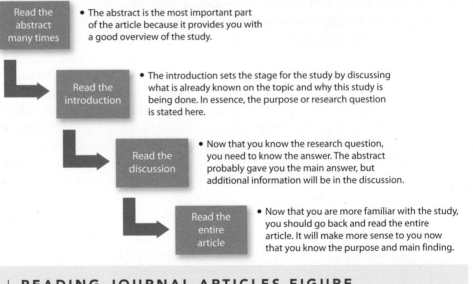

Read the abstract many times
- The abstract is the most important part of the article because it provides you with a good overview of the study.

Read the introduction
- The introduction sets the stage for the study by discussing what is already known on the topic and why this study is being done. In essence, the purpose or research question is stated here.

Read the discussion
- Now that you know the research question, you need to know the answer. The abstract probably gave you the main answer, but additional information will be in the discussion.

Read the entire article
- Now that you are more familiar with the study, you should go back and read the entire article. It will make more sense to you now that you know the purpose and main finding.

READING JOURNAL ARTICLES FIGURE
TIPS ON READING A JOURNAL ARTICLE

PEER-REVIEWED JOURNAL ARTICLES QUICK QUIZ

1. What is a peer-reviewed research article?
2. What are the main sections of a research article?
3. In what order is it recommended that you read a research article?

Critical Thinking

Critical thinking is one of the most important skills needed in life. Increasing critical thinking skills is a goal of every college or university. Likewise, critical thinking is a skill that is highly valued by employers. Throughout your college experience, you will have many opportunities to build critical thinking skills.

What Is Critical Thinking?

Critical thinking has been defined as the ability "to think in a sophisticated manner—to ask questions, define terms, examine evidence, analyze assumptions, avoid emotional reasoning, resist oversimplification, consider alternative interpretations, and tolerate uncertainty" (Wade, 2008, 11). While there are numerous definitions of critical thinking, Dunn, Halonen, and Smith (2008) noted that most definitions have the following themes:

Ehrman Photographic/Shutterstock.com

cate_89/Shutterstock.com

- Exploring and considering multiple perspectives and interpretations
- Examining and evaluating evidence
- Engaging in self-reflection
- Drawing conclusions

Critical thinking is a learning task that requires actively taking in, evaluating, and using information. Critical thinking is obviously an important part of our everyday life and plays an especially important role in the decision-making process. According to constructivism, a learning theory, students can't learn by simply memorizing facts. Instead, students must actively construct or create knowledge, making connections between new information and what has been previously learned (Dennick, 2012). "In other words, students arrive with pre-existing 'constructs,' and in order to learn, must modify these existing structures by removing, replacing, adding, or shifting information in them" (Hartle, Barviskar, & Smith, 2012, 31).

Researchers have examined how students change their thinking during the college years. Perry (1970), for instance, studied intellectual development in college and discovered that students at the beginning of their college careers were more likely to think of information as being right or wrong, while students near graduation were more likely to recognize the complexity of information and the importance of considering many factors when evaluating the accuracy of information. In other words, college students move from simplistic to complex thinking. Based on the work of Perry and several others, West (2004) identified the following four stages of intellectual development:

- Stage 1 (Absolute): Believes that there is a right and wrong answer. Also believes that professors or other authority figures know the correct answer.

- Stage 2 (Personal): After discovering there is not always a correct answer, believes that opinions are what really matter. Knowing is therefore based on personal experiences.
- Stage 3 (Rules-based): Values rules to compare and judge opinions or claims but will resort back to opinions when rules do not apply.
- Stage 4 (Evaluative): Uses more formal strategies to evaluate opinions and evidence. Can explain the process behind the evaluation, defending conclusions drawn.

The college experience fosters these high-level thinking skills and moves students toward the evaluative stage. The more open you are to looking at information from multiple perspectives, the more likely it is that you will develop these high-level cognitive skills. Challenge yourself to go beyond your personal opinion and to carefully examine the evidence.

CRITICAL THINKING QUICK QUIZ

1. What does it mean to be a critical thinker?

2. What are the four stages of intellectual development?

Bloom's Taxonomy

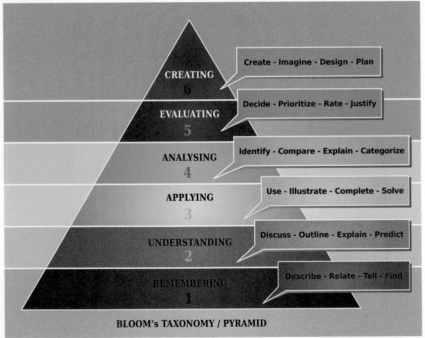

BLOOM's TAXONOMY / PYRAMID

artellia/Shutterstock.com

One of the most well-known figures in the world of critical thinking is Benjamin Bloom (Anderson & Kratwohl, 2001). Basically, Bloom identified the various levels of knowing. He encouraged educators to think about what they really wanted students to be able to do with the information being learned. Did they want their students to simply memorize or remember the information, or did they want them to engage in a higher-level task where they had to apply the information to a new situation or make a judgment based on what was learned?

Being able to remember information is the first step. In order to engage in more complex cognitive tasks, you will need to know about the subject matter. The other levels are understanding, applying, analyzing, evaluating, and creating. Each cognitive task builds on prior skills and is more challenging in nature. The concepts in the upper levels of the pyramid, analyzing, evaluating, and creating, are often thought of as critical thinking skills. One of the best ways to develop critical thinking skills is through questioning. See Critical Thinking Questions Table for some examples of questions you can ask yourself to help you think more critically.

CRITICAL THINKING QUESTIONS TABLE
Questions Aligned to Bloom's Taxonomy That Promote Critical Thinking Skills

Bloom's Taxonomy Levels	Questions to Promote Critical Thinking
Remembering	• What basic knowledge do I need to know?
Understanding	• How does this information relate (compare/contrast) to other information I already know? • How could I explain these concepts?
Applying	• How could this information be applied in different situations? • What are the potential positive and negative consequences of this information? • How useful is this information?
Analyzing	• What evidence or proof exists for or against the idea or finding? • What potential biases exist? • What distinguishes this finding from other findings?
Evaluating	• Why might this be true? • What other explanations might there be? • What would someone who disagrees with the finding say? • How consistent is this finding? • How does this finding or idea add value to the current knowledge base in the field? • Based on this knowledge, what recommendations would you make?
Creating	• How would this information guide your actions? • How might you modify or adapt products based on this information? • How can you take this information and create an original product? • How can this information be used to benefit others?

Creating is the goal. Based on what you've learned (working all the steps of the pyramid), your professors are going to want you to create academic products such as papers and presentations. As a professional, your employer will also likely want you to create products such as an advertising campaign, a lesson, or a written report. Thus, you need to be able to remember, understand, apply, analyze, and evaluate information in order to be successful at creating academic and professional work. It's important for you to know that it takes time and effort to get to the top of the pyramid. As you do so, you'll discover that your thinking patterns will shift from simplistic to sophisticated. Using the process described in the next section, you'll be developing these higher-level thinking skills in no time!

BLOOM'S TAXONOMY QUICK QUIZ

1. What is the basic premise behind Bloom's taxonomy?
2. According to Bloom, what are the different levels of knowing?
3. What would be an example of remembering and creating?

The Process of Becoming a Critical Thinker

So how do you develop critical thinking skills? For starters, you need to focus on three foundational conditions. You need to know related content (knowledge base), believe in your ability to engage in critical thinking (self-efficacy), and be motivated to learn (desire/drive). The following two learning conditions are then needed: challenging learning opportunities and support. Once all of these conditions have been met, you will be able to easily engage in productive, high-level thinking. See Becoming a Critical Thinker Figure for an overview of this process. The process is cyclical in nature. Productive thinking increases knowledge, self-efficacy, and motivation. These increased foundational skills, combined with a challenging and supportive learning environment, lead to even more productive thoughts and actions.

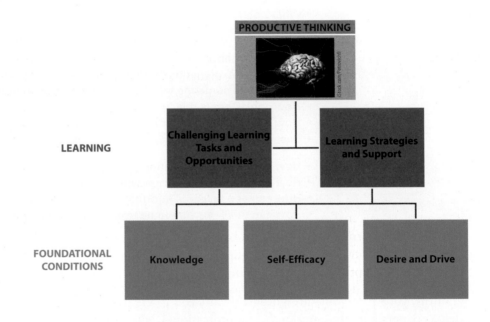

| **BECOMING A CRITICAL THINKER FIGURE**
THE PROCESS OF BECOMING A CRITICAL THINKER

Foundational condition 1: Knowledge. As indicated in Bloom's taxonomy (Anderson & Kratwohl, 2001), the first step is to remember the course content you are learning. Neuroscience research has demonstrated that it is easier to learn new information when you connect it to something you already know (Goswami, 2008). Thus, the more you know, the easier it is to learn. It's impossible to become a critical thinker without knowing a lot of information (Willingham, 2009). In college, you'll be constantly building this knowledge base because there is so much new information to learn—definitions, theories, concepts, and other important information in each field you are studying.

You are obviously entering college with knowledge. While you are in college, you add to or modify your current knowledge base. In some courses, you'll be exposed to content that you have not yet encountered. In other courses, you may discover new information about a familiar concept or may even be challenged to think about whether or not what you know is accurate. In fact, questioning the accuracy and usefulness of information is an essential part of being a critical thinker. Critical thinkers don't take information at face value, but instead challenge, question, and seek out additional information before determining whether or not the information presented is accurate and has value.

Foundational condition 2: Self-efficacy.

Becoming a critical thinker involves more than just cognitively processing information. Our beliefs about ourselves also matter. The second foundational condition is self-efficacy. Self-efficacy refers to your belief about whether or not you can successfully complete a task such as critical thinking (Bandura, 1997). If you think you will be able to do a task successfully, you will be much more likely to put in the effort needed and will also be more likely to keep trying even if you experience some difficulties along the way. The way in which we think about ourselves and our abilities undoubtedly drives our actions.

Foundational condition 3: Desire and drive.

The third foundational element is your desire and drive—otherwise known as motivation. You may know a lot about a topic and think you can do a critical thinking task successfully but not be interested in doing so. Let's face it—critical thinking takes work. Why would you want to do the task if you don't think it's important or worthy? When you perceive the task as valuable and meaningful, you are more likely to have the desire and drive to work toward the upper levels of Bloom's taxonomy.

Learning condition 1: Challenging learning tasks and opportunities.

There are two learning conditions needed for the development of critical thinking skills: challenging learning tasks and support to help you successfully complete the challenging tasks. Let's discuss challenging learning tasks first. Some of these learning challenges will be a natural part of your college experience. For example, your professors will require you to engage in a variety of learning tasks such as in-depth discussions, debates, research papers, and presentations. Designed to facilitate the development of critical thinking skills, many of these learning tasks will have question prompts similar to the ones listed in Socratic

SOCRATIC QUESTIONS TABLE Developing Critical Thinking Skills (based on the work of Paul, 1990 and Strang, 2011)	
Purpose	**Socratic Questions**
Clarifying explanations	What do you mean by . . .? How does this compare and/or contrast to . . .? What are the potential advantages and disadvantages of . . .?
Questioning assumptions	What other explanations might exist? What are the assumptions behind this statement or finding?
Exploring additional evidence	How can I find out more about this topic? What additional evidence might support or refute this idea?
Multiple perspectives	What would someone who disagrees say? What are the cultural implications?
Real-world implications	What are the potential consequences or implications of this? What is a real-world example of this?
Self-reflective processes	Why does this matter? What is the importance of this information? What are the unanswered questions?

Questions Table. If this is not the case, you can still ask yourself these Socratic questions to help you think more critically. Make the most of these opportunities; they facilitate deep learning and critical thinking skills.

You will also want to take advantage of challenging learning opportunities outside of the classroom. For instance, you can seek out opportunities to work with faculty on research or other projects, become a leader of a club or organization, participate in campus-wide events, or get involved in community service projects. Many of these activities force (or at least strongly encourage) you to view the world from multiple perspectives. Research has shown that these out-of-class experiences can sometimes play a more important role in developing critical thinking skills than traditional in-class learning experiences for many students (Loes, Pascarella, & Umbach, 2012).

Learning condition 2: Learning strategies and support. It is important that you are supported as you strive to achieve success with the challenging tasks just discussed. Learning is a social activity and we learn best when others assist us with tools and general support.

Professors, for example, can support you in many important ways, such as providing you with a good foundation of information, supplying guidelines about assignments (maybe even rubrics or models), and being available during office hours or by e-mail. Professors can also pose challenging questions that require you to think about the issues from different perspectives and dive more deeply into research and theory. There are many other campus supports such as librarians and tutors available as well. Your classmates may also become a part of your support team. We learn best when we interact with others (Goswami, 2008), so be sure to reach out to your support system, especially those who will challenge you, as needed.

Once you've got the foundational and learning conditions met, critical thinking will happen naturally. Your background and experiences will constantly play a role in your thinking. As your critical thinking skills develop, you'll find yourself automatically analyzing and evaluating information to create amazing presentations, papers, and other work.

PROCESS OF BECOMING A CRITICAL THINKER QUICK QUIZ

1. What are the three foundational conditions needed to become a critical thinker?
2. What are the two learning conditions needed to become a critical thinker?

CHAPTER 1

Chapter Summary: Note-Taking Model

Instead of traditional chapter summaries, this text uses various note-taking models to capture the key concepts from each chapter. This chapter's summary is modeled using the Cornell Method. There are several ways to use this section:

- **Preview:** Read the model before reading the chapter to familiarize yourself with the content.
- **Compare:** Compare the notes you took on the chapter to the model provided.
- **Study:** The model along with your notes and other course materials are great resources for studying.

Cornell Method Model

Why attend college? What are the benefits of a college education?	College graduates are: • more likely to have strong decision-making and critical thinking skills that are needed personally and professionally • happier, less depressed, and physically healthier • more engaged in community • better parents • more likely to be employed and earn higher salaries
Decision-making: What is the process for making good decisions?	Step 1: Keep your goal(s) visible—ask, "What do I want?" Step 2: Gather relevant information—ask, "What do I need to know?" Step 3: Creatively identify and explore possible options—ask, "What are my options?" Step 4: Evaluate options—ask, "What are the pros and cons?" Step 5: Decide and take action—ask, "What is my decision?" Step 6: Assess whether your choice supported your goal and was effective—ask, "Was this decision a good one?"
Information literacy: What information do you need and is it valuable?	Information literacy refers to your ability to determine what information is needed, finding that information, and then evaluating the value and relevance of that information. Information literacy is a skill needed in careers (90% of college graduates reported using information literacy skills at least once a month). Good questions to ask are as follows: • Who might be an expert or credible source for this information? Why? • What was the purpose of this information and did the purpose influence its creation? • Who deserves credit for the information? • What conclusions can be made based on this information? • What are various perspectives on this topic? • What information would be most useful? How can I find this information?
	Evaluating websites: The CRAAP test • Currency • Relevance • Authority • Accuracy • Purpose

	Peer-reviewed research—scholarly theoretical or research work that has been deemed worthy of publication by professionals in the field. • Parts of a research article: abstract (summary), introduction (purpose and research question), method (how study was conducted), results (answer to research question), and discussion (importance of key findings) • Reading journal articles: Read abstract several times, then introduction and discussion, and finally the entire article
Critical Thinking: What is it and how do you become a critical thinker?	• Critical thinking is high-level thinking, which involves considering many perspectives, evaluating evidence, monitoring and reflecting, and making judgments or conclusions • Constructivism theory focuses on how one creates knowledge by connecting new information to what's already known—active learning is a must! • Four stages of intellectual development: absolute right or wrong; personal opinions matter most; rules; formal evaluative strategies • Bloom's taxonomy—different levels of knowing (remembering, understanding, applying, analyzing, evaluating, creating)
	Process to become a critical thinker: • Knowledge—need to know about a subject in order to think critically about it; add to or modify current knowledge • Self-efficacy—belief about whether one can successfully complete a task; high self-efficacy increases effort and achievement • Desire and drive—motivation is higher when tasks are perceived to be valuable and meaningful; need to care about the task and commit to it • Challenging tasks—assignments, class activities, out-of-class activities (work with faculty on research, leader of club, community service project) • Support—strategies to help learn and complete academic tasks; reach out for help

SUMMARY: Going to college has many benefits. College graduates are more likely to be mentally and physically healthy, be more involved in their communities, be satisfied with their work, and earn higher salaries. College graduates are also good decision makers, know how to find and use information effectively, and engage in critical thinking. The process of becoming a critical thinker begins with knowledge, believing in oneself, and caring about the task, and then requires challenging tasks and support. College promotes the development of these high-level skills by providing challenging learning opportunities and high levels of support.

Setting Goals and Choosing a Career Path

Shoot for the moon. Even if you miss, you'll land among the stars.

—*Les Brown*

Armadillo Stock/Shutterstock.com

1 What are the benefits of setting short- and long-term goals?

2 What are the characteristics of effective goals?

3 How do we make career decisions?

4 How can career theories guide or influence our actions?

5 What contributes to career indecision and what can we do to move toward a decision?

6 What should you know about yourself before making career decisions?

7 How can you learn about various careers?

Exploring the Research in Summary

Research Study Citation

Morisano, D., Hirsh, J. B., Peterson, J. B., Pihl, R. O., and Shore, B. M. (2010). Setting, elaborating, and reflecting on personal goals improves academic performance. *Journal of Applied Psychology*, 95(2), 255–264.

INTRODUCTION: THE RESEARCH QUESTION

What question did the researcher seek to answer?

Colleges are interested in developing interventions that will help students complete college successfully. Having effective goals is one area that has been associated with student success. In this study, Morisano, Hirsh, Peterson, Pihl, and Shore (2010) investigated the effectiveness of a goal intervention on academic success. The research question was: Does participating in a goal-setting intervention lead to positive academic outcomes such as improved GPA?

METHOD: THE STUDY

Who participated in the study? What did the researchers ask the participants to do?

College students who were struggling academically were asked to participate in the research study. A total of 85 full-time students participated. Official grades were collected before the intervention and then one year later. Students were randomly assigned to the goal-setting intervention or another general intervention that did not address goals. The intervention was done online and lasted about two and a half hours. Students were then asked to complete a questionnaire 16 weeks later.

RESULTS: THE FINDINGS

What was the answer to the research question?

There were three main findings. First, students in the goal group had higher GPAs after the intervention. Specifically, the average GPA for the goal group was 2.91, while the average GPA for the non-goal group was 2.25 (see Goal Intervention GPA Figure). Second, students in the goal group were less likely to drop classes than students in the non-goal group. Finally, the goal group had less negative emotions at the end of the study.

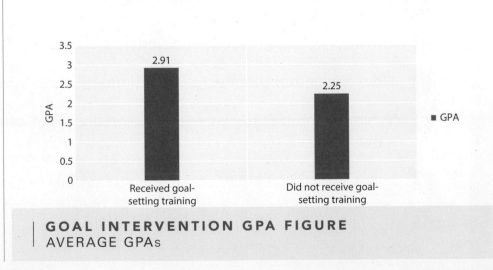

GOAL INTERVENTION GPA FIGURE
AVERAGE GPAs

DISCUSSION AND SO WHAT FACTOR

How can YOU use this information as a student?

This research provides evidence that goal setting is an important part of student success. Students who know how to set and use goals are more likely to succeed. Professors of student success or first-year seminar courses can teach students how to create effective goals. This can be taught in person or through online methods. Brief instruction and support on goal setting can be extremely effective. Students, especially those who are struggling, could benefit from seeking out support to create and use personal goals.

Setting Goals

Goals are an important part of life. We all set goals. However, some of us are more effective at doing so than others. Setting effective goals can increase the likelihood that you will successfully achieve them. Exploring the value of goal setting and strategies to do so effectively will help you meet with success.

Importance of Goal Setting

There is a substantial body of research that shows us that goals are connected to success (Locke & Latham, 2002). This is true in both the personal and career aspects of your life. Would you exercise more if you set a goal for yourself? Would your business sell more if there was an established target goal? The answer to both of these questions is yes! Setting short- and long-term goals can increase motivation and effort. This results in increased achievement.

Marilyn Volan/Shutterstock.com

Goal setting is particularly important in the world of academia, where there is a strong connection between goal setting and academic achievement (Moeller, Theiler, & Wu, 2012). Researchers have found that students often earn the grade they set as their initial goal (Perlman, McCann, & Prust, 2007). Thus, students striving for A grades often earned A's while students aiming for a C grade often earned a C at the end of the course.

Unfortunately, Bishop (2003) reported that 85% of college students indicated they were not taught how to set effective goals (as cited in Moeller, Theiler, & Wu, 2012). The good news is that a relatively brief training session on goal setting can be incredibly effective. Morisano, Hirsch, Peterson, Pihl, and Shore (2010) found that students who participated in a goal-setting intervention had significantly better grade point averages than students who did not receive goal training (2.91 GPA compared to 2.25 GPA).

iStock.com/nzphotonz

In addition to increasing achievement levels, goal setting has also been connected to overall well-being. In a 17-year-long study, Hill, Jackson, Roberts,

Lapsley, and Brandenberger (2011) found that both initial goals and goal development growth during young adulthood predicted well-being in adulthood. Specifically, they found that having high-level goals at the start of college and increasing pro-social (e.g., helping others, serving the community) and career goals during college was connected with improved well-being in later adulthood.

Long-term goals are important because they provide us with a big-picture view of where we want to be in our future. Long-term goals can take anywhere from several months to many years to accomplish. Some examples of long-term goals include: graduating from college with a 4.0 grade point average, earning a doctoral degree, or gaining employment in the career field of your choice.

Long-term goals are valuable, but they are often not enough. Identifying short-term goals can help you make steady progress toward your long-term goals. Short-term goals are goals that you can complete within days, weeks, or months. Your short-term goals are often considered steps toward your long-term goal. Let's look at the example of achieving a 4.0 GPA when you graduate. To increase the likelihood of achieving this goal, you could set the following short-term goals:

- Earn 90% or higher on practice quizzes when studying.
- Earn an A on the first test.
- Meet with the professor and identify a topic for your research paper.
- Consult a librarian for assistance and locate the five to ten sources needed for the paper.
- Write a first draft and get it reviewed by a campus tutor.
- Use feedback from the tutor to revise the paper.
- Earn an A on the research paper.

Research has shown that our motivation and effort is often higher when we set short-term goals (Schunk, 1990). These short-term goals are often referred to as proximal goals because the distance between where you are now and where you need to be in order to achieve the goal is much shorter than it is for long-term goals. It is often easier to be motivated when a reward is closer versus farther away.

Another benefit of short-term goals is the opportunity they give us to monitor our progress toward our long-term goals. As you would expect, students who monitor their progress are more likely to achieve their goals (Heikkilä & Lonka, 2006; Kitsantas, Winsler, & Huie, 2008). If you discover that you are not on track to achieve your long-term academic goal, you can modify your study habits, seek support from a tutor, or increase the amount of time you spend studying. These actions increase the likelihood of goal achievement. If you don't take time out to check on your progress, you won't know what adjustments to your actions are needed.

BENEFITS OF EFFECTIVE GOAL SETTING

- Increased academic achievement
- Increased likelihood of staying in college
- More positive emotions
- Improved well-being later in life
- Increased success overall

IMPORTANCE OF GOAL SETTING QUICK QUIZ

1. If you aim for a B grade in a course, what grade will you be most likely to earn?
2. What are three benefits of effective goal setting?
3. What is the value of short-term goals?

The ABCS of Setting and Implementing Effective Goals

So now you know that goal setting is extremely important and learning about how to set effective goals is a worthwhile activity. But what makes a goal effective? There are several frameworks that exist for goal setting. One well-known framework is the SMART (Specific, Measurable, Achievable, Realistic/Relevant, and Time-based) goal. Although this framework is quite popular, there has been little research investigating its effectiveness (Day & Tosey, 2011). While this SMART framework does contain important elements that are supported by research, such as goals being specific, findings about some factors in this model have been mixed. For example, unrealistic goals may not be detrimental (Linde, Jeffrey, Finch, Ng, & Rothman, 2004), and in fact may result in higher amounts of effort and success (De Vet, Nelissen, Zeelenberg, & De Ridder, 2013). The SMART goal framework is also missing some key factors. For instance, Zimmerman (2002) argues that self-efficacy, your belief in your ability to successfully complete a task, and intrinsic interest are integral parts of the goal-setting process and these factors are not addressed via SMART goals. This framework also doesn't address the importance of developing challenging goals despite challenge being one of the most important goal characteristics (Locke & Latham, 2002).

DeeaF/Shutterstock.com

Understanding this, let's consider another framework: the ABCS of effective goal setting and implementation. See Effective Goal Setting Table for a description of this framework. This approach to goal setting includes important affective and cognitive factors such as self-efficacy and motivation. There is also research support for every factor within this model. Let's take a look at this framework and the research support behind each component.

EFFECTIVE GOAL SETTING TABLE		
The ABCS of Effective Goal Setting and Implementation		
A	**Aim High**	Challenging goals are best! The higher you aim, the higher you will achieve.
B	**Believe in Yourself**	Self-efficacy is important. If you believe in your ability, you will be more likely to put forth the effort needed.
C	**Care and Commit**	Being motivated matters! Believing your goal is important and being committed to achieving it leads to more success.
S	**Specify and Self-Reflect**	Having a specific goal is connected to successful outcomes. This allows for easier monitoring and reflection, important parts of the process.

Aim high: Challenging goals are best!   The higher you aim, the higher you will achieve. Locke and Latham (2002) conducted an extensive review of 35 years of research on goal setting in a variety of contexts (i.e., personal, business, academic). One of their major findings was that "the highest or most difficult goals produced the highest levels of effort and performance" (Locke & Latham, 2002, p. 706). You are more likely to achieve more when you set challenging goals.

While there is strong evidence for setting challenging goals, there is mixed research on whether these challenging goals need to be realistic or not. Realistic goals are within your reach and are achievable, while unrealistic goals are quite grandiose and may be impossible or next to impossible to achieve. Some research has found negative outcomes associated with setting unrealistic goals. Brusso, Orvis, Bauer, and Tekleab (2012), for instance, found that having unrealistic goals led to negative outcomes such as poorer performance and lower-level goals in the future. However, others have not found harmful outcomes associated with unrealistic goals and suggest that likelihood of achievement may not be an important element of effective goals (Linde, Jeffrey, Finch, Ng, & Rothman, 2004).

Realistic or moderate goals are often suggested because student success professionals are concerned about the emotional cost associated with not achieving the goal. In other words, if you do not achieve a high-level goal, how will you feel? Will not achieving the goal negatively impact you? Reynolds and Baird (2011) conducted an interesting study that investigated this issue. Basically, they wanted to find out whether or not there was a "downside" to establishing challenging goals. They asked adolescents and young adults to indicate the highest level of education they planned to achieve. They then followed these students (almost 13,000 at the beginning of the study and almost 5,000 students at the end of the study) for 13 years to see what level of education they did, in fact, achieve. As you can see in Analyzing Challenging Goals Figure, they found that approximately half of those who participated achieved their educational goal while 43% fell short of their goal. Only 8% of participants exceeded their goal. Thus, it is not typical to go beyond the goal you set. Another reason to aim high from the start!

In addition to finding out information about their education level, Reynolds and Baird (2011) also assessed depressive symptoms. They did not find any evidence of an emotional cost associated with not achieving goals. In other words, the participants who did not achieve their educational goal did not have more

ANALYZING CHALLENGING GOALS FIGURE
PERCENTAGE OF PARTICIPANTS WHO ACHIEVED THEIR EDUCATIONAL GOAL

symptoms of depression than participants who did achieve their educational goal. Interestingly, they found that participants who had higher expectations at the start had lower levels of depression, even if they did not reach their goal!

Aiming high or creating challenging goals leads to the best outcomes. Given the limited research and mixed findings on the topic of realistic or unrealistic goals, it may not be worth your time to worry about whether or not it's realistic. Instead, focus on challenging yourself.

Believe in yourself: Self-efficacy is key!

Self-efficacy is your belief in your ability to successfully complete a task (Bandura, 1997). According to researchers, self-efficacy plays an important role in goal setting (Zimmerman, 2002). In other words, your beliefs about yourself shape the goals you set. Research has found that students who believe in themselves and exhibit high levels of self-efficacy set more challenging goals (Cheng & Cheou, 2010). Students who have low self-efficacy unfortunately set less challenging goals and, as you know, this can result in lower levels of achievement.

Successful experiences are one of the best ways to increase your self-efficacy. Researchers have found that individuals with a history of success will be more likely to challenge themselves with higher goals in the future (Spieker & Hinsz, 2004). One way for you to keep focused on your successful experiences is to keep track of your accomplishments. For example, if you've performed well on a paper or project, earned Dean's List status, or received an award, document these success stories and refer back to them often. Keeping your successful experiences front and center can help you build your self-efficacy.

In addition to playing a role in goal development, self-efficacy also impacts goal accomplishment. If you believe that you can achieve your goal, you are much more likely to succeed. Why? You are more likely to work at something when you believe you can successfully complete the task. If you have low self-efficacy, you may avoid the task or not invest as much effort into it. This connection between self-efficacy and achievement was demonstrated in a research study conducted by Komarraju and Nadler (2013) in which they discuss how high self-efficacy enables students to continue to work and persist in spite of difficulties or failures.

Care and commit: Motivation matters!

Caring or being motivated to achieve the goal along with a strong commitment to do what it takes to succeed at the goal are important parts of the goal-setting and implementation process. Not surprisingly, students who are more motivated to achieve a goal are more likely to do so. Research conducted by Goodman et al. (2011) found that intrinsic motivation is the best predictor of academic success. Intrinsic motivation refers to factors within a person such as curiosity, interest, enjoyment, and excitement that encourage the person to start or continue doing a task (Deci & Ryan, 1985). Choose goals you care about and you'll be more likely to achieve them.

Once you choose a goal you care about, you must be committed to achieving it. Being committed means you do what it takes to achieve the goal. Angela Duckworth (2016), a renowned psychologist, has conducted several studies that show caring and commitment are related to successful outcomes. She refers to these qualities as grit or the passion and perseverance to complete tasks (Duckworth, 2016). In other words, commitment means you will put in the effort needed in order to successfully reach your goal. Evidence for the importance of commitment comes from research conducted by Seijts and Latham (2011). In their study, participants had to indicate their commitment level to successfully complete a business simulation exercise. There was a significant relationship found between commitment and performance. Participants with higher levels of commitment performed much better than participants who were not as committed to the goal. Turner and Husman (2008) found this to be particularly important when students experienced setbacks or failures.

Some interesting research suggests that you might want to keep this commitment to yourself though. Gollwitzer, Sheeran, Michalski, and Siefert (2009) found that when we share our goal with others, we experience satisfaction similar to the positive feeling we have when we achieve a goal. As a result of prematurely experiencing this sense of satisfaction, we don't work as hard and do not accomplish as much. On the other hand, if we make the commitment but keep it to ourselves, we are more likely to work hard toward the goal so that we can experience this positive feeling upon completing the goal.

Specify and self-reflect: Monitoring your progress is important!

Specific, measurable goals are connected to successful outcomes (Roney & Connor, 2008). Locke and Latham (2006) report that over 1,000 studies found specific (and high level) goals lead to the best performance. Specific goals are stated in measurable terms, defining the standard that will be used to judge whether the goal was accomplished. In other words, it will be very easy for you or someone else to know if you have achieved your goal if it is specific.

Many students often say that they will "do their best" as an academic goal, but unfortunately, this type of goal is not effective. "Do your best" goals don't work because there is no specific target identified. This results in less effort being exerted and lower performance. Locke and Latham (2002) found that "when people are asked to do their best, they do not do so" (p. 706). Students with specific academic goals such as "I will earn a 4.0 GPA this semester" will exert more effort than students with an "I'm going to do my best" goal. Specificity then leads to higher levels of achievement.

Specific goals also allow for easier monitoring of progress. Self-reflection on your progress is an important part of goal setting and achievement. Let's look at the "I will earn a 4.0 GPA this semester" goal again. To determine whether you are on track with this goal, you can look at your grades thus far. Are your current grades consistent with your desired grade? Grade calculation apps or websites can help you understand your current grade and what grades are needed on future assignments and exams in order for you to reach your goal. If, on the other hand, your goal was to "do well" or "do your best," how would you be able to assess this progress? While no one could argue with the spirit of this goal, it is next to impossible to know whether you have achieved it. Do you need to get all A's on your assignments? Do you need to earn passing grades on assignments and tests? Are D's evidence of support with this goal? Hopefully you are discovering the importance of being specific and how this makes it much easier for you to see if you are on track to accomplishing your goal.

As you evaluate your progress, you may need to make modifications or adjustments. For instance, if you were aiming for an A in your biology class and you currently have a B average, you will probably want to increase your studying time and perhaps even add new learning strategies into your daily routines so that you can achieve your goal. Students who actively monitor their progress and make adjustments as necessary are more successful than those who do not engage in self-reflection (Schloemer & Brenan, 2006; Zimmerman, 2002).

ABCS OF GOAL SETTING QUICK QUIZ

1. What are the ABCS of setting and implementing effective goals?
2. What is the emotional cost associated with setting challenging goals that you do not accomplish?
3. Do "do your best" goals work? Why or why not?

Career Exploration and Decision-Making

Choosing a career path is probably one of the biggest decisions college students face. Your career choice guides your choice of major. It also influences the courses you select and the experiences or opportunities you seek out. Engaging in career exploration will help you determine a career path that is aligned to your values, interests, and abilities.

Christopher Futcher/E+/Getty Images

How Do We Make Career Decisions?

Most of us won't have just one career but rather will likely have numerous careers during our lifetime. According to the Bureau of Labor Statistics (2015), the average person will have 11.7 jobs throughout their life. Thus, while having a career direction or path will make it easier for you to determine a college major and experiences you want to pursue, it's important for you to think broadly about what you are passionate about and how this may translate into success in a variety of careers. Because you are likely to have numerous positions over the course of your professional life and many career opportunities you will encounter in the future may not even exist today, identifying a specific career goal may not be as important as identifying a career pathway. A career pathway is a broader vision of what career field or type of profession you'd like to pursue. For example, health care or business would be considered career pathways. Within each career pathway, there will be many options that will likely match your goals and interests.

iStock.com/CreativaImages

For many students, deciding on a career path can be overwhelming. Your career is an important part of your identity. Establishing your identity is a developmental crisis that all adolescents and individuals in early adulthood must struggle with, according to Erikson's theory of psychosocial development (Woolfolk, 2013). James Marcia, a renowned developmental psychologist, has described different identity statuses, emphasizing that identity achievement requires both exploration and commitment (Myers, 2014). See Marcia Identity Statuses Table to see how these identity statuses can be applied to career decision-making.

MARCIA IDENTITY STATUSES TABLE
Marcia's Identity Statuses Applied to Career Decision-Making

Identity Status	Exploration	Commitment	Description
Identity moratorium	Yes	No	Actively exploring career options but has not yet decided; may be overwhelmed or anxious
Identity foreclosure	No	Yes	Career decision is made with little to no exploration; often decision is made based on parental influence or to avoid anxiety
Identity diffusion	No	No	Not yet invested in the career decision-making process
Identity achievement	Yes	Yes	Career path has been identified after careful exploration of many career options

According to the classic work of Parsons (1909), the three key steps involved career decision-making are the following:

1. Knowing about yourself
2. Knowing career information and opportunities
3. Using information about yourself and world of work to decide on a career path

While this classic framework is still used as a general guideline to help students or others make career decisions, we know that career decision-making is not this simple. It is a much more complicated process. Self-awareness and career information are still critical parts of the process, but there are many other factors that influence our decisions.

Greenbank (2011) found that students tend to rely on intuition and readily available information from friends and family rather than actively engaging in a thorough process of exploring available career information. Not surprisingly, family and friends play a significant role in our decision-making, with parents often playing the most significant role (Chope, 2002; Phillips, Christopher-Sisk, & Gravino, 2012; Workman, 2015). Significant others, other relatives, and teachers also impact our career decisions. In a study conducted by Phillips, Christoper-Sisk, and Gravino (2012), many students reported that family or friends gave them a suggested career option to explore, with some indicating they were pushed or strongly encouraged to pursue a certain career path. Your parents and other family members probably know you well and understand what matters to you, so their input and guidance will be particularly useful. These findings suggest that career decision-making is a very personal process and as with all decisions, the role of and impact on others needs to be carefully considered. See Personal Network Career Influence Figure for a visual presentation of who influences our career decisions.

It is obviously more likely for you to consider careers that you know about or are visible to you. Two primary ways we become aware of possible career options is through role models and experiences. Role models play a critical role in career decision-making (Nauta & Kokaly, 2001). We often learn about career options because we have interacted with people in these fields. For instance, by going to school,

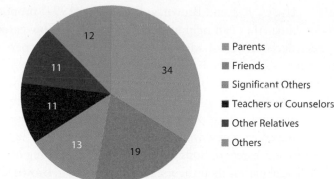

12	■ Parents
11	■ Friends
34	■ Significant Others
11	■ Teachers or Counselors
13	■ Other Relatives
19	■ Others

PERSONAL NETWORK CAREER INFLUENCE FIGURE
WHO INFLUENCES CAREER DECISIONS?

Source: Adapted from Phillips, S. D., Christopher-Sisk, E. K., and Gravino, K. L. (2001). Making career decisions in a relational context. *The Counseling Psychologist*, 29, 193–213. Retreived from http://dx.doi.org/10.1177/0011000001292002.

you are exposed to teachers and school administrators and by going to the doctor's office, you are exposed to doctors, nurses, and receptionists. We also learn about careers from people we know who are in these career fields. For instance, perhaps you have a neighbor who is a fragrance chemist, someone who studies odor molecules to develop perfumes, or a member of your church who is a voiceover artist, someone who is the voice for a cartoon character, a documentary, radio show, etc.

Role models also provide us with vicarious learning experiences that can directly impact career decisions (Lent, Brown, & Hackett, 1994). In other words, we can learn from watching others be successful. For example, hearing others talk about how much they enjoy their job or seeing them get recognition or an award for their work can inspire and influence us. We are more likely to pursue a career path if we have seen others achieve and do well, especially if we perceive the role models to be similar to us in some way (Quimby & DeSantis, 2006). This may be particularly important with career options that are predominately associated with males or females. In other words, having a female role model and/or mentor in engineering may increase the likelihood that a female student will pursue this traditionally male career path. Similarly, having a male role model in a field such as nursing that has traditionally been a female career path may make it more likely for a male to choose this field.

Our experiences also play an important role in the career decision-making process. Direct or vicarious exposure to work-related activities influences our career decisions (Lent et al., 2002). When we take on tasks, we can quickly discover what we enjoy and what we don't enjoy. According to social learning theory (Bandura & Walters, 1963), we also learn from watching others. When we observe others do a task, we experience emotions and reactions such as becoming interested and excited or frustrated and disinterested. We can therefore learn a lot about ourselves and our preferences by trying out new tasks and by watching others do so. This is why it is so important to seek out new opportunities, especially in work environments, that interest you. The more you take advantage of experiential learning opportunities and interact with professionals in the field, the more access and exposure you will have to work-related activities for various careers. These direct or indirect experiences can be very helpful to you as you engage in the career decision-making process.

Social cognitive theory. Lent, Brown, and Hackett (1994) proposed a social cognitive theory of career that can help us better understand how career interests develop, how career decisions are made, and what contributes to persistence and high-level performance. One of the basic premises behind this theory is that situational factors can play a major role in our decision-making. Situational factors can include the people with whom we interact and experiences. For example, others in our life can make suggestions about careers, provide us with job opportunities, and encourage us. When we take on new work experiences, we not only learn new skills but also are exposed to new career options and benefit from watching others perform job tasks. This is the social part of their theory. In addition, Lent, Brown, and Hackett (1994) believe that cognitive factors also play a central role in career decision-making. Specifically, they believe that goal setting, expectations, and self-efficacy really matter when it comes to career decision-making. After we set and reach a goal, what do we expect to happen? In other words, what is the reward or outcome of actually achieving the goal? If we value this reward or outcome, we will be more likely to pursue this path. If we don't value the outcome, we may not be inclined to go down this path.

Self-efficacy or our belief in our ability to successfully complete tasks also plays a major role in the career decision-making process (Lent, Brown, & Hackett, 1994). We are not likely to pursue careers that we do not think we will be successful in. On the other hand, we are much more likely to pursue a career path when we believe that we will be successful. As you'll recall, this refers to the "B" in the ABCS of goal-setting framework. See Self-Efficacy Table for a summary of factors that influence self-efficacy. According to this social-cognitive framework, our career interests are shaped by our beliefs and social experiences. For example, it is more likely for us to be interested in a task if we think we will succeed at it and believe that by doing so, positive things will happen. We are also more likely to believe this if we have experienced success previously or we have seen others experience success. When others in our life believe in us and value our career choices, this too positively impacts the career decision-making process.

SELF-EFFICACY TABLE
Factors That Influence Self-Efficacy

Factors	Description
Personal accomplishments	Experiencing success will increase self-efficacy while failure experiences will likely decrease self-efficacy.
Vicarious experiences	When we observe other people who are similar to us achieve success, our self-efficacy increases.
Social persuasion	We can be influenced by others encouraging and believing in us.
Physiological reactions	Our physical reaction when participating or completing a task also influences our self-efficacy. When we experience excitement or exhilaration, we will likely elevate our self-efficacy while, on the other hand, if we are exhausted or drained after completing a task, our self-efficacy can drop.

(Lent, Brown, & Hackett, 1994)

Happenstance learning theory. Krumboltz (2009), a social learning psychologist, believes most career decisions are the result of happenstance. According to happenstance learning theory, career journeys don't necessarily follow a predicted path but rather happen as a result of planned and unplanned events. Krumboltz and Levin (2004) discovered that many people are employed in careers that they did not plan to enter. In fact, they found that very few people followed a planned, predictable path and that many individuals were employed in areas that were not directly connected to their college major. Rather, individuals often choose careers based on experiences, networking, and being open to new opportunities. Because of this, Krumboltz (2009) is less interested in students deciding on a specific career and is more interested in whether they "engage in an active lifestyle to generate unexpected events, to remain alert to new opportunities, and to capitalize on the opportunities they find" (p. 152). Krumboltz and Levin (2004) believe that people who engage in action steps discover many excellent career opportunities. Here are some examples of action steps you can take:

- Talk to others (professors, friends, family, and coworkers) about career options.

- Take a variety of courses in college and talk with professors and classmates about your career aspirations.

- Participate in clubs and organizations and talk with the club advisors and members about your career goals.

- Seek out work experiences in a variety of settings and talk to coworkers about career issues.

- Participate in an internship program to gain experience in a work environment in your field of interest.

- Engage in a service learning project.

- Conduct informational interviews with individuals from different careers.

- Ask others you meet at social events, conferences, and club meetings about their career journey.

Person-environment fit. One of the most well-known career theorists is Holland (1997). His theory focuses on a person-environment model. According to this theory, interests, personality types, and work environments can be characterized according to six basic themes: realistic, investigative, artistic, social, enterprising, and conventional (see Holland's Hexagon Figure). The basic premise of the person-environment theory is that if you can identify a work environment or career that matches well with your personality and interests, then you will be satisfied with your career choice (Smart, Feldman, & Ethington, 2006). Holland refers to this as congruence. The better the match between your personality and interests, and the work environment and tasks, the higher the level of congruence (Leung, 2008). Higher levels of congruence have been connected to higher levels of satisfaction. Research studies have shown that there is indeed a connection between interest, job task, and satisfaction (Jagger, Neukrug, & McAuliffe, 1992; Nauta, 2010).

HOLLAND'S HEXAGON FIGURE
HOLLAND'S HEXAGON ON PERSON-ENVIRONMENT FIT

Reproduced by special permission of the Publisher, Psychological Assessment Resources, Inc., 16204 North Florida Avenue, Lutz, Florida 33549, from the *Self-Directed Search Technical Manual* by John L. Holland, Ph.D., Copyright 1985, 1987, 1994. Further reproduction is prohibited without permission from PAR, Inc.

MAKING CAREER DECISIONS QUICK QUIZ

1. According to social cognitive theory, what influences career decisions?
2. According to happenstance learning theory, what influences career decisions?
3. According to person-environment fit theory, what leads to satisfaction in careers?

Career Indecision

iStock.com/Nastia11

It is not uncommon for students to enter college unsure of what major or career to choose. Some researchers have found that 70% of traditional-aged students (high school student or recent graduate) and 65% of older students are undecided about their career choice (Albion & Fogarty, 2002). If this is the case for you, you are certainly not alone. Some career theorists argue that deciding on a specific career may not be necessary, but rather determining what actions will lead to a satisfying career and personal life matters most (Krumboltz, 2009). Edmondson (2016) argues that students should major in happiness, meaning that students should choose a major that matches their interests and values instead of trying to chase the latest employment trend or identify a major that is associated with a high salary. He believes that when students choose a major that they are passionate about, success will follow. Discovering what matters to you and what will bring meaning to your life and the life of others will help you identify a major and actions you can take to have a successful career.

Although choosing a college major will make it much easier for you to determine what classes you'll need to take, making a decision without engaging in active exploration will not lead to the best outcome. The key is to take actions that will help you explore your options before ultimately deciding on a career pathway. With all of the academic tasks on your plate, it is easy to put off the work associated with career exploration. However, there is no doubt that you will make a better decision if you make career exploration a priority and engage in actions that will help you determine a career pathway.

While it is important for you to explore before committing to a career path or major, choosing a major aligned to your career goals sooner versus later can help you stay on track with your graduation timetable. Waiting too long before choosing a major may have negative consequences in terms of time and money. It may take longer for you to earn a certificate or a degree. Taking longer to graduate also means you will be paying more tuition and perhaps more room and board, which can add to your student loan debt.

It is worth noting that choosing a major is not the same as choosing a career. In some cases, such as nursing, you will need to choose a major that is directly aligned to your career goal. However, in many cases, you can enter your career path through a variety of majors. For example, if you want to become a police officer, the major that would likely come to mind is criminal justice and this is, of course, a great option, but other majors such as psychology, sociology, communications, or a foreign language could also set you up for success in this field. It is therefore more important to identify a career path and then determine which major can best help you reach this goal.

As you are discovering, career decision-making is complex. As a result, many researchers have studied the career decision-making process and what difficulties might arise during the process. Gati, Krausz, and Osipow (1996), for instance, identified three primary types of career decision-making difficulties:

1. Lack of readiness. Some individuals may not be motivated to make a decision and engage in the career exploration process. Others may have a difficult time making decisions in general.

2. Lack of information. Individuals may lack information about themselves (e.g., interests and values), career information, or how to find information that will be helpful in this process.

3. Inconsistent information. Individuals may struggle to make a decision because the information they have is not consistent. For example, maybe you are excited about the job tasks and salary when reading about it online, but when you talk with professionals in the field, their description of the tasks and salary is not as positive. In addition, career options could cause internal or external conflict. An example of internal conflict could be if a career option matches many of your important values but conflicts with one value that is very important to you. An external conflict, on the other hand, could occur when your career choice doesn't match what your family or significant other had in mind for you.

Seeking professional guidance from career counselors who are experts at helping you with this process is recommended, especially if you are uncertain about your career goals (Greenbank, 2010). Unfortunately, only 8% of the students in a study conducted by Vertsberger and Gati (2015) reported meeting with career advisors even though this service was available free of charge. Students instead tend to get most of their career information from friends and family (Greenbank & Hepworth, 2008). While using your network is certainly important, seeking guidance from career specialists can also be quite helpful, especially if you are struggling with the career decision-making process. A career specialist can help increase your motivation to engage in the career exploration process, help you find additional information, or help you navigate and interpret inconsistent information.

Another benefit of reaching out for help is that you will be less likely to change your major if you work with a career expert (Vertsberger & Gati, 2015). As you can imagine, changing your major can sometimes increase the amount of time and money needed to graduate with a degree. Thus, investing your time and effort in this process now so that you make a choice after exploring options will help you save time and perhaps money in the future. You will also be more likely to choose a career path that will make you happy.

CAREER INDECISION QUICK QUIZ

1. What are three primary types of career decision-making difficulties?
2. How can career specialists help with career decision-making?

Self-Assessment

Jacek Dudzinski/Shutterstock.com

The career exploration process involves self-assessment (considering your personality, values, abilities, and interests), finding career information (such as educational requirements, job tasks, salary), and taking action. It's no surprise that self-assessment is an important part of the process. The more you know about yourself, the better you can make decisions about your future. Personality, values, interests, and abilities will all play a role in career decisions. Even if you have a clear career goal and have declared an academic major, engaging in self-assessment can be a worthwhile activity. As a result of this process, you may feel more confident with your chosen career path, be clearer about what specialty area within a chosen field best fits for you, or you might question your initial goal and be interested in exploring different options. Think about how your values, abilities, personality, and interests can guide your career decision-making. Research-based assessment tools to help with this are available in MindTap and online.

Exploring your values. Exploring your values is a great place to begin the career exploration process. Values are a driving force in our decisions (Balsamo, Lauriola, & Saggino, 2012; Hall, Hladkyj, Perry, & Ruthig, 2004; Sargent & Domberger, 2007). Values refer to what matters to you or what is high on your priority list of importance. Examples of career values include the following:

- Being able to help others or make a difference in society
- Functioning independently
- Room for creativity
- Working alone
- Working with others
- Salary
- Prestige
- Job security

- Engaging in a variety of tasks
- Having consistent, predictable job tasks
- Working in a competitive, fast-paced work environment
- Working in a calm work environment
- Flexible hours
- Consistent schedule, such as 9–5 work day
- Having reliable and likeable coworkers
- Having fair and responsive supervisors
- Opportunity for advancement
- Recognition for achievements
- Opportunity to use strengths or talents
- Supportive work environment—easy to access help when needed
- Travel opportunities
- Leadership opportunities—managing or supervising others

Your values may change over time. For example, you might value the opportunity to travel now, but if you have a family in the future, you might then place a higher value on family time, and traveling may no longer appeal to you because it might mean you will miss out on important family events. While it is difficult to predict what will matter to you in the future, it is a good idea to think about what might be important to you in 5, 10, or even 20 years from now.

Unless you are in an extremely difficult situation, you will likely not take a job or enter a career that conflicts with your value system. For example, a person who is totally against smoking probably would not take an otherwise ideal job at a tobacco company. In other words, if a position clashes with your values, it will likely be a deal breaker.

Exploring your abilities. Your skills and abilities are also important considerations as you engage in career decision-making. Research has shown that ability is linked to career success (Judge, Hurst, & Simon, 2009). Most of us would prefer to go into a career that builds on our strengths instead of focusing on our weaker areas.

Gardner's (1983) theory of multiple intelligence is a great way to start thinking about your abilities and strengths. He identified several different types of intelligence:

1. **Linguistic**—ability to use language
2. **Logical-Mathematical**—ability to use logic and solve mathematical problems
3. **Spatial**—ability to perceive spatial relationships
4. **Bodily-Kinesthetic**—ability to use your body to perform tasks
5. **Musical**—ability to comprehend and create music
6. **Intrapersonal**—ability to engage in self-reflection
7. **Interpersonal**—ability to engage in social behavior
8. **Naturalistic**—ability to identify patterns in nature
9. **Existential/Philosophical**—ability to think deeply about philosophical questions such as the meaning of life

It is important to note that Gardner (1983) does not place a higher value on one type of intelligence as compared to another. Rather, he believes all types of intelligence are valuable and worthwhile. Gardner (1983) viewed these types of intelligences as being on a continuum, with everyone having some level of intelligence in each area but being stronger in some areas than others. As you can see, this view of intelligence is fairly comprehensive in nature. This theory provides you with a great way to focus on where your strengths lie. Thinking about your strengths can help you choose a career that builds on these strengths, maximizing career success.

Employers are looking for both technical skills related to the career field and soft or transferable skills that are important in most, if not all, careers. Technical skills vary from career to career. For example, teachers need to be able to write lesson plans while pharmacists need to know how medications may interact with one another. Transferable or soft skills can be used across all careers and include being able to communicate and work well with others. In a study conducted by Robles (2012), employers indicated that soft skills are very important. Specifically, employers were asked to rate 10 soft skills. As you can see in Valued Soft Skills Figure, all of the skills were highly valued by employers, with integrity and communication skills being the most important. You can increase your ability in these areas by seeking out assistance and relevant opportunities. For instance, if you want to increase your verbal or communication skills, take additional courses in this field, work with your professor or a tutor, or participate in activities where you can develop and use these skills.

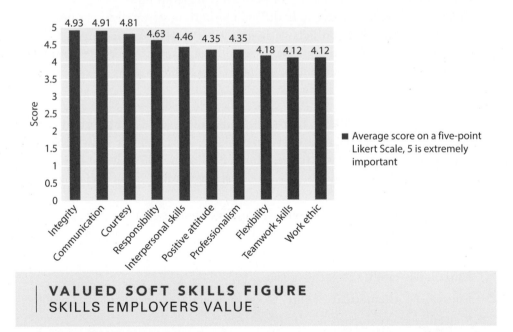

VALUED SOFT SKILLS FIGURE
SKILLS EMPLOYERS VALUE

Exploring your personality and interests. Another important part of the process is to explore your personality traits and how these traits may play a role in your career decision-making. Personality factors have been connected to career choice (Warr & Pearce, 2004) as well as career success (Rode, Arthaud-Day, Mooney, Near, & Baldwin, 2008). While there are several personality theories, McCrae and Costa's (1990) Big Five Personality Factor trait theory is one of the most well-known and researched theories. According to this theory, there are five distinct personality factors or characteristics (the mnemonic OCEAN can help you remember them). The factors are on a continuum, meaning you will be low, moderate, or high on each dimension. See McCrae and Costa Personality Table for an overview of the Big Five Personality Factors.

MCCRAE AND COSTA PERSONALITY TABLE — Big Five Personality Factors		
Mnemonic	**Personality Factor**	**Description**
O	**O**penness	Like to try new things and enjoy doing a variety of activities
C	**C**onscientiousness	Responsible, organized, careful, and self-disciplined
E	**E**xtraversion	Enjoy the company of others, social, fun to be around
A	**A**greeableness	Cooperative, trusting of others
N	**N**euroticism	Worry a lot, anxious, high strung

As previously discussed, Holland's person-environment theory emphasizes personality and interests and the importance of matching one's personality and interests to job tasks and work environment. See Holland's Theory Table for a description of each of the six themes and a few career choices linked to each one. Your top three personality types or interest areas are often referred to as your Holland code (i.e., SEC for Social, Enterprising, and Conventional). To find out your code, you can take an interest inventory. The Strong Interest Inventory and the Self-Directed Search are two very well-known interest inventories based on Holland's (1997) theory. Stop by the career center at your college and see if it has career interest inventory resources available to you. There are also many resources available that describe careers using Holland's coding system. For example, O*NET OnLine (https://www.onetonline.org/) lists Holland's code for various occupations.

HOLLAND'S THEORY TABLE — Holland's Theory and Related Careers		
Theme	**Description**	**Careers**
Realistic	Athletic, prefers working with things and outdoors	Pilot, florist, laboratory technician
Investigative	Scientific thinker, prefers working with ideas	Biologist, researcher, computer systems analyst
Artistic	Creative, prefers unstructured situations and working independently	Artist, journalist, photographer
Social	Helper, prefers working with others	Teacher, speech pathologist, psychologist
Enterprising	Leader, prefers to influence and persuade others	Sales manager, buyer, politician
Conventional	Detail-oriented, prefers clerical and structured tasks	Administrative assistant, editorial assistant, tax accountant

Source: Adapted from: http://www.myfico.com/Downloads/Files/myFICO_UYFS_Booklet.pdf.

To more fully understand your personality, you may want to consider taking more comprehensive personality assessments. You can contact your Career Services department to explore your assessment options and to discuss the career decision-making process. The Myers Briggs Personality Assessment is one of the most widely used personality assessments and it is often recommended by career counselors (Kennedy & Kennedy, 2004). It summarizes your psychological preferences for interacting with the world. Knowing your preferences can aid you in the career decision-making process. For example, if you are someone who is extroverted, getting your energy from others, it will be important that you choose a career where you will have the opportunity to be around others. See Myers Briggs Table for an overview of the personality factors associated with this assessment tool.

MYERS BRIGGS TABLE
Myers Briggs Personality Factors

Extroversion: Gets energy from the external world (others, activities)	**Introversion:** Gets energy from one's internal world (thoughts, ideas, emotions)
Sensing: Prefers paying attention to what can be seen or sensed (what is real)	**Intuition:** Prefers to consider what might be rather than what currently exists
Thinking: Prefers to take in and organize information logically	**Feeling:** Prefers to take in and organize information based on personal values and emotions
Judgment: Prefers a life that is planned and well-organized	**Perceiving:** Prefers a life characterized by spontaneity and flexibility

Source: Adapted from: Hirsh and Kummerow (1992) as cited in Kennedy and Kennedy (2004).

CAREERS AND YOUR SELF-ASSESSMENT

- Values—What is important to you? What will be important to you in the future?
- Abilities—What are your overall strengths? What are your soft or transferable skills? What technical skills do you have for various career choices?
- Personality—How would you describe your personality? What careers might fit best with your personality?
- Interests—What do you like to do? What is your Holland code? What types of careers might match your interests?

SELF-ASSESSMENT QUICK QUIZ

1. What role do values play in career decision-making?
2. What's the difference between technical and soft skills?
3. What are the Big Five personality factors and how does personality influence career choice?

Learning about Careers

Now that you've considered your values, abilities, personalities, and interests, it's time to explore career information. Knowing the education or training requirements, job tasks, salary information, or other important information about various careers will help you with the career decision-making process. It's difficult to know if a career is a good match for you if you don't know much about the profession. Finding and evaluating career information is therefore important.

Because it is impossible to thoroughly explore every possible career option, career decision makers only typically search a manageable number of options (Gati & Tikotzki, 1989). For some, the challenge is to narrow the options because too many careers match their values and interests. If this is the case for you, you will want to spend some time and energy on really thinking about your values and what matters to you. In other words, you will want to prioritize your values and identify the core values that matter the most to you. You can then use your core values as way to screen potential options, eliminating career options that do not match your values until you have a list that is manageable (Gati, 1986).

However, some of you may begin the process with a narrow list of values or interests and this can result in a short list of career options to pursue. If your list is too narrow, you will likely miss out on exploring options that could potentially be good matches for you. Seeking out new opportunities and experiences, talking with others, and exploring online career information resources can help you identify potential options you might not have previously considered. For some, expanding the list before strategically evaluating options is a critical step. You can meet with a career specialist to help you expand or narrow your list.

There is a wealth of information on careers available. As you know, the information literacy challenge is determining what information you need and then sifting through the vast amount of information out there to find it. Two of the most widely used information-gathering strategies related to career exploration are reviewing career websites and conducting informational interviews.

Career websites. The first and most comprehensive strategy is to use websites or database systems that have packaged the information you are looking for into brief career summaries. Career counselors or librarians at your college can assist you with finding information about the careers you would like to investigate. There is an incredible amount of career information available on the Internet. As you know, you'll have to carefully evaluate the credibility of websites before you accept the information as being accurate. Here are just a few credible resources you may want to explore:

- Occupational Outlook Handbook (www.bls.gov/ooh) (see Occupational Outlook Handbook Figure)
- Career One Stop (www.careerinfonet.org)
- O-NET (http://online.onetcenter.org)
- Ferguson's Career Guidance Center (www.fofweb.com/Careers)
- National Career Development Association www.ncda.org

Career websites provide you with basic information about the educational and other requirements needed to enter the career, an overview of job tasks, and

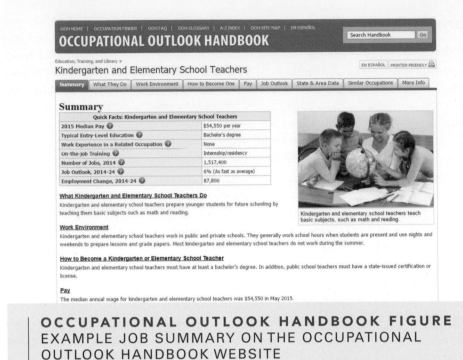

OCCUPATIONAL OUTLOOK HANDBOOK FIGURE
EXAMPLE JOB SUMMARY ON THE OCCUPATIONAL
OUTLOOK HANDBOOK WEBSITE

Source: U.S. Bureau of Labor Statistics.

responsibilities, salary, and job outlook. Job outlook refers to the number of job openings expected in the future. Most of the data presented on career websites are based on national data, so it's important for you to know that some of the information may vary significantly across different geographic areas. After gathering general information from these national resources, be sure to also look for information specific to where you plan to work. Salaries and job opportunities, for instance, can vary significantly based on location. See Teacher Salaries Table for an example. Use websites such as salary.com for more specific information related to your geographic location.

In addition to seeking out general information about different careers, you may also want to consider searching online to see what positions in your field of interest are available. Websites such as indeed.com or monster.com can work well for this purpose. Conducting a job search now can give a sense of the type and

TEACHER SALARIES TABLE Example Salaries for Elementary School Teacher	
Data Source	**Median Salary ($)**
National Average (*Occupational Outlook Handbook*)	54,550
New York City, NY (Salary.com)	64,208
Rapid City, SD (Salary.com)	50.566

Source: Retrieved January 7, 2017, from http://www.salary.com and http://www.bls.gov/ooh/education-training-and-library/kindergarten-and-elementary-school-teachers.htm.

number of positions available in the career path that interests you and provide you with valuable information about skills and experiences you will need to develop during college. Look at the job requirements so that you can determine what types of experiences you will want to seek out during college to build a strong résumé. This increases the likelihood that you will be offered a position in the field of your choice in the future. Perhaps you might even come across part-time opportunities that you are able to take advantage of now!

Informational interviews. While websites can provide you with a very clear overview of the career, informational interviews can give you a more personal look at the career. "An informational interview is a brief meeting between a person who wants to investigate a career and a person working in that career" (Crosby, 2010, 22). The goal of the interview is to learn about the career, not land a job. The first step is to find someone working in your field of interest. Here are some tips to find professionals in careers you would like to explore:

- Ask your family and friends if they know anyone in your field of interest.
- Ask your professors, especially those in the major related to your career choice, if they would be willing to meet with you or connect you to a professional working in the field.
- Check with your alumni office on your campus—alumni may be willing to help you explore career options.
- Social media sites such as LinkedIn can help you find a professional who is willing to do an informational interview with you.

Once you identify a person to interview, reach out to that person to request his or her participation in the informational interview. While most individuals are interested in helping college students with career decision-making, it's important for you to realize that professionals can be very busy. You may want to have several individuals in mind to interview in case someone doesn't respond or is unable to do the interview due to other responsibilities.

It is important to conduct yourself professionally before, during, and after your informational interview. Prior to the interview, generate a list of questions you would like to ask. You should respect the professional's time—the interview shouldn't last more than 15 to 30 minutes. Keep your questions to a minimum and prioritize the most important ones. Here are some questions you might consider:

- How did you get started with this career?
- Describe a typical day in your position.
- What do you most enjoy about your career?
- What are the challenges associated with this career choice?
- What suggestions or advice do you have for someone who is interested in this field?

On the day of your interview, be sure to dress professionally. You want to make a good impression, as this is also a networking opportunity. Arrive on time and end the interview on schedule. In addition to thanking the person at the end of the interview, send a formal thank you e-mail or letter once you return home.

These personal conversations can provide you with wonderful, rich information; however, it is not advisable to rely solely on this approach because the experience of one person may not be consistent with the experiences of others. As always, take in information from a variety of sources and look for themes that emerge. This leads to a more comprehensive understanding of the career field.

CAREER INFORMATION QUICK QUIZ

1. What are some examples of credible career websites and what type of information will you find on these sites?

2. What is an informational interview and why is it valuable?

Chapter Summary: Note-Taking Model

Let's summarize what you've learned in this chapter. The matrix model is used for this chapter. Remember, it is not expected that your notes will look like this right after class or reading. It takes time to organize your notes and repackage them. It is time well spent, though, because you learn the content better as you organize it and you'll have a fabulous foundation from which to study for your exams! There are several ways to use this section:

- **Preview:** Read the model before reading the chapter to familiarize yourself with the content.
- **Compare:** Compare the notes you took on the chapter to the model provided.
- **Study:** The model along with your notes and other course materials are great resources for studying.

Matrix Notes Model

Use the ABCS of Setting and Implementing Goals to Achieve Success	
Aim high	Goals should be challenging because the higher you aim, the higher you will achieve
Believe in yourself	If you believe you can reach your goal, you will be more likely to succeed.
Care and commit	Being passionate about your goal and making a commitment to achieve increases success.
Specify and self-reflect	You will be more likely to achieve success if your goal is specific in nature. To help you achieve your goal, it's important to regularly monitor your progress and make changes as needed.

How Do We Make Career Decisions?	
Social-cognitive theory	As social beings, important people in our life can influence career decisions by encouraging us or by watching others in various careers. Decisions are also based on our self-efficacy, which refers to whether we believe we can successfully achieve a task
Happenstance theory	Planned and unplanned events influence our career decisions. Being open to experiences and seeking out new opportunities is recommended.
Person-environment fit	We make career decisions based on our personality and interests.

Career Indecision			
Reasons for Indecision	Lack of readiness	Lack of information	Inconsistent information

What's Involved in Career Exploration?

Career Exploration Activities	Information Needed	Where to Access this Information
Self-assessment	• Values • Abilities • Personality • Interest	• Self-assessment surveys • Discussion with career specialist
Learning about careers	• Basic information about careers (tasks, educational requirements, salary) • Personal experiences in the career	• Websites such as *Occupational Outlook Handbook* (www.bls.gov/ooh) • Informational interviews

PART 2

STRATEGIES AND SKILLS FOR SUCCESS

CHAPTER 3

Building Academic Skills

> All the so-called "secrets of success" will not work unless you do.
>
> —*Author Unknown*

1. What memory techniques work best? How can you apply these techniques to your study practices?

2. What reading methods work best?

3. How can you get the most out of being in class? What note-taking approach works best?

4. Which study strategies work best? Which study strategies are least effective?

5. What is the testing effect? How can you use this approach to have long-lasting learning?

6. Why is teaching such a powerful learning tool? How can you engage in teaching while studying?

7. How can you use organizing strategies to increase learning?

James Woodson/Getty Images

Exploring the Research in Summary

Research Study Citation

McDaniel, M. A., Howard, D. C., and Einstein, G. O. (2009). The read-recite-review study strategy: Effective and portable. *Psychological Science,* 20(4), 516–522.

INTRODUCTION: THE RESEARCH QUESTION

What question did the researcher seek to answer?

Which reading strategy (re-reading, note-taking, or read-recite-review) works best?

METHOD: THE STUDY

Who participated in the study? What did the researchers ask the participants to do?

The researchers conducted two experiments. In both experiments, 72 college students were assigned to one of the following three groups:

- Re-read (students read the passages twice)
- Note-taking (students took notes on the passages while reading, but were not able to use notes at the time of testing)
- 3R: Read-recite-review (students read the passages once, then recited what they remembered, and finally read the passages again to review, determining if they accurately captured all of the information)

All of the students read several passages and then answered test questions about what they read immediately after the task and then again one week later. Some of the questions were fact-based and others required higher-level cognitive skills such as inference and problem-solving.

RESULTS: THE FINDINGS

What was the answer to the research question?

Students who used the 3R method performed better on the fact-based recall questions as compared to the note-taking and re-reading groups (see Reading Strategy Free Recall Figure). This finding was true for the immediate test and the testing that occurred one week later. The students in the 3R method and note-taking strategy groups performed equally well on problem-solving tasks, both performing better than the re-reading group. However, the 3R method was less time-consuming (13.4 minutes in experiment 1 and 21.5 minutes in experiment 2) than the note-taking method (17.5 minutes in experiment 1 and 25.4 minutes in experiment 2). The re-reading group took an average of 9.2 minutes in the first experiment and 20.9 minutes in the second experiment (see Reading Strategy Time to Completion Figure).

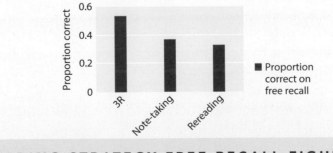

READING STRATEGY FREE RECALL FIGURE
PROPORTION CORRECT ON FREE RECALL

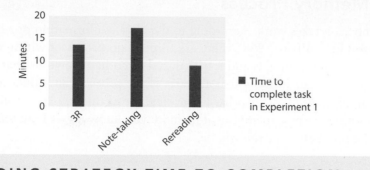

READING STRATEGY TIME TO COMPLETION FIGURE
TIME TO COMPLETE TASK (EXPERIMENT 1)

DISCUSSION AND SO WHAT FACTOR

How can YOU use this information as a student?

These findings show that simply reading and re-reading your textbook will not lead to high performance on exams. The 3R method is the best option to maximize your success. The note-taking strategy is also very effective for more challenging test items. The act of recalling information, verbally or through writing, is what will really assist you with mastering the material. The 3R method does not take much longer than simply re-reading the chapter (less than a minute in the second experiment), and it leads to much better results. It therefore seems very worthwhile to add in this additional step of reciting what you recall before you read the material again. In your classes, you will have to master much more information than what was asked of students in this study. Taking notes, while not looking at the book, may therefore be the best strategy to use so that you can refer to and use these notes when you are studying. If you are crunched for time, though, simply adding in a verbal recall activity can work!

How Memory Works: Building Foundational Knowledge

In college, you are exposed to extraordinary amounts of new information. Each course you take will be packed with new concepts and theories. As a college student, you are expected to engage in many sophisticated cognitive tasks, such as critically evaluating information and applying newly learned material to various situations. You need to know and remember key foundational information in order to engage in higher-level thinking tasks. In other words, gaining content knowledge is a must—it not only makes it easier for you to learn more in the future but also helps you get ready to tackle challenging cognitive tasks.

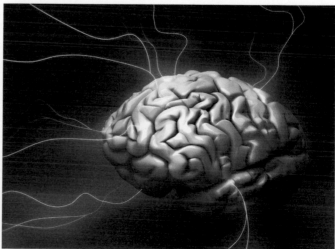

The Memory Process

iStock.com/bulentozber

Remembering takes work. According to the classic information processing model (Atkinson & Shiffrin, 1968), there are three main processes within our memory system: encoding, storage, and retrieval. Research has shown us that this process is multidirectional, meaning that all parts of the process can influence other parts (Willingham, 2009). Our prior memories, for example, play a role in how we encode and store new memories. The more you know about how these processes work, the more efficient you will be!

Encoding.
Encoding refers to how we get memories into our memory system. To purposefully encode material, start by paying attention to it. We are constantly exposed to sensory information. For example, today in class your professor was probably talking to you about a topic (memory perhaps!), your classmates were taking notes, students were walking in the hallway, and the projector in the classroom may have been making a humming noise. You have to decide what information is worthy of your attention. Our past experiences can influence this process. If we have previously found information to be useful, it will be more likely that we will attend to content that seems similar in nature. Likewise, if we have discovered that information has not been useful, we are less likely to attend to related content. While much of these attentive processes happen without effort or work, it is, of course, more likely for us to hold onto to content if we actively attend to it. Thus, if you are actively and purposely attending to what your professor says during a lecture, it is much more likely for this content to get encoded and stored in your memory system.

Multisensory approaches to learning can assist you in encoding information more effectively (Myers, 2014). For instance, if you encode information using both visual and auditory input, you have increased the likelihood that the information gets into your memory system. This dual-encoding process also makes it more likely that you will find the information in your memory system when you need it. You have probably had the experience where you could not remember something for an exam, but then all of a sudden, you were able to visualize where it was in your notebook. In this example, the visual encoding process helped you retrieve the information. Using more than one sense to input information into your memory system will improve your encoding and retrieval. While we naturally use all of our senses to take in new information, intentional interventions can improve memory. For instance, as you are learning a new concept, thinking of a related image can improve memory for that concept.

Storage.
The second part of the memory process is storage, which refers to how we hold onto and save our memories. Most of us have had the awful experience of typing a paper (the words got into the computer—they were encoded) and then turning the computer off without saving it. Saving information in our memory system is the same idea. Within your memory storage system, you have two main subsystems: working memory and long-term memory. Willingham (2009) nicely visualizes this process via a simple model shown in Memory Figure.

Let's discuss long-term memory first. The great news about long-term memory is that it seems to last forever and appears to have an endless amount of room (Myers, 2014). Unlike your computer hard drive, which has limited capacity, your brain allows you to store more information than you will ever need during

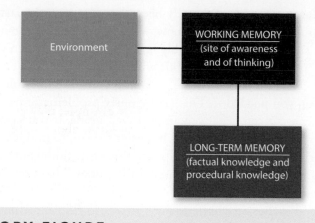

MEMORY FIGURE
A SIMPLE MODEL OF MEMORY

Source: Figure 6: Just about the simplest model of the mind possible from Willingham, D. T. (2009). *Why Don't Students Like School? A Cognitive Scientist Answers Questions About How the Mind Works and What It Means for the Classroom*. San Francisco, CA: Jossey-Bass. Figure 6, Page 11

your lifetime. Long-term memory is clearly the goal when it comes to knowledge related to college, but it takes effort for content to get there.

To get information into long-term memory, working memory is needed. Working memory refers to the work space of your brain where new information is temporarily held. Psychologists used to think that memory was like a one-way street. First, you encoded a new piece of information, and then you stored it temporarily until you housed it permanently in long-term memory. However, research has shown us that our memory system is much more interactive in nature (Woolfolk, 2013). What we already know plays a big role in how we learn new information. We search our long-term memory for information that might help us encode or store the new information. Let's take a look at an example. If you are trying to learn the names of your classmates, you will likely think about others you know with names or features similar to your classmates. This prior knowledge can help you bring the new knowledge into your memory system and keep it there.

Working memory is limited in terms of duration and capacity. In other words, we can only hold onto information for a short period of time, often only seconds, and can only hold onto a few chunks of information at a time. A famous psychologist, George Miller, demonstrated this limited capacity through a research experiment. He asked participants to remember a list of nonsense syllables (so the words could not be simply linked to other memories) and found that the average number of items participants could remember was 7 ± 2. In other words, we can only hold five to nine items in short-term memory at a time (Miller, 1956). This is not good news, since your professors will likely expect you to remember much more than that from each lecture. Don't panic just yet! We are able to move content into the long-term part of our memory system when we actively work with the new content. For example, we can look for connections between the new content and what we've previously learned or prior experiences we've had. We also organize or chunk information so that we can accommodate more than five to nine pieces of information at a time. An example would be a phone number. Typically, we remember area codes as one chunk rather than three independent numbers. Actively working with the information and using memory strategies can help you hold on to important concepts you need to know.

Retrieval. Retrieval has traditionally been thought of as the last stage of the memory process. To show what you know, you retrieve or find the memories you have previously stored. You have probably had the experience when you knew you saved a document in your computer, but when you needed it later, you couldn't locate it. This is called retrieval failure, meaning you were not able to find what you needed when you needed it. This is obviously problematic when it happens during a test because it can negatively impact your grade. If you saved your document in a folder with a clear title, it will be easier for you to find it later. Organizing your memories mentally can also help you efficiently find what you need when you need it. Think of your brain as a mental file folder. The more organized the content, the easier it will be to retrieve.

As mentioned earlier, it will be easier for you to find information that was encoded with a multisensory approach. Using a non-academic example, pretend that you need to get to your friend's house. If you only know one way to get there, you will be in trouble if the road you need to travel is closed. However, if you know two ways to get there, you will be able to take the other path to get there. A multisensory approach provides you with many pathways to find the content you need.

MEMORY PROCESS

- Encoding—Getting information into your memory system
- Storage—Saving information
- Retrieval—Finding stored information when you need it

MEMORY PROCESS QUICK QUIZ

1. How has our understanding of memory changed?
2. What strategies are useful during the encoding stage?
3. How much information can we typically hold in working memory?

Memory Strategies

Now that you are more familiar with how the memory process works, it's time to discuss memory strategies that help you get information into your long-term memory system. This information will help guide your study practices. In this section, we'll be discussing rehearsal, elaboration, chunking, mnemonics, and retrieval practice.

iStock.com/South_agency

Rehearsal. Information in your working memory quickly disappears if you are not actively using the information. Rehearsing or reviewing helps you hold on to your memories. Let's look at an example. If someone tells you a phone number and you don't have your cell phone or a piece of paper handy, it is very likely that you will forget it unless you do something active with the information. One of the easiest strategies to use is to repeat or rehearse the phone number until you can document it somewhere. If you continually rehearse it without being interrupted, you will likely be successful at recalling the number accurately.

Rehearsal is a good start to remembering, but if you only rely on this technique, you'll be disappointed with how much you'll remember. Karpicke and Blunt

(2011) found that students overestimated the effectiveness of the rehearsal or restudying strategy. Many students use rehearsal when they review their notes in preparation for an exam. As you review your notes, the content will become more and more familiar. However, familiarity doesn't equal learning. It does, unfortunately, lead to increased confidence that may, in turn, lead you to stop studying too soon and ultimately not perform as well as you would like on the exam. While rehearsal is an important memory strategy that can work well as a first step, you'll want to combine rehearsal with other more powerful strategies (such as elaboration, chunking, and testing yourself) to ensure that you develop long-lasting memories related to the content being learned.

Elaboration.

Elaboration is when you attach meaning to new content being learned (Myers, 2014). Whenever you learn something new, you change the neural networks in your brain. Elaboration allows you to start with neural connections that already exist and then modify and add neural connections to incorporate the new information.

To elaborate, find connections between information you know and new information you are learning. You can also find connections between new concepts you are learning. Examples are a great way to accomplish this task. When a professor addresses a topic, you can search your long-term memory to find an experience that fits the concept. For example, if your professor lectures about how to do an effective presentation, you can think about your prior experiences with giving or watching presentations. Activating these memories helps you take in the new information because this new content connects to your existing neural pathways. You therefore don't need to spend energy on developing a new pathway. There is strong research support for the elaborative memory technique (Cheung & Kwok, 1998; Gadzella & Baloglu, 2003; Hall et al., 2004).

Chunking.

One of the most effective memory strategies is chunking. Chunking is a memory strategy that simply means organizing the information into manageable, meaningful units or chunks. Using the chunking technique allows you to go beyond the approximately seven items you can typically manage in working memory. For example, let's assume you are trying to recall the following letters: GPSPCDVDWIFI. This can be a tricky task because there are 12 letters to recall and we are typically only able to recall approximately seven items at a time. However, if we chunk these letters into meaningful units such as GPS PC DVD WIFI, the task becomes much easier and it will be much more likely that we can recall all the letters. Researchers have found that chunking study strategies are linked to high grades in college (Gettinger & Seibert, 2002; Gurung, 2005; Lammers et al., 2001).

Chunking is apparent in many places in the college setting. In your textbooks, for example, your authors create large chunks called chapters. Within each chapter, authors use headings to chunk smaller amounts of information. Any time you are using a hierarchy such as an outline, you are chunking. The most important topic is on top; related topics are under it. Remember, chunking simply means organizing the information into manageable amounts of information that are meaningful in some way.

Mnemonics.

Mnemonics are memory tools that help you remember large chunks of information. They have built-in retrieval cues that come in very handy when you need to access your memories (Myers, 2014). Acronyms and sentence or acrostic mnemonics are two of the most frequently used types of mnemonics. Acronyms are made when you take the first letter of the different concepts you need to memorize and create a word from those letters. Let's look at some examples. Do you recall learning ROY G BIV? The letters in this mnemonic stand for the colors of the rainbow. SQ3R (Survey, Question, Read, Recite, and Review) is another example of an acronym. Sentence or acrostic mnemonics are made when you create a sentence or phrase; the first letter of every word stands for a concept that you need to remember. Do you recall learning Please Excuse My Dear Aunt Sally? This refers to the order of operations in math. Although it can be time-consuming to create mnemonics, they can help you create long-lasting memories for information you need to know.

Retrieval practice.   Retrieving information from long-term memory is a powerful memory tool (Karpicke & Roediger, 2006). The act of retrieving information strengthens memories. Let's discuss some ways you can use this strategy. Several reading methods use this approach. For example, the second R in 3R and SQ3R reading methods are examples of how you can practice retrieving information as you read. The second R stands for recite. This is where you remember what you read without looking at the book. Any time you are recalling content, you are using retrieval practice. Quizzes, tests, or exams are also opportunities for you to engage in retrieval practice. To use this as a learning tool, though, you'll need to use these strategies while studying, not just during class.

MEMORY STRATEGIES QUICK QUIZ

1. Which memory strategy is the least effective?
2. Which memory strategies work best?

Active Reading Strategies

Courtesy of Suzanna LoPorto

There are two primary ways you will be learning new information in college: participating in class and reading your textbooks. Class time is limited, and there are many important concepts and theories that you will need to learn. Professors will therefore expect you to get the important additional information you need from the textbook. Reading and, more importantly, using your textbook as an information resource has been found to be positively connected to grades (Rawson et al., 2000).

You've probably discovered that college textbooks can sometimes be challenging to read. A research study conducted by Williamson (2008) found that even students who were reading very well as graduating high school seniors experienced a big drop when it came to comprehending a college-level textbook. This is because college textbooks are much more complex and students will often not know much about the subject matter. Too often students report reading their textbooks only to feel that they have wasted their time because learning didn't take place. Perhaps you too have had the experience that you spent time reading a page but really had no idea what you've just read. The good news is that there are several strategies you can use to increase your reading comprehension. To learn, you must make reading an active process. You can make reading an active process by building prior knowledge and using effective reading strategies such as the 3R and SQ3R method.

Power of Prior Knowledge

Researchers have found that one of the best predictors of how well you will be able to comprehend what you read is not how well you read but instead how much you know about the subject. This was illustrated in a classic study conducted by Recht and Leslie (1988). In their study, students were assessed in terms of their reading skills and their knowledge of baseball. Students were then asked to read a passage on baseball. After reading the passage, students were asked to answer questions related to the story and to re-create the story nonverbally. As you would imagine, the students who were good readers and who knew a lot about baseball performed the best. Similarly, the students who were poor readers and did not know much about baseball had the poorest performance on the tasks. However, the fascinating findings were that the students who were good readers but had low baseball knowledge performed almost as poorly as the poor readers with low baseball knowledge, while the poor readers with high baseball knowledge performed almost as well as the good readers with high baseball knowledge. The key finding of this study is that prior knowledge about baseball was the best predictor of reading comprehension (Recht & Leslie, 1988). In other words, prior knowledge matters more than reading skills.

iStock.com/baramee2554

As a college student, you will likely be reading textbooks about subjects you may not know much about. While this will make it more challenging to comprehend the textbook content, there are several strategies you can use to help you get the most out of reading. The table of contents is a great resource because it provides you with an outline of the chapter content. As you know, the table of contents clearly identifies the big ideas of the chapter. This can provide a helpful organizational context for the information you will be reading. Another simple, yet powerful strategy is to read the end of the chapter summary first, before reading the chapter itself. The summaries can serve as previews for the chapter much like a movie preview. The key points from the summary will help you take in the more detailed information from the chapter. With textbook content that is particularly challenging, you might want to search for a video on the topic before you read the chapter. Some publishers may provide related videos, but if this is not the case, ask your professor for online resources or search the Internet for related videos or general information on the topic. While your professors won't want you to use sites such as Wikipedia as sources for academic products, this type of website can be helpful to provide you with a very basic background on the topic before you read the more detailed textbook. Remember, the goal is to build some background knowledge so that it will be easier for you to understand the assigned reading. Thus, these general resources are simply beginning steps to take prior to reading the chapter.

PRIOR KNOWLEDGE QUICK QUIZ

1. What did the research by Recht and Leslie (1988) tell us about reading comprehension?

2. How can you build your prior knowledge before reading?

The 3R and SQ3R Reading Methods

iStock.com/Manczurov

One simple yet effective reading strategy is the 3R method (McDaniel, Howard, & Einstein, 2009). The 3R method involves the following three steps:

1. Read the material.
2. Recite the material—close the book and say what you remember (or better yet, write it down!).
3. Review or read the material again (add to your notes, filling in missing content and/or write key concepts in the text, a process called annotating).

Active readers use the 3R technique after reading small sections of a chapter. Research tells us that we need to be actively involved with information as we go along rather than waiting until the end of a chapter (Linderholm, 2002; Rawson, Dunlosky, & Thiede, 2000). It is therefore best to identify a short section of the chapter to read using this method rather than trying to use this technique with an entire chapter at once.

After reading the identified section, close your book before you begin the second step—recite. During the recite step of the process, you simply recall what you just read without looking at the text. It is really important that your book is closed during the recite part of the process so that you are truly retrieving the information from your memory. Closing the book before you take notes forces you to put the information into your own words. This results in increased learning (Dickinson & O'Connell, 1990). This is much more effective than copying textbook language into your notes. Copying does not require much attention or engagement and is not very effective when it comes to learning. On the other hand, this "close the book and summarize the information in your own words" strategy will tap into higher-level cognitive skills and definitely increase your understanding of the material.

During the third R, review, you go back and review how well you summarized the content. If you missed any content, this is the perfect opportunity to add to your notes, filling in any information gaps. During this process, you may also want to jot down page numbers so that you can easily use the text as a reference when you are studying. For example, you might be studying a concept and not fully understand the definition or example you wrote down. If you also wrote down the page number, you will be able to quickly get back to that section of the text to review the concept in more depth. If you didn't write the page number down, you may waste time looking for that concept in the text. During this part of the process, you might also want to annotate the textbook. Annotating simply means you are writing some of your notes in the text itself, often in the margins. Your notes are therefore connected to the text. To annotate, you can summarize a key concept, note how this concept relates to something you already know, or write your reaction to the content.

Another well-known reading strategy is the SQ3R method. You will notice that there are two letters or steps added to the process. With this technique, you must:

1. Survey
2. Question
3. Read
4. Recite
5. Review

For the first step, survey, you preview the chapter. Survey means you scan the chapter as a whole and take in the big picture. Start by looking at the table of contents for the assigned chapter, headings, images throughout the chapter, and the chapter summary. Doing this provides you with an overview of the chapter content. It sets the stage for you by helping you understand the organization of the information that will be presented in the chapter.

The second step in SQ3R involves creating questions about the content. You have probably already discovered that this textbook comes with chapter opener questions that appear on the first page of every chapter. If your other texts do not have this feature, create your own questions based on the survey you did of the chapter. What questions do you think will be addressed in the chapter? What are you curious about after scanning the chapter? Searching for answers to questions is an active reading strategy and will result in increased learning. The final three steps involve the same read, recite, review steps of the 3R method. Research has shown that the SQ3R method has been connected to increased reading comprehension (Artis, 2008) and improved exam performance (Carlston, 2011).

3R AND SQ3R QUICK QUIZ

1. What are the similarities between the 3R and SQ3R reading methods?
2. What are the differences between the 3R and SQ3R reading methods?
3. What should you do during the second R in the 3R and SQ3R reading methods?

Highlighting

Most college students highlight their texts as they read. Researchers have found that students comprehend what they read at higher levels when important text is highlighted (So & Chan, 2009). Unfortunately, most students are not engaging in good highlighting practices. Because students are novice learners and do not know a lot about the textbook content, it is extremely difficult for them to differentiate the important from the less important and determine what to highlight. As a result, students either highlight too much or too little. This obviously does not result in increased learning and has been found in some cases to even result in poorer performance (Dunlosky, Rawson, Marsh, Nathan, & Willingham, 2013; Gier, Kreiner, & Natz-Gonzalez, 2009). Thus, ineffective highlighting is worse than not highlighting at all.

iStock.com/eyefocusaz

Some researchers have found that teaching students to highlight or underline main ideas works. For example, Hayati and Shariatifar (2009) found that students who participated in a one-hour training session on how to highlight effectively performed well on a reading comprehension test. Students were taught to read the passage first without highlighting and then to go back and underline the main ideas. As you can imagine, it would be next to impossible to truly figure out what is important on a first read of a passage or article. Thus, don't pick up your highlighter, if you want to use this technique, until the last R, reviewing, of the 3R or SQ3R methods. This way you will be deciding what is most important after you have already interacted with the text a couple of times. If you are still unsure about what is or isn't important, rely on other strategies instead and avoid highlighting.

In order to benefit from highlighting, you must bring attention to the important points. The more familiar you are with the content, the easier this task will be for you. Check out the Identifying Important Points Table for tips on how to identify the important points when reading a chapter. As you've noticed, this section on active reading has been highlighted. This can serve as a model for you.

IDENTIFYING IMPORTANT POINTS TABLE Identifying Important Points When Reading	
Survey or preview the chapter and other resources	• Look at the table of contents. • Skim chapter to find headings, subheadings, key terms, visual images, and graphs. • Read the summary at the end of the chapter. • Check out PowerPoint slides or other handouts given to you by the professor. • Create questions about the content if this has not already been done for you by the author.
Identify a section of the text to read	• Don't try to read an entire chapter at once. • Break up the reading task into manageable chunks (sections with headings or subheadings work well).
Read and recite	• Read the identified section. • Write down the main points, using your own words. • Think about how this information might fit in with the other chapter content or previously learned content.
Review time	• Review the section you just read. • Use your highlighter to draw attention to the concepts you just identified. • Limit the amount that you allow yourself to highlight to one to two sentences per paragraph or section.
Make reading social	• Partner with a classmate before class and compare what you've identified as important. • Explain why you highlighted what you did and your partner can do the same.

HIGHLIGHTING QUICK QUIZ

1. Is highlighting an effective reading strategy?
2. How can you highlight more effectively?

Tom Peterson

Note-Taking

To get the most out of your class experiences, you will want to be prepared, be ready to participate, and will need to take good notes. Your notes serve as an excellent study tool. You will likely forget most of what you learned in class unless you take good notes and actively use or repackage these notes after class.

Preparing for and Participating in Class

Attending class is obviously an important first step in learning college-level material, and research has shown that attending class is in fact one of the best predictors of academic success (Jones, 1984; Thatcher, Fridjhon, & Cockcroft, 2007). Classroom lectures, discussions, and other classroom-based tasks are essential learning activities. Physical presence alone is obviously not enough. To make the most of your time spent in class and maximize the learning that takes place there, you'll need to be prepared and ready to participate. Being prepared will make it easier for you to be cognitively engaged during class, which is associated with increased learning (Mayer, 2009).

Preparing is important in all areas of our life—learning is no exception. Would an athlete go to an athletic event without training for it? Would an actor perform in a play without practicing his lines first? Of course not! Many students believe that learning begins when they walk through the classroom door and the professor begins to lecture, but this is not the case. Professors expect you to be ready to take in the information presented during class. Being ready to take in the information involves more than just bringing the appropriate note-taking materials to class. To get ready to learn, review the syllabus, read the chapters and other materials, and complete assignments before heading off to class. This will provide you with the background knowledge you need to be an active participant in class and to take effective notes. Research conducted by Strage et al. (2002) shows that students who read before class and who took good notes while reading and during class had higher levels of success than students who did not. As you read, you can also jot down questions you may have about the concepts you've read and do not fully understand.

By reading the material prior to class, you set yourself up for a successful class experience. You will be familiar with the terminology and concepts that will be discussed by your professor. If you go to class and you don't have any background knowledge about the topic, everything the professor says will be brand new to you, and you will likely feel the need to write it all down. As you attempt to quickly write down as much as you can, you may miss more than you catch. If, on the other hand, you are familiar with the terminology being used by your professor, you won't feel the pressure to write everything down and it will be easier for you to determine what is most important. Knowing what information is available to you via the textbook can also help you decide what must be written down during class. For example, if you recall seeing the definition of a term in your textbook, you may opt not to write it down during the lecture and instead focus on the examples and applications that may not have been in the book.

Being ready to take effective notes requires more than academic preparation. It also involves your attitude and motivation level. You need to be mentally ready to take in the information. For example, it is best if you've had a good night's sleep the night before class, ate a good breakfast, and maybe even exercised a bit that morning. Having a positive mindset about the class, even if it's not one of your favorites, also helps you prepare for good note-taking. Focus on the importance of doing well in the class and the connection between your performance in this course and your academic and career goals.

Learning is an active process and requires more than attendance and listening. While in class, you can participate in a variety of ways. Asking questions in class is a great way to get involved and shows the professor that you're interested in learning. Don't ask a question for the sake of asking, instead ask questions to clarify and expand on what you are learning. Not everyone is comfortable asking questions in front of the class, and it is certainly not the only way you can be an active learner. You can also be engaged by jotting down personally meaningful examples or questions that you plan to look up or ask others (professors, classmates, or other students) after class. This may be particularly important in large lecture classes where high participation levels may not always be possible. Mayer's (2009) research shows us that cognitive engagement is what matters most.

Regardless of the approach you use, you want to show the professor that you are attending to and processing the information through your behaviors. You can do this by using nonverbal communication such as eye contact, nodding, facial expressions, and note-taking. Your posture can also communicate your level of involvement. Students who are sitting up and leaning forward send the message "I'm interested and engaged," while students who slouch and sit back send the opposite message. These nonverbal behaviors provide your professor with feedback about your level of attentiveness and interest. Professors notice your behaviors, even in large lecture classes.

ACTIVELY PARTICIPATING IN CLASS

- Read the chapter and other reading assignments prior to class.
- Complete all written or other assignments prior to class.
- Write down questions you have about the material you've read or have previously discussed in class.
- Ask questions that seek to clarify and expand on what you are learning.
- Take notes and jot down examples and questions.
- Maintain good eye contact with the professor, tracking him or her as he or she lectures.
- Sit up and lean forward to communicate you are interested and engaged.

PREPARING FOR AND PARTICIPATING IN CLASS QUICK QUIZ

1. Why is it a good idea to read chapter content before class?
2. How can you show your professor that you are interested in learning?

Note-Taking Methods

stock_photo_world/Shutterstock.com

Why do we need to take notes? Research has shown us that we will forget information quickly if we do not actively use it (Myers, 2014). See Forgetting Figure for a visual image of how quickly we can forget information.

To prevent forgetting, you need to take action. Taking good notes during class will help you remember important lecture content. Research shows that note-taking is linked to test performance (Peverly, Brobst, Graham, & Shaw, 2003). It is important to note, however, that it is not the act of note-taking that helps you remember but rather how you use these notes after class. This was illustrated in an interesting study by Knight and McKelvie (1986) where students were assigned to different learning conditions. Some students were provided with lecturer notes while others took their own notes or did not take notes at all. The results showed that studying from notes was connected to the highest performance, with those who studied from lecturer notes performing the best. This result highlights the

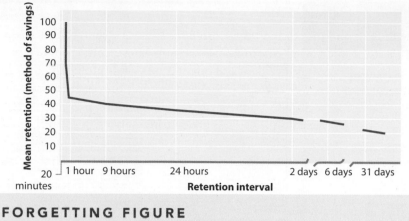

FORGETTING FIGURE
EBBINGHAUS FORGETTING CURVE
This graphic illustrates that we quickly forget information if we do not actively use it. Most (over 50%) will be forgotten within hours. It is therefore essential that we actively work with the information and take good notes!

Source: From Ellis, *From Master Student to Master Employee*, 5th ed. Boston, MA: Cengage, p. 187. Copyright © 2017 Cengage Learning, Inc. Reproduced by permission, www.cengage.com/permissions.

importance of having good notes to study from when preparing for a test or exam. Interestingly, students who did not review their notes did not perform any better than students who didn't take any notes at all. This finding emphasizes that the act of note-taking doesn't result in learning, but rather that learning happens when you use your notes as a study tool. One particularly effective after-class strategy is to combine your notes from the lecture and the readings. Organizing concepts from your notes enhances your learning.

There are several different note-taking methods. Some students prefer to take notes in their notebook, while others like to use technology tools such as their laptop or tablet for note-taking. There are also many note-taking apps such as Evernote that students find useful. Try different methods until you find the one that works best for you. As you know, capturing key content during the lecture is important and will help you have the content you need when it is time to study.

Note-taking shouldn't be an in-class activity only. Taking notes on the reading prior to class is important. Repackaging your notes after class to combine your notes from the reading and from the lecture is an excellent use of your time. Because this is a high-level cognitive task, this action can be considered a study technique. In fact, some of the most effective note-taking methods such as the matrix or concept map are best used after class when you have time to think deeply about the content. You may therefore use one note-taking method during class and then a different note-taking method after class. This approach is very effective.

Note-taking apps There are many note-taking applications such as Evernote (see Evernote Figure) and Google Notes where you can capture and store information from a variety of mobile devices and keep your notes organized in one place. With these tools, you can take pictures of text or images and combine these pictures with other notes you take. For instance, you may want to take a photograph of a complex problem on the board and save it with your other notes for the class. Don't forget to get approval from your professor before taking any photographs.

EVERNOTE FIGURE
EVERNOTE NOTE-TAKING APP

Source: Evernote Corporation.

Some applications also allow you to easily share notes with others. Working collaboratively can help you and your classmates have the strongest, most complete foundation from which to study. Imagine if you and a classmate both took notes using two different methods during class and then afterward you shared these notes with one another via a note-taking application. You would now not only be more likely to capture more content but would also have this information packaged in two different ways. This could be incredibly helpful to both of you as you study for exams.

The options for online note-taking grow every day, so explore options and try different approaches out to see what works best for you. Be sure that the tool you choose allows you to easily organize and use the notes you create. While there are many bells and whistles available, sometimes the simplest applications are the most powerful. One word of caution with electronic note-taking choices is that you have to be self-disciplined to avoid the temptation to multitask. Stay focused on the class material and avoid using your laptop or tablet for nonacademic tasks that distract you from your goal.

Linear notes. The linear note-taking method (see Linear Notes Figure) consists of phrases, sentences, or perhaps paragraphs. In many cases, linear notes look like a series of sentences that capture the conversation that took place. This method is not recommended because it does not use strategies that have been shown to be effective. For example, linear notes tend to not have an organizational structure, making it difficult for you to see which concepts are most important and how concepts are connected to one another. Unfortunately, this method is frequently used by students because it is very easy to use this method during class. If this is the note-taking method that you have been using,

> Linear notes typically consist of information in sentence format. In most cases, it is difficult to identify what is most important because there is little or no organization of the information. Students using this style simply try to capture a written record of the lecture, filling up page after page in their notebook.

LINEAR NOTES FIGURE
LINEAR NOTE-TAKING
METHOD

try a different method and see if it helps you better achieve your goals. If you want to rely on this method during class, be sure to take your notes and repackage them into a more effective format after class.

Traditional outline. With the traditional outline format, the main headings appear toward the top left of the page, and subheadings and information about the subheadings are indented and written below the main headings. This traditional method also allows one to easily see the structure of the lesson (see Outline Figure). While this may be easier to use in class, it can sometimes be difficult to determine the main headings. If your professor shares PowerPoint slides ahead of time, this might help you identify the main points or ideas, making it easier for you to organize content during class. Research has shown that the outline method of note-taking approach leads to good recall of the information but is not as effective as the matrix approach (Kiewra et al., 1988).

Digital notes. Using a laptop or tablet in class opens up many more possibilities for note-taking. For example, your professor might share his or her PowerPoint slides with you and you can type your notes right into this document, so your notes correspond directly to the slides created by your professor. Remember PowerPoint slides are organizational and visual tools, not comprehensive summaries, so it will be important for you to take notes even if you are provided with the slides.

Using a standard word processing program such as Microsoft Word is another way to take notes. Many of us are much faster at typing than writing, so you will likely capture more content using this approach. Typing notes also allows you to use the many organizational tools, like different font sizes, colors, highlighting, and images (see Digital Notes Figure). After class, you can use technology to reformat your notes to bring attention to important points. You can also easily add matrixes, charts, or visual images to increase the effectiveness of your notes.

```
Title: _____
   I.    Major Point
            A. Supporting Detail
            B. Supporting Detail

   II.   Major Point
            A.  Supporting Detail
            B.  Supporting Detail
                1.  Additional Detail
                2.  Additional Detail
```

OUTLINE FIGURE
TRADITIONAL OUTLINE FORMAT

Use larger fonts or color to draw attention to key points

Supporting details can be in smaller font

Bulleted lists can be used:
- Detail
- Detail
- Detail

When making tables, bold headers so they stand out.

Column 1 Header	Column 2 Header	Column 3 Header
Column 1 details	Column 2 details	Column 3 details
Column 1 more details	Column 2 more details	Column 3 more details

DIGITAL NOTES FIGURE
SAMPLE DIGITAL NOTES

CORNELL METHOD FIGURE
THE CORNELL METHOD

Cornell method. The Cornell method is another effective note-taking method. (Pauk & Ross, 2008; see Cornell Method Figure). In this method, you draw a vertical line about one-third of the way across the paper and then only take notes on the right-hand side. The left-hand side remains blank at first. After class, you use the left side, known as the cue area, to identify the headings and subheadings and provide organizational structure to your notes. You can also indicate areas that are not clear to you so that you will remember to revisit these concepts as needed. The bottom area of each page is then used for the purpose of summarizing the information. The summary can simply be a paragraph or two, highlighting the important concepts of the chapter or lesson. Similar to the cue section, the summary section can be completed after class.

Concept maps. Another method is concept mapping (see Concept Map Figure) or visually graphing your notes. This method emphasizes visual connections between concepts. With this method, you indicate the main idea and put a bubble or box around it. A hierarchical approach (more important topics on top) is often used, but a variety of approaches can work. Concepts that are connected to the main idea are put in different, often smaller boxes, with lines connecting the boxes that are related to one another. Most students find it difficult to accomplish this type of note-taking during a lecture and instead use it when they get home from class as they reorganize their notes in a personally meaningful way. Research has found that students who create concept maps have higher levels of academic achievement as compared to those who do not use this approach (Chiou, 2008). There are several different computer programs and applications for tablets available that can help you create visually effective concept maps.

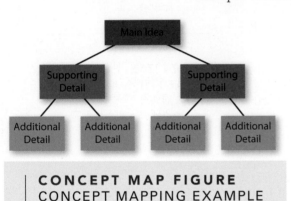

CONCEPT MAP FIGURE
CONCEPT MAPPING EXAMPLE

Matrix notes. According to research conducted by Kiewra et al. (1988), the matrix note-taking approach (see Matrix Figure) works the best. For the matrix method, you create a table where the main topics are on the top and subtopic headings are listed on the left. For example, if you were going to use this note-taking approach to summarize the different note-taking methods, you could list the methods (i.e., Cornell, concept map, outline, matrix, and digital notes down the first column on the left and subtopics such as description, advantages, and disadvantages across the top (see Matrix Notes Example Figure). You then take pertinent notes in each box. Advantages of this approach include focusing on the connections between concepts and the easy-to-read visual format. It is particularly useful for comparing and contrasting concepts or theories. It is often very difficult to use this approach during class because you may need more processing time to figure out the best organizational topics and to see how concepts are connected. However, packaging your notes after class in a table or matrix is a great idea. It gets you thinking more deeply about the concepts and also provides you with a fabulous tool for studying.

Overall Topic	Main Topic I	Main Topic II	Main Topic III
Sub-Topic I			
Sub-Topic II			

MATRIX FIGURE
MATRIX NOTE-TAKING APPROACH

	Description	Advantages	Disadvantages
Note-taking apps	Electronic version of notes on tablet or other device.	Can use images and organizational tools. Easily share notes with classmates. Can search for key terms or concepts.	Some apps have a fee. May take time to learn how to use the app. Need access to technology.
Linear	Series of sentences with little to no organization.	Easiest method to use during class because you capture the content without organizing it.	Least effective method—difficult to study from.
Outline	Main headings appear on the left and subheadings are indented.	Easy to use during class. Easy to see major headings.	May be difficult to determine major headings during class.
Digital notes	Typed notes using programs like Microsoft Word. Can include organizational (e.g., larger font) and visual (e.g., graphs, pictures) tools.	Typing is faster than writing. Easy to reorganize after class. Many tools available to draw attention to key points.	Need to make sure battery on laptop or tablet is charged. Need technology access to use notes.
Cornell	Draw a line one-third of the way down the page. Take notes to the right of the line. Go back and fill in headings on the left-hand side. At the bottom of each page, summarize the main points.	Headings bring attention to concepts. Summary helps focus attention on key points.	The right-hand side may end up not being well organized—could look like linear notes.
Concept map	Visual map of concepts. Large circles or boxes represent most important concepts. Lines represent connections between concepts.	Easy to see visual connections between concepts.	Difficult to create during class when new information is presented. With complex concepts, maps may become overwhelming.
Matrix	Table format that visually shows connections. Works especially well for comparing and contrasting.	Research has shown that this is the most effective note-taking method. Very easy to read format and can easily see connections between concepts.	Time-consuming to create because it requires thinking about the topics first. May not be easily done during class.

MATRIX NOTES EXAMPLE FIGURE
MATRIX NOTES EXAMPLE ON DIFFERENT NOTE-TAKING METHODS

NOTE-TAKING METHODS QUICK QUIZ

1. Which note-taking method works best?
2. Which is the least effective note-taking method?
3. When is it best to take notes using a concept map or matrix?

Note-Taking Tips

iStock.com/FatCamera

Many students struggle with deciding what to write down and how to effectively capture the important information. Professors often lecture for an entire class period. It is neither possible nor productive to write down everything the professor says. However, capturing well-organized, comprehensive notes on the key concepts will serve you well (Carter & Van Matre, 1975; Knight & McKelvie, 1986).

Use the clues offered by your professor to help you determine what is important. Sometimes professors make statements like "This is important," but in most cases, you have to look for subtler clues. Here are some ways that your professor sends you the message that a particular part of the lecture is important:

- Spending a lot of time on the topic
- Repeating the information
- Providing several examples
- Talking in a louder voice or with more passion
- Writing on the board or presenting information on a PowerPoint slide

See Tips Table for general note-taking tips and strategies.

TIPS TABLE Note-Taking Tips and Strategies	
Examples	Write down details and examples to help the material come to life when you are studying.
PowerPoint slides	If your professor provides you with a copy, print them and bring them to class or bring your tablet or laptop with the slides uploaded. If printing, consider printing three per page so that you have room to take notes. PowerPoint slides typically give you only the organizational structure, so you still need to take comprehensive notes.
Pause to summarize	Write a brief summary of what you have learned during or after class to help master the material (Davis & Hult, 1997).
Take notes on all learning activities	Take notes on readings, lectures, discussion, videos, and all other learning activities that take place in and out of the classroom.
Emphasize key points	Use a larger font, highlighting, boxes, or graphics, like a star, to bring attention to key points.
Repackage your notes after class	Since it is often difficult to organize notes during class, spend time after class putting your notes into a more effective format such as a matrix or table. Technology tools can be very effective. Combining your lecture and reading notes helps you create a comprehensive study tool.
Study your notes	Remember, notes are not worthwhile unless you use them. Be sure to use them almost daily!

NOTE-TAKING TIPS QUICK QUIZ

1. What professor actions might indicate a topic is important?
2. If your professor provides you with the PowerPoint slides, what should you do in terms of note-taking?

Studying Strategies

Studying is an interesting concept. What do you mean when you say that you have studied? Studying is most often connected to exams, but studying is really a much broader activity in college. For the purposes of this text, we define studying as any activity that promotes learning. Learning activities occur both in and out of the classroom. For example, in class, you may participate in discussions and activities, listen to lectures, watch videos, and so forth. Outside of the classroom, you read textbooks and additional readings as assigned, complete papers and other assignments, and prepare for exams and presentations.

Monkey Business Images/Shutterstock.com

Although it is important that you make a significant time commitment to studying, time alone does not seem to translate into higher grades (Gurung, 2005). You need to use study strategies that work. Unfortunately, many students rely on study techniques that do not work very well. Reviewing notes, text, and other resources, for instance, is the most commonly used study technique by college students (Gurung, 2005), but it is not the most effective one. Students often overestimate the importance of pure rehearsal and review, and underestimate the importance of other more effective techniques such as testing yourself (Karpicke & Roediger, 2006) and integrating organizational strategies into study practices (Lynch, 2007). Learning about which strategies work best will help you make the most of your study time.

We Are All Multisensory Learners

Many of you have probably heard of learning styles such as auditory, visual, and kinesthetic. Since the validity of learning styles has been called into question by several researchers because of the lack of research evidence (Krätzig & Arbuthnott, 2006; Pashler, McDaniel, Rohrer, & Bjork, 2008; Rohrer & Pashler, 2012), we will focus on a research-based multisensory approach to learning. Neuroscience research, for example, has shown that we are more similar than different in terms of how we learn best and that we typically learn best when we are using multiple senses (Goswami, 2008; Willingham, 2009). In other words, you remember more if you see, hear, and do something with the information. This is because you are engaging different neural pathways at the same time, which strengthens learning and memory.

kurhan/Shutterstock.com

Visual images appear to be particularly powerful in the learning process. Based on numerous experimental studies, Mayer (2009) found that adding an image to text resulted in significantly better memory for the concept. Other researchers have found that we are able to process pictures more quickly and efficiently than words (Seifert, 1997), and our memory for pictures is better than it is for words (Foos & Goolkasian, 2008). This phenomenon is referred to as the picture superiority effect and is connected to the encoding and retrieval processes (McBride & Dosher, 2002). Paying extra attention to the graphs, charts, and images that connect to the content you are learning and studying is therefore a good approach. Your textbooks are filled with these powerful images and you can also create visual matrixes, charts, or other images to maximize your learning.

Another way to engage in multisensory learning is to take advantage of the interactive exercises and tools available on the textbook publisher's website (i.e., MindTap). Most textbooks come with a wealth of online studying resources, so be sure to ask your professor what is available to you. After reviewing over 60 studies, Smetana and Bell (2012) found that engaging in computer-based simulation exercises online helped students master content. Similarly, researchers have found that playing academic digital games is another powerful way to learn (Clark, Tanner-Smith, Killingsworth, & Bellamy, 2013). Not surprisingly, technology tools such as simulations and games activate many of our senses simultaneously. In addition, these tools typically provide you with instant feedback about your performance. As a result, you are more likely to learn more.

MULTISENSORY LEARNERS QUICK QUIZ

1. What does the research say about learning styles?

2. What is the picture superiority effect?

Testing Your Knowledge

AmmentorpDK/Getty Images

One of the most effective ways to learn is by testing your knowledge (Einstein, Mullet, & Harrison, 2012; Karpicke & Roediger, 2006). This is known as the testing effect. Most of us don't think of tests as learning opportunities but rather as the final step in learning—showing what you know. However, tests can be used for both purposes. We can demonstrate knowledge when taking a test, but we will also learn from testing our knowledge. The testing effect was illustrated by a classic study conducted by Karpicke and Roediger (2006). In this study, students were randomly assigned to one of the following three groups:

- Study, Study, Study, Study
- Study, Study, Study, Test
- Study, Test, Test, Test

In all groups, students were asked to learn content from a passage. The first group of students was given four study sessions of five minutes each to learn the content. Participants in the second group were given three five-minute study sessions and then were asked to write down what they could recall from the passage. Students in the last group was allowed to study the passage content for five minutes and then had three opportunities to write down what they recalled. On a delayed recall test, students in the Study, Test, Test, Test group performed the best, recalling 61% of the content. The Study, Study, Study, Test group remembered 56% of the content while the Study, Study, Study, Study group performed the worst, remembering only 40% of the passage content (see Testing Effect Figure). This research shows us that the act of retrieving information strengthens our memories. It therefore makes sense for us to use testing as a studying strategy if we want to really learn the content and remember the information in the future. To put this research into practice, pretend you have a test after every class and quiz yourself on that content several times.

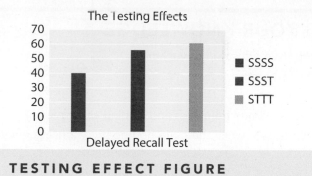

The Testing Effects

TESTING EFFECT FIGURE
RESULTS OF THE TESTING EFFECT STUDY

Source: Adapted from Roediger, H. L., & Karpicke, J. D. (2006). Test-enhanced learning. *Psychological Science,* 17(3), 249–255. doi:10.1111/j.1467-9280.2006.01693.x

Most students are not aware of how much testing improves learning and as a result, they do not use the testing technique often enough (Einstein, Mullet, & Harrison, 2012). However, testing your knowledge has been found to be even better than other proven strategies such as creating concept maps (Karpicke, Butler, & Roediger, 2009). Integrating testing into your studying practices will most definitely help you learn course content.

Even if your professor doesn't give you quiz opportunities, you can take charge of your learning by taking online quizzes (which may be available via your textbook publisher's website) or by creating your own quizzes based on your text and notes. Working with a classmate or study group to test one another is a great way to put the testing effect into practice. There are online platforms such as Quizlet that allow you to share and co-create quizzes with your peers.

Another great way to test yourself is to use good old-fashioned flash cards. While some students like to use index cards for this purpose, there are also many apps or online tools that can also be used. The advantage of using an app is that it is accessible on your phone, so you can study anywhere, anytime. While many use flash cards as a tool to learn vocabulary terms, flash cards can also be used for many other tasks. For example, you can use flash cards for higher-level cognitive tasks by writing questions on one side and comprehensive answers on the other side. The immediate feedback about whether or not your response was correct can inform your study practices.

Many students who use flash cards make use of their study time by putting aside the concepts they believe they know well so that they can focus their studying on the more difficult concepts. This sounds like a good strategy, but it may not lead to the best outcome. Kornell and Bjork (2008) conducted a series of experiments on flash card use and found that dropping cards from the study pile was not beneficial. In fact, dropping cards resulted in poorer performance. Studying the material several times makes it more likely for the content to stay in your long-term memory. So while you may need more time on cards with content you don't yet know well, it is still important to review all the cards several times.

Another way that you can put the testing effect into practice is by engaging in a "Dusting off the Cobwebs" exercise. To engage in this exercise, recall everything you can remember from the prior class or reading for that week without looking at your notes, book, or other materials. Once you've remembered as much as you can, pull out your notes and other resources to fill in any gaps. This act of practicing retrieval strengthens the memory and makes it more likely that the concepts find a home in your long-term memory. Doing this exercise with a classmate enhances your learning even further because you can then discuss what you learned.

TESTING YOUR KNOWLEDGE

- Pretend you have a test after every class.
- Frequently take practice tests.
- Use flash cards.
- Recall what you learned from class and reading assignments.
- Learn from mistakes while there are no negative consequences.

TESTING YOUR KNOWLEDGE QUICK QUIZ

1. What is the testing effect?
2. How can you put the testing effect into practice?

Teaching to Learn and Study Groups

Monkey Business Images/Shutterstock.com

Another extremely powerful way to learn is to teach the content to someone else (Galbraith & Winterbottom, 2011; Rubin & Hebert, 1998; Srivastava et al., 2015). Being able to teach the content to someone else requires a high level of understanding. It is therefore likely that you will spend more time and energy learning the content if you need to teach it. When preparing to teach the content, you'll need to summarize the information in your own words and identify meaningful examples of the concepts. These are both very effective learning strategies, so it's not a huge surprise that these preparatory actions will be beneficial to you. Research has shown that although this is a challenging task, students who taught their peers indicated that this activity helped them learn and increased their confidence with the content as a result of teaching the material to another student (Johnson, Robbins, & Loui, 2015; Srivastava et al., 2015).

One effective way to use this study approach is to participate in a study group where different members take turns teaching content to one another. For example, you could each choose a section of a chapter to teach to the other study group members. This process would require you to prepare well so that you can clearly communicate your assigned part of the chapter to your peers. You will also need to be able to effectively answer questions posed and will therefore need to deeply engage with course content in order to teach content to a peer. Being cognitively and socially engaged increases learning (Garrison, Anderson, & Archer, 2000; Prince, 2004).

Research has shown that students who study with other students outperform students who learn alone (Schmidt & Moust, 1998). Students report finding study groups to be valuable (Plecha, 1998). The three main benefits identified by students in this study were increased motivation, increased support, and the opportunity to clear up confusing concepts (Hendry, Hyde, & Davy, 2005). However, not all study groups work out well. Be sure your study group is a manageable size. Shimazoe and Alrich (2010) recommend a group size of three to four members. A small group size makes it more likely that your group will stay on task and work out well. Let's discuss strategies you can use to make study groups work for you.

1. First, it is important that you are working with other students who share your commitment to learning and success.

2. All members need to be prepared. Millis (2002) emphasizes the importance of all group members being individually accountable for learning when engaged in group work. In other words, everyone needs to contribute. One way to address this issue is to assign a task to do prior to attending the study group session. For example, each member might need to come ready to teach a section of the chapter. Doing independent work first helps everyone be ready to discuss topics more deeply, maximizing your study group time (Sarfo & Elen, 2011).

3. Establishing ground rules and roles helps keep all of you focused on the task at hand. An example of a ground rule could be that the first 10 minutes are purely social and then you will start focusing on the topic of study. Another example could be that all members need to either come to the session prepared or post materials in an online space prior to the study session in order to stay in the group. See Study Groups Table for some examples of group roles. Rotate roles so that different members have different responsibilities each time.

STUDY GROUPS TABLE
Study Group Roles

Role	Tasks
Agenda maker	Identifies the topics to be covered and what all members should do to prepare for the study session. The agenda should be distributed to group members approximately a week in advance. This might involve assigning each member a section of the chapter or content to teach others during the study group.
Facilitator	Starts the study session, makes sure everyone participates, and keeps the conversation moving along productively. The facilitator may begin with unclear concepts and then move into the other content areas identified on the agenda.
Time keeper	Ensures the study session time is maximized by following the schedule and keeping group members on track.
Quiz creator	Creates 5 to 10 quiz questions about the material. This gives members an opportunity to benefit from practice retrieval and also helps members of the study group assess how well they are learning the content.

TEACHING TO LEARN AND STUDY GROUPS QUICK QUIZ

1. Why is teaching a good study strategy?
2. Is it more productive to study alone or in a group?
3. What strategies can make study groups function more effectively?

Organizing and Making Connections

Organizing has been found to be one of the most effective study strategies because it pushes you to engage in deeper processing of the information (Gadzella & Baloglu, 2003; Gurung, 2005; Hall et al., 2004). Organizing goes beyond being organized and keeping your study materials neat and tidy. Dickinson and O'Connell (1990) described organizing as a mental process whereby students:

- put information into their own words
- create links between concepts via a hierarchical structure
- create examples to help the concepts come alive

When comparing high- and low-performing students, Dickinson and O'Connell (1990) found that high-performing students spent approximately one hour or more per week studying. They also found that high-scoring students spent an average of 43.13 minutes organizing compared to only 10.28 average minutes per week by the low-scoring group. Interestingly, high- and low-performing students spent similar amounts of time reading and reviewing (see High Performers Figure). Thus, the difference lies in total study time and the use of organizing as an important study strategy.

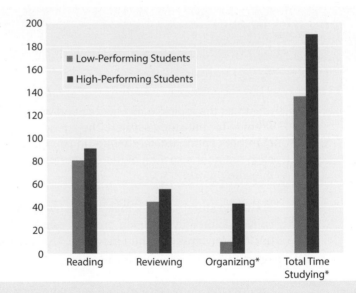

HIGH PERFORMERS FIGURE
AVERAGE TIME ON TASKS (IN MINUTES) FOR LOW- AND HIGH-PERFORMING STUDENTS

There are a few reasons that these organizing actions matter so much. By putting information into your own words, you are engaging in a high-level cognitive task that demonstrates your understanding of the content. When you frequently summarize newly learned concepts using your own words, you will discover how much this can increase learning. By identifying connections between concepts, you are also more deeply engaging in the learning process. Learning is enhanced when new concepts are linked to previously learned content (Goswami, 2008). Seeing the relationships between new information and previously learned information enhances and strengthens learning. Finally, by identifying examples, you are attaching meaning to the content. This is a concept called elaboration. Elaboration refers to the process of identifying meaningful examples and experiences related to content being learned. Engaging in elaboration has been connected to increased learning (Hamilton, 1997). Refer to the Study Strategies Table for a brief summary of effective and ineffective study strategies.

STUDY STRATEGIES TABLE An Overview of Effective and Ineffective Study Strategies	
Most Effective Study Strategies	**Least Effective Study Strategies**
Testing yourself Teaching others Organizing information Using all senses, especially images	Looking over or reviewing notes Highlighting too much or too little

An effective study plan consists of the following five approaches:

1. **Use a multisensory approach to learning.** Using a multisensory approach will increase the likelihood that you effectively encode and retrieve information. Because memory for images is more powerful than it is for words, identifying and using relevant images will help you learn the content.

2. **Organize.** Use organizing techniques to create an effective study guide. Create written notes by putting key concepts into your own words, identifying examples, and finding connections between concepts you are learning. Combine the notes you took during class and while reading the chapter into one comprehensive document that makes explicit connections between concepts being learned. Use an effective format such as the matrix table and concept map, or tools (bold, larger font) to bring attention to the most important points.

3. **Review.** Next, review your organized notes. For optimal performance on the exam, review your notes multiple times over the course of several different study sessions. Spaced practice, studying many times over a period of time, works best (Schwartz, Son, Kornell, & Finn, 2011).

4. **Test.** Now, quiz yourself over and over again. Use publisher-provided assessments when available or create your own. Track your progress and modify your studying habits as needed.

5. **Teach.** Finally, teach the content you've learned to someone you know. Teaching is an extremely powerful way to learn!

ORGANIZING QUICK QUIZ

1. According to Dickinson and O'Connell's research, what were the similarities between high and low performers?

2. How do Dickinson and O'Connell (1990) define organizing?

CHAPTER 3
Chapter Summary: Note-Taking Model

Let's summarize what you've learned in this chapter. The concept map model is used for this chapter. Remember, it is not expected that your notes will look like this right after class or reading. It takes time to organize your notes and repackage them. It is time well spent, though, because you learn the content better as you organize it and you'll have a fabulous foundation from which to study for your exams! There are several ways to use this section:

- **Preview:** Read the model before reading the chapter to familiarize yourself with the content (the S in SQ3R).

- **Compare:** Compare the notes you took on the chapter to the model provided.

- **Study:** The model along with your notes and other course materials are great resources for studying.

Concept Map Model

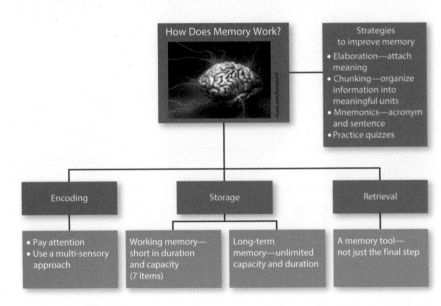

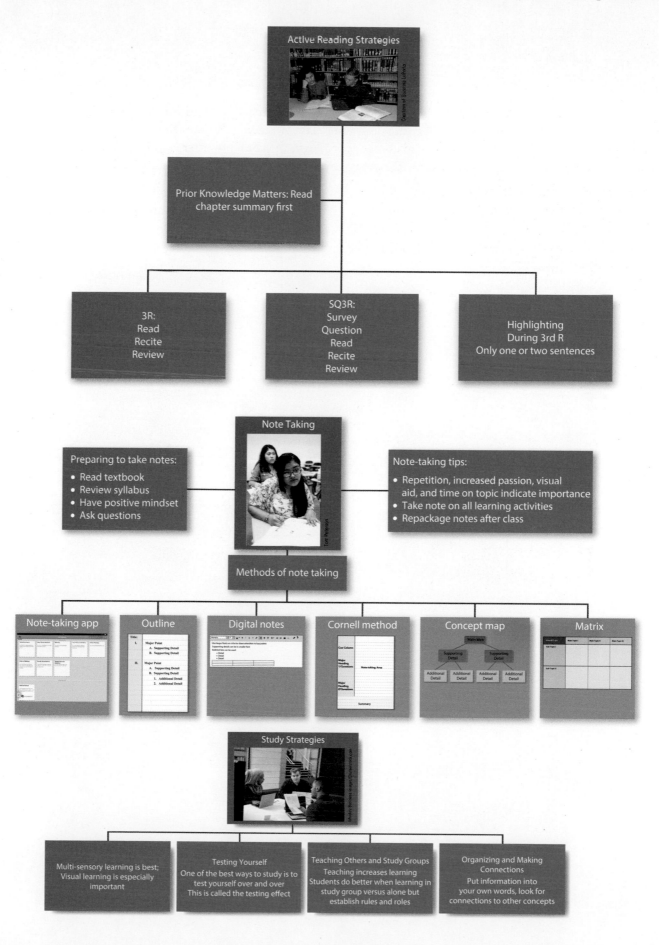

Strengthening Soft Skills

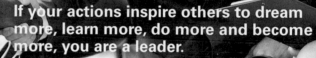

If your actions inspire others to dream more, learn more, do more and become more, you are a leader.

–John Quincy Adams

1 What behaviors demonstrate professionalism?

2 Does working while attending college positively or negatively impact school performance?

3 What is the best way to combat procrastination and meet deadlines?

4 Does multitasking work?

5 What is emotional intelligence?

6 How can you build teamwork and collaboration skills?

7 What do effective leaders do? How can you develop leadership skills?

Exploring the Research in Summary

Research Study Citation

Clark, G., Marsden, R., Whyatt, J. D., Thompson, L., & Walker, M. (2015). 'It's everything else you do…': Alumni views on extracurricular activities and employability. *Active Learning in Higher Education*, 16(2), 133–147. doi: 10.1177/1469787415574050.

INTRODUCTION: THE RESEARCH QUESTION

What question did the researcher seek to answer?

Recognizing the need for students to develop essential soft skills desired by employers, Clark et al. (2015) were interested in the role that extracurricular activities play in the development of soft skills. Their research questions can be summarized as follows:

1. Are soft skills more likely to be learned through extracurricular activities or as part of degree requirements?

2. Are all extracurricular activities equal in terms of developing soft skills?

3. What role do extracurricular activities play in gaining employment?

METHOD: THE STUDY

Who participated in the study? What did the researchers ask the participants to do?

A survey focused on extracurricular activities and the impact of these activities, if any, on employment was e-mailed to 14,538 alumni who graduated from Lancaster University between 1990 and 2010. The survey reached 14,215 alumni, was opened by 5,095, and a total of 620 alumni completed the survey. Those who responded to the survey were also invited to participate in an interview. A total of 320 agreed to be interviewed and the researchers selected 25 from the list that represented diversity in terms of extracurricular activities, occupations, gender, and years since graduation. A total of 18 interviews were conducted.

RESULTS: THE FINDINGS

What was the answer to the research question?

The first research question focused on where soft skills were learned, from extracurricular activities or as part of degree requirements. Results indicated that skills were learned from both extracurricular activities and course requirements, but alumni reported that skills learned from extracurricular experiences (communication skills, interpersonal skills, and self-confidence) were most critical to landing their first job. Interestingly, extracurricular and academic experiences led to different skill sets. For example, more alumni reported learning planning and analytical skills, time management, problem-solving, and creativity from their degree program. However, alumni reported that extracurricular activities led to increased skill development in almost all of the other areas (communication skills, interpersonal skills, self-confidence, decision-making, and leadership). Refer to Soft Skill Development Figure for an overview of the findings.

The second research question focused on whether all types of extracurricular activities resulted in the same skill set. All types of extracurricular activities enhanced interpersonal skills, while most also improved self-confidence and leadership skills. However, alumni did report that certain activities facilitated the development of some skills more than others. For example, paid employment was the only activity that developed business awareness. Confidence was most

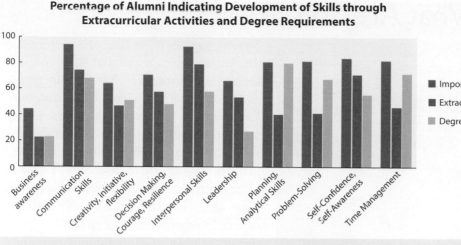

Percentage of Alumni Indicating Development of Skills through Extracurricular Activities and Degree Requirements

SOFT SKILL DEVELOPMENT FIGURE
IMPACT OF EXTRACURRICULAR ACTIVITIES AND DEGREE REQUIREMENTS ON SOFT SKILLS DEVELOPMENT

developed through sports and interpersonal skills were most developed through social groups or organizations.

The last major research question focused on whether extracurricular activities played a role in employment. Survey and interview data indicated that participating in extracurricular activities did help graduates gain employment and perform well in the position. More specifically, 64% of the alumni indicated that the extracurricular activity helped them land their first job and 57% indicated that skills developed from participating in extracurricular activities helped them perform well on the job. Alumni consistently reported that participating in extracurricular activities helped them develop skills above and beyond those developed through the curriculum requirements.

DISCUSSION AND SO WHAT FACTOR

How can YOU use this information as a student?

This research illustrates that the college experience involves much more than completing degree requirements. In order to learn and develop the soft skills that are desired by employers, participate in extracurricular activities. Since different types of activities can build different skills, consider participating in more than one type of activity. Participating in extracurricular activities such as sports, social clubs, arts- or music-related opportunities, volunteer work, or paid employment can enrich your college experience and help you build skills that will serve you well now and in the future.

What Are Soft Skills?

Rei and Motion Studio/Shutterstock.com

Success requires more than just content-specific knowledge, expertise, and skills. Soft skills are also very important. Soft skills are general skills that are needed in life and in many careers. Examples of soft skills include professionalism, work ethic, oral and written communication skills, interpersonal skills, time management, problem-solving, and leadership. Soft skills are often referred to as transferable skills because these skills transfer across many different careers. In other words, you can easily apply or transfer your soft skills from one position to another, even if the positions are in very different career fields. For example, having excellent communication and interpersonal skills will serve you well in most, if not all, positions.

Technical skills (sometimes called hard skills), on the other hand, are more career-specific. Examples of technical skills include using a special cooking technique if you are a chef or using a special software editing tool if you are a video editor. Technical skills are less likely to be useful in different career paths. In other words, if the chef changes careers and decides to work in video editing, the cooking technique that was critical as a chef will probably not have any value in the new position. Technical skills are, of course, also important, but employers are often more willing to train you on the technical skills needed for the position if you are walking in with excellent soft skills. This is likely due to soft skills being more challenging and time-consuming to learn. Based on extensive research, Ericsson, Prietula, and Cokely (2007) note that "experts are always made, not born" (p. 2), meaning that it takes a tremendous amount of time, purposeful practice, and learning from feedback to develop and master skills. This is particularly true for soft skill development. You don't learn to be a good communicator or a leader in a day or even in a semester. These skills develop over time.

Research has shown that soft skills really matter in terms of being successful (Bowles, Gintis, & Osborne, 2001; deCarvalho & Junio, 2015). Employers value soft skills. Eighty-six percent of mid-level to top-level executives surveyed agreed that soft skills are very important to success in the world of work (Deepa & Seth, 2013). In a survey conducted by Career Builder, 77% of the human resources professionals who responded to the survey indicated that soft skills were as important as hard or technical skills and 16% indicated that soft skills were more important than hard skills (as cited in Russo, 2015).

Employers also often place a higher value on soft skills as compared to grades when making hiring decisions (Jones, Baldi, Phillips, & Waikar, 2016). It is important to note that this does not necessarily mean that employers do not value academic achievement, but rather that the soft skills are often what sets a candidate apart from the others. In other words, many applicants applying for the same position as you may have very high grades, so while having high grades may help you get noticed, having evidence of soft skills will help you stand out among other high-achieving applicants, thereby making it more likely for you to get a job offer. Thus, it is not surprising that colleges and universities are focused not only on building your knowledge but also on helping you develop essential soft skills. "In a fast-changing world, education has to prepare learners to act intelligently, skillfully, and with good judgment when they meet the unexpected" (Claxton, Costa, & Kallick, 2016, p. 61).

What skills are most valued by employers? Based on an employer survey conducted by Barrington, Wright, and Casner-Lotto (2006), the four most important skills needed by employees were:

- Professionalism and work ethic
- Oral and written communication
- Teamwork and collaboration
- Critical thinking and problem-solving

Integrity, communication, and interpersonal skills are among the most highly valued skills by employers (Robles, 2012). Other soft skills that have been identified as important by employers include confidence, planning and organizational skills, and decision-making skills (Archer & Davison, 2008).

It's not just about what employers think though—college graduates have also reported that soft skills were important in landing their first job and with performing well in their career. Specifically, college graduates indicated that communication and interpersonal skills along with self-awareness and confidence were the most important skills when it came to getting their first job after graduation, noting that these skills also helped them meet with success once hired. Interestingly, these graduates said that extracurricular activities really helped them develop these skills (Clark, Marsden, Whyatt, Thompson, & Walker, 2015).

SOFT SKILLS

- Professionalism
- Time management
- Planning and organizational skills
- Work ethic
- Decision-making
- Oral and written communication
- Teamwork and collaboration
- Leadership
- Critical thinking
- Problem-solving

SOFT SKILLS QUICK QUIZ

1. What are soft skills?
2. What soft skills do employers value most?

Professionalism

michaeljung/Shutterstock.com

Employers expect their employees to act professionally. What does this mean? Professionalism refers to behaviors in the workplace that communicate that you are:

- Committed to achieving goals
- Responsible
- Hardworking
- Honest
- Respectful
- Mindful of boundaries
- A team player

Professionals care about the mission of the organization and want to do their part to help the company or organization achieve its desired goals. This point was highlighted by Cottringer (2015) when he noted that "a professional attitude involves a diligent, conscientious approach to doing what is necessary to help the organization demonstrate its values and accomplish its goals" (p. 26). Commitment to the mission of the organization happens naturally if the organizational mission aligns with your values. This is why it is important to learn about an organization before you accept a job offer. Choosing positions where you will be able to perform tasks that match your values makes it easier for you to engage in behaviors that demonstrate professionalism. Being professional at school means caring about and valuing education, your courses, your professor, and your fellow classmates.

Being responsible means that your employer, professors, and colleagues can count on you. Responsible individuals show up on time, do whatever is needed to complete a task, and ultimately successfully complete those tasks. Responsible individuals are also responsive, always answering e-mails and providing information requested in a timely fashion. Professionals will work hard and typically go above and beyond in order to achieve a successful outcome. In other words, individuals with professionalism exhibit pride in their work and are willing to do what it takes to meet with success, demonstrating a high level of work ethic. As a result, the final product is polished, professional, and on target.

Honesty and integrity are also essential components of professionalism. Employers want employees who will act ethically. Ethics refers to whether choices are morally right or wrong. Our personal, social, and cultural values play an important role in our decision-making (Flaming, Agacer, & Uddin, 2010; Lincoln & Holmes, 2010). Making ethical decisions involves working through the decision-making process, carefully thinking through the potential impact of your decision. Focusing on ethics during decision-making increases the likelihood that you will make ethical choices (Winston & Bahnaman, 2008). Engaging in honest, ethical actions promotes a positive image of yourself and your organization. It will also make it more likely that others will trust you. For example, if you have access to company information, like a new product being developed, and your friend works for a competitor, it would be unethical to share what you know with him or her if this product hasn't been publicly announced.

Additionally, when mistakes happen, professionals acknowledge the mistake, take responsibility for their actions, and develop a plan to address the issue at hand.

Individuals who exhibit professionalism are polite, respectful, and courteous of others. Being friendly is a simple, yet powerful way to demonstrate professionalism. Demonstrating professionalism also involves doing your part to create an effective learning or working environment by minimizing distractions. For example, turn off electronic devices such as cell phones to avoid disturbing others, like coworkers and classmates, as research has shown that distractions can negatively impact others (End, Worthman, Mathews, & Wetterau, 2010).

Professionals continue demonstrating respect even during conflict. When a conflict arises, disagreements are discussed calmly by listening to the viewpoints of others and using appropriate language to communicate ideas and concerns. If the conflict escalates, professionals will seek the guidance and support of someone, such as a supervisor, who can assist with resolving the conflict.

Professionals are mindful of boundaries and are able to determine which actions or behaviors are appropriate in which situations. For example, although you may become friends with coworkers, it is important that you keep your relationship professional while at work. This doesn't mean you can't discuss anything personal at work. An important part of getting to know your colleagues and establishing and maintaining good working relationships is sharing some personal information. For example, you may choose to share some general information about your family and significant other, your interests, hobbies, and activities you engage in. However, one of the most common unprofessional actions in the workplace is sharing too many details about your personal life, especially if you were involved in actions that would not be viewed positively by your colleagues or employer (Rawes, 2014). When sharing personal information, it is best to share experiences and activities that are positive in nature.

Likewise, professionals recognize that there is a difference between professional and social communication. While informal communication strategies such as emojis or abbreviations may be fine to use in social situations, these strategies are probably not appropriate in professional environments. As an example, let's take a look at e-mail communication. Although you may be very accustomed to texting friends, professors and employers will likely prefer e-mail and will probably not appreciate you using text language such as abbreviations ("u" for "you").

It is best to begin e-mails with a salutation, such as "Dear Professor Harrington." If you are unsure about how to address your professor, refer to your syllabus. If your professor listed his or her name as Dr. Harrington, then use this as your salutation. When uncertain, use "Professor." Next, clearly express your thought or question, being sure to check your spelling and grammar before you send it. Also use a closing, such as "Sincerely, Ashley Smith" (see Professional E-mail Etiquette Figure). Students should send e-mails from their school account and should clearly indicate the course and section number (PSY 123-10), as professors have many students in many different courses and this will help them respond appropriately. When interacting with potential or current employers, it is important to use an e-mail account that is professional. If necessary, create a new e-mail account. If possible, have your name included in the e-mail address.

```
⤴Send  ⤓  🔗 ☺   Importance Normal ▾   Options None              ▾   Close  ⊙ Help
📖 To:      charrington@cengagelearning.edu
📖 Cc:
📖 Bcc:
Subject:    PSY 123-10 Question about today's lecture
Attachments:
```

Dear Professor Harrington,

I found today's lecture on memory fascinating. As I was reviewing
my notes and reading the chapter, I am not quite sure if I fully
understand the concept of elaboration in memory. I would like to
schedule an appointment with you to discuss this concept further.
Unfortunately, I have another class during your office hours
tomorrow. Would you be available on Thursday after 12:30 or Friday
morning to discuss this concept? Thank you for your assistance.

Sincerely,
Ashley Smith
PSY 123-10

PROFESSIONAL E-MAIL ETIQUETTE FIGURE
EXAMPLE OF E-MAIL TO PROFESSOR

Cengage Learning, Inc.

PROFESSIONALISM QUICK QUIZ

1. What does professionalism mean?
2. What are some behaviors that demonstrate professionalism?

Time and Project Management

iQoncept/Shutterstock.com

Effective time management, and relatedly project management, are soft skills that are connected to successful personal, academic, and professional outcomes. Ineffective time management is one of the most cited obstacles to student success. Numerous research studies have shown the relationship between time management and success, providing evidence that effective time management is related to higher levels of achievement (Kitsantas et al., 2006; Macan, Shahani, Dipboye, & Phillips,1990; Thompson, Orr, Thompson, & Grover, 2007).

You may have heard the expression that we are all equal in terms of time. We all get 24 hours each day. However, some of us are more productive than others when it comes to using our time. Some of us really struggle in this area. In order to make the most of your 24 hours per day, you can ask yourself the following questions:

1. Am I using my time in a way that is consistent with my values and goals?
2. Do I have good work–school–life balance?

3. Am I able to effectively plan and engage in actions so that I am successfully completing personal, academic, and professional tasks in a timely fashion?

4. How might I improve my use of time?

Matching Use of Time with Values and Goals

Perhaps the most important question you should be asking yourself about time management is whether or not you are using time in a way that is consistent with your goals and values. Your goals and values indicate what really matters to you. It therefore makes sense that your actions (i.e., your use of time) should match your goals and values. Unfortunately, this is not always the case. For instance, some students may say they want to earn high grades but then do not spend enough time studying and completing learning activities outside of class and instead spend a significant amount of time socializing or engaged in other activities.

Praethip Docekalova/Shutterstock.com

Getting an accurate picture of how you currently spend your time can help you determine which activities in your life are taking up the most time, whether these activities are aligned to your goals, and where adjustments might be needed (Nonis, Philhours, & Hudson, 2006). A powerful way to get a clear picture of how you currently use your time is to do what many call a time diary, documenting how you spend your time over the course of a week. Becoming aware of your patterns can help you change behaviors. Documenting actions is a widely used strategy by individuals who would like to change behaviors. For example, nutritionists often ask clients to track what they eat and how often they exercise, and financial advisors often ask clients to track and document their spending patterns. These tracking actions can help you understand your current practices. Tracking your time will help you better understand how you use your time so that you can determine if you need to make any adjustments.

To get even more out of this exercise, categorize your use of time. In other words, determine how much time was spent studying, working, socializing, sleeping, etc. in total for the week. Categorizing your time can help you better understand patterns associated with your current use of time and will help you determine whether or not you are using your time in a way that is consistent with your goals and values. It is obviously much easier to achieve goals if we use our time in a way that supports progress and achievement, rather than distracts from goal accomplishment.

When you evaluate your time, you may discover that you are engaging in activities that are not connected to your goal. In many cases, this will be due to a time trap, an activity that takes up a lot of your time and is typically unproductive in nature. Some examples of time traps are using social media sites, such as Facebook, surfing the Internet, texting, watching television, or playing games. Not surprisingly, researchers have found that successful students spend less time on time traps, such as watching television and hanging out with friends (George, Dixon, Stansal, Gelb, & Pheri, 2008). Although it is important to engage in social and relaxing activities, it is easy to lose track of how much time we spend on these time traps. Often, it will be much more time than we originally planned on spending. Perhaps you have had the experience where you went to briefly check your Facebook page only to discover that an hour passed by and you never returned to your studying. There are several strategies you can use to reduce your time spent on these nonproductive time traps:

1. Simply raising your awareness of your personal time traps can be helpful. You can also ask your friends and family to remind you to get back on track if they see you distracted by a time trap.

2. Self-imposed time limits are a good strategy. For instance, determine how long you would like to spend on the activity and then set a timer, or alarm on your cell phone, for that amount of time. This external reminder can help you stick to your plan and avoid letting the time traps take you on a detour from your goals. This strategy helps you take charge of your time.

3. Use fun activities as a reward for must-do activities. For example, if you work on your presentation for an hour, reward yourself with one of your favorite time traps. Give yourself approximately 10 minutes for your reward, such as socializing time on a social media site, and then get back to your academic tasks.

TIME AND PROJECT MANAGEMENT QUICK QUIZ

1. Why is it a good idea to track how you spend your time?
2. What are time traps?

Work–School–Life Balance

iStock.com/marekuliasz

In today's world, we are all being pulled in many different directions. Family and friends want to spend time with us, professors want us to read and complete significant learning projects, and employers may want us to work more hours or complete tasks by a certain deadline. While making school a priority will increase the likelihood that you complete your degree in a timely fashion, school may not always be your top priority if you have important family and work responsibilities that also demand your time. Research shows that work–school–life balance is one of the biggest stressors facing students (El-Ghoroury, Galper, Sawaqdeh, & Bufka, 2012). To achieve work–school–life balance, you don't have to necessarily choose between these different responsibilities. Rather, successful individuals have learned to effectively juggle their many different roles, finding balance among these competing needs and responsibilities. The key will be to keep your goals front and center.

It is important to note that balance doesn't necessarily mean that you will spend the same amount of time on the different parts of your life. Given the complexities of life, the amount of time you spend on different activities or priorities will often fluctuate. For example, school will demand more of your time during the crunch time at the end of the semester, work might demand more of your time if a project deadline is looming, and family may need more of your time if a family member is ill. Thus, work–school–life pressures change over time. Sometimes, these pressures can collide, with different areas of your life demanding increased attention at the same time. For example, if you work in retail, employers often need employees to put in more hours during the holiday season, which happens to be at the end of the fall term when academic pressures are highest. When faced with this challenge, your short- and long-term goals can help you determine your priorities and guide your actions. Remember, you and your employer do not necessarily share the same goal. Your employer will be looking out for the best interest of the company, while you have to look out for your best interest and what will help you achieve your personal, academic, and career goals. Staying focused on what matters most to you can help you decide which tasks require more of your time and attention.

Working has been cited by student success professionals as one of the biggest obstacles to student success, and some research supports this claim. For example, Lammers, Onwuegbuzie, and State (2001) found that students who worked 23–60 hours per week studied less, had poorer concentration, slept less, and had increased absences in classes with optional attendance. Other researchers have also found that working negatively impacted academic success (Kulm & Cramer, 2006; Stinebrickner & Stinebrickner, 2004). However, not all research has found negative outcomes associated with working (Nonis & Hudson, 2006), and some research has even found that working can have positive outcomes. Dundes and Marx (2006), for example, found that students working 10–19 hours per week spent more time studying and performed better than students who didn't work at all or worked 20 hours or more per week. In addition to the financial benefits, working can also help you build your skills, give you an opportunity to network with others, and create situations that demand you become good at time management (Larkin, LaPort, & Pines, 2007). Thus, according to this research, a balanced approach to work and school is best.

How can you balance your many different responsibilities? For starters, you can decide if everything that is on your plate needs to stay on your plate. Make a list of all of your primary responsibilities and decide how important each one is to you. It may be that you need to take something off your plate entirely or ask for help with it. For example, students often work more hours than needed and this may negatively impact academic goal performance. To help you manage your many responsibilities, consider the following time and project management tips offered by Shellenbarger (2009):

1. Make a to-do list of all tasks that need to be completed, documenting deadlines and determining the importance of each task.
2. Organize all content related to each task or project.
3. Develop a schedule to complete tasks.
4. Stay focused on one task at a time to maximize the use of your time.

WORK–SCHOOL–LIFE BALANCE QUICK QUIZ

1. Based on the research, what are the pros and cons associated with working while attending college?
2. What strategies can you use to have good work–school–life balance?

Meeting Deadlines

As a college student, you will have lots of deadlines to meet. This is also the case in the world of work. Developing and using time management strategies can help you complete tasks on schedule.

Make a prioritized to-do list. Although simple in nature, creating a to-do list of tasks you must complete is a powerful planning and organizational strategy. To-do lists help you see the big picture of what you need to accomplish. Research

has found that students who use a to-do list tool are more likely to complete tasks ahead of schedule (Cavanaugh, Lamkin, & Hu, 2012). To-do lists can include personal, academic, and professional tasks. According to Shellenbarger (2009), your to-do list should include deadlines associated with the task and the level of importance of each task. There are many electronic tools available that allow you to easily organize your to-do list by deadlines and/or importance.

One of the biggest mistakes people make when creating a to-do list is to simply write down large projects such as writing a research paper. It is much more effective if you break large assignments down into smaller tasks, just like you've broken a long-term goal into short-term goals. This requires you to think about what steps you'll need to take in order to complete the assignment or task. If you are uncertain, reach out to your professor, a tutor, or a librarian for help with identifying the smaller tasks associated with this big project. Breaking down the larger task into smaller action steps makes the task seem more manageable and will reduce the likelihood that you will procrastinate. It is also very rewarding to check "done" for a task on your to-do list, and you don't want to wait until the end of the semester to experience this positive feeling!

Once you have identified all of the tasks you need to complete, you'll want to focus on the importance of each task. This process is called prioritizing tasks and is an essential part of effective time management. While there are many factors that will guide your decision-making about which tasks deserve your priority attention, your values and goals should be the driving focus here. In other words, you should give higher priority status to tasks that help you achieve your goals.

For academic tasks, the syllabus can be a great guide to help you start prioritizing. In the syllabus, you'll find information about the nature of the assignments, their due dates, and how much the assignment counts toward your final grade. Grading can communicate the importance of an assignment. Assignments that count more are probably more important than assignments that do not count much toward your final grade. However, all assignments are important and can help you achieve the course learning goals. If your syllabus does not provide you with the information you need, ask your professor for this information. Meeting with your professor, advisor, or counselor can help you evaluate the tasks and decide on a time management plan that will help you successfully complete all assignments in a timely fashion.

Develop a schedule. Success doesn't happen by chance; success comes as a result of planning and hard work. Planning is an essential part of developing effective time management skills. Students who plan out their studying activities perform better academically (Krumrei-Mancuso, Newton, Kim, & Wilcox, 2013). There are a variety of planning tools available to assist you with this process. Many find apps or other online calendars work best for them, while others prefer good old-fashioned paper calendars. While there are pros and cons associated with different planning tools, the key is for you to choose a calendar tool that you will use regularly. It's a good idea to refer to your calendar at least once a day.

Scheduling time to study or work on assignments/tasks is essential. Think about it: Don't you usually go to activities that are scheduled? For example, most of us go to our job and classes as per our schedule. However, some students struggle with completing out-of-class activities on time. One of the main reasons for this phenomenon is that class time is built into your schedule, but assignments are not. Scheduling out-of-class academic time helps you stay on track toward your academic goal. Block out time on your calendar to complete all of your assignments and learning tasks, including study time. Professionals often use this technique, scheduling working meetings or time to independently work on projects.

Tracking how long tasks take you to complete will definitely help you plan well. For example, knowing that it takes you three hours to complete a reading assignment means that you need to find three hours in your schedule for this task. If you only allotted one hour for a task that actually required three hours, you would have to re-adjust your schedule and you may not get to another important project. By tracking how much time you actually spend on the various tasks, you will make future planning easier.

Sometimes unplanned events happen and impact our plans. For instance, you may get sick and be unable to complete academic tasks. Working ahead of the due dates instead of waiting until the last minute will make it easier for you to adjust and still meet deadlines. A good rule of thumb is to pretend all assignments or projects are due several days or even a week earlier than indicated on your syllabus.

When planning your schedule, you'll want to consider the priority you gave it on your to-do list. Additionally, you'll want to think about the difficulty level of the tasks. There's some debate among student success professionals about whether you should start with easy or difficult tasks. Although students recognize the need to spend more time on tasks that they perceive to be difficult as compared to easy, they often spend their time on easy tasks (Son & Metcalfe, 2000). However, when students thought they had a lot of time, they did focus on the more difficult tasks (Son & Metcalfe, 2000). Thus, your perception of how much time you have may be one of the deciding factors. If you only have an hour or less, study the easy material. If you have several hours or more available, consider diving into the more challenging material. Shellenbarger (2009) also suggests that you plan to work on challenging tasks when you have the most energy. In other words, if you are a morning person, take on difficult or challenging tasks in the first part of your day.

Some students find that starting with the easy tasks really helps them get started, and the success of achieving a task, even if it is a simple one, motivates them to continue working on more demanding academic tasks. Other students, however, find that if they don't focus on the challenging work first, they lose interest and motivation when it comes time to begin the difficult tasks. Individuals who have this experience may prefer to work on the challenging tasks at the start of their study session when they have the most mental energy to take on these tasks that are more difficult. Notice your own habits around completing easy and difficult tasks, and make changes as needed to successfully complete assignments or tasks on schedule.

Combat procrastination. Procrastination refers to putting tasks off, often until the last minute. In fact, it is often the impending deadline that finally prompts action. When the deadline is in the distance, little or no action is taken. Most of us have procrastinated at one time or another, and college is a place where it is easy to fall into this pattern of behavior. Procrastination typically happens when we are faced with a task that is challenging or time-consuming. It is easier to avoid than to do. Making matters worse, our avoidant behaviors are rewarded, making it less likely that we will start the work we need to do. For example, let's imagine you are sitting in your room trying to decide if you should start your research paper. If you don't have much experience with writing a research paper, you may question your ability to do so. The more you think about the research paper, the more anxious you feel. You decide to first update your social media site. The moment you start working on your social media site, your anxiety lessens. You start to feel better as you forget about the paper. This feeling of being less anxious is very rewarding. Because it was rewarding to avoid the research paper, you will likely procrastinate again the next time you contemplate whether you should begin. Despite this, procrastination can actually increase your stress level and ultimately has the potential to reduce your academic performance, so it is important to use strategies that combat procrastination.

The good news is that there are some simple strategies than can help you combat procrastination. Converting big and difficult assignments or projects into small and manageable ones is one of the best ways to combat procrastination. This is because we are more likely to start tasks that seem doable and can be accomplished in a relatively short time. Combat procrastination by identifying several small tasks such as developing an outline, finding sources, and writing a section of a paper instead of listing a research paper on your to-do list. Another effective strategy to reduce procrastination is to set up a reward structure that makes you feel good about being productive and helps you get tasks done. In other words, give yourself a reward for accomplishing a task on your to-do list. Small rewards can increase your motivation to keep working on tasks (Cameron, Pierce, Banko, & Gear, 2005). Your rewards need to match your work level. In other words, it is productive to allow yourself 10–15 minutes of fun after working for 45 minutes to an hour. However, it would not be productive if this was reversed and you had 45 minutes of fun after 15 minutes of work!

COMBATING PROCRASTINATION

- Break big tasks down into more manageable ones.
- Reward yourself for taking action!

MEETING DEADLINES QUICK QUIZ

1. Why are to-do lists helpful?
2. What should be the most important factor you consider when prioritizing tasks?
3. What is one of the best ways to combat procrastination?

Avoid Multitasking: Single-Task It!

Branislav Nenin/Shutterstock.com

In today's world, we often hear the term *multitasking*. Appelbaum, Marchionni, and Fernandez (2008) distinguish between two types of multitasking: task-switching and dual-tasking. Task-switching refers to switching back and forth between two or more tasks. In other words, your attention shifts from one task to another. An example of task-switching would be reading and texting. Dual-tasking, on the other hand, refers to simultaneously working on two or more activities. An example of dual-tasking is having a conversation while cleaning your room.

According to research conducted by Carrier, Cheever, Rosen, Benitez, and Chang (2009), students today report multitasking much more than students of previous generations. Most people think they are fairly effective at both types of multitasking and that this leads to increased productivity. However, research has provided us with strong evidence that shows us that tasks take more time, not less, when we multitask. In an experiment conducted by Bowman, Levine, Waite, and Gendro (2010), it was found that students who engaged in instant messaging (IM) while completing a reading task took much longer to read the passages. This increase of time needed to complete the reading task did not include the time spent on IMing. In fact, students who engaged in IMing while reading took 22%–59% longer to read, not including the IMing time (Bowman et al., 2010). This is not an isolated finding. Other research has also found that individuals who multitask take much longer to complete tasks (Applebaum, Marcionni, & Fernandez, 2008; Fox, Rosen, & Crawford, 2009).

In addition to increasing the amount of time it takes us to complete tasks, there are other negative outcomes associated with multitasking. In their review of the research in this area, Appelbaum, Marcionni, and Fernandez (2008) found that multitasking can also increase your stress, increase the likelihood of you making more errors, and decrease your ability to be creative and make good decisions. You may also reduce your opportunities to feel a sense of accomplishment because you are working on several tasks but may not be completing them as quickly or as well as if you had worked on one task at a time.

Multitasking is particularly problematic in college classrooms when students are learning new content and skills. Researchers have found that multitasking in class is detrimental to learning (Junco, 2012; Wood, Zivcakavoa, Gentile, Archer, De Pasquale, & Nosko, 2012). Wood et al. (2012), for instance, found that there was a negative impact on learning when students used technology during class for social reasons (e.g., Facebook). Learning opportunities during the lecture were lost when attention was focused on the social task. Multitasking isn't just detrimental for you, it also negatively impacts others. Distractions such as a ringing cell phone can result in you and your fellow classmates missing important information in your notes and performing more poorly on the exam (End, Worthman, Mathews, & Wetterau, 2010). Researchers found that students sitting near a multitasker in class who was using a laptop for nonacademic reasons also suffered negative consequences (Sana, Westin, & Cepeda, 2013). Thus, our multitasking actions can have negative effects on others too.

Individuals who multitask are also less likely to enjoy a task. In an interesting study conducted by Oviedo, Tornquist, Cameron, and Chiappe (2015), it was found that individuals who used Facebook while watching television were less likely to enjoy the television experience as compared to individuals who only engaged in one task—television viewing. Multitasking can therefore negatively impact us personally, academically, and professionally.

Instead of multitasking, it is better to engage in what we call single-tasking. In single-tasking, you give your full attention and effort to one task at a time. Based on the research just reviewed, you can see how this approach can actually save you time. By focusing on one task at a time, you are able to really concentrate on it, which is particularly important for tasks and projects that are cognitively complex.

The single-tasking approach allows you to make the most of all the tasks you do. When you're studying, keep focused on studying. When you're having fun, keep focused on having fun. When you're working, focus on doing the best job possible. Sharing your attention between multiple tasks will probably result in frustration and having to spend more time than needed on the tasks. Your enjoyment related to the tasks may also be reduced. Focusing on just one task at a time is recommended (Shellenbarger, 2009). Concentrate on what you are doing at the moment and enjoy and learn from it. Practicing single-tasking will be beneficial to you personally and professionally.

SINGLE-TASK IT STRATEGIES

- Remove distractions—turn off notifications for e-mail, phone, or social media.
- Give your full attention to the current task.
- Write down other tasks you are thinking about so that you can relieve yourself of the pressure of remembering them.

MULTITASKING QUICK QUIZ

1. What are the two types of multitasking?
2. Does multitasking work?
3. What are the academic consequences of multitasking during class?

Interpersonal Skills

Monkey Business Images/Shutterstock.com

Being able to work effectively with others is essential from a personal and professional standpoint. Relationships are a key part of our lives. Being able to effectively communicate and collaborate with others is a skill that is highly valued by employers. These relational skills will also help you with your personal relationships.

Communication and Conflict Management

Communication is an extremely important skill and is the basic building block of relationships. Communication involves listening and clearly expressing your thoughts, ideas, or needs. Doyle (2016) nicely captures the key com-

Monkey Business Images/Shutterstock.com

munication skills that will be helpful to you in the world of work. See Communication Skills Table for a list and description of these essential communication skills. Practicing these skills will also help you communicate more effectively with your family, significant other, and friends.

Listening sounds like a simple task, but it's not. Most of the time, we engage in what we like to call half-listening, which means we hear the person talking, but we also focus on other activities at the same time. In other words, we are not engaging in single-tasking behavior but rather are attempting to multitask (listening while checking e-mails, watching television or a video on our phones, making dinner, playing video games, etc.). Although this half-listening can sometimes work, it tends to become problematic when the conversation is important. You may miss important messages and the other person will likely not feel very important or valued.

COMMUNICATION SKILLS TABLE
10 Essential Communication Skills

Skill	Description
1. Listening	Active listening is when you are giving someone your undivided attention, really focusing on what they are communicating. As you actively listen, you can ask questions to clarify what is being said if you don't fully understand and periodically paraphrase what was said to be sure you are fully understanding.
2. Nonverbal communication	Most of what we communicate happens from how we communicate rather than what we communicate. Be mindful of your body language, facial expressions, and tone as you communicate with others.
3. Clarity and concision	Before communicating an important idea, plan what you want to say. This will make it more likely that you will be able to clearly communicate your ideas in a brief and concise manner. Brief, concise messages are more likely to be heard and understood.
4. Friendliness	Others will respond more positively when you communicate messages in a friendly, positive way. Simple actions such as a smile can enhance the communication process, making it more productive.
5. Confidence	It is more likely that others will respond positively to your ideas and messages if you communicate them with confidence. When you believe in your ideas, others will also be more likely to believe in your ideas.
6. Empathy	Empathy refers to being able to see the world from the perspective of another person. It doesn't mean you have to agree with the other person's perspective or point of view, but others will appreciate it if you can demonstrate that you understand how they see the issue.
7. Open-mindedness	Others will feel respected and valued when you demonstrate that you are open to different perspectives and ideas. This will also often result in more creative and positive outcomes.
8. Respect	Everyone wants to be treated with respect. There are a variety of ways you can send a message of respect including removing distractions, giving the other person your undivided attention, and thanking the person for sharing his or her thoughts and ideas.
9. Feedback	Being able to give and receive feedback is important. If you are in a position where you need to provide feedback to others, it is important to specifically share what the person is doing well and where and how improvements can be made. Feedback helps you grow and improve, so when you are given feedback, identify ways to take the feedback and put it into action.
10. Picking the right medium	In today's world, we communicate in so many ways: face-to-face conversation, online virtual meetings, e-mail, phone, text, and more. Determining the best mode for the communication is important. While technology tools such as e-mail can be very efficient, much can be lost because the nonverbal element of communication is missing. If a conversation is really important, it might be best to have the discussion face-to-face.

Source: Adapted from Doyle, 2016

Real listening, also referred to as active listening, requires that you give your full attention to the person. This means you eliminate barriers such as your phone, the computer, or other distractions. As you listen, you focus on the message that is being communicated. You also encourage the person to continue talking by sending nonverbal messages such as maintaining eye contact and nodding, which show you are listening. Asking relevant questions and paraphrasing, which basically means summarizing what you hear in your own words, are also powerful communication tools. When you paraphrase or summarize what was said, this gives the other person the opportunity to let you know if you accurately heard the message. If not, the person can clarify so that you can better understand. Engaging in active listening communicates that the person you are listening to is important to you. Others will likely appreciate the time and energy you spent listening. When you listen and gain a good understanding of the person's ideas or concerns, you are then positioned well to engage in problem-solving if needed.

Being able to clearly articulate your ideas and concerns is also an important communication skill. What you say and how you say it can impact whether or not your message is heard and understood. Consider both the verbal and the nonverbal messages you are communicating. Words matter. Using negative or judgmental language can cause the other person to become defensive. As a result, the person will likely focus on making his or her case instead of listening to your experiences, ideas, or feelings. For healthier and more successful conversations, use "I messages," messages that focus on you and your experiences, rather than making judgmental comments about others. For example, instead of using a judgmental statement such as "You are such a jerk," you can instead communicate how you feel by stating "I felt hurt and unimportant when you canceled our date." Using "I messages" will result in more positive communication. Communicating your ideas in a clear, concise manner also will increase the likelihood of your messages being heard.

Nonverbal communication can either support or contradict verbal communication (Bonaccio, O'Reilly, O'Sullivan, & Chiocchio, 2016). An example of nonverbal communication supporting verbal communication would be a smile or look of joy when sharing good news. Examples of nonverbal communication contradicting verbal communication could be if you were crying while stating you are happy or saying you are fine when you look irritated or angry. Researchers have found that we are generally accurate in making judgments based on nonverbal communication. For instance, Naylor (2007) found that judgments about job performance and personality were accurately predicted from a photograph where only minimal nonverbal communication was being communicated.

In addition to being able to communicate well with others, being able to effectively manage conflicts when they arise is important from a personal and professional standpoint. It is important to note that some conflict is positive; discussion and debate can promote the development of good ideas and improved outcomes. However, often times conflict can negatively impact relationships and the working environment. It is therefore important to address conflict when it arises and to learn skills to help you manage situations involving conflict. As you would imagine, employers desire employees who are able to engage in effective conflict management.

There are several steps involved in managing conflict effectively. First, it is important to clearly define the problem or source of conflict. This typically involves all parties sharing their point of view and making a genuine effort to listen and understand the situation from the perspective of the other person or persons involved. It is critical that emotions are managed well during this process because when emotions run high, the situation can quickly escalate. To promote effective conflict resolution, all parties should share behavioral or objective data linked to their feelings or thoughts and avoid judgmental and overly emotional communication. For example, you might say, "When you look at the computer or your phone when I'm speaking, I feel unimportant" instead of saying "You don't care about me." Next, possible solutions need to be discussed, with pros and cons being evaluated. Then, a solution or decision will need to be made. There may be times that an outside party, such as someone from human resources if the conflict is taking place in a work environment, will need to come in and serve as a mediator, helping the parties involved come to a solution. Finally, a timeline for assessing the effectiveness of this resolution needs to be established. By following up and evaluating whether the solution had the desired effect, it can make it less likely for future conflict in this area to develop or if additional conflict does arise, you will be better equipped to manage it well.

Rahim (2002) describes five different styles of handling conflict and notes that different styles will work best in different situations.

1. The **integrating style** is particularly effective when dealing with problems that are complex in nature because it uses a problem-solving approach. Individuals using the integrative style will have all parties share their perspectives and suggestions for effectively dealing with the issue at hand and then look to find a solution that works for all parties involved. With this approach, everyone works together to identify the best solution, which might be the solution offered by one person or could be a new solution that resulted from the conversation.

2. The **obliging style**, which basically means you defer to the other party and agree to their solution, can work well if the issue being discussed isn't of high importance to you as it will lead to a quick resolution and not distract you from other issues that are of more importance to you.

3. Individuals using a **dominating style**, on the other hand, are completely focused on their point of view and desired solution such that the opinions of others are not valued. While on the surface, this seems like a problematic style, Rahim (2002) notes that it can be effective with minor decisions or conflicts, or when harm may result if a different solution is chosen.

4. Those with an **avoiding style** typically try to avoid conflict and are not likely to confront a colleague about a topic that could create conflict. While this approach will not work when decisions need to be made, avoiding the situation while emotions cool off can be beneficial, especially if there is no urgency or need to resolve the conflict immediately.

5. Individuals who use the **compromising style** get all parties involved in sharing solutions and the outcome typically involves a give and take by all parties. In other words, a compromise is reached. This style works best during negotiations between different groups or when both parties have equal power. With this approach, the goal is to find a way for everyone involved to get something that he or she wanted.

There is some conflict in all relationships, so it is unrealistic to expect that you can be in a relationship that is conflict free. However, by practicing the communication skills just discussed, you will be able to effectively deal with conflict when it arises. Just like any other problem that comes up, it is sometimes useful to reach out for professional assistance. Remember that psychologists, counselors, and other campus supports are available to you.

COMMUNICATION AND CONFLICT MANAGEMENT QUICK QUIZ

1. What is active listening?
2. What role does nonverbal communication play in communicating messages?
3. What are the five different styles associated with managing conflict?

Emotional Intelligence

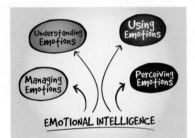

dizain/Shutterstock.com

Emotional intelligence can be defined as perceiving, understanding, and managing your own emotions as well as the emotions of others (Schutte & Loi, 2014). Individuals with high levels of emotional intelligence can skillfully interpret facial expressions and other nonverbal messages sent by others and are aware of the messages they are communicating to others. Managing these emotions is a key component of emotional intelligence. In terms of managing your own emotions, this means using effective coping strategies. In other words, to be emotionally intelligent means you are capably using stress management techniques so that negative emotions do not get in the way of you being productive.

Being emotionally intelligent also involves managing the emotions of others. This involves recognizing the feelings of others and determining how your behaviors can positively impact the situation. In some cases, this may mean giving a person some space and knowing that now may not be the right time to ask a question or make a request because the person is frustrated or angry. Recognizing when someone is in a good mood is also an important part of being emotionally intelligent. In these cases, the timing might be perfect to pitch a new idea or make a request.

Having high levels of emotional intelligence has been connected to positive academic and career outcomes. For example, researchers have found emotional intelligence to be a predictor of whether or not students graduate. Specifically, Sparkman, Moudling, and Roberts (2012) found that social responsibility, impulse control, and empathy were strong predictors of graduation. Empathy refers to the ability to identify and understand the feelings of another person. Impulse control refers to the ability to refrain from acting on feelings immediately and being able to manage one's emotions. Social responsibility refers to one's ability to work collaboratively with others to engage in meaningful and productive actions that benefit society.

Researchers have also found emotional intelligence impacts success in the workplace. Schutte and Loi (2014), for instance, found that employees with high levels of emotional intelligence were more likely to be engaged and satisfied. When employees have high levels of emotional intelligence, conflicts are more easily resolved and done so in more productive ways (Hopkins & Yonker, 2014).

Emotional intelligence has been found to be particularly important in some positions. For example, Lopes (2016) found that the relationship between emotional intelligence and performance was strongest for managers, customer service positions, and healthcare providers. As you can imagine, being able to manage emotions in these positions is particularly important.

Research shows that emotional intelligence can be learned. Lopes (2016) conducted a thorough review of the studies on this topic and concluded that there is strong evidence that training related to emotional intelligence competencies works. Based on this review of the literature, Lopes (2016) recommends that training focus on managing and expressing emotions and that training be offered in the context of projects rather than in isolation. Here are some strategies to improve your emotional intelligence:

1. Increase the awareness of your emotional reactions and how you communicate when you are experiencing different emotions. Notice how others react to you when you are happy, sad, or angry.

2. Practice good stress management on a daily basis, increasing the use of strategies when emotions are more intense.

3. Notice the emotional reactions of others. How do your friends, family members, or coworkers act when they are happy, sad, or angry? Pay close attention to how your response or behaviors impact their emotions and behaviors.

4. Engage in behaviors that have a positive impact on the mood or behaviors of others.

5. Meet with a counselor or psychologist if you would like to better manage your own emotions and the emotions of others in your life.

EMOTIONAL INTELLIGENCE QUICK QUIZ

1. What is emotional intelligence?
2. Can emotional intelligence be learned?

Teamwork and Collaboration: The 5R Approach

Being able to effectively work with others is another important skill that will serve you well personally and professionally. In college, you will likely work with your classmates on various types of projects. Research has shown that there are many benefits to group projects such as improved communication and interpersonal skills, increased knowledge and deeper thinking, and higher levels of motivation and achievement (Hansen, 2006). This is particularly true when students are taught about how to function effectively in groups before being required to do so, as evidenced by a research study conducted by Cranney, Morris, Spehar, and Scoufis (2008). Thus, assignments that require you to work in groups are great experiences because they will give you opportunities to develop essential skills desired by employers.

iStock.com/Rawpixel

To develop teamwork and collaboration skills, it is important that you approach group work productively. Unfortunately, students sometimes approach group work from a divide and conquer mindset, believing that each member of the group should be assigned a part of the project and should work independently on that part of the project to minimize the workload for all involved. This is not the best approach though. Group work is not designed to reduce your workload, but rather is a social learning opportunity where you can develop skills and support one another as you work toward a goal. Approaching group work from a collaborative framework is best. Collaboration, which means working together to achieve a desired outcome, is the key to effective group work. When using a collaborative approach, members will likely have different leadership roles or more responsibility for certain parts of the project, but the work is still primarily done with others in the group. When you work collaboratively, you will typically produce a higher quality product.

Groups don't always function well and this can be quite frustrating to all members involved. One of the most frequently cited problems with group work is when not everyone does his or her fair share of the work. Sometimes there is a member or two who do not do any of or very little of the work. This is referred to as social loafing (Hansen, 2006). Other problems cited by researchers are a lack of skills, lack of group leadership, and behavioral or attitudinal problems (Hansen, 2006). When these problems exist, frustration levels can run high, relationships can become strained, and teamwork skills are not developed. Fortunately, there are effective strategies you can use in groups to help you have a productive, positive experience.

In order for groups to function effectively, there are several key strategies that need to be used. The 5R approach to group work describes these strategies (see 5R Table). By applying these strategies, you are more likely to have positive experiences and develop essential teamwork and collaboration skills. These skills are not only essential in college but also in the world of work.

5R TABLE
5R Approach to Effective Group Work

The 5R Approach to Group Work	Description
Establish **R**apport	Get to know group members.
Determine **R**ules	Agree upon ground rules for working in the group.
Determine **R**oles	Assign roles such as group leader, note taker, visual aid leader, finishing touch specialist, and rehearsal director.
Get **R**eady to work and support one another	Work individually on tasks before meetings. Come prepared and challenge one another with questions to more deeply explore content.
Remember to evaluate	Monitor progress and address conflict immediately.

Establish rapport. Before you begin working on the task at hand, it is important to take some time to get to know your group members. When engaging in group work as a student, ask one another about career goals, interests, work experiences, and why he or she is taking this class. Knowing something about each member can help you understand his or her perspective better. The amount of time you spend on this part of the process will vary depending on the nature and length of your group work. Edmunds and Brown (2010) suggest that spending time on this activity promotes a positive social climate for the group. You are more likely to be productive if group members have established a good working relationship where members respect and value one another.

Develop group rules.

Establishing ground rules is "probably the most important, yet overlooked, action needed to create an effective group" (Armstrong, 2004, p. 34). Rules set clear expectations and provide members with a way to handle conflict that may arise. It is one of the best ways to prevent problems.

All group members should participate in the creation of the group rules. Rules may relate to communication and respect as well as to contributions and deadlines. It is particularly important to establish a timetable for completing the major tasks associated with the project. Some suggested group rules are:

- Attend all group meetings or call or text if there is an emergency and you must miss a meeting.

- Come prepared to meetings, having read materials and produced what was expected according to an established timetable.

- Respond to e-mail, text, or other communication within 24 hours.

- Respect one another at all times.

Assign group roles.

In addition to ground rules, establishing group roles for each member can help groups function productively. The nature of these roles will vary depending on the assignment. Group roles provide clarification of expectations for each member. Students report that having assigned roles within the group is valuable (Wise, Saghafian, & Padmanabhan, 2012). Roles promote individual accountability. This can reduce the likelihood of social loafing, one of the biggest problems associated with group work. Social loafing refers to instances when a group member sits back and allows other members to do all of the work. These members are, in essence, getting a free ride. Assigning roles helps to ensure that all members contribute to the final project and that the work is evenly distributed. Here are some possible roles for a group that is working on a presentation:

- *Group leader*—Arranges meeting schedule, facilitates group meetings while allowing all members an opportunity to discuss their thoughts, and helps make sure there is an even distribution of work.

- *Note taker*—Takes meeting notes and shares the notes with everyone, clarifying tasks assigned to members.

- *Visual aid leader*—Takes work from other group members and puts it together into one cohesive document or presentation.

- *Finishing touch specialist*—Reviews the document or presentation and any handouts for errors, and makes sure the product matches the assignment expectations.

- *Questioner*—Asks group members questions about their contributions, often playing the role of devil's advocate to encourage all members to explore the content more deeply. This role is particularly important because it encourages critical thinking.

- *Rehearsal director/timer*—Organizes the rehearsals and the timing of the presentation, maybe even videotaping it for review.

Get ready to work and support one another. Once rules and roles are established, it is time to start working on the project. One of the biggest challenges associated with group work is finding times when all members are available to meet. You may want to consider using technology tools for scheduling and communication purposes. For example, tools like Doodle (doodle.com) help determine optimum group meeting times. There are also apps where you can assign tasks, keep track of progress, and share documents (e.g., Trello, Wiggio). You probably also have communication tools within your course learning management system. Using these tools provides a way for members who can't make a meeting to still share their contribution electronically and to "catch up" afterward.

To make the most of your face-to-face meeting time, be sure to assign tasks that need to be completed prior to the meeting. Researchers have found that doing work individually before gathering as a group improves functioning and increases productivity (Sarfo & Elen, 2011). Identify tasks that need to be completed prior to your group meeting. For example, what should members read to prepare for the group meeting? Should members take notes or create an outline prior to meeting? Completing tasks such as these can help you have a more productive meeting.

In addition to considering what needs to be done prior to the group meeting, you should think about how to make the most of the meeting itself. During the meeting, support one another by making sure all group members understand the material. Explain course concepts to one another. Teaching someone else content is one of the most effective ways to learn (Schwartz, Son, Kornell, & Finn, 2011). Thus, teaching the content can help you (the "teacher") and the other group members who are struggling with understanding the concept. It's a win-win situation!

Challenging one another with questions is also important because it fosters critical thinking skills for all members. Wise, Saghafian, and Padmanabhan (2012) found that having questioner and devil's advocate roles in a group enhanced the learning experience. Strang (2010) also found that students learned more when they asked each other challenging questions. Some examples of challenging questions are the following:

- What would be another example of this concept?
- Why do you think that is the case?
- How does this relate to....?
- What data support or contradict this idea?
- What are other possible explanations?

Remember to evaluate. As with all of your work, monitoring your progress is a must. As a group, refer back to the timetable you established at the start of your project. Are you on track to achieve the goal by the deadline? If not, readjust the schedule by establishing new deadlines. Consider not only task completion, but also the quality of the product you are creating. Plan to complete the project at least several days in advance of the due date. This way, if there are any events that make it difficult for members to get together (e.g., weather, illness), you'll still be able to complete your assignment on time.

In addition to evaluating progress as it relates to the group, it can also be helpful to evaluate the progress and effectiveness of individual group members. Hughes, Toohey, and Velan (2008) note, "For students to develop skills in teamwork, team members must learn to give and receive feedback effectively" (p. 5). Thus, incorporating peer feedback about individual performance into the evaluation process can enhance skill development. Feedback that is specific and constructive, providing suggestions on how to improve, is most useful.

TEAMWORK AND COLLABORATION QUICK QUIZ

1. What is the 5R approach to group work?
2. What are some examples of group rules?
3. What are some examples of group roles?

Diversity and Cultural Competence

Diversity refers to the differences among and between individuals. Although most people immediately think of ethnicity and race when they hear the word *diversity*, it is a much broader concept than that. For starters, we can talk about diversity in terms of culture, economic status, cognitive abilities, sexual orientation, gender, and age. Disability is another type of diversity. Some disabilities will be obvious, such as a person who has mobility impairments and needs to use a wheelchair or a person who is visually impaired and has a guide dog. Other disabilities are invisible to the eye and are not easy to detect. For example, a person could have a learning disability or attention deficit hyperactivity disorder. It is important for you to know that while the disability does impact that person, it does not define the person. This is true for individuals without a disability, too. One strength or weakness does not define you. The same goes for other types of diversity. While our race, gender, and sexual orientation are essential parts of our identity, being a part of a group or population doesn't tell the whole story about us. We will often identify with several groups and will also have our own unique family and individual values and beliefs that define us. Knowing someone's diverse background is important, but getting to know the individual is equally, if not more, important. For many college students, college may be the first time they have the opportunity to interact on a daily basis with other individuals whom are very different from them in a variety of ways. Perhaps this is the case for you.

Rob Wilson/Shutterstock.com

As we live in a diverse world, developing cultural competence is important. Cultural competence is understanding and being able to effectively interact with others from different cultures. Burcham (2002) identified a total of six attributes of cultural competence that are identified in the literature most consistently, namely, cultural awareness, cultural knowledge, cultural skill, cultural sensitivity, cultural interaction, and cultural understanding (as cited in Shen, 2015, p. 311).

Developing cultural competence often involves the following:

1. Learning about various cultures and populations
2. Becoming more aware of your own beliefs and attitudes and how these beliefs impact you and others
3. Developing skills to effectively work with others who may be very different from you

In other words, becoming culturally competent will likely result in changes to your knowledge, attitudes, and behaviors. Reducing stereotypes and prejudice is also an important part of being culturally competent. Stereotypes are judgments you make about a person based on beliefs you have about a group that he or she belongs to. Prejudice refers to your feelings or attitudes about a group or members of a group. Not surprisingly, stereotypes and prejudice can negatively impact performance of group members (Wolfe & Spencer, 1996). In fact, even the fact that stereotypes exist can negatively impact someone's performance. Psychologists call this stereotype threat. Stereotype threat refers to the worry or risk that you will confirm that a negative stereotype about a group you belong to is true based on your actions or performance (Palumbo & Steele-Johnson, 2014). Let's take a look at an example. One gender stereotype is that women don't perform as well as men on mathematical tasks. As a result of this stereotype, women often perform more poorly on tests related to mathematical skills due to the pressure associated with trying not to confirm this stereotype. Researchers have found that emotions, particularly negative emotions, often play an important role in this process (Mangels, Good, Whiteman, Maniscalco, & Dweck, 2012). See Reducing Stereotype Threat Table for research-based strategies identified by Casad and Bryant (2016) that can reduce stereotype threat and the negative consequences of it.

REDUCING STEREOTYPE THREAT TABLE Strategies to Minimize the Impact of Stereotype Threat on Performance	
Environmental strategies	Surround yourself with positive images and examples of success of others who are similar to you. Using the gender stereotype of math as an example, have photos and success stories of women being successful on mathematical tasks and in careers that require high-level mathematical skills.
Role models and peer group	Find role models or even mentors who are similar to you. When possible, attend events with others who are similar to you so that you are not the only one representing your group. Engage in group work that requires all members to work toward a common goal. Surround yourself with others who value you and provide you with feedback that is performance-based.
Attribution training	Meet with a counselor or psychologist or attend a workshop focused on attribution training. Attribution training targets our perception of what contributes to our success or failure and helps us focus on internal, changeable factors such as effort.

Source: Adapted from Casad & Bryant, 2016

Becoming culturally competent and learning to work collaboratively with others from diverse backgrounds and cultures can enrich your overall experiences and increase your successful career experiences. Discovering the cultural norms and customs associated with different cultural groups increases your diversity knowledge. Research has shown that diversity education that focuses on increasing knowledge of different cultures is effective (Kulik & Roberson, 2008). Learning experiences that include experiential learning are most effective (Bezrukova, Spell, Perry, & Jehn, 2016). Diversity training has also been linked to attitudinal and behavioral changes, although these changes are not always long-lasting (Bezrukova et al., 2016). Ongoing diversity training or experiences may therefore be needed.

According to Caligiuri and Tarique (2012), the following competencies are critical to being a leader in a global, multicultural context:

1. **Reduced ethnocentrism or valuing cultural differences.** Caligiuri and Tarique (2012) state that ethnocentrism refers to when individuals place a higher value on their own cultural perspective, viewing other perspectives and cultures as being inferior, noting that ethnocentrism negatively impacts work relations.

2. **Cultural flexibility or adaptation.** Caliguiri and Tarique (2012) describe cultural flexibility as being willing and able to engage in behaviors and activities that are consistent with a culture other than your own. In other words, culturally flexible individuals are willing to approach tasks in ways that may be very different from what they are used to doing.

3. **Tolerance of ambiguity.** Tolerance of ambiguity refers to being able to handle and manage new or unpredictable situations that may arise, which are more likely to occur when you are working with others from different cultures.

Research findings show that all three of these competencies, reduced ethnocentrism, cultural flexibility, and tolerance for ambiguity, are qualities of effective global leaders and that these competencies can be developed by increasing our interactions and experiences with others from different cultures (Caligiuri & Tarique, 2012). Thus, you can build your cultural competence by seeking out opportunities to interact and work collaboratively with others from diverse backgrounds. You can also increase your cultural competence by taking courses on diversity or participating in workshops or conferences with a diversity focus; however, finding learning opportunities that include experiential components will work best. Thus, it is important to not just seek out learning opportunities but to also seek out experiential learning opportunities so that you can interact with others who are different from you. Seeking out these opportunities regularly will increase your cultural competence.

It is human nature to seek out people who are similar to us. There's a level of comfort associated with being with people who are more alike than different from you. However, interacting with others with different backgrounds and abilities will certainly enrich your experience as a college student, help you develop cultural competencies, and better prepare you to live and work in a diverse world. By interacting with others, you will be less likely to stereotype or pass judgments about a person based solely on group membership. Researchers have found that when you work in diverse groups on a task that requires cooperation, prejudice is reduced and you are more likely to view your peers positively (Walker & Crogran, 1998; Wolfe & Spencer, 1996). Likewise, others will be less likely to pass judgments about you. Interacting with others with different perspectives also exposes us to varied viewpoints that contribute to the development of more sophisticated thinking. As Schreiber and Valle (2013) note, "collaboration with diverse others can be a vehicle for developing an appreciation of personal and cultural differences" (p. 396).

Leadership

Employers often indicate that leadership is a highly desired skill, but what does it mean to be a leader? Being a leader means you influence or persuade others to do the work needed to achieve a goal. McCallum and O'Connell (2008) note that "leadership involves the ability to build and maintain relationships, cope with change, motivate and inspire others and deploy resources" (p. 152). Leaders have many

excellent soft skills, interpersonal and communication skills being especially important.

Leaders typically take charge of a project, discovering the best ways to utilize the expertise of the members of the group in order to best accomplish the task at hand. Leaders focus on the goal or desired outcome and encourage team members to share their ideas about how to best reach that goal. Using their organizational skills, leaders map out possible pathways to accomplish the task based on the ideas presented by group members. Leaders emphasize the importance of the task and how collaboration will lead to the best outcome. Leaders routinely provide positive feedback and encouragement to motivate all members to fully invest in the process. Leaders also emphasize the importance of celebrating accomplishments.

Many might say that leadership is an innate skill, believing you are a born to be a leader. However, research negates this statement. Rather, research shows us that leadership skills are learned. The secret to developing expertise in a skill such as being a leader is years of deliberate practice with the support of a coach or mentor (Ericsson, Prietula, & Cokely, 2007). Deliberate practice involves more than just improving skills you have; deliberate practice also requires that you go beyond your comfort zone and practice skills you don't yet have. For example, if you are not an inspirational speaker, a skill often associated with being a leader, you can become one by practicing this skill with the support of a professor or mentor. Stretching and challenging yourself to engage in new skills is an essential part of becoming a leader.

While there are many different types of leaders, the transformational leader is often most desired by employers. A transformational leader inspires others to engage in creative and collaborative problem-solving aimed at achieving a common goal that is highly valued by all members of the team. Arnold (2017) conducted an extensive review of the literature and found a positive relationship between transformational leadership and the psychological well-being of employees. Thus, many will benefit when a company hires a transformational leader.

According to Bass, there are four primary characteristics associated with being a transformational leader:

1. **Charismatic.** Transformational leaders are role models whom others admire and want to follow. They clearly and passionately articulate a vision that immediately makes sense to others.

2. **Inspiring and motivational.** Transformational leaders exude enthusiasm about their vision and get others excited about making this vision a reality.

3. **Intellectually stimulating.** Transformational leaders not only share their ideas but also encourage others to consider creative ways to meet with success and actualize the shared vision.

4. **Respectful of individual differences.** Transformational leaders care about the individuals with whom they work. They attend to the needs and ideas of all members of the group and create a supportive working environment where varying ideas and approaches are respected and appreciated (as cited by Stewart, 2006).

How do you develop leadership skills? Becoming a leader obviously requires much practice and time on task. Take advantage of opportunities you have in and outside of the classroom to work with a group of peers. As with all other skills, the more you practice, the better you will become at being a leader.

One of the most important first steps in becoming a leader is to self-reflect on your core values and what matters most to you. It will be much easier to develop leadership skills when you are working on a project that is consistent with your values. Leadership begins with vision and your values will shape your vision. Ask yourself, "What is it that you want to accomplish and why?" This will obviously depend on what you are leading. For example, you may be deciding on a community service project for a club or perhaps you need to choose a service learning project or presentation topic for a collaborative group project in one of your classes. Whatever the task at hand, finding value and meaning in projects is essential. For example, if you care deeply about increasing opportunities for elementary school students in disadvantaged areas, you could develop a program or participate in an already established program to increase opportunities for children in these areas. Once you've identified your vision, you'll want to think about why others would get excited about this goal. Clearly identify the reasons that this project matters so much and why actualizing the vision is so important. Effective leaders ensure that everyone knows the rationale behind the goal (Seijts & Latham, 2011).

To determine the best way to make your vision a reality, you'll want to use your listening skills. Ask others to share their ideas and actively listen to their thoughts and ideas. Good leaders listen more than they talk. Good leaders are also inclusive, giving all members of the group the opportunity to speak and be heard. Listening will not only provide you with numerous ideas to consider, it is also a very effective way to show you respect and value others on your team. As you listen and get to know members of your team, you can also begin to discover the talents and skills of each member. You may even want to ask members about their strengths and how they believe they can best contribute to the project. For example, perhaps someone has skills in design and could develop the promotional materials or visual aids for the project. When all members of a team genuinely feel respected and valued and believe they can make a significant contribution to the project, the team is much more likely to function more effectively.

Good leaders also have time management and planning skills. In other words, they will develop a timeline for completing tasks so that the project is completed on schedule. Along the way, the leader will ask team members to provide status updates on progress and encourage problem-solving when issues arise. Regularly reporting on progress helps all members be accountable and engaged. When problems arise, leaders engage all members in identifying potential solutions. Throughout the process, leaders provide positive feedback and encouragement and of course celebrate successfully completing the project (Seijts & Latham, 2011).

LEADERSHIP QUICK QUIZ

1. Is leadership an innate skill or is it learned?
2. What are the characteristics of a transformational leader?

CHAPTER 4 | Chapter Summary: Note-Taking Model

Let's summarize what you've learned in this chapter. The Cornell model is used for this chapter. Remember, it is not expected that your notes will look like this right after class or reading. It takes time to organize your notes and repackage them. It is time well spent, though, because you learn the content better as you organize it and you'll have a fabulous foundation from which to study for your exams! There are several ways to use this section:

- **Preview:** Read the model before reading the chapter to familiarize yourself with the content (the S in SQ3R).
- **Compare:** Compare the notes you took on the chapter to the model provided.

- **Study:** The model along with your notes and other course materials are great resources for studying.

Cornell Method Model

What are soft skills?	Skills that are important in many different careers and in life. Examples include: • Professionalism • Time management • Interpersonal skills • Leadership Different from technical skills that are more specific to careers
What does professionalism mean?	Engaging in behaviors that communicate you care about achieving goals, are honest and responsible, hardworking, and a team player
What time management strategies work best?	Improve time management • Evaluate your time and determine if you are spending your time in a way that matches your goals • Avoid time traps, activities that take up a lot of your time and do not help you achieve your goals Achieve Work–school–life balance • Evaluate whether you need to do all you are doing (e.g., working) • Prioritize and spend more time on important tasks Meet deadlines • Make a to-do list with specific tasks, prioritizing most important tasks • Create a schedule • Break large tasks into small ones to combat procrastination Avoid multitasking • Multitasking is not effective; often takes longer to complete tasks, tasks may not be completed as well, and less enjoyment is experienced • Single-task it, focusing on one task at a time

| What interpersonal skills are important to employers? | Communication and conflict management

• Actively listen—remove distractions and give your undivided attention to the task
• Monitor nonverbal communication to make sure you are sending consistent, clear messages
• Brief is often better when communicating
• Be respectful and open to ideas of others
• Provide feedback that is specific and meaningful
• Choose the right medium for communication; sometimes face-to-face communication is best
• Conflict resolution involves identifying the problem, all parties sharing their perspectives, a discussion of possible solutions, selecting a solution and then evaluating whether that solution worked
• There are different styles for handling conflict: integrating, obliging, dominating, avoiding, and compromising

Emotional intelligence

• Being able to identify, understand, and manage your emotions and the emotions of others

Teamwork and collaboration

• Being able to work effectively with others
• 5R approach to group work: establish Rapport, develop group Rules, assign group Roles, get Ready to work and support one another, and Remember to evaluate

Diversity and cultural competence

• Many types of diversity such as race, ethnicity, gender, economic status, sexual orientation, age, disability
• Cultural competence is ability to interact effectively with individuals and groups from other cultures
• Increase cultural competence by engaging in experiential learning opportunities to learn about different cultures, become more aware of your own beliefs and attitudes, and develop skills
• Stereotype threat is pressure or worry you experience because you don't want to engage in actions that confirm a negative stereotype about a group you belong to |
| What does it mean to be an effective leader? | Leaders influence or persuade others to do what is needed in order to accomplish a goal

There are four characteristics of a transformational leader, a leader who inspires others to engage in creative collaboration to achieve a goal that is valued:

• Charismatic
• Inspiring and motivational
• Intellectually stimulating
• Respectful of individual differences |

SUMMARY: Soft skills, such as communication and teamwork, are skills that are needed across many different careers. Employers consistently indicate that they prefer candidates who possess soft skills. College is an opportunity to develop soft skills such as good time management, communication, collaboration, and leadership. While you will develop some of these skills through coursework, it is a good idea to participate in extracurricular activities, as these skills are often best learned through out-of-class experiences.

CHAPTER 5

Demonstrating Knowledge and Skills

This is your moment to shine. Embrace it.
—John Smith

Tom Peterson, Middlesex County College

1 Why is it important to first focus on the purpose of an academic task?

2 What is academic integrity? Why does it matter?

3 When do you need to use citations? How do you cite sources?

4 What steps are involved in writing a paper?

5 How can you engage your audience when giving a presentation?

6 What makes a visual aid effective?

7 What do the best students do when they take a test?

Exploring the Research in Summary

Research Study Citation

Issa, N., Schuller, M., Santacaterina, S., Shapiro, M., Wang, E., Mayer, R., & DaRosa, D. (2011). Applying multimedia design principles enhances learning in medical education. *Medical Education*, 45(8), 818–826.

INTRODUCTION: THE RESEARCH QUESTION

What question did the researcher seek to answer?

Does learning increase when PowerPoint slides are based on multimedia learning principles?

METHOD: THE STUDY

Who participated in the study? What did the researchers ask the participants to do?

Medical students (n = 130) participated in a lecture on shock as part of their curriculum. Ninety-one students participated in the revised PowerPoint condition, where the PowerPoint slides were developed based on multimedia research. A total of 39 students participated in the lecture where the original PowerPoint slides were used. The revised PowerPoint condition used the multimedia principle (use images rather than words), the signaling principle (draw attention to main points), and the coherence principle (only include essential content).

Pretests were given prior to the lecture so that groups could be compared on prior knowledge. One hour after the lecture, a posttest was administered to assess learning that took place during the 50-minute lecture.

RESULTS: THE FINDINGS

What was the answer to the research question?

Both groups had similar levels of background knowledge and both groups had experienced significant learning as a result of the lecture. However, the students in the revised PowerPoint condition outperformed the students in the original PowerPoint condition on a posttest measuring how well they remembered the lecture content. See PowerPoint Multimedia Principle Figure illustrating test performance.

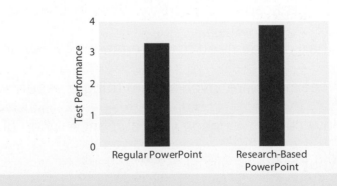

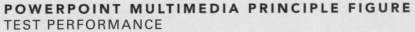

POWERPOINT MULTIMEDIA PRINCIPLE FIGURE
TEST PERFORMANCE

DISCUSSION AND SO WHAT FACTOR

How can YOU use this information as a student?

These findings show that the multimedia principles identified by Mayer (2009) really do work in the classroom setting. When creating PowerPoints or using multimedia, it is important to only put the essential information on the slides and to use images rather than words whenever appropriate to do so. Eliminating distractions, such as animations, can also increase learning. This research reminds us of the importance of visual images and that PowerPoints are visual aids, not papers on slides.

Purpose of Academic Tasks

In college, you will be completing numerous academic tasks such as papers, presentations, and tests in every course you take. Understanding the "why" behind these assignments is important because it can increase your motivation and help you successfully complete the task. As you'll recall, the primary purpose of higher education is to create citizens who can use knowledge and skills learned to make positive, significant contributions to society. The curriculum or course requirements have been developed to help you learn the knowledge and skills needed to be a productive citizen. The combination of general education and major specific coursework allows you to learn and develop skills that are essential in life and all careers (i.e., communication and critical thinking skills) and gain the more specific background knowledge and skills that will be needed in your field of interest. In academia, we call these big goals of the curriculum program outcomes. Program outcomes define what graduates of each major should be able to know, think, or do.

Constantin Stanciu/Shutterstock.com

Every course has course-level outcomes that are connected to these larger program outcomes. Course-level outcomes outline what students will be able to know, think, or do as a result of taking the course. Think of it this way—course-level outcomes define the purpose of the course and act as steps that will help you achieve the overall program outcomes (goals for graduates). A lot of thought goes into determining what courses will be required and why. The same is true for the assignments and academic tasks within each course. Professors often spend countless hours creating assignments that are aligned to the course-level outcomes or goals. In other words, every assignment will help you build knowledge and skills that will ultimately help you achieve the course and program goals or outcomes. Hence, the purpose of assignments is to help you develop skills needed to reach your goals and be a productive citizen.

Learning is the goal. By focusing on learning as the primary purpose of assignments, you will learn more and achieve at higher levels. Researchers have found that students who have learning goals and view assignments as learning opportunities have high levels of motivation and achievement (Grant & Dweck, 2003; Valle et al., 2003). Learning goals focus on acquiring knowledge and skills. Sanders (2012) contends that becoming a learner is the primary purpose of higher education, noting that "Mastering the process of learning through study, analysis, and experimentation is much more important than the details of what you learn" (p. 12). Although it is more productive to have learning goals, some students have what is called performance goals and focus primarily on their academic performance, which in many cases refers to their grades, rather than their learning. Researchers have found that students who focus primarily on their performance or grades are less likely to use deep learning strategies and consequently do not perform as well as those with learning goals (Valle et al., 2003). This may be due, in part, to students with learning goals doing whatever it takes and persevering when faced with challenges in order to achieve their goal of learning, while students who focus on performance or grades may just put in the minimal work needed to earn the desired grade. This is not to say that you shouldn't care about your grades. The reality is that grades do matter, especially if you need to maintain a merit-based scholarship or you are interested in pursuing a graduate degree. However, putting learning as your priority, rather than grades, will increase the likelihood that you will learn more while achieving higher grades.

Before you begin working on an assignment or academic task, focus on the purpose for the task. Having a clear understanding of the purpose of the task will help you determine how to best approach and learn from this opportunity. For example, if you are taking a quiz that is designed to help you build foundational knowledge in the subject area, memory strategies can help you learn and remember key concepts. If, on the other hand, the purpose of the quiz or test is to determine how well you can apply concepts learned to real-world situations, your study approach will have to go beyond memory strategies, incorporating application practice. Similarly, the purpose of writing assignments can vary significantly. For example, the purpose of a research paper might be to synthesize or summarize the research on a topic while the purpose of a reflection paper might be for you to engage in self-regulation, the process of monitoring your progress and making adjustments as needed. While there will be some similarities to how you approach both of these writing tasks such as writing an outline, draft, and revising your work, there will also be several differences in how you should approach each task based on its purpose. For the research paper, you will need to conduct a thorough, broad-based literature review on the topic, identifying and evaluating sources. For the reflection paper, you may need to instead look at the evidence related to your academic progress and engage in reflection about your performance.

To learn more about the purpose of an assignment, review the syllabus, especially the section on learning outcomes for the course. Some professors will explicitly communicate how the assignments are related to the course learning outcomes or goals. If this is not the case, look for the link between the assignment and course goals and ask your professor for clarification if needed. Carefully read all of the assignment details as this often provides you with a clear purpose and understanding of the assignment. In some cases, professors may also provide you with a rubric or other grading criteria. While you should focus more on learning versus grades, grading rubrics can provide you with information about assignment expectations and what knowledge and skills you will need to demonstrate. Focusing on the purpose and expectations associated with assignments will help you develop an effective learning approach and successfully complete the assignment.

PURPOSE OF ACADEMIC TASKS QUICK QUIZ

1. What are program and course learning outcomes, and what is their relationship to assignments?

2. Why is it important to have learning goals?

3. How can you find out the purpose for an assignment?

Academic Integrity

Before you turn in any work for a course, it is important to understand academic integrity. You will want to become familiar with what it means to engage in academically honest work and the college policies related to academic integrity. Learning about academic integrity will make it less likely for you to unintentionally engage in dishonest actions.

What Is Academic Integrity?

Academic integrity refers to engaging in academically honest behaviors. It involves doing your work without using unapproved aids and creating your own academic product, such as a paper or presentation, while giving appropriate credit to those who shaped and influenced your work. Giving credit to these sources for their contributions is a must and involves using in-text citations and a reference or works cited page. Academic dishonesty can be intentional or unintentional, but either way it can have significant negative consequences. One of the best ways to avoid unintentional dishonest actions is to fully understand plagiarism and cheating. See Academic Dishonesty Table.

Ivelin Radkov/Shutterstock.com

3D_creation/Shutterstock.com

Academic integrity benefits everyone at college. It is important for others to have a positive image of your college or university so that the work you and others do there is valued. Negative mindsets about your institution or program that stem from dishonest actions can be detrimental to both current and future students. For example, negative views about your institution may result in fewer outside learning opportunities for students, such as yourself, or reduced employment options for graduates. Local businesses and other community services are less likely to partner with an institution with a questionable image. As you can see, it is important for everyone at the institution to value integrity and encourage honest behaviors. McCabe, Butterfield, and Trevino (2012) found that peers had a major influence on whether or not students cheated. Specifically, they found that students were less likely to cheat when they thought their peers were being honest and would not approve of cheating behavior. You can help promote a positive culture on your campus by caring about academic integrity and talking about the importance of it with your peers.

ACADEMIC DISHONESTY TABLE
Types of Academic Dishonesty

Type of Academic Dishonesty	Definition	Examples
Plagiarism	Presenting someone else's work as your own.	• Putting your name on a work (entire paper or small sections) that someone else created. • Not using quotation marks when using another person's words. • Using quotation marks when using another person's words but not citing the source. • Only changing a few words in a sentence even if you cite the source. • Paraphrasing the idea of another person and not citing the source. • Submitting the same paper or work in two different classes without professor approval—this is referred to as self-plagiarism.
Cheating	Engaging in any activity that gives you or another student an unfair advantage.	• Using unapproved materials or resources when completing an assignment or exam. • Working collaboratively when an assignment is supposed to be completed independently. • Discussing exam content with another student who hasn't taken the exam yet.

Your character and learning matters much more than the grades you earn (Sanders, 2012). The goal of assignments such as papers and presentations is for you to learn content and develop skills. View these tasks as opportunities for you to build your knowledge and enhance important skills. When students are dishonest, they lose out on valuable learning that will help them perform well in their career. While a degree may be the minimum requirement for a position, employers are really much more interested in the learning that was connected to completing this degree.

There are several ways to avoid engaging in dishonest academic actions. Perhaps most importantly you should focus on learning. Students who care about learning are more likely to engage in honest behaviors (Miller, Shoptaugh, & Wooldridge, 2011). Preparing well for tests and using good time management on assignments also makes it less likely that you will be tempted to be dishonest. Learning about academic integrity and how to effectively cite sources can help you avoid unintentional dishonesty (Belter & du Pré, 2009). Finally, don't forget to seek out help from others when needed. Sometimes students engage in dishonest actions when tasks are challenging. The better approach is to seek the help you need so that you can learn the knowledge and skills associated with the task while also being honest.

STRATEGIES TO HELP YOU BE ACADEMICALLY HONEST

- Know the definitions of plagiarism and cheating.
- Focus on learning as your goal.
- Prepare well for exams.
- Use effective time management strategies.
- Learn how to cite sources appropriately.
- Consult tutors, librarians, and professors as needed.

WHAT IS ACADEMIC INTEGRITY? QUICK QUIZ

1. What is the definition of academic integrity?
2. Why is academic integrity important?

Citing Sources and Paraphrasing

Citing sources is important regardless of the product you are creating. Most students know that they need to document the source when writing a paper, but they may not realize that media tools such as PowerPoint also need to include citations on slides as well as on a reference list. You can't use images, videos, or other media tools without giving proper credit. Be sure to include citations on all of your academic products. Unfortunately, in a study conducted by Howard, Serviss, and Rodrigue (2010), it was found that 94% of the papers reviewed did not cite a source for information that was clearly not common knowledge. If you neglect to cite the source, this is considered plagiarism, so it is very important that you learn when and how to cite sources appropriately. When in doubt, cite it!

aboikis/Shutterstock.com

To avoid plagiarism:

- Cite all ideas unless they are purely your own or are considered common knowledge, which means that most people would know the information.

- If you are using someone else's exact words or other work, be sure to use quotes, which clearly indicate that this is the direct work of someone else. Since your professor wants to hear your ideas, use quotes from others sparingly.

- Always cite the source whenever you are paraphrasing someone else's thoughts or ideas.

How you cite sources depends on the format and style your professor expects. Different disciplines use different styles. The Modern Language Association (MLA) and the American Psychological Association (APA) are two of the most common citation styles used in college settings. With both styles, it is essential that you provide citations in the body of the text, with a complete citation on the Works Cited or References page. There are many Internet resources that can help you get your source information into the correct format. You can also use writing resources such as *Keys for Writers* (Raimes & Jerskey, 2011). Check out the Citation Examples Table for an example of APA and MLA citations.

CITATION EXAMPLES TABLE
Examples of Citations: APA and MLA

	APA	**MLA**
Paraphrase	College students will typically be expected to use either MLA or APA style in their papers (Harrington, 2019).	College students will typically be expected to use either MLA or APA style in their papers (Harrington 141).
Quote	"The Modern Language Association (MLA) and the American Psychological Association (APA) are two of the most common citation styles used in college settings" (Harrington, 2019, p. 141).	Harrington indicated that "the Modern Language Association (MLA) and the American Psychological Association (APA) are two of the most common citation styles used in college settings" (141).
Works Cited	Harrington, C. (2019). *Student success in college: Doing what works* (3rd ed.). Boston, MA: Cengage Learning.	Harrington, Christine. *Student Success in College: Doing What Works*. 3rd ed., Cengage Learning, 2019, p. 141.

Keeping track of your sources helps you cite them appropriately. Whenever you take notes from a book, article, or website, write down the entire citation next to the content. In most library databases, you'll see a citation tab where the citation appears in a variety of formats (see Citation Figure for an example). You can then copy and paste the citation into your notes, making it easier for you to cite your sources when you are finalizing your paper or presentation. It is important to note though that these tools are not always completely accurate, so you should double check the formatting of citations you get from online tools.

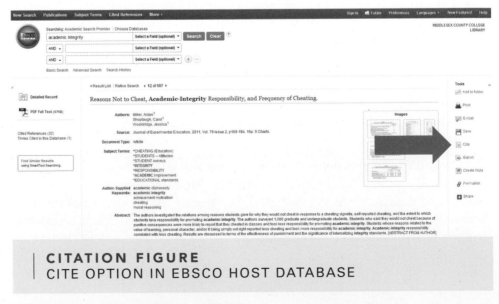

CITATION FIGURE
CITE OPTION IN EBSCO HOST DATABASE

Source: EBSCO accessed via Middlesex County College

When it comes to paraphrasing ideas from others, researchers have found that students are not always paraphrasing effectively. Howard, Serviss, and Rodrigue (2010) found that most students cited sentences from sources rather than citing the sources themselves. Paraphrasing is about summarizing ideas in your own words, so you should be paraphrasing ideas from an entire article, not just from a sentence within an article. In fact, in the 18 papers they reviewed, none included a summary of a source, defined by Howard, Serviss, and Rodrigue (2010) as "restating and compressing the main points of a paragraph or more of text in fresh language and reducing the summarized passage by at least 50%" (p. 181). Instead students relied on changing a few words and inserting synonyms. This study suggests that students may not be fully reading or comprehending the source material. Paraphrasing is a skill that gets better with practice. It is most difficult to paraphrase when you don't understand the content. In these instances, be sure to get help from a tutor, librarian, or professor. Accessing help not only helps you avoid plagiarism but also helps you learn the content!

Learning how to paraphrase well also reduces the likelihood that you will unintentionally plagiarize. Paraphrasing involves more than just changing a few words in a sentence. It involves summarizing someone else's idea in your own words. When you write your summary, close the book or minimize the window if using a computer when capturing the content. This way you will not be tempted to copy words used in the original. This strategy decreases the likelihood that you only change a couple of words.

CITING SOURCES AND PARAPHRASING QUICK QUIZ

1. When do you need to cite sources?
2. What is the definition of paraphrasing?

Papers and Presentations

Papers and presentations are wonderful opportunities for you to develop your communication skills. Being able to effectively communicate orally and through your writing is a skill that will serve you well personally and professionally. In fact, communication is one of the most desired skills by employers (Robles, 2012). Papers and presentations are also great opportunities to build your information literacy and critical thinking skills (Albitz, 2007; Breivik, 2006).

Courtesy of Suzanne LoPorto

Developing a Plan

Good organization is an essential element of papers and presentations. It is not uncommon for students to start writing or creating a PowerPoint presentation without first mapping out the organizational structure of the paper or presentation. This is not advisable. Would you go on a trip to a place you've never visited without

Goodluz/Shutterstock.com

directions, a map, or GPS? Probably not! Knowing where you are headed and how you plan to get there is important when writing papers or creating presentations.

Begin by focusing on your outcome or destination. Why did your professor assign you this paper or presentation? What is the goal or purpose of it? Consider writing the assignment down in your own words to help you fully understand the task. Having a very clear understanding of the professor's expectations will assist you in knowing what you need to accomplish. Carefully review rubrics (detailed explanations of how assignment will be graded) if provided, and ask your professor for clarification as needed. As you work on the project, it is a good idea to periodically review the assignment and its purpose.

If you have the freedom to choose the focus for the paper or presentation, the next step will be to select a topic. Students often underestimate what is involved in this process and the importance of choosing well. Identifying a topic that is too broad seems to be the most common student mistake (Head & Eisenberg, 2009). Suppose you choose stress management as a topic for a presentation. This topic is too broad because it covers many subtopics. You may soon become lost in the vast amount of information available on stress management, and, as a result, you may not have a focus for your assignment. Broad topics often lead to papers or presentations that are general in nature, not providing the level of depth and detail expected at the college level.

One way to help you narrow your search is to focus on specific populations. For example, you could focus on stress management in children, college students, individuals about to have surgery, or unemployed individuals. In addition to narrowing your search by population, you could also zoom in on one aspect of the topic. Perhaps you want to learn about a particular stress management technique, such as progressive muscle relaxation, or you want to know more about the connection between stress and heart disease. You could even combine the specific population and aspect approach by looking at the connection between stress and heart disease in the unemployed population. After you engage in this process, you will have a clear, concise topic that provides you with focus and direction, making it much easier to create a fabulous paper or presentation.

Choosing a clearly defined topic helps set the stage for your success. See Identifying a Topic Table for some ideas about how to choose a topic.

IDENTIFYING A TOPIC TABLE Strategies to Identify a Well-Defined Topic	
Identifying a Well-Defined Topic	**Strategies**
To get started	• Look at the table of contents in related textbooks. • Review chapters that catch your interest, focusing on the subheading topics. • Google topics that capture your interest, looking for specific areas you could target. • Go to broad sources like encyclopedias, but don't stop there. • Conduct a literature search in the library databases.
To further define your topic	• Use search features that are built into database search engines (see Search Features Figure). • Focus on specific populations or aspects of the topic. • Identify key words related to the topic (see Key Words Figure). • Work with a librarian or your professor for additional tips.

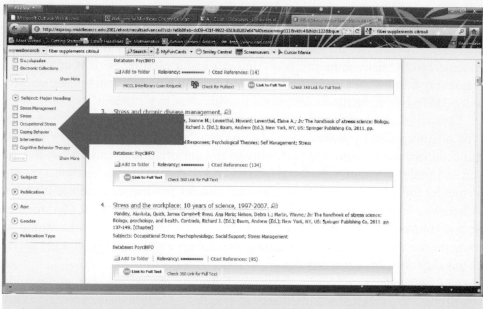

SEARCH FEATURES FIGURE
SUGGESTED SEARCH CATEGORIES

Source: © 2011 American Psychological Association

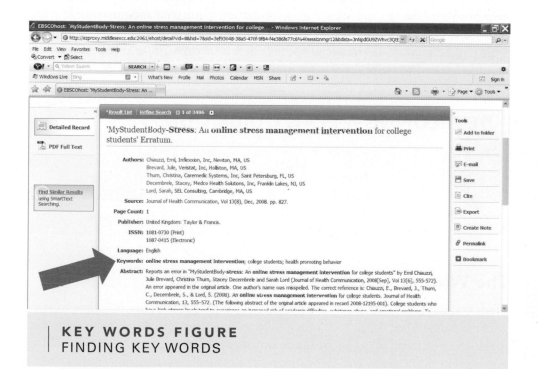

KEY WORDS FIGURE
FINDING KEY WORDS

Source: © 2011 American Psychological Association

The next step is to map out the path you will take to get to your finished product. You can use a variety of organizational tools, such as outlines or concept maps. Researchers have found that using tools, such as graphic organizers, improved writing skills (Brown, 2011). List the main concepts you will address as the major headings in an outline or as large circles in a concept map. Then, add subtopics and details. Think about how the topics are connected and which concepts are most important. As you work on the outline, be sure to keep in mind the intended audience. For example, are you preparing this assignment for your professor who is an expert in the field or are you preparing it for your classmates? If your audience is not very familiar with the information you will be writing or presenting on, you will need to be sure to define terms and provide clear explanations.

You will then need to use your information literacy skills to determine what type of information you will need to complete the assignment, find the needed information, and evaluate the credibility of the information found. In most cases, you will find more information than you will need. As you know, there are a variety of sources for information including journals, books, newspapers, and the Internet. Where you look for the information will depend on the task at hand and whether or not your professor has any specific requirements about sources. Learning to navigate the vast amount of information available is a skill and you will get better at this skill with time and practice.

The best place to go for assistance with finding the information you need is the library. While visiting the library in person is ideal because you can easily ask the reference librarians for assistance as needed, many college students rely on the online databases that can be accessed from almost anywhere. If you need help while working online, you'll be happy to know that many college libraries offer telephone and Internet support. In fact, you may even have 24/7 online access via tools like chat. However, traditional in-person assistance is still the best type of help around! Use this assistance in combination with your information literacy skills to locate everything you may need to complete your paper or presentation. This will help you build important skills needed in your future career, where you will likely need to write reports for and give presentations to bosses, coworkers, and clients.

DEVELOPING A PLAN QUICK QUIZ

1. What is the first step when developing a plan for a paper or presentation?
2. What is the most common mistake students make when selecting a topic?

iStock.com/jacoblund

The Writing Process

Once you have mapped out an organizational plan for your paper, it is time to start writing. Remember, this is just a first draft, so focus on getting your thoughts and ideas documented. Take the ideas you outlined and expand on them, describing concepts in more depth and providing more detailed explanations. There's plenty of time later to make modifications and edits.

Here are some suggestions for when you write your paper:

1. Begin with a strong opening. Your opening should clearly address the purpose of the paper and your main idea. It should also gain the reader's attention and interest. After reading your first paragraph, your professor should have a very clear understanding of the purpose and scope of the paper and should be excited to read it. Your opening sets the stage for the rest of the paper.

2. To stay on track as you start writing, keep your outline or concept map in front of you. As you work, review it regularly. This can help ensure that you address all of your key points. You may find that you need to modify your original plan as you start working and discover that there were additional points that you would like to include. This, of course, is not a problem. Your paper or presentation will likely grow and develop as you continue to work on it. Just be sure that you revisit the actual assignment periodically to be sure that you have met all of the expectations set forth by your instructor.

3. End with a strong conclusion that summarizes the key points. The conclusion or summary is your opportunity to remind the reader of the main ideas presented in your paper. It refocuses the reader back to your most important points. This last part of the paper is often what is best remembered, so make the most of this section.

First drafts are not final products; they are just the beginning. Once you have completed a draft, the critical process of revising and proofreading begins. You will be surprised at how much you are able to improve upon your initial work, especially if you take a flexible approach to writing. As you begin writing and revising your work, you may discover that you need to find additional sources to support the ideas you are presenting. You may even decide that you want to make changes to your organizational plans, restructuring your paper to some extent (Council of Writing Program Administrators, National Council of Teachers of English, & National Writing Project, 2011). Although finding information and creating an organizational plan were initial activities, you may need to revisit these steps as you engage in the revision process. Making changes and adding information often results in a better paper. See Writing Process Figure.

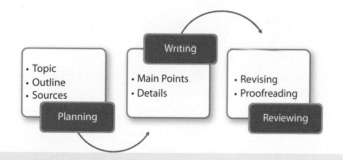

WRITING PROCESS FIGURE
THE FLEXIBLE WRITING PROCESS

Revising a paper involves adding, deleting, and modifying the information in your first draft for the purpose of improvement. Before reviewing and revising your work, it is often a good idea to give yourself a little space from the project. In other words, don't expect to plan, write, and review your assignment in one day. Instead, allow yourself time to reflect on what you've done before you begin revising it. You are often tired by the time you reach the end of the first draft. Take a day or so to rest and reenergize and you will find that this results in being able to revise and proofread more effectively.

When revising your work, first look at the big picture and then focus on the details. Wallace (1990) conducted an interesting research study where college students were asked to revise a written document. Half of the students were simply told to revise it, while the other half were first given an eight-minute lesson on how to effectively revise work. The lesson focused on the importance of:

- Reading the entire written work before making any revisions
- Considering the document as a whole
- Emphasizing global factors, such as the intended audience, purpose, and general organizational structure

Students who participated in the brief revision training created documents that were judged to be of higher quality compared to the students who were simply told to revise the work.

As you review and revise, focus on whether your primary message was clearly communicated. The purpose of each section or paragraph should be easy to identify. Investigate whether your main ideas were supported by details and examples and backed up with citations. Did you provide the reader with enough information and examples to get your point across? It is also important to explore whether it will be easy for the reader to see the connections between topics you discussed. Adding transition statements such as "next" or "as a result" can assist the reader in seeing the connections and will make your paper flow well. It should be easy for the reader to follow your thought process.

Once you are finished, give yourself some more space and revise it again. To produce high-quality work, you will go through several drafts. By carefully engaging in this review process, you will enhance your work to create a polished product that reflects your knowledge and skills.

REVISION TIPS AND STRATEGIES

- Start by reviewing the assignment expectations.
- Allow time (a day or so) to elapse before beginning the review process, and again between drafts.
- Carefully review the document, focusing on what is actually in the paper and not just what you think you wrote down.
- Review it from a global perspective, focusing on whether you clearly addressed your key points in an organized fashion.
- Look for supporting details and examples.
- Determine whether or not you need to find additional information on the topic.
- Find your thesis statement for each paragraph.
- Explicitly make connections between concepts being discussed.
- Review the organization of the paper and make modifications as needed.
- Be sure you cite everything except your own ideas and general knowledge.

The final step in the process of writing an academic paper is proofreading. When you proofread your work, you check for accuracy and the presence of grammatical or spelling errors. This is when you shift from the global focus to the more specific focus. Take advantage of resources that can help with this step. Your computer, for instance, has many built-in tools that can help you with the proofreading process. The most obvious ones are the spelling and grammar checks that are often turned on automatically. Experiment with the other tools like Outline View in Word documents to check out your organizational structure. Use other resources such as a text from your English class to help you with the proofreading process.

This is also a great time to go back over your written work and be sure that you have not unintentionally plagiarized. Ask yourself the following questions:

- Did I provide in-text citations according to MLA, APA, or other professor expectations?
- Did I always cite information that was not my own idea or general knowledge?
- Did I use quotes and citations when using the words of another?
- Did I include a Works Cited or Reference page with complete citation information using MLA or APA style?

Remember, you can also seek tutoring or writing support. Tutors don't typically proofread or edit your paper for you, but they will assist you with becoming good at these tasks yourself. Research has found that consulting with a tutor can contribute to improved performance on writing tasks (Oley, 1992).

WRITING PROCESS QUICK QUIZ

1. How would you describe the writing process?
2. When revising your work, what should you focus on first?

Presentations

Presentation skills are important in college and beyond. In addition to having well-organized content from credible sources, you also need to know how to effectively communicate this information verbally and via a visual aid. In other words, the presentation has two primary components: the content and the delivery of the content.

Matej Kastelic/Shutterstock.com

Managing performance anxiety. When most students hear the word "presentation," they often start to feel anxious. Performance anxiety is normal. Some anxiety is desirable because it motivates us to perform our best. However, for some students, anxiety can spiral and become debilitating. When anxiety becomes debilitating, your performance is negatively impacted (Raffety, Smith, & Ptacek, 1997).

The most effective way to manage performance anxiety is through preparation. It is easier to feel confident and less anxious when you know you've adequately prepared for the task ahead of you. For example, Menzel and Carrell (1994) found that the amount of time spent preparing for a speech was significantly linked to how well students performed on the presentation. Specifically, they found that all of the following were positively connected to high-level performances:

- Total time preparing for the speech
- Total time spent practicing
- Amount of time spent on preparing the visual aid
- Total number of rehearsals
- Time rehearsing silently
- Time rehearsing out loud

You can use a variety of rehearsal methods when preparing. For instance, you can rehearse in front of a mirror, in front of family members or friends, or in front of anyone else who is willing to listen! As you practice, try avoiding filler words such as "umm" and monitor the time it takes you to do the presentation. At the end of your presentation, ask the audience for feedback. In addition to overall feedback, try asking content-based questions to see if the members of your audience understood the material you presented. This is a great way to assess your effectiveness. You can also encourage audience members to ask questions of you so that you can become comfortable responding to questions before the actual presentation.

Beginning and ending strong. There is a concept in the world of public speaking called the *Golden Rule* (Sellnow, 2005) that involves:

1. Telling the audience what you are going to say
2. Saying it, and then
3. Telling the audience what you just said

By using this approach, your presentation includes a strong opening and conclusion. The opening sets the stage for the audience by preparing them for what's to come. Priming or talking about what's coming next gets the audience ready to take in or encode the information you will be presenting. Effective presentations begin with a strong opening that grabs the attention of your audience and draws them into your presentation. Make the start of your presentation interesting and informative. After just the first few minutes, your audience members should have a clear understanding of what you will be discussing, understand why are you discussing it, and be interested in hearing more. There are several opening strategies or hooks that you can utilize. Here are some examples of hooks:

- Interesting statistics that speak to the importance of the topic
- Stories that help the audience connect to the material on an emotional level
- Audience involvement through questioning techniques or activities
- Humor (when used appropriately)

After you are finished presenting your content, go back and summarize the key points from your presentation. A strong conclusion is essential. Audience members can often get overwhelmed by the amount of information presented, especially when presented in a short period of time. By drawing their attention to the main points, you increase the likelihood that they walk away with the most important content. We are most likely to remember the first and last part of the presentation. This is referred to as the primacy and recency effect (Myers, 2014). Be sure to start and end strong!

Audience engagement. Audience engagement refers to the involvement and attentiveness of your audience members. Maintaining good eye contact is a great way to stay connected to your audience. Practice and preparation play a key role because it is very difficult, if not impossible, to have good eye contact when you are not well prepared. The more comfortable you are with the material, the less likely you will feel a need to look at your notes or the PowerPoint slides when presenting. When presenters have their back to their audience as they read their slides, attention and interest drop significantly. Putting just images or a couple of key points on the slide provides a simple, clear focus for the audience while allowing you the opportunity to maintain eye contact as you elaborate on the topic. By discussing instead of reading, you keep the interest of your audience and exude a level of confidence that is sure to impress your professor!

Use active learning strategies throughout your presentation to keep the attention of your audience and make it more likely they will remember the concepts. As the presenter, you want to help your audience members focus on what is most important. Even with short presentations, there is often a lot of information being communicated. When there are several presentations given during one class period, this can quickly result in students being overloaded with information. To avoid this, try the following strategies to emphasize or highlight important concepts:

- Comment on the importance of the topic.
- Become more animated or change your voice pattern.
- Repeat the information.
- Use a dramatic pause.
- Connect concepts to a gesture or image.
- Spend a significant amount of time on the topic.
- Use several examples.
- Share stories related to the material.
- Use visual tools like charts or graphs.

Active learning techniques move the learner from a passive to an active role. While student presentations are generally short in duration, you can still find quick ways to promote the active role for your audience. Many strategies may take only a minute or two but can significantly help your audience process and remember the information you are sharing with them. Here are some active learning strategies:

- Give a brief one- or two-question quiz.
- Poll the audience, using a show of hands, about their opinion or experiences.
- Pause for questions or brief comments.
- Ask members to engage in an independent written self-reflection activity (What have you learned from the presentation so far? What questions do you have?)
- Encourage the audience to do a Turn and Talk, turning to a classmate and summarizing what they have learned from the presentation.

Using multimedia effectively. Researchers have conducted many studies to explore what type of PowerPoint slides or other multimedia tools works best. Mayer (2009), in particular, has conducted numerous experimental studies investigating best practices in multimedia. See Multimedia Best Practices Table for research-based strategies based on Mayer's (2009) work.

As you are discovering, creating a visual aid that consists primarily of an image can increase learning. There are some presentation tools that you can use that will put this research into practice. For example, the Pecha Kucha method, an alternative to Power Point, requires students to select primarily images for their slides and they are expected to spend only approximately 20 seconds on each slide.

MULTIMEDIA BEST PRACTICES TABLE
Best Practices for Using Multimedia

Principle	Description
The Multimedia (or what we like to call Images are Powerful) Principle kurhan/Shutterstock.com	According to Mayer's (2009) research, adding an image significantly increased learning. According to this research, a fabulous slide could simply include a title and an image or graph.
The Coherence (or what we like to call the Less is More) Principle FOCUS totallypic/Shutterstock.com	Students often add background music, sounds, or even videos, believing these make the presentation more effective. However, Mayer (2009) found that these additions can actually reduce learning, because they distract and overload the brain and do not help the learner differentiate between important and less important content. Instead, keep the slides focused on one or two main points.
The Signaling (or what we like to call the Bring Attention to Main Points) Principle Test Performance Einstein, Mullet, & Harrison, (2012)	According to research conducted by Mayer (2009), highlighting or emphasizing main points through tools such as arrows or larger, bold font increased learning.
The Personalization (or what we like to call the Conversational Language) Principle Syda Productions/Shutterstock.com	Mayer (2009) found that learning improved when simple conversational language was used instead of more formal language. Avoid complex terminology and use easy-to-understand explanations (this is why we've renamed the principles!).
The Modality (or what we like to call the Be Quiet) Principle Yuricazac/Shutterstock.com	Basically, Mayer (2009) found that when learners were presented with a lot of text and the presenter spoke about the topic, less learning took place. He attributed this to split attention. The learner is not sure whether they should listen or read—both are competing for the learner's attention. To increase learning, use only images or very few words with a narrated description. If there is a need to put a lot of words on the screen, then let the learner read the slide silently and "be quiet." After giving them ample time to take in the information, you can then discuss additional content on that topic.

Source: Based on the work of Mayer (2009).

Beyer (2011) found that the Pecha Kucha presentation approach can be effective. Another tool within PowerPoint that is often overlooked is Smart Art. Sometimes an image won't best capture the content, so words are needed. However, we know that bullets are not very effective on a slide. One solution is to use Smart Art to visually package the key words. See Smart Art Figure for an example.

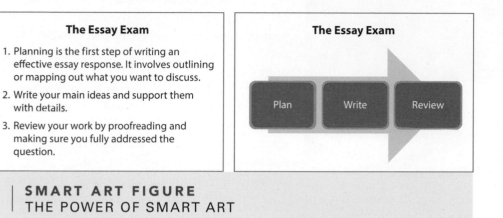

SMART ART FIGURE
THE POWER OF SMART ART

After you finish your presentation, reflect on your performance to maximize learning and enhance your skill development. Researchers found that students who watched and reflected on videos of their presentations produced higher-quality presentations as compared to students who did not watch and reflect on their initial performance (Sterling et al., 2016). This reflective practice also resulted in higher levels of confidence. Specifically, Sterling et al. (2016) found that students who engaged in these reflective practices felt more confident in their ability to prepare and conduct presentations as well as being more able to differentiate between effective and ineffective presentations.

TIPS FOR EFFECTIVE PRESENTATION DELIVERY

1. Practice! Practice! Practice!
2. The Golden Rule: Tell your audience what you will say, say it, and then tell them what you said.
3. Grab their attention with a good hook.
4. Maintain eye contact with your audience.
5. Integrate active learning techniques, such as brief quizzes, questions, or discussions.
6. Create effective visual aids.
7. End with a compelling conclusion.

PRESENTATIONS QUICK QUIZ

1. What is the best way to combat performance anxiety?
2. What are some strategies you can use to engage the audience during a presentation?
3. What PowerPoint strategies did you learn from Mayer's (2009) multimedia research?

Test-Taking Strategies

Robert Kneschke/Shutterstock.com

Testing is a powerful way to learn. If you didn't take tests, you probably wouldn't learn as much. Let's assume you are taking a psychology course. Before class, you read your textbook and take notes on the key psychological theories. During class, your professor lectures about psychological theorists, shows you brief videos, and has you engage in group discussion about the theories. Is learning happening here? It certainly ought to be! But wait…. Think back to what you learned about how memory works. If it all ends here and your professor does not test you on the material, you probably wouldn't do anything with the material after class. As you know, studying the material after class is necessary to promote learning and reduce forgetting. Exams are great learning opportunities that require you to be engaged with the content.

While there is no substitute for studying and preparation, there are some test-taking techniques that can help you perform your best. There are several research-based approaches to use during tests. For example, having a positive mindset and focusing on your successful experiences can help you perform better. Nelson and Knight (2010) conducted an interesting study where they found that students who were instructed to think and write about a successful experience before taking a quiz had less anxiety and better performance when compared to students who were instructed to write about their morning. It is therefore a good idea to recall a successful experience before taking an exam.

Multiple-Choice Tests

iStock.com/PeopleImages

While most students prefer multiple-choice tests over short-answer or essay exams (Tozoglu, Tozoglu, Gurses, & Dogar, 2004), multiple-choice tests can be quite challenging. Many multiple-choice test questions require you to apply knowledge learned. Even if you know you will be taking a multiple-choice test, it is recommended that you pretend it is a short-answer test. Why? Research has found that students put forth more effort when expecting a short-answer versus multiple-choice exam (Balsch, 2007). This is probably because students perceive multiple-choice tests to be easier even though they can be just as challenging.

Fortunately, we have research to guide your test-taking behaviors during multiple-choice tests. According to research (LoSchiavo & Shatz, 2002; McClain, 1983), all of the following test-taking strategies are connected to better exam performance:

- **Anticipating answers**. Read the question and come up with an answer before looking at the possible choices. This approach forces you to pay attention to the question, and spending time on the question can reduce the likelihood of errors. For instance, missing even one word in a question could set you up to choose the incorrect response. It is common for students to quickly skim the question and then dive into the answers, particularly when anxiety levels are high. In this situation, there is often not enough energy directed at the question itself; it is very difficult to choose a correct answer for a question you don't fully understand. By forcing yourself to come up with the answer, you must focus on the question. To help you avoid peeking at the responses (because let's face it—it's very tempting!), cover up the answers with a piece of paper or your hand. You will be less likely to fall victim to the distracter items since you are looking for a particular answer. Distracter items have been specifically designed to take you off track, but if you are clear on the question and have formulated your own answer, you will be more likely to answer correctly.

- **Reading all choices**. You have probably had an experience where you thought your answer was correct, but your professor indicated that another choice was the better option. If you don't read all of the choices, you won't be able to compare your choice with the other possibilities to determine which is best.

- **Eliminating wrong answers**. Eliminating wrong choices helps to visually remove options you are no longer considering. This can save you time because you won't be tempted to reread and rethink the answer options that you know are incorrect.

- **Skipping difficult questions**. If you spend too much time on a difficult question, you may not have enough time to answer questions that might be much easier for you. Before you move on, make your best guess based on the investment you've already made in case you don't have time to return to it later. Skipping difficult questions can also help reduce anxiety. Spending time on difficult questions brings attention to what you don't know, making you more anxious. Skip the difficult questions and find the ones you know to increase your confidence and decrease your anxiety. You may also come across questions later in the exam that trigger a memory, helping you correctly answer the original, difficult question.

- **Writing on the exam to highlight key terms, draw figures or diagrams, and mark questions**. Researchers have found that writing on tests was positively linked to academic performance. Specifically, students who highlighted key concepts, marked questions needing further thought, and drew figures or charts performed better than students who did not engage in these tasks during the exam (LoSchiavo & Shatz, 2002). You can also jot down mnemonics or other key information you've studied, which is sometimes referred to as a data dump. Writing down connections between concepts or images in a way that is meaningful to you can also be productive. Underlining key words in the question helps you understand the main focus of the question, while drawing lines through answer options you've eliminated keeps you focused on good answer choices.

- **Changing your answer if you have good reason**. You have probably heard the advice "Stick to your gut, and go with your first answer." If you have heard this advice before, you may be surprised to find out that research suggests that changing your answers is often a good, not bad, idea. It is important to note that although this issue is discussed quite a bit, the reality is that students don't change their answers very frequently. Specifically, Di Milia (2007) found that a little over half of the students in the study did switch answers, but only for approximately 2% of the questions.

Research indicates that students make more wrong to right switches than right to wrong switches when changing their answers (Di Milia, 2007). Shatz and Best (1987) also found that answer changing can have a more positive than negative impact on academic performance, as long as there was a good reason for the change. Specifically, individuals who changed their answer because they misread the question or because of a clue discovered later in the exam made a wrong to right change in 72% of the cases. When guessing was identified as the reason for the switch, students were about as likely to make wrong to right as right to wrong changes. Based on this research, change your answer whenever you have a good reason. Although switching your answer based on guessing doesn't put you at a big disadvantage in terms of outcome, it takes time away from the other exam questions, so it is therefore not a good practice.

MULTIPLE-CHOICE EXAM TIPS

- Prepare as if you were taking an essay exam.
- Carefully read questions while removing answers from view.
- Highlight key terms.
- Anticipate the answer before reviewing options.
- Read all answer options.
- Eliminate wrong responses.
- Skip difficult questions.
- Write on your exam if permitted to do so.
- Change your answer if you have a good reason for doing so but not if you are only guessing.

MULTIPLE-CHOICE TESTS QUICK QUIZ

1. What strategies do high performing students use when taking a multiple-choice test?

2. Is it a good idea to change your answer when taking a multiple-choice test?

Short-Answer and Essay Exams

Kate Aedon/Shutterstock.com

Short-answer and essay exams give you the opportunity to show off what you know and to articulate and apply your knowledge. You are generally not confined to focusing on one piece of information as you might be in a multiple-choice test question. Instead, you can use your knowledge about the topic to produce a good response.

Unfortunately, most students don't feel confident taking essay exams (Sommer & Sommer, 2009). Research suggests, however, that despite their dislike of the essay exam, students do not perform worse on essay exams as compared to multiple-choice exams (Skinner, 2009). Rather, students tend to perform equally well on exams, regardless of the format.

You can increase your confidence as well as your essay-writing skills with these three main steps involved in writing a good essay response:

1. Planning
2. Writing
3. Proofreading

All good products start with a plan. The same is true for a good essay response, which is a product of your knowledge. Unfortunately, students often forget this important step when answering short-answer or essay questions and start to dive into their response without first thinking about how to best respond. The first step is to fully understand the question. Read the question carefully, underlining key words to keep focused on what the question is asking. For example, if it says compare and contrast, you need to discuss both similarities and differences between the concepts. Despite how thoroughly you discuss the similarities, if you forget to address the differences, it could result in losing half the points!

Timing is an important part of the planning process. Before you begin, know how much time you have for each question. Simply divide the amount of time you have to complete the test by the number of questions, and this tells you how much time you have for each question. It also gives you a sense of how much detail your professor is expecting. For example, if you have 30 minutes for a question, your professor is likely expecting a pretty sophisticated product with a lot of details. If, on the other hand, you only have 10 minutes for a question, your professor will not be expecting quite as much detail and depth.

Spend approximately one-fifth of the time you have for the question on this planning stage. Think about what you want to say and how you plan to organize your thoughts. Consider making a quick outline or concept map before you start writing. Start by jotting down the main points you would like to cover and then add details that support these points.

The majority of your time will be spent on writing the response. Begin with a strong opening that directly relates to the question. This is often referred to as a thesis statement. This allows the reader to know where you stand with the issue or what you believe is most important.

Each subsequent paragraph should also have a clear opening sentence that tells the reader about the focus for that paragraph. Add more specific information about the topic through examples and supporting details. Writing an organized response is important.

Ending with a strong conclusion is an effective way to reiterate or emphasize your main point. Be sure you use this opportunity to leave the reader with a clear understanding of what you perceive to be most important. It is what the professor will remember most when grading your exam, so show what you know!

Although you will probably get excited as you write the conclusion, and you may even breathe a sigh of relief that you are finished, don't put your pen down yet! There is one more very critical step you must do before you hand in your exam—proofreading your work! You should give yourself approximately one-fifth of the time you have to complete the question for this important step.

Begin this part of the process by rereading the question, carefully focusing on what is being asked. It is not uncommon for students to get off track when answering a question, writing about concepts that were not directly asked about in the question. Also, make sure that you have answered all the subparts of the question. Check off each sub-question as you review your response so that you are absolutely certain that you gave a complete response. If you miss something, it could negatively impact your test score.

Next, check your organizational structure, spelling, and grammar. Ask yourself the following questions:

- Are your ideas clearly connected?
- Did you provide support for your opinion?
- Did you check and double-check your spelling and grammar to be sure your response is error free?

When reviewing your organization and flow, read your response slowly and carefully. As you proofread, you may read what you thought about as opposed to what actually made it to the paper. To combat this issue, read slowly and really focus on the words written on the page.

ESSAY WRITING TIPS

- Read the question carefully.
- Plan effectively by jotting down main ideas and supporting details.
- Begin with a strong opening that sets the stage for your response.
- End with a solid conclusion that directs the reader back to your main point.
- Read the question again and check off the parts you answered.
- Proofread for spelling, grammar, and organization.

SHORT-ANSWER AND ESSAY EXAMS QUICK QUIZ

1. What are the three steps associated with writing a good response to a short-answer or essay question?

2. How much time should you spend on each step if you want to write a good essay response?

Take-Home and Online Exams

iStock.com/Maica

Take-home and online exams, although sometimes similar in format, can be a very different experience from in-class exams. Online exams are being used more and more frequently even in on-ground (traditional, in-person) classes, so it is likely that you will encounter this type of test during your time as a college student. Part of the reason for online or take-home exams is that these options do not take away from learning time during class.

While many students often report less anxiety when taking tests outside of the classroom setting (Stowell & Bennett, 2010), it is important that you still prepare well. Take-home and online exams can be quite challenging in nature and students often underestimate how much studying and preparation is needed, which can obviously result in poor performance. It is likely that you will have to go beyond memorization (the lowest level of Bloom's taxonomy) and engage in higher-level critical thinking skills. Thus, you want to be sure that you have a strong foundational knowledge in the course content before you start working on the exam. In addition to being challenging, take-home or online exams may also be more time-consuming than traditional tests. Because the testing is taking place outside of the classroom, the professor is not limited to the amount of time allowed for class. It is therefore essential that you carve out enough time to successfully prepare for and complete the exam. Look at your syllabus or ask your professor for details about the testing process so that you can plan accordingly.

Knowing what to expect with these different test formats is important. Online testing can vary quite a bit from class to class. It's important to know the technology requirements and be sure you are using a computer and web browser that matches these testing requirements. You may also want to know the procedure should you have a technology problem when completing the test.

Before an online test, ask how the test will be set up. One professor may allow you only one attempt at the test while another professor may allow you take the quiz or test more than once. In some cases, you'll be able to go back and change your answers, while in other cases you will not be permitted to do so. Some online quizzes or tests may also be timed while others may not. When tests are timed, a clock is often running on the computer screen. Some students find this to be distracting or anxiety-producing, while others believe it helps them with their time management during the exam. You may also benefit from asking your professor if there are any practice test opportunities, which allow you to get comfortable with this testing format before it counts toward your final grade.

Many online testing programs will immediately grade your test upon completion. You should also find out whether you will have an opportunity to review your results to see which questions you answered correctly and incorrectly. Remember, learning from your mistakes is a great way to increase your knowledge!

As with all testing, it is essential that you uphold the academic integrity of the course and engage in appropriate test-taking behaviors when completing take-home and online exams. Be sure you are clear about what materials, if any, you are permitted to use. Using unapproved materials or sharing exam content with other students is considered cheating. To avoid the temptation to engage in academically dishonest behaviors, be sure you practice good studying skills and focus on the goal: learning. Strong preparation leads to successful outcomes—no matter what the test format!

TAKE-HOME AND ONLINE EXAMS QUICK QUIZ

1. How do take-home and online exams differ from traditional exams?
2. Can you use materials and resources when taking an online exam?

CHAPTER 5 — Chapter Summary: Note-Taking Model

Let's summarize what you've learned in this chapter. The Digital Notes model is used for this chapter. Remember, it is not expected that your notes will look like this right after class or reading. It takes time to organize your notes and repackage them. It is time well spent, though, because you learn the content better as you organize it and you'll have a fabulous foundation from which to study for your exams! There are several ways to use this section:

- **Preview:** Read the model before reading the chapter to familiarize yourself with the content (the S in SQ3R).

- **Compare:** Compare the notes you took on the chapter to the model provided.

- **Study:** The model along with your notes and other course materials are great resources for studying.

Digital Notes Model

Helvetica ∨　14 ∨　▪ ∨　**B** *I* U̲ S̶ {}　☑ ☰ ☰　🔗 📎 ⬠　⊞ —　☰ ∨　More ∨

Chapter 5 Demonstrating Knowledge and Skills

Purpose of Academic Tasks

- Assignments are designed to help us achieve the course and program learning goals/outcomes.

- Focusing on learning rather than grades will lead to higher levels of motivation and achievement.

Academic Integrity

- Care—integrity impacts the image of the institution, character is more important than grades, learning is increased with integrity.

- Avoid unintentional dishonesty—know definitions of plagiarism and cheating, focus on learning over grades, prepare well, know how to cite sources, seek help as needed.

- Cite sources
    - When? Any time you use the ideas or work of another person. Don't need to cite when using own ideas or if it is common knowledge.
    - Citation styles—use in-text citations and a Reference/Works Cited page
      ✓ APA
      ✓ MLA

- Paraphrasing—summarizing someone else's idea into your own words (more than just changing a few words), takes time to learn.

Papers and Presentations

Choose a topic

• Be specific—avoid topics that are too broad in nature.

• Use resources—table of contents, Google, literature review in library databases (use features to select specific populations or aspects of the topic).

Writing process

• Goal - focus on the purpose of the task.

• Organize → use outline or graphic organizer to map out organizational structure that identifies main ideas and supporting details.

• Start and end strong—get reader interested from the start; summarize key points at the end of the paper.

• Be flexible—when revising, you may discover you need more information or a new (or modified) organizational structure.

• Review work—start by focusing on the big picture (goals of assignment and main ideas); then look at the details (proofreading); seek help as needed.

Presentations

• Prepare well → reduces anxiety, easier to engage audience and improve performance.

• Start and end strong → use a hook (interesting story, statistic) to gain interest from audience; summarize key points at end to refocus audience on what is most important.
    • The Golden Rule = tell them what you are going to say, say it, tell them what you said.

• Emphasize main points—repeat, use examples, tell stories, increase volume.

• Use brief active learning strategies—poll audience, quiz, Turn and Talk.

• Create powerful visual aids; use tools like Smart Art

Multimedia Principles (Based on Mayer's work)	Description
Less is More	Avoid distracting transitions or animations; focus on primary points
Bring Attention to Main Points	Use arrows, large font to draw attention to main ideas
Conversational Language	Use conversational language on slides; avoid jargon or formal language
Be Quiet	If you need to use a lot of words, allow audience to read the slide; don't "talk over" it

Chapter 5 Demonstrating Knowledge and Skills

Test Taking

Multiple-choice tests

- Anticipate answers.
- Read all choices.
- Eliminate wrong answers.
- Skip difficult questions.
- Write key terms on test and mark up questions.
- Change answer if good reason for doing so.

Essay questions

- Read question carefully.
- Pay attention to time.
- Plan out response—what key points should you make?
- Strong opening and conclusion.
- Stay on track—give main ideas and supporting details that address question.
- Proofread.

Take-home and online exams

- Can be challenging and time consuming.
- Prepare well.
- Maintain academic integrity.

SFIO CRACHO/Shutterstock.com

PART 3

BEING SUCCESSFUL: PLANS AND PERSEVERANCE

Mapping Your Path to Success: Plans and Action Steps

Find meaning and relevance in all that you do, and you will never wonder about the value of your existence.

—Kathryn Suk

1. Why is it important to meet with your advisor and develop an academic plan? What should be included in your academic plan?

2. What are the benefits of studying abroad, participating in service learning, and doing internships?

3. What impact might social media have on your future employment? How can you create a professional online presence?

4. What is an elevator speech and why is it important?

5. Why is networking important? How can you expand and strengthen your current network?

6. How can your financial choices now, including paying for college, impact you in the future?

7. How can you establish and maintain a good credit score? What benefits are associated with a high credit score?

Exploring the Research in Summary

Research Study Citation

Celio, C. I., Durlak, J., & Dymnicki, A. (2011). A meta-analysis of the impact of service-learning on students. *Journal of Experiential Education*, 34(2), 164–181.

INTRODUCTION: THE RESEARCH QUESTION

What question did the researcher seek to answer?

Service learning is incorporating community service into a course in a way that aligns to the course goals. How do students who engage in service learning benefit from the experience?

METHOD: THE STUDY

Who participated in the study? What did the researchers ask the participants to do?

The researchers surveyed the literature on service learning and conducted a meta-analysis. A meta-analysis is a method used to look at results across studies, identifying consistent themes that emerge. To locate studies on this topic, the researchers searched library databases for articles published between 1970 and 2008. Only studies that were written in English, integrated the service learning with academic curriculum, compared students in service learning coursework to students not in service learning coursework, and focused primarily on service learning were included. A total of 62 studies were analyzed. Sixty-eight percent of these studies targeted the college population. This represented 11,837 students in total. Results were "organized into five main categories: (a) attitudes toward self, (b) attitudes toward school and learning, (c) civic engagement, (d) social skills, and (e) academic achievement" (Celio, Durlak, & Dymnicki, 2011, p. 170).

RESULTS: THE FINDINGS

What was the answer to the research question?

There were five main benefits of participating in a service learning experience. Two themes related to attitude. Students who participated in service learning had more positive attitudes toward themselves and also toward school. This meant that these students had higher self-esteem and self-efficacy and were more engaged in their learning. Service learning participants also had higher levels of civic engagement, better social skills, and performed better academically. These students were more likely to believe they have responsibilities as a citizen, have leadership and social problem-solving skills, and achieve higher grades. Outcomes were even better when the service learning project was directly linked to the course learning goals and included reflection activities.

DISCUSSION AND SO WHAT FACTOR

How can YOU use this information as a student?

These findings show the powerful impact of participating in service learning projects. It is strongly recommended that you seek out courses that incorporate service learning into the curriculum and give you reflection opportunities. Talk to your advisor to learn about these opportunities on your campus. If there are not many opportunities for service learning, you may want to get involved in college-wide committees (such as student government) to raise awareness about the importance of service learning.

Creating an Academic Plan

Academic planning involves mapping out when you will complete all of the academic requirements needed for graduation, identifying which electives to take, and determining what additional learning opportunities such as co-curricular activities or study abroad you would like to take advantage of as a college student. Planning can also help you complete your degree in a timely fashion. As you know, you'll need to complete a variety of required courses in order to graduate and many of these courses are sequential in nature. This means that there will likely be some courses that need to be taken in a certain order. If you don't take courses that are required in the beginning of the sequence early on

alphaspirit/Shutterstock.com

in your college journey, you may have difficulty graduating on schedule. Mapping out an academic plan will help you see when courses will need to be taken so that you can stay on track with your graduation timeline. In addition, there may be amazing opportunities such as internships or study abroad experiences that need to be planned well in advance.

Connecting with Your Advisor or Academic and Career Mentor

Most, if not all, colleges or universities will assign you an advisor, who is typically a faculty member in your career of interest or a professional who is well-informed about the field. Colleges and universities use a variety of different job titles to describe this position such as advisor, counselor, student development specialist, mentor, and coach. We will use the term *advisor* in this section as it is still the most widely used title, but it is important for you to know that the advisor is not there to simply provide you with advice. Rather, advisors serve as your academic and career mentor, helping you determine your academic and career goals and then assisting you with mapping out a plan to achieve these goals. In other words, advisors will guide you through the process, but you will ultimately determine your goals and actions.

iStock.com/Jovanmandic

Too often, students rely solely on information from their peers instead of getting information from campus experts such as advisors. While it is a good idea to use all of your resources, it's important for you to know that your advisor has professional and institutional expertise that your friends may not have. Advising is connected to successful outcomes. For example, students who use advising services, as compared to students who do not, have higher grade point averages (Kot, 2014). In addition to performing better academically, students who regularly meet with their advisor are also more likely to continue in college (Ryan, 2013).

As your academic and career mentor, your advisor serves in a variety of roles. Some might think that the primary role of advisors is to help students navigate the curriculum and select courses needed for graduation. However, advisors are so much more than registration assistants. Using their professional experiences and background, advisors provide you with a wide array of support and services. Advisors can engage you in self-assessment, help you identify your goals, help you develop strategies to monitor your progress and achievement, connect you to academic and career resources, encourage and support you, and help you make networking connections. By meeting with your advisor, you'll also be better informed of opportunities aligned to your goals so that you can take full advantage of the offerings and experiences at your college. For example, advisors can share information about upcoming events related to various career fields or new internship opportunities. In a study conducted by Christian and Sprinkle (2013), students noted that advisors also provided students with motivation. This can be particularly helpful and important if you are struggling with an academic task or are feeling overwhelmed. Your advisor or academic and career mentor can serve as a great source of support throughout your college journey and beyond.

HOW ADVISORS OR ACADEMIC AND CAREER MENTORS CAN HELP YOU

- Help you determine your interests, values, and abilities
- Assist with identifying possible career pathways
- Provide access to academic and career resources
- Inform you of academic and professional opportunities
- Provide encouragement and motivation, especially when challenges are encountered
- Expand your network
- Assist with course selection
- Serve as a member of your support system

CONNECTING WITH YOUR ADVISOR OR ACADEMIC AND CAREER MENTOR QUICK QUIZ

1. Why is it a good idea to meet with your advisor?
2. How can your advisor assist you?

Understanding Curriculum Requirements

iStock.com/LemonTreeImages

Most students want to know the answer to the following question: What courses do I need to take in order to graduate? Knowing the curriculum structure at your institution provides you with valuable information you can use to make good academic choices. While curriculum structure will of course vary from institution to institution, there are some common elements that are generally true at most institutions. Most bachelor's degree programs can be broken down into three main components: general education or core requirements that all students must take regardless of selected major, major courses in your area of interest, and electives (see Degree Requirements Figure). The general education or core requirement structure varies from college to college. However, most colleges and universities require standard categories such as communication, math, sciences, social sciences, and humanities. Students who understand curriculum structure will be more likely to graduate on schedule because they will choose courses that fulfill graduation requirements.

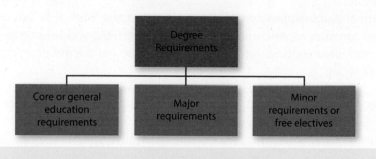

DEGREE REQUIREMENTS FIGURE
STRUCTURE OF DEGREE REQUIREMENTS

If you begin your college journey at a community college, you will first work toward an associate's degree. This is the equivalent of half of a bachelor's degree and primarily involves taking general education courses and a few courses in your major. The associate's degree is often referred to as a two-year degree and the bachelor's degree as a four-year degree, although some students take longer than two or four years to complete their degree requirements, so this language is not always appropriate or accurate. You don't make it to the graduation ceremony based on how long you are a student or the number of credits you have earned though. Instead graduating is based on whether or not you have completed the courses and other requirements, such as internships, required to graduate.

In order to complete your degree, you will need to take approximately 15 credits per semester and may even need to take some summer courses. The number of courses will vary based on your institution and major-specific requirements. This is why it is so critical to understand curriculum and degree requirements.

General education and major-specific coursework. In addition to knowing what courses are required for graduation, it is also important to ask, "Why do I need to take these courses in order to graduate?" Some students struggle with understanding the value and purpose of general education or core courses that may not on the surface seem to be directly related to their major, but research has found that general education courses are beneficial. Specifically, a liberal arts education has been found to positively connect to lifelong learning, intercultural effectiveness, the ability to be a leader, and overall well-being (Seifert et al., 2008).

Taking courses in many different fields and viewing the world through multiple perspectives also helps you to become a critical thinker. Interpersonal skills, leadership, and critical thinking are important skills in most, if not all, careers. The general education coursework is designed to help you develop general knowledge and skills that will help you be a productive citizen while also benefiting you in your desired career. Understanding the value of general education course and major requirements can increase your motivation to succeed.

Every discipline or field requires specific skills and background knowledge in order to be successful, and faculty members have carefully designed learning experiences and courses that will prepare you for a career in your field of interest, or provide you with the necessary foundation for success in graduate studies. Taking the required coursework in your declared major will help you learn the discipline-specific knowledge and skills related to your area of study. For example, careers in the health field will require significant coursework in the sciences while mathematical and business courses are essential in the field of business. Related internships or other experiential learning opportunities may also be required. For example, students majoring in education will need to participate in several student teaching experiences.

Elective options: Minors and double majors.

With the free elective category, you will likely have several options. You can minor in a different subject, taking numerous courses in that academic discipline; double major, completing the requirements for two academic majors; or simply take a variety of courses in many areas of interest.

A minor is a great way to gain a more in-depth knowledge in an area of interest while still having some free electives to explore other areas as well. Some students may opt to complete two minors. While the number of requirements can vary significantly from one college to another, minor requirements are typically equivalent to half of the courses required for a major. Some colleges or universities may require you to select a minor while this is optional at other colleges.

Students who want to explore two fields in depth can often double major. Having a strong in-depth foundation in two different disciplines can expand your career options. However, one of the challenges associated with a double major is being able to complete all requirements on schedule. While this is typically possible, good planning will be essential. In addition, you won't have many other opportunities to explore different areas of interest since you won't likely have many, if any, free electives. Meet with your advisor or academic and career mentor to discuss your options, exploring the pros and cons associated with double majors and minors.

Sequence and plan.

Meeting with your advisor or academic and career mentor to map out your plan will help you see the "big picture" related to your course and other degree requirements such as internships. This can be particularly important when there are courses that need to be taken in a particular order, which is the case when courses have prerequisites or corequisites.

Prerequisite courses are courses that must be taken before you will be allowed to register and take another course. For example, English I is typically a prerequisite for English II and Introduction to Psychology is often a prerequisite for most other psychology courses. In some instances, there could be four or more courses that need to be taken in a specific order. This is often the case in majors such as nursing, foreign language, and mathematics. In these situations, if you don't start the first course in the sequence early enough, you may not be able to graduate when originally planned.

Corequisites are courses that you need to take at the same time, or before, as another desired course. Corequisite requirements can also impact the sequencing of your courses. This is why it is so critical that you start meeting with your advisor during your first semester. Effective planning will help you meet your goals in a timely fashion.

You can find information about prerequisites, corequisites, and sequencing issues related to your curriculum in your college catalog, on a curriculum sheet, or in the online student information system used at your institution. Ask your advisor or academic department for assistance if you have difficulty finding the degree requirements for your major or have questions about the required courses or experiences. Most colleges have mapping or planning tools built into their student information systems, the online system you use to register for classes. This means that you will probably be able to log in to the college or university system and develop an academic plan online. Many systems allow you to try out "what-if" scenarios. For example, the online system may be able to map out how your plan would change if you decided to change your major, opted not to take summer courses, or if you needed to go to school part time due to personal or family issues. This feature can also show you how a minor or double major would fit into your plan.

Course format: Online courses.

In addition to deciding which courses to take, you will also have to decide which course format will work best for you. While most of your courses will still be offered in a traditional in-person format, many colleges also offer online courses as an alternative format. As you can imagine, online coursework is quite different from the traditional classroom experience. In order to know whether this type of course is a good fit for you, you'll need to know how online learning works.

Most online classes are asynchronous in nature, which means that you complete the coursework at whatever time of day works best for you as long as you complete the tasks on schedule. In the asynchronous course, you are not expected to be online at the same time as the rest of your class. Synchronous courses, on the other hand, require that all members of the class log in on certain days and times. In this type of learning environment, the professor may give a live online lecture where you can ask questions and participate as you would in a typical classroom setting or may have live online discussion or chat sessions. In essence, the class still meets at regularly scheduled times, but the meeting is online instead of in person.

ONLINE COURSE TERMINOLOGY

- Asynchronous online course—Class members are not scheduled to be online on the same day and time; work is completed at any time of the day as long as it is submitted on time.
- Synchronous online course—Class meets on scheduled days and times, but the meeting is online rather than in person.

One of the primary learning activities in an online class is the discussion board, where you converse with other students about the course content. Your professor typically gets the conversation started by posing a question and then students are expected to integrate content from the text and other materials into the discussion. Online conversations typically go into much more depth than conversations that take place in a classroom setting (Guiller, Durndell, & Ross, 2008). This is because you are able to reflect on the content and search for information to guide your contribution to the conversation when participating in an online discussion. For this reason, you may find that some of your professors for your in-person classes may also require online discussions to support the learning that takes place during class.

In addition to online discussions, your professor may also post videos or narrated lectures. These tend to be much briefer than what typically takes place in a traditional classroom but are sometimes an online lecture of an entire class.

As with all classes, you have to do a variety of assignments and take quizzes and exams. Some professors might have you take the exam online, while others may require you go to campus or a testing location to take the exam in person. Online courses can vary quite a bit, so it is a good idea to reach out to the professor for specific information about the course you're considering taking.

You might ask, "Do students learn as much in online courses?" While the data on this is mixed, there is evidence that students can have an equally satisfying and productive learning experience in online courses (Driscoll, Jicha, Hunt, Tichavsky, & Thompson, 2012). Some researchers have even found that students perform better in online courses. Poirier and Feldman (2004), for example, found that online students outperformed students in a traditional in-person class on a proctored in-person exam. Similarly, Guiller, Durndell, and Ross (2008) found that students engaged in more critical thinking during online as opposed to face-to-face discussions.

Some students think that online courses will be easier, require less work, or will be less time-consuming than traditional courses. This is not the case! The goals and expectations of the class are the same. The delivery method is just different. You will spend approximately the same amount of time on learning activities in both types of classes. Some students may even find online learning to be more time-consuming because it may be more difficult for them to identify the key points without the benefit of an in-person lecture (Tham & Werner, 2005).

In an online learning environment, reading and writing tasks often replace the listening and speaking tasks that occur in traditional classroom environments. Since reading and writing can be more time-consuming, this too can increase learning time in online courses. However, you can spread out your learning by working on your online class a little each day, making it more manageable. Waschull (2005) found that being self-disciplined was the best predictor of success in online coursework.

Although the nature of the communication between faculty and classmates is obviously very different in an online class, connection is still important. Reio and Crim (2006) suggest that making connections can be more challenging in an online environment because there is no access to important nonverbal elements of communication. Others, however, have argued that online environments might allow you to get to know one another better. For example, in a study conducted by Bruss and Hill (2010), it was found that there is more self-disclosure in online conversations than there is in face-to-face conversations. This may be particularly true for students who are less likely to participate in traditional classroom settings. See Online Asynchronous Coursework Table for an overview of advantages and disadvantages of online courses.

Online courses are not for everyone. Unfortunately, many students struggle with this learning modality and as a result, withdrawal rates for online courses are often higher than withdrawal rates for traditional in-person courses. However, many students find that online courses work very well for them and as a result are quite successful in online courses. Lee and Choi (2011) reviewed the research in this area and found that the following factors were associated with *successfully* completing online coursework:

- Higher GPA
- Upper-level students with some background in the course content
- Prior experience with online coursework

- Good time management skills
- Confidence with technology skills
- Having a high internal locus of control
- Higher levels of motivation
- Higher self-efficacy

ONLINE ASYNCHRONOUS COURSEWORK TABLE
Advantages and Disadvantages of Online Asynchronous Coursework

Advantages	Disadvantages
Convenient—You can "go to class" at whatever time of day works best for you.	**More difficult to identify main points**—Online coursework likely includes a lot of content that you will need to navigate, and it is easier for faculty to emphasize main points in a live lecture.
Flexible—It won't conflict with another course you want to take.	**Easy to forget to "go to class"**—Since it is not in your schedule, you have to be disciplined and schedule class time.
Save travel time—No time is spent on getting to and from class.	**Technology problems may arise**—Technology or Internet problems may make interfere with completing coursework.
Higher-level discussions—You can refer to course materials prior to participating in a class discussion, making it more likely that you are critically thinking about the content.	**Missing immediate feedback during conversation**—You may not be as engaged during an online conversation and won't have access to important nonverbal cues.
Opportunity to review course content—You can listen to lectures posted online more than once if needed.	**Delay in getting questions answered**—If you have a question while watching a narrated PowerPoint or video, you will most likely have to wait for an answer.
Possibly more social connections—You may get to learn more about your classmates because everyone must participate and students may self-disclose more in an online conversation.	**Social connections may be less personal**—You may not feel as personally connected to your classmates because you only interact electronically with one another.

UNDERSTANDING CURRICULUM REQUIREMENTS QUICK QUIZ

1. What are the typical requirements needed to earn a bachelor's degree?
2. What's the difference between a double major and having a major and minor?
3. What are some of the pros and cons associated with online courses?

Exploring Experiential Learning Opportunities

lightpoet/Shutterstock.com

Your academic plan needs to consist of more than just a list of when you will take required courses. For starters, you will also want to consider what experiential learning opportunities you'd like to pursue. Experiential learning typically refers to learning skills and knowledge beyond what the traditional classroom experience offers. Examples of experiential learning opportunities include internships, service learning, and studying abroad. Your college or university may require you to participate in one or more types of experiential learning in order to graduate. If you are not required, you will still want to explore these amazing opportunities and determine whether you would like to take advantage of these incredibly valuable experiences.

According to a national survey, 52% of college students are participating in experiential learning experiences (Association of American Colleges & Universities, 2010). Many college graduates report that their experiential learning experiences were the most valuable part of their college experience (Stone & Petrick, 2013). In addition, employers often indicate that they are more likely to hire college graduates with experiential learning experiences (Association of American Colleges & Universities, 2010). If you are planning to do an internship or study abroad, determining which semester or semesters you'd like to engage in these learning activities will help you develop a plan that allows you to benefit from these experiences while still graduating according to your desired timeline.

Internships. Internships are opportunities for you to gain work experience in your field of study while also earning credit toward graduation, allowing you to apply what you have been learning in your coursework to a real work environment. Based on a review of 57 different studies, Velez and Giner (2015) found that internships benefit students, employers, and colleges and universities. Students benefit through increased employment opportunities, improvement of skills needed in their future career, and receiving help related to the career decision-making process. Internships are also connected to an increased likelihood of being employed full time after graduation and earning higher salaries (Blair & Millea, 2004; Gault, Leach, & Duey, 2010).

By hiring interns, employers benefit from their enthusiasm, creative ideas, and eagerness to learn new skills. It also costs less to hire an intern versus a professional staff person, so it is a financial savings to employers. Employers value interns who exhibit timeliness, initiative, commitment to quality work, and who accept criticism (Gault, Leach, & Duey, 2010). Internships also provide companies with an opportunity to see if an individual is a good fit for a permanent position after his or her graduation. As you can imagine, many employers prefer to hire a current intern or former intern for a full-time position over an external candidate whom they have never met.

Colleges and universities benefit from internships because they are seen as essential marketing tool to attract students. Thus, internships can enhance the college or university's reputation. Students are more likely to attend colleges and universities with strong internship programs.

Most students participate in internships in their junior or senior years of college, but there may be opportunities to get involved with this type of experience even as a first-year student or as a sophomore. Gaining internship or related work experience earlier versus later can help you determine if you are on the best career path because internships are a great way to engage in the career exploration process. Working in your desired field or an atmosphere near others who are working in careers you want to explore is a great way to get a first-hand look at the working environment. This hands-on learning experience may validate your career choice, strengthening your desire to work in the field. Or, you may discover that this career is not what you expected and you may even decide to change your major or career goal. Either way, the experience is valuable.

By participating in an internship program, you not only learn technical or career-specific skills, but you can also learn many transferable or soft skills, such as being able to write and speak well, think critically, or communicate well with others, which you need in any career field. In a study conducted by Barnett (2012), students who took advantage of internship opportunities learned the importance of communication, autonomy, and teamwork, leaving their internship with more realistic expectations about what it takes to be successful in the workplace.

Students who participate in internships are also better prepared for the job search process. For starters, internships can provide you with valuable work experience that can strengthen your résumé. Students who participate in internships have better interviewing skills and get more job offers (Weible, 2009). This may be due in part to the networking that frequently takes place during an internship. While you are working, you can make connections with others who can help you prepare for interviews, inform you of opportunities, and even recommend you for available positions.

Not surprisingly, employers prefer to hire college graduates who have work experience (Gualt, Leach, & Duey, 2010; Sulastri, Handoko, & Janssens, 2015). College students who participate in internship programs are therefore more likely to be employed after graduation. In a study conducted by Callanan and Benzing (2004), it was found that 51% of seniors who did an internship had a job offer after graduation while only 13% of students who did not do an internship had secured a job.

In addition to internships, another way to gain work experience in college is cooperative education programs, often referred to as co-ops. Co-ops are often full-time, paid practical working experiences, whereas internships are generally part-time and may be paid or unpaid. Both internships and cooperative education programs can take place during a regular fall or spring semester or during a summer session. Consult with your advisor or the career services department to find out what types of internships and/or cooperative education programs are available at your college or university.

Study abroad. Studying abroad involves going to another country to learn and continue your studies. When you study abroad, you are not only immersed in the culture and language of another country, but will continue to make progress toward your degree requirements because you will be taking college courses. Many colleges offer study abroad opportunities in a variety of formats such as full semester or year-long experiences, and briefer summer, winter, or even spring break experiences.

While some students may eagerly jump at study abroad opportunities, others may be more hesitant to do so. This new learning experience may be outside your comfort zone, but remember, learning and critical thinking skills often increase when you are open to new experiences. When deciding if studying abroad is the right choice for you, consider the research. In a study conducted by Hadis (2005), students who studied abroad reported having a sense of increased independence and being more open-minded. More recently, Earnest, Rosenbusch, Wallace-Williams, and Keim (2016) found that students who studied abroad had increased cultural awareness and competency. Living in a different culture can lead to increased knowledge and appreciation of others. It is also much easier to learn another language if you are immersed in the language. Individuals who studied abroad were also more likely to focus on learning rather than grades, and many reported it to be one of their most powerful learning experiences (Stone & Petrick, 2013). The skills developed while studying abroad will serve you well in all aspects of your life.

Service learning. Service learning is another way to learn beyond the classroom walls. "Service learning is a teaching and learning strategy that integrates meaningful community service with instruction and reflection to enrich the learning experience, teach civic responsibility, and strengthen communities" (National Service-Learning Clearinghouse, 2013). Learning skills and knowledge about the course content is a key component and the service is integrated into the course curriculum. Students find service learning to be quite rewarding because they know that they are making a difference through their community service work. Although volunteer work is very important and valuable, service learning is much more than volunteer work. In service learning projects, both the targeted community and the student benefit (DeLaune, Rakow, & Rakow, 2010). For example, Trail-Ross (2012) required students in a gerontology course to facilitate programs in an Adult Day Program for the elderly. This project not only benefited the individuals at the Adult Day Program but also assisted the students with learning about this population and building communication skills, both learning goals of the course.

Explore service learning opportunities at your college. Investigate whether your college has a service learning office or explore the college website for information about which courses include the service learning component. Service learning can be incorporated into most courses, so discover the possibilities at your institution. Academic advisors are a great resource; be sure to reach out to yours.

BENEFITS OF PARTICIPATING IN SERVICE LEARNING

- Increased self-esteem and self-efficacy
- Increased engagement in learning
- Improved academic performance
- Increased civic engagement and responsibility
- Improved social problem-solving skills

EXPLORING EXPERIENTIAL LEARNING OPPORTUNITIES QUICK QUIZ

1. Why are internships or co-ops valuable?
2. What are the advantages of studying abroad?
3. What is service learning?

Career Planning: Discovering the Power of Networking

Although you are just beginning your college journey and are several years away from starting your career, there are many important actions you can take now to set yourself up for career success in the future. Research has shown that planning and networking has a long-term positive impact on career success (DeVos, DeClippeleer, & Dewilde, 2009). Developing your network and networking skills will help you achieve your goals.

Importance of Networking

Networking is one of the most powerful ways to be proactive in the career planning process. Networking involves establishing

and maintaining personal and professional relationships with others. As Addams, Woodbury, and Addams (2010) point out, networking is not a one-way street where students just receive mentoring and guidance from professors and other professionals, but rather should be a two-way street where both parties benefit from the relationship. In academia, faculty can benefit when students bring new perspectives and intellectual curiosity to situations and can assist with research or other projects. Students benefit from individualized learning experiences with an expert and access to opportunities that may arise.

Networking is related to social capital, which "refers to the collective value of all social networks and the trust, reciprocity, information, and cooperation generated by those social networks" (Timberlake, 2005, p. 35). Another way to think about social capital is to focus on the structure and associated benefits of your relationships. Many opportunities present themselves through our relationships. You've probably heard the expression, "Who you know matters more than what you know," meaning that your connections will be one of the most important factors in helping you get hired for a desired position. Many react to this expression with a sense of discouragement and perhaps even outrage at the injustices related to this phenomenon. However, a more productive reaction is to figure out how you can better position yourself for career success by increasing your network and building your social capital.

Sundheim (2011) takes this a step further and argues that networking is about who knows you and suggests engaging in actions that help you stand out from a crowd. For example, others will likely notice if you have a strong work ethic and are passionate about what you do. Levin (2016) believes that the key element related to successful networking is your character and whether others like you. We are all more likely to go above and beyond for people we like and admire, and for those who seek to use their talents for the greater good rather than only being concerned with personal gain. Thus, you are more likely to meet with success when you genuinely respect and care for others in your network rather than being primarily concerned with how the relationship will benefit you.

It is important to note that social capital is not only influenced by the number of connections or relationships you have but the nature and strength of these relationships.

In other words, quality matters more than quantity (PRNewsWire, 2013). It is therefore important to really get to know others and for others to really get to know you. If someone recommends you for a position, their reputation is at stake. The more they know and trust you, the more likely it is that they will be willing to take this risk and recommend you for a position when the time comes (Violorio, 2011). College is an opportunity to build your social capital and make connections with professors, classmates, and other professionals on campus. Individuals with larger and stronger networks are more likely to be employed (Van Hoye, van Hooft, & Lievens, 2009) and have higher salaries, salary growth, and career satisfaction (Villar, Juan, Corominas, & Capell, 2000; Wolff and Moser, 2009).

"What you know" also really matters, despite what the adage says. Higher grades have been linked to success at finding a job after graduation (Sulastri, Handoko, & Janssens, 2015). When professionals in your network know about your skills and talents, they will be more likely to make you aware of opportunities related to your career interest and recommend you for a position. While a professional contact might be able to help you get an interview, you will obviously need to have strong background knowledge and skills in order to be offered the position and to ultimately perform well in the position. Gaining knowledge and skills will undoubtedly increase job opportunities and ultimate success in your desired career path.

Networking is a skill and it takes time to develop it. Developing and enhancing your networking skills while in college is therefore critically important. Violorio (2011) suggests that networks be established long before it is time to engage in the job search process. As with all relationships, time is needed to develop trust and foster professional relationships, and as a college student, you have many opportunities to form new connections and strengthen existing relationships.

Most colleges and universities offer many resources that can assist you with developing this important networking skill set and making connections with others, such as a career center. Students often wait until it's time to begin a job search to visit the career center, but career centers often offer many other services that will benefit you earlier, such as developing networking skills and finding experiential learning opportunities. McCorkle et al. (2003) suggest that students connect with the career centers at their college sooner versus later. This is because students who seek out assistance with networking skills benefit from doing so. According to results from the annual Gallup-Purdue University study of college graduates, graduates who visited a career center at their college at least once were more likely to be working full time. Specifically, 67% of college graduates who visited a career center were employed full time as compared to 59% of graduates who did not visit the career center (as cited in New, 2016).

IMPORTANCE OF NETWORKING QUICK QUIZ

1. What is networking?
2. What are the benefits associated with networking?

Creating a Professional Presence

You never know what experience or relationship might lead to a great opportunity. It is therefore really important that you are always putting your best foot forward, making positive first impressions. As you know, first impressions can be long-lasting (Clayson, 2013). In other words, your actions today have long-term positive

Twin Design/Shutterstock.com

or negative consequences. As a college student, engage in actions that demonstrate your work ethic and values. You might be surprised at how much others will take note of your actions. Your professor or classmates will likely remember it if you go above and beyond to help someone else out or if you create an amazing paper, presentation, or project that really stands out.

Social media. If you are like most students, social media is probably an important part of your life. College students spend a lot of time on social media sites, such as Facebook, Twitter, and Instagram. Although most students do not believe it is appropriate for employers to use social media in hiring decisions (Sánchez Abril, Levin, & Del Riego, 2012), it is likely that a future employer will look at your online presence. In other words, your social media actions can impact you both personally and professionally.

Employers are using social media more and more as part of the hiring screening process (Grasz, 2009). According to a 2012 survey, 93% of recruiters reviewed the social profile of a candidate before making a hiring decision, and 55% reported reconsidering a candidate after doing so (Jobvite, 2014). Facebook, Twitter, and LinkedIn are the most frequently checked social media sites (Mader, 2016). Posts with sexual content, alcohol, drugs, profanity, and spelling or grammar mistakes were viewed negatively by recruiters, while volunteering and donating to charity were viewed positively by recruiters (Jobvite, 2014). In an experiment conducted by Bohnert and Ross (2010), it was found that individuals with a Facebook page that had an alcohol emphasis were less likely to be offered job interviews and were offered lower salaries than individuals with professional or family-oriented Facebook pages. Employers *do* have the right to access public information about a candidate and can choose not to hire someone with questionable character or moral values (Sánchez Abril, Levin, & Del Riego, 2012). Many employers have reported that they did not hire candidates due to content found on social media sites. See Social Media Figure for social media-related reasons for not being offered employment.

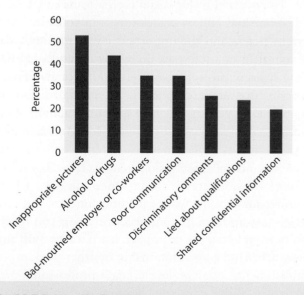

SOCIAL MEDIA FIGURE
SOCIAL MEDIA REASONS FOR NOT BEING OFFERED EMPLOYMENT

Source: Adapted from Grasz (2009).

Knowing your social media presence is important. Google yourself to determine what information about you is available on the Internet. Review your social media posts, especially those that are available to the public. What messages do your photos and posts send about you? Who are your "friends" or "connections" and what do these relationships say about you? Based only on the information available via the Internet, how would someone describe you? If an employer was viewing this information, how might your social media presence influence whether or not he or she would hire you for a position? While some may question whether information on social media sites predicts performance on the job, some researchers have found that information obtained from social media sites is in fact useful. For example, researchers have found that personality factors can be determined to some extent by reviewing social networking sites (Kluemper & Rosen, 2009).

If your social media presence is not communicating the professional message that you want future employers to see, take actions now to change and improve your social media image. First, be sure to check your privacy settings and make decisions about what information you want public versus private. It is important to note, however, that your online friends or connections may share information you post or may even create their own posts about you. Thus, if there is something that you definitely don't want public, it may be best to avoid putting this information on the Internet at all. It may also be important to limit your online friend group to those whom you truly trust to help you convey a positive social media image. Talking with your friends about the importance of having a professional image can also help. You will also want to delete photos or comments that may not be viewed positively by an employer. Moving forward, when you post something on a social media site, ask yourself whether you would be comfortable with a future employer or colleague reading or seeing that information. These actions can help you avoid a negative social media presence.

Social media can also positively impact your future. For example, you can use social media to create a professional online presence, learn about careers, and network. LinkedIn, Twitter, and other social media tools can help you learn more about your field of interest. Follow professionals in your field of interest to help you explore current trends and the important issues in the field. Discover what professionals in your field of interest are doing. By investigating the experiences of others such as the types of projects they are working on, which conferences they are attending, or what they are reading about, you can learn a lot. You may want to explore the possibilities of getting involved in similar activities. For example, you could join a professional organization or attend a local or national conference.

Social media sites such as LinkedIn were created to help you establish a professional online presence and make professional connections. If you don't already have a LinkedIn account, consider creating one. Once you have a LinkedIn account, start sharing a professional photo, your accomplishments, and professional interests. For example, post updates to your account when you receive an award or honor, successfully complete a major project, learn a new skill that is relevant to your field of interest, or land a great internship or other work experience. By sharing your accomplishments, you are developing a professional presence on social media. This can have positive consequences now and in the future. Someone in your network who notices your hard work and accomplishments might reach out to you about a related opportunity. In addition, when employers see a long history of professional activities and accomplishments, this can increase the likelihood of you being offered a position.

In addition to helping you create a positive social media presence, sites such as LinkedIn can help you make professional connections, thus expanding your network (Strehlke, 2010). Students report using online tools such as LinkedIn to find or research jobs and to make professional connections (Gerard, 2012). In a study conducted by Peterson and Dover (2014), students reported positive experiences with using social media for career purposes, noting that using social media led to job offers. While it might be relatively easy for you to increase your network using technology, it is important to remember that quality really matters when it comes to networking. It is therefore not about making as many connections as possible, but rather developing meaningful relationships with others, keeping in mind that both parties should be benefiting. Before sending or accepting requests to be connected, remember that you can be judged by the peers or colleagues with whom you choose to interact. Who we choose as our "friends" or "connections" says a lot about who we are as a person.

Social media can also impact you after you've been hired. Companies may monitor your social media presence, making sure that your actions are consistent with the company image. For example, some companies may prohibit you from making negative comments about the company. While this is certainly a privacy issue, Sanchez Abril, Levin, and Del Riego (2012) reviewed legal cases and reported "it seems that U.S. employers may legally canvass social media sites for information on employees and candidates and act on the basis of the information found therein" (p. 95). Familiarize yourself with the social media policy at your place of employment to avoid engaging in actions that could jeopardize your employment.

CREATING A PROFESSIONAL SOCIAL MEDIA PRESENCE

- Delete inappropriate posts.
- Check privacy settings and review what is public.
- Use a professional photo and e-mail address.
- Before posting, ask yourself if you would be comfortable with a future employer seeing the post.
- Create a LinkedIn account.
- Follow professionals in the field.
- Share your accomplishments via social media.

Crafting an elevator speech. As you work toward creating a professional presence, it is important to think about what talents and skills you have to offer. One productive way to summarize your key strengths is to develop an elevator speech. An elevator speech is a very brief description of your skills and goals. Elevator speeches are often only about 30 seconds long (de Janasz & Forret, 2008), brief enough for you to share on a quick elevator ride. The advantage of developing an elevator speech is that it forces you to determine which strengths and values are most important to highlight. Your elevator speech should clearly communicate key information about yourself in a way that sparks interest and questions.

The elevator speech can be used as your introduction when you meet new people. You may want to develop different elevator speeches for different audiences. Going through this exercise can also help you determine the most important

ELEVATOR SPEECH TABLE Tips on Creating Your Elevator Speech	
1. Keep it simple and short.	Using simple language and avoiding complex jargon can make it easier for others to take in and understand your strengths, especially when pressed for time. Because we live in a world full of busy people, short messages are more likely to be heard.
2. Focus on one or two key accomplishments.	An elevator speech is not the time to share all of your accomplishments; your resume is the better place for a comprehensive list of your achievements. Instead, share one or two actions you took that resulted in successful outcomes.
3. Be creative and use your imagination.	Following public speaking guidelines, use a hook to grab the attention of others. Effective elevator speeches leave others wanting to hear more about you.
4. Know your audience.	Make connections between your strengths and what matters to the person with whom you are speaking. Because priorities and values will vary from person to person, you will want to create different versions of your elevator speech.

Source: Based on Howell's work (as cited in Hughes, 2010).

factors to highlight in your online profiles. See Elevator Speech Table for tips on creating your elevator speech. You can search online to find a variety of sample elevator speeches.

CREATING A PROFESSIONAL PRESENCE QUICK QUIZ

1. How do employers use social media?
2. How can you develop a professional presence online?
3. What is an elevator speech? What are some strategies that will help you develop an effective elevator speech?

Expanding and Strengthening Your Network

maxstockphoto/Shutterstock.com

Networking is one of the primary ways to find employment and to advance up the career ladder. Research clearly shows that having a strong network is associated to higher levels of employment, higher salaries, and increased career satisfaction (Van Hoye, van Hooft, & Lievens, 2009; Villar, Juan, Corominas, & Capell, 2000; Wolff & Moser, 2009). Students who are more confident in using social networks are more likely to be successful (Villa, Juan, Corominas, & Capell, 2000). There are many ways you can increase and strengthen your professional network. The more you engage in networking behaviors, the more confident and skilled you will become.

Expanding your network. Building a professional network takes time. Planning can help you engage in experiences that will help you develop this network. For example, join a club, organization, or sport. Becoming an active participant or leader of a club, student organization, or sport is a great way to develop skills and make connections to others who share your interests. Students who are engaged in campus activities not only make connections to the faculty advisor or coach but also build strong relationships with their peers. Your peers will likely become your colleagues in the future, so fostering great relationships now can benefit you now and in the future. Not surprisingly, research has shown that students who are involved in extracurricular activities are more likely to find employment (Sulastri, Handoko, & Janssens, 2015). This is likely due both to networking and skill development.

Another great way to build your network is to take advantage of college- or community-sponsored events. For example, colleges will often host job fairs. Too often, students wait until the end of their college career before taking advantage of these great opportunities. By attending job fairs now, you can not only build your network, but can also discover what employers in your field of interest are looking for in their employees. Knowing the desired skills and abilities being sought by employers puts you in a great position because you can take action steps early to build these skills.

You may also want to consider joining professional organizations related to your career interests. If you need assistance with finding professional organizations linked to your goals, ask your advisor, a faculty member, or search the Internet. Many professional organizations have a student network within the larger structure and have several ways for you to learn about the profession. For instance, you might want to sign up for a newsletter, subscribe to a journal, or follow the organization on social media. If the organization sponsors a conference or meeting, consider attending. This is an excellent way to learn about careers and connect with professionals in the field. In fact, researchers have found that there is connection between career success and attending conferences, business-related gatherings, and other in-person networking events (DeVry, 2015).

Mentoring relationships. One way to start networking is to seek out a faculty or professional mentor. If you haven't already done so, investigate the areas of expertise for the faculty in your declared major. Determine which faculty member is engaged in work that matches your interests and values. For example, perhaps a faculty member is looking for an assistant to help with a service project for a non-profit organization or a research project on biofeedback.

Once you've identified a possible mentor, request a meeting to discuss his or her work and explore mentorship possibilities. Consider asking yourself the following questions before you request a meeting:

- What are your academic and career goals?
- What do you want to know about his or her work?
- How does his or her research and other interests fit with your interests and goals?
- Why are you asking this person to be your mentor?
- How would this mentoring relationship benefit this other individual?

Remember, because mentoring is a mutually beneficial relationship, you will want to think about and communicate how you can contribute to the relationship. This is where the elevator speech you developed will come into play. Being able to briefly share your goals and talents can help the faculty member understand why are you seeking out this mentorship opportunity and how he or she could benefit from the relationship. When you approach the professor, you can ask questions about his or her work and briefly highlight how you might be able to support his or her work in some way.

If you are given the opportunity to work side by side with a faculty member, you will be learning valuable skills while also developing a professional relationship. You will learn skills more quickly when you are supported by a mentor, especially when your mentor provides you with constructive feedback about your skills and performance (Ericsson, Prietula, & Cokely, 2007). You never know what doors might open as a result of this relationship. For instance, you might be invited to attend or even copresent on the project at a professional meeting or conference in your field of interest. You could also be invited to coauthor a publication. Be open to experiences and opportunities that come your way!

While professors make great mentors, you may also want to seek out a mentoring relationship with a professional who works full time in your field of interest. For example, if you are interested in becoming a lawyer, you may want to find a mentor who practices law in a specialty area that interests you. Many students will naturally develop professional mentor relationships through internships or other related experiences; however, you can still seek out this type of mentoring relationship even if you are not currently an intern. Consider reaching out to the alumni office on your campus for assistance with identifying a potential mentor in your field of interest. Alumni are often very interested in helping out students from their alma mater. The Career Services department on your campus is another great resource to help you identify a professional mentor.

In addition to finding a mentor, you will likely find it rewarding to be a mentor. Many colleges and universities have peer leadership or similar opportunities where you can serve as a mentor for other students. You might be surprised to learn that givers, individuals who contribute and assist others without expecting anything in return, tend to be the most successful people (Grant, 2013). In addition to the personal satisfaction typically associated with being a mentor, you will also likely gain additional skills such as listening and problem-solving by serving in this important role. As you assist your mentee with decisions, you will likely improve your own decision-making, information literacy, and critical thinking skills.

See Mentoring Table for a list of benefits associated with having and being a mentor.

MENTORING TABLE **Benefits Associated with Having and Being a Mentor**	
Benefits of Having a Mentor	**Benefits of Being a Mentor**
• Develop your network • Knowledge and skill development in field of interest • Increased motivation • Access to opportunities	• Develop your network • Personally rewarding • Soft skill development

Strengthening your network. Relationships take work. Once you have developed a solid network, it is important that you develop a plan to keep your network strong. If you see a professional contact at a meeting or event, reach out and have at least a brief conversation to find out how he or she is doing. Another simple but powerful strategy is to make a quick phone call or send a text or e-mail. The more frequently you interact with and support members of your network, the stronger the relationships will be. Small gestures such as sending a quick thank-you note when someone shared his or her wisdom or advice with you can go a long way.

Networking is a skill that you will use throughout your career. Many professionals are able to climb the career ladder and accomplish more with networking. Relationships matter. It is therefore important to nurture the relationships in your network. Focus on how you can provide ongoing support and encouragement to others in your network. Members in your network will likely do the same for you. Watch how professionals engage in networking. Forret and Dougherty (2001), for example, found that survey respondents with an average of 15-years of work experience still engaged in many networking behaviors such as:

- Maintaining contacts (giving out business cards, sending thank-you notes)
- Volunteering for tasks that have high visibility (important committees or assignments)
- Participating in community events (events and projects)
- Professional activities (attending or speaking at conferences, writing articles or blogs)

As you can see, strengthening your network can take even more time and effort than expanding your network. However, it is time well spent. Having a solid network provides you with a strong support system. A strong network can also give you access to new career opportunities. Focus on the most important members of your network and spend the time and energy needed to keep these relationships strong.

EXPANDING AND STRENGTHENING YOUR NETWORK QUICK QUIZ

1. How can you expand your network?
2. Why is it beneficial to have a mentor?
3. What can you do to strengthen current relationships in your network?

Job Search Tips

Creating a resume that highlights your accomplishments is one of the most important tasks associated with searching for a job. A resume is a snapshot of your professional skills and accomplishments, and is used by hiring managers to decide if you should be interviewed for an open position. Hiring managers or committees will likely be reviewing hundreds of applications for each job posting. It is therefore important that your resume is clear, easy to read, and highlights your most important work experiences or accomplishments.

SFIO CRACHO/Shutterstock.com

While the content and substance of your experiences matter most, organization and visual appeal are also important. There are many resume templates available online that you can use to get started. You'll find that most accomplishments or job experiences are presented in reverse chronological order, meaning your most recent experiences are at the top. This approach makes it easy for a hiring manager to see the timeline of your work experience to determine how long you were at different places of employment and whether you have taken on more challenging roles and responsibilities over time. However, some resumes are functional or skill-based versus chronological. A functional resume focuses on skill sets versus work experience. It is suggested that you meet with a professional in Career Services to review your resume to be sure it will capture the attention of hiring managers. See Resume Table for a list of what is typically included in a resume.

RESUME TABLE
What to Include in a Resume

Contact information	Include name, phone number, and e-mail address (be sure you are using a professional e-mail). May also include a link to a personal Web page.
Summary statement	Although this is not required, providing a brief one-paragraph summary of your key accomplishments and goals can help gain the attention of employers. Think of this as your written elevator speech.
Education	Indicate your college or university and date (or expected date) of graduation. If you graduated with honors, you can note this in this section.
Experience	This is often presented with most recent work experience first. You can include both paid and volunteer experience, which is also valuable. Provide place and dates of employment along with a brief description of what you accomplished in this position. Use action verbs and add outcome data that demonstrate your success where possible.
Extracurricular and community involvement	Share how you have been an engaged member of the community, noting leadership roles and key skills developed.
Awards and honors	If you have received any special honors or awards, include a section to highlight these accomplishments.

Remember that employers will be looking not only at your academic qualifications but also at your work experiences and extracurricular activities (Cole, Rubin, Field, & Giles, 2007). This is why it is important to begin working on your resume now even if you are not trying to find employment. Thinking about what experiences you'd like to showcase on your resume can help you determine which opportunities to seek out as a college student.

When applying for a job, customizing your cover letter and resume will increase your chances of getting noticed and being offered an interview (Violorio, 2011). In other words, you will want to highlight different experiences and skills based on what the employer is looking for in a candidate. For example, if you are applying for a position that requires significant data analysis, you will want to emphasize jobs and other related experiences that involved working with data. Identify achievements related to the position and highlight them. In the cover letter, which accompanies your resume and is written to the hiring manager, you should directly address job requirements and duties outlined in the job posting and how your related experiences match these tasks and responsibilities. In essence, your cover letter is another way to emphasize why you're a great fit for the job.

Although many students seeking employment after graduation often spend countless hours using Internet-based search tools to find employment, networking is much more likely lead to a professional job offer. In fact, according to Koss-Feder, approximately 70%–80% of jobs are found through networking rather than advertisements (as cited in de Janasz & Forret, 2008). It is therefore important to communicate your career goal to your network and ask members of your network to inform you about any potential opportunities. There are many "hidden" job opportunities, jobs that are never advertised but are instead filled through connections (Violorio, 2011). Thus, one of the best job-hunting strategies is to use your network.

While you will want to devote more time to networking since it is more likely that this will lead to a job offer, you may still want to engage in some online search strategies. Some professionals suggest that you focus on just a few companies rather than randomly applying to numerous positions. This strategy allows you to better understand the organization, which will help you determine if it is a good match for you.

Knowing the organization or company values will also serve you well during the interview process. Hiring managers or committees will expect you to know about their company, and a high level of knowledge shows that you have done your homework and are being strategic with your job search. Since you have researched the company, it is more likely that the values and tasks associated with the position align with your personal values and interests. This is important for both you and the company since the company will want to invest in a person who will likely be happily employed and stay in the position for the long term.

Once offered a job interview, you will want to prepare, prepare, and prepare some more. As previously mentioned, researching the company to learn about its mission, values, and structure is essential. You will also want to practice answering questions you might be asked. This is a great time to reach out to the Career Services department on your campus. Many campuses offer students the opportunity to engage in mock interviews, which can be incredibly helpful. Identifying specific examples or scenarios you have experienced will add strength to your responses. After the interview, follow up with a strong thank-you note or e-mail that reaffirms your interest in the position and provides a brief summary of your skills and qualifications (Vilorio, 2011).

SUMMARY OF JOB SEARCH TIPS

- Create a resume that is well-organized and clearly communicates your key accomplishments.
- Write a customized cover letter that communicates your interest and explicitly shows a connection between the required job duties and your experiences and accomplishments.
- Focus on your network as this is most likely to lead to job offers.
- Rather than sending your resumes to hundreds of employers, identify employment opportunities and companies that match your values, interests, and abilities.

- Research companies prior to applying and interviewing.
- Prepare and practice prior to your official interview.
- Send a follow-up thank-you note that communicates your continued interest in the position.

JOB SEARCH TIPS QUICK QUIZ

1. How do most people find jobs?
2. What will make your resume and cover letter stand out?
3. How can you prepare for a job interview?

Financial Planning

isak55/Shutterstock.com

As a college student, you will make many financial decisions that will impact you today and, perhaps even more importantly, in the future. Financial factors are often one of the biggest obstacles that prevent students from completing their degree requirements (Robb, Moody, & Abdel-Ghany, 2012). In fact, one-third of the students who drop out of college do so because of financial reasons (Johnston & Ashton, 2015), so planning for financial success while in school is critical.

Most students rely on student loans in order to be able to attend college. The Institute for College Access and Success (2013) reported, "Seven in 10 college seniors who graduated in 2012 had student loan debt, with an average of $29,400 for those with loans" (p. 1). While college is a very good investment in your financial future, having too much debt can be stressful and impact your ability to qualify for loans, such as mortgages, in the future. You will therefore want to minimize your debt to the extent that this is possible. Keep in mind that while loans are an important resource, understanding the terms of the loan and how long it can take to pay off the loan is also important, as is understanding the long-term impact of other financial choices you make while a college student. For example, some students leave college not only with student loan debt but also with significant credit card debt. Students who engage in good planning and decision-making related to financial choices are more likely to succeed (Johnson, & Ashton, 2015).

Financing Your Education

iStock.com/calvste

College students rely on a variety of financial aid supports in order to attend college, not just student loans. Many colleges offer need-based or merit-based scholarships or grants. Need-based funding is based on your financial situation. In order to be considered for this type of aid, you will need to complete federal forms commonly referred to as the FAFSA (Free Application for Federal Student Aid). The FAFSA paperwork needs to be completed every year and is used to determine your eligibility for federal aid, including grants, work-study, and loans. Most traditional-aged students will need to provide financial documents and information from their parents or guardians. If you are older or are not dependent on your parents or guardians, you will likely be able use your own finances to fill out this form. Many colleges offer students assistance with completing this paperwork. If you need assistance with this task, reach out to the financial aid office.

You may also be receiving merit-based scholarships. Merit-based scholarships are offered to students with exceptional academic performance. Some scholarships are one-time scholarships, meaning you receive the funding only once or toward one year of college. Other scholarships are renewable, providing you with funds for up to four years of college. Often, there are grade point average or other requirements that must be met in order to continuing receiving the funding. If you are receiving a scholarship, it is important for you to know the terms of the scholarship and whether or not it is renewable.

Contact your financial aid office or visit websites such as Fastweb.com or Scholarships.com to learn about additional scholarship opportunities for which you can apply. If you are planning to transfer to a different institution, be sure to contact its financial aid department to inquire about scholarship opportunities for transfer students. Many colleges and universities offer scholarships specifically for transfer students. Investing your time to explore possible scholarship opportunities might pay off!

Many students, who would otherwise not be able to go to college, finance their education through student loans. Student loans are therefore an incredible resource. One of the primary differences between grants or scholarships and loans is that loans must be paid back. In other words, if you take out a student loan, you are borrowing the money while you are in need of assistance and then you will be expected to pay it back upon graduation (or if you stop attending college). Generally, you must start paying loans back about six months after you stop attending school (graduation or no longer attending). There are two kinds of student loans: federal loans, which require you to fill out a FAFSA, and private loans. It is recommended that you apply for federal loans first, and use private loans only after you've exhausted all other options because private loans often have higher interest rates and payments may be required immediately even though you are still a student.

Before you take out a loan, it is important for you to understand how loans work and how they will impact you financially after graduation. Loans are comprised of principal and interest. Principal is the amount you borrowed and interest is the additional amount you are paying to the lender as a service fee for lending you the money. Loan repayment plans typically front-end the interest costs. In other words, when you start paying your loan back, most of your initial payments will be toward interest and not the principal of the loan. This means the overall amount that you owe doesn't decrease significantly in the earlier years of the loan.

According to Kantrowitz, a general rule of thumb is that if your total student loan debt is less than your starting salary, you will likely be able to pay it off within 10 years (as cited in Ashford, 2014). The average student loan debt is approximately $30,000 (Bidwell, 2014). According to a national survey, the average starting salary for college graduates in 2016 was projected to be just over $50,000 (Poppick, 2015). If your situation is similar, you will be able to repay your loans within the 10-year period with payments of approximately $300.00 per month. As the size of your loan grows, the repayment becomes more significant. See Loan Repayment Table for some examples of how long it can take to repay student loans

LOAN REPAYMENT TABLE Examples of Student Loan Repayment Schedules and Costs			
Student Loan Amount	**Monthly Payment**	**Approximately, How Many Years to Pay It Off?**	**Approximately, What Will Be the Total Interest Paid?***
$30,000	$300.00	10	$6,500.00
$60,000	$600.00	10	$13,100.00
$100,000	$1,000.00	10	$21,800.00

*Based on 4% interest rate.

Knowing the specific terms associated with your loan is very important. Some loans (subsidized) don't accrue interest while you are a student, meaning the amount you borrowed will be the same amount you owe at the time you have to start repaying the loan. Other loans (unsubsidized) start to accrue interest from the moment you sign on the dotted line. In this case, by the time you finish school, your loan amount will be more than what you originally borrowed.

Loans can have either variable or fixed ratio interest rates. Variable rates tend to be very attractive because they are often low at first, but as their name implies, the rate can go up or down at any time. Fixed ratios, on the other hand, are predictable because they are locked in, meaning your interest rate remains the same throughout the duration of the loan. Most federal student loans are fixed while private loans are often variable. The interest rate on the loan is incredibly important because when rates change on a variable interest loan, your monthly payments will also change. It can therefore be more challenging to engage in budgeting. It is strongly recommended that you meet with a professional in the financial aid office at your college so that your student loan questions can be answered and you can understand the terms of your loan.

Borrow only what you need. You may qualify for a loan that will cover expenses beyond tuition costs. While having some extra cash for books or other related expenses can seem like a good idea at first, remember that you will be paying interest on this money. Whenever possible, consider paying for smaller expenses as you go along. This helps keep you from graduating with an astronomical amount of debt.

FINANCING YOUR EDUCATION QUICK QUIZ

1. What is the difference between need- and merit-based aid?
2. What is the difference between subsidized and unsubsidized loans?
3. How much would your monthly payment be on a $30,000 loan versus a $100,000 loan if you wanted to pay it off in 10 years and the interest rate was around 4%?

mstanley/Shutterstock.com

Return on Investment

While college can be expensive, analysts have shown that education has a high return on investment. Return on investment refers to the financial benefits associated with investing your money in something such as education or the stock market. In other words, when someone is asking about return on investment, he or she is basically asking the question, "Is this a worthwhile investment that will lead to financial gain?" According to Abel and Deitz (2014), the return on investment for a college degree is much higher (14%–15% over the past 10 years for a bachelor's degree) than other financial investments such as stocks that typically have a return rate of approximately 7% or bonds that have a typical return of 3%. In other words, education is one of the best financial investments one can make, often resulting in more financial gain than investing in the stock market.

Although getting a degree does significantly increase your earning potential (Julian & Kominski, 2011), the total cost of an education is an important consideration. Abel and Deitz (2014) discussed two types of costs associated with getting an education: direct costs and opportunity costs. Direct costs are any costs associated with obtaining the degree. Tuition, fees, and books are examples of direct costs. Opportunity cost, on the other hand, refers to what is lost as a result of attending college. The best example of an opportunity cost is the wage that you would have earned if you were working instead of attending college. Going to school part-time can often have a higher opportunity cost than attending full-time. This is because part-time students spend more years in college and although part-time students earn some income while in college, the pregraduation salaries are typically significantly lower than the postgraduation salaries. Graduating within four years can decrease both direct and opportunity costs.

Return on investment can vary by institution and by career field. While it may cost more to attend some colleges or universities, the return on investment might be higher. You can visit websites such as payscale.com to better understand the return on investment at different schools and for different majors. Ash (2014) outlines the following steps to calculate the return on investment for college:

1. Determine the net price for the college you are or will be attending. The net price is the total cost of tuition, books, fees, and room and board minus any grants or scholarships you receive.

2. Determine the approximate debt you will have upon graduation. In other words, how much will you have to borrow by the time you graduate?

3. Find out how long it will take you to earn the degree. Unfortunately, only approximately 59% of undergraduates earn a bachelor's degree within six years (as cited in Ash, 2014). Attending college as a full-time student is advisable if at all possible.

4. Investigate your earning potential upon graduation. There are many websites that can help you identify starting and average salaries for various majors or careers.

5. Identify missed opportunities for income. For example, if you are attending school full-time, you will be missing out on a full-time income.

Considering all of these factors will help you determine if the investment is worth it. As mentioned previously, earning a college degree has a high return on investment. However, it is best if you can earn a degree without having significant debt upon graduation. Evaluate the pros and cons of attending more expensive colleges and universities.

Many of you may be attending a community college, which is a terrific way to get a quality education without accumulating as much debt. The average tuition and fees for community college are less than half of the tuition and fees at the public, four-year colleges. Specifically, in 2013–14, the average annual community college tuition and fees were \$3,260 while the average annual tuition and fees at the four-year public colleges were \$8,890 (AACC, 2014). You might be surprised to learn that "nearly half of all undergraduates attend community college" (AACC, 2014, p. 1). Community colleges have high returns on their investment, and starting at a community college before transferring to a four-year school can also be a way to reduce debt.

RETURN ON INVESTMENT QUICK QUIZ

1. What does return on investment mean? Does education have a good return on investment?

2. What is the difference between direct and opportunity costs?

Establishing Good Credit

Andrey_Popov/Shutterstock.com

Based on your financial behaviors, you will be assigned a credit score. A credit score communicates how well you are managing your finances. Thus, it can help others, such as banks, determine the level of risk associated with loaning you money. Credit scores are used to determine eligibility for loans, interest rates, or even reward programs. It is therefore very important to have a good credit score. Scores range from 350 to 850, and a score of 700 or higher is typically considered good while 800 or higher would be considered excellent. There are several agencies that conduct the credit evaluations to determine your score (FICO, 2011). These agencies determine your credit score based on several factors including:

- payment history (on-time vs. late payments), 35%
- amount owed (debt), 30%
- length of credit history (when first financial account was opened), 15%
- new credit (new accounts), 10%
- type of credit (variety in account types) 10%

The better your credit score, the more likely it is that you will be eligible for a loan or for a loan with the best interest rate. You are also more likely to get higher limits that will allow you to make big purchases, such as buying a car or home.

There are several ways to earn a good credit score:

1. **Paying bills on time.** The most important way to build good credit is through on-time payments of bills. You can set up automatic payments from your checking account to be sure that you are not late or do not miss payments.

2. **Getting a credit card.** If you don't already have a credit card, you might want to consider getting one or two, keeping in mind that it's not a good idea to open too many credit card accounts though.

3. **Using your credit card wisely.** It is important to consider how much you owe on a credit card compared to your limit. The limit is the maximum amount you can charge. Maxing out your credit cards or charging close to the credit limit lowers your score. A good suggestion is to charge up to 25% of your limit. So if you have a \$1,000 credit limit on a credit card, don't charge more than \$250, and be sure to pay your bills on time (FICO, 2011).

Getting a credit card can be a wise financial decision, as long as you are responsible. The Credit Card Act of 2009 makes it more difficult for college students under 21 to get a credit card though. In order to do so, you'll either need your parent to cosign for you or you'll have to show proof that you are able to pay the credit card bill (Prater, 2010). Since you are only going to get one or two accounts, choose your credit card carefully. Thoroughly review the terms and conditions associated with the card. Several credit cards offer reward programs such as miles for flying or cashback, but factors such as the interest rate matter more.

Remember, credit card companies are in the business of making money. They charge fees, such as annual maintenance fees, late fees, and interest on your purchases. They only require that you pay a minimum amount each month, and the interest charges quickly increase your debt. In fact, if you are only able to pay the minimum amount each month, it will take a very long time to pay off the entire balance and get out of debt. If you have a credit card balance of $1,000, make the minimum payment of $20 per month, and have an annual interest rate of 18%, it would take you over seven years to pay it off and you would pay almost $1,800 to the credit card company (nearly double the original amount). This is obviously an extreme example, but it exemplifies how important it can be to pay off your credit card bill each month. Apps or online credit card calculators (http://www.creditcards.com/calculators/) are good resources if you want to see how long it will take to pay off a debt. See Evaluating Credit Cards Table for an overview of the advantages and disadvantages of credit cards.

EVALUATING CREDIT CARDS TABLE
Advantages and Disadvantages of Credit Cards

Pros	Cons
Builds credit if bills are paid on time, which will help later when making big purchases such as a mortgage for a home.	Interest adds up quickly.
Tracks spending habits easily.	If you don't pay off your balance each month, you will be paying more for the product because of interest.
You get the product now.	If you don't pay the balance on time, it negatively impacts your credit score.
Rewards may be associated with credit card use (e.g., cashback or airline miles).	Can easily create long-term debt if not paid off each month.

ESTABLISHING GOOD CREDIT QUICK QUIZ

1. Why is it important to have a good credit score?
2. What can you do to establish good credit?

Financial Planning and Budgeting

Zadorozhnyi Viktor/Shutterstock.com

Even though we know that engaging in short- and long-term financial planning is beneficial, most of us do not focus enough time and energy on this important task. College students are particularly guilty of not engaging in financial planning, probably because many college students don't have much money to "plan" with! Yet, the financial choices you make today can have significant, long-lasting consequences.

As with all planning, it is best to start with the end in mind. What is your long-term financial goal? For most of us, we want financial security, meaning we want to be able to afford to live the lifestyle we would like and not experience financial stress. As you know, education is the single most important action you can take to make this goal a reality. It is therefore really important to think about short-term financial goals that will ensure that you can pay for college.

Reviewing your plan to pay for your education is a great place to start. If you don't already know, find out the schedule of payments for your tuition bill and important deadlines, such as the deadline to apply for financial aid. Students typically receive financial aid packets that are fairly consistent from one year to the next unless circumstances have significantly changed, but you are still required to complete the FAFSA each year. Your short-term plan could also include searching for scholarship opportunities. As you would expect, tuition and other fees are likely to increase during your time as a college student, so it may be important for you to factor in approximate increases. Once you know the amount you'll need to pay for tuition, books, and other fees, plus the financial aid or scholarships you are receiving, you will then be able to determine how much additional money will be needed in order to pay for your college education. If you do not have enough financial aid to cover your educational expenses and you do not have family who is willing and able to provide financial support, you will likely have to work in order to pay the tuition bill. Some students will have to attend part-time due to financial issues and to allow time to work in addition to school. However, it is important to remember the opportunity cost associated with taking longer to graduate. Meeting with a financial expert to help you figure out the best way to pay for college is recommended.

College is probably not your only expense. Most college students have other expenses such as their car or cell phone. You'd probably also like to have some money for fun too! You will be faced with many financial decisions as a college student. For example, many students may need to decide if they are going to purchase a car, lease a car, or rely on public transportation options. To make this decision, you'll need to weigh the pros and cons associated with each option. For example, if you purchase the car, it will be yours once you are finished making the payments, but high monthly car payments may require you to work more hours and then you may not be able to graduate on schedule. In many cases, leases are much less expensive, but this may not be a great option if you drive far on a regular basis because most leases have mileage limits each year. While some individuals really like the leasing option because you are always driving a relatively new car, it is important to note that you will also always have a monthly car expense since it is not your car at the end of the lease. Public transportation might not be as convenient, but in many cases, public transportation can be less expensive, depending on how often you need it. Not owning or leasing a car means that you don't have to pay for car insurance, which is sometimes equivalent to or even more than the monthly car payments. In addition, you'll also save on gas. With new public transportation options such as ride-sharing programs, or daily or hourly car rental options, more and more students are choosing this method for getting around. The key is to consider the short- and long-term financial implications of each option.

When making financial decisions, it is important to make logical choices that result in positive consequences. However, we often make emotionally based decisions. Mood definitely plays a significant role in decision-making, especially when making big purchase decisions (Gardner, 1985). As emotions go up, logic drops down (see Emotions-Logic Connection Figure). This is particularly problematic when you are making decisions with big price tags such as buying a car. If you are getting excited about a car, for example, you need to know that the logical part of your brain will not be as functional as it would be if your emotions were neutral.

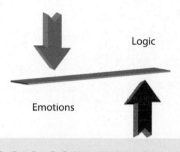

EMOTIONS-LOGIC CONNECTION FIGURE
HOW EMOTIONS AND LOGIC CONNECT

Wait before making a big purchase. With the passage of time, your emotions tend to become less intense, which allows you to make more logical decisions. This is why the car salesperson pressures you to make a decision now. The salesperson knows that you are more likely to sign the contract when your emotions are high, so he or she will push you to sign on the dotted line today. To increase your excitement, the salesperson will have you sit in a car that is your favorite color and tell you all about the bells and whistles. If you leave and your emotions decrease in intensity, your logic returns and you are more likely to make a financially wise decision.

Budgeting is another important concept to help you make good financial choices. The concept of budgeting is pretty simple: Determine how much money you have coming in, deduct required expenses, and then decide what to do with any additional monies. Unfortunately, when we do this exercise, many of us discover that our expenses exceed our income. This is how debt begins to accrue because many will use their credit cards in this situation.

When budgeting, it is important to take a good look at our expenses. Finding ways to reduce your monthly expenses can have long-term positive consequences. Too often, we simply continue paying whatever monthly fee is being charged; however, it is a good idea to periodically shop around and renegotiate pricing. For example, you will want to be sure that you take advantage of things like bundling discounts. Insurance companies will reward you for purchasing more than one type of insurance through their company, often giving discounts if you use their company for auto and home or rental insurance. Technology companies do this too—if you purchase Internet, phone, and television services through the same provider, you will likely benefit from a bundled rate. In addition to investigating bundling discounts, you may also want to shop around to see if your current provider is giving you the best rate. You can even start with your current provider to see if there is a better rate it will offer you. Many companies will do this because they don't want to lose your business. Otherwise, look into pricing options at other companies. Although it might take some of your time to contact different car insurance companies or cell phone providers, sometimes you can save a significant amount of money. Thus, shopping around can be a worthwhile activity.

When looking at your monthly expenses, it is also a really good time to evaluate whether all of your expenses are essential. For example, instead of paying a membership fee for an outside gym, use the on-campus fitness center. Look for other places where you can reduce spending. For example, do you stop to get a cup of coffee at Starbucks before heading off to class? If so, how much money could you save each month or in a given year if you started brewing your own coffee? Small actions can have a big impact on your financial future. The money you save through these actions can help you balance your budget, so you don't start accruing more debt or you could even start saving for the future.

FINANCIAL PLANNING AND BUDGETING QUICK QUIZ

1. Why is financial planning important?
2. How do emotions play a role in financial decision-making?
3. What are some strategies you can use for staying within your budget?

CHAPTER 6

Chapter Summary: Note-Taking Model

Let's summarize what you've learned in this chapter. The concept map model is used for this chapter. Remember, it is not expected that your notes will look like this right after class or reading. It takes time to organize your notes and repackage them. It is time well spent, though, because you learn the content better as you organize it and you'll have a fabulous foundation from which to study for your exams! There are several ways to use this section:

- **Preview:** Read the model before reading the chapter to familiarize yourself with the content (the S in SQ3R).

- **Compare:** Compare the notes you took on the chapter to the model provided.

- **Study:** The model along with your notes and other course materials are great resources for studying.

Concept Map Model

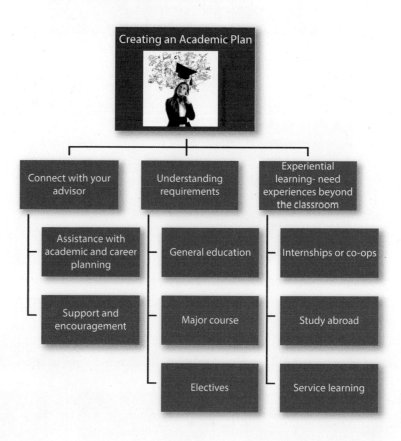

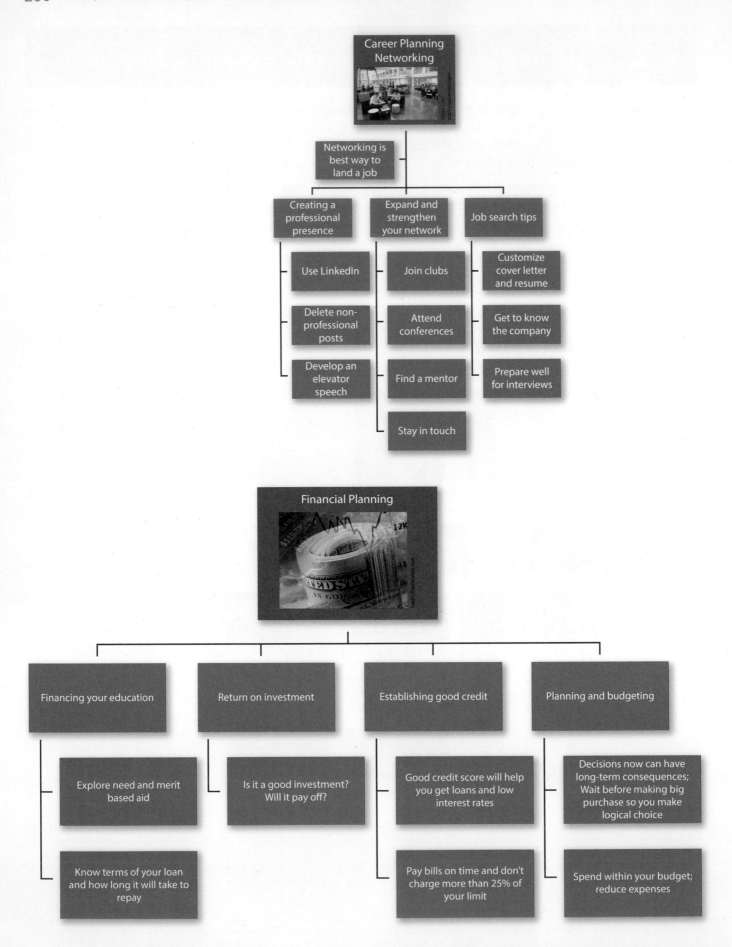

Staying on Track and Celebrating Success

You're on the road to success when you realize that failure is only a detour.
—*Source Unknown*

1 What is academic self-regulation? What strategies can help you determine whether or not you are on track to achieve your goals?

2 How do successful students interpret their mistakes or failure experiences?

3 What motivates us to continue moving toward our goals, especially when challenges arise?

4 What stress management techniques work?

5 What do resilience, growth mindset, and grit have to do with success?

6 What role do our thoughts and our support system play in our success?

7 Why is it important to celebrate success?

Exploring the Research in Summary

Research Study Citation

Iglesias, S. L., Azzara, S., Squillace, M., Jeifetz, M., Lores Arnais, M. R., Desimone, M. F., & Diaz, L. E. (2005). A study on the effectiveness of a stress management programme for college students. *Pharmacy Education*, 5(1), 27–31.

INTRODUCTION: THE RESEARCH QUESTION

What question did the researcher seek to answer?

Knowing that college students often experience stress, Iglesias et al. (2005) explored whether teaching students how to manage stress was effective. Specifically, the research question was: Does a stress management program for undergraduate students decrease stress levels?

METHOD: THE STUDY

Who participated in the study? What did the researchers ask the participants to do?

A total of 136 second-year college students completed a questionnaire about a variety of psychological factors such as stress and anxiety. Eighty-nine of these students indicated they wanted to improve their stress management skills and a group of 10 students was randomly selected to do so. The other students had an opportunity to participate after the study was over. The selected students participated in a stress management program that taught them about various coping skills such as deep breathing, relaxation, visual imagery, time management, and challenging thoughts. In addition to completing the questionnaire, these students also had their psychophysiological stress levels measured through saliva and a computer-based polygraph. Stress levels were assessed prior to and after the intervention.

RESULTS: THE FINDINGS

What was the answer to the research question?

At the end of the stress management program, students had lower levels of stress and anxiety. This was evidenced by lower scores on anxiety inventories and lower levels of salivary cortisol. See Stress and Anxiety Levels Figure.

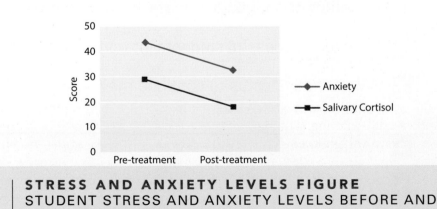

STRESS AND ANXIETY LEVELS FIGURE
STUDENT STRESS AND ANXIETY LEVELS BEFORE AND AFTER PROGRAM

DISCUSSION AND SO WHAT FACTOR

How can YOU use this information as a student?

These results suggest that learning about stress management techniques does reduce stress levels in college students. College students can take advantage of stress management workshops or individual counseling to learn how to use techniques such as relaxation, deep breathing, visual imagery, time management, and shifting negative thoughts. Workshops on these topics may also be offered through the counseling or student activities office. Learning these skills can improve your ability to manage stress and can also positively impact learning in general.

Reflecting on Progress

Creating goals and mapping out a plan to achieve those goals is important, but a plan is not enough. Monitoring your progress toward goals will increase the likelihood that you will meet with success. Too often, this important part of the process is forgotten. This reflection process is even more important when we face obstacles or challenges. Regularly engaging in self-regulation, the process of setting goals, monitoring progress, and making modifications as needed, will help you meet with success.

Real Deal Photo/Shutterstock.com

Self-Regulation

Engaging in academic self-regulation helps you stay on track with your goals and will increase your likelihood of success. "Self-regulated learners are those who are able to monitor their abilities and employ strategies to improve upon their learning" (Cohen, 2012, p. 901). According to Schloemer and Brenan (2006), self-regulation involves the following three steps:

1. Setting goals

2. Monitoring progress toward these goals

3. Making changes as needed so that the goal can be realized

Arcady/Shutterstock.com

Research shows that students who engage in self-regulatory actions before, during, and after learning activities or tasks are more likely to meet with success and achieve at high levels (Cohen, 2012; Ketonen, Haarala-Muhonen, Hirsto, Hanninen, Wahala, & Lonka, 2016). Successful students regularly engage in academic self-regulation (Schapiro & Livingston, 2000; Schloemer & Brenan, 2006). The self-regulation process has also been found to be connected with better adjustment to college (Park, Edmondson, & Lee, 2012) and being better able to think critically (Uzuntiryaki-Kondakci & Capa-Aydin, 2013). Thus, it is a good idea to frequently ask yourself, "How am I doing?" See Self-Regulation Figure for an illustration of the academic self-regulation process.

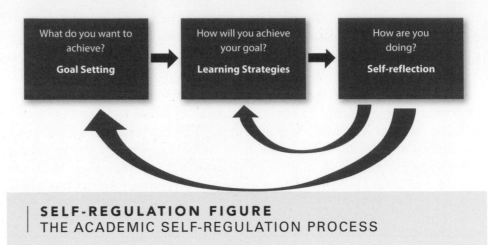

> **SELF-REGULATION FIGURE**
> THE ACADEMIC SELF-REGULATION PROCESS

Self-reflection, the process of pausing to carefully consider the progress you have made toward your goals, is at the heart of the self-regulation process. Chen (2011) found that it was beneficial for students to answer this question, "Am I reaching my goals through the strategies I created?" (p. 30). There are a variety of strategies that you can use to monitor your progress. According to Bercher (2012), there are two main types of feedback that you can use to assess your academic progress: cognitive and outcome feedback.

Cognitive feedback. Feedback plays an important role in learning. Cognitive feedback occurs *during* the homework or studying process. It involves you making judgments about your progress to guide your behaviors. In other words, assessing your progress toward studying for an exam can help you decide how much more you need to study and which concepts or topics you should target.

The challenge with cognitive feedback is that it is sometimes difficult to know if your assessment is accurate. Whenever possible, rely on outside indicators such as your performance on online practice quizzes or flashcards to help you make more accurate judgments. See Cognitive Feedback Table for sample questions you can ask yourself to help monitor your progress while completing assignments or studying.

COGNITIVE FEEDBACK TABLE
Self-Reflective Questions to Monitor Progress

Assignments	Studying
1. How well do I understand the assignment?	1. Is the amount of time I am spending on studying enough?
2. How well is my approach to completing this assignment working?	2. What learning strategies are working well? Where are improvements needed?
3. What other strategies or approaches might also work well or even better?	3. How easily can I recall the information when studying? Do I recall all of the information I need to know when using flashcards or similar techniques?
4. Do I need help with the task? If so, who would best be able to assist me? What resources are available to me?	4. How well can I clearly explain the concepts I am learning to others?
5. How does my draft compare to any models or rubrics that were provided?	5. How am I performing on practice quizzes?
6. Am I on track to complete the assignment on schedule?	6. Would seeking help assist me in achieving my goal? If so, whom should I reach out to for help?

Outcome feedback. After you receive a grade or other feedback from your professor, you'll want to engage in reflection, using this outcome feedback to guide your future actions. Once you get your exam grade, for example, it is important to continue to engage in the self-reflection process (Bercher, 2012). Ambrose, Bridges, DiPietro, Lovett, and Norman (2010) encourage students to explore why they received the grade that they did using an activity called the exam wrapper. The exam wrapper activity requires students to reflect not only on their studying behaviors but also on the nature of the errors made. It basically involves answering many questions about your preparation and performance in order to guide your future studying behaviors. You can also engage in this process after receiving a grade on an assignment. See Outcome Feedback Table for questions to ask yourself after you receive specific feedback on your performance. Outcome feedback can play an important role in helping you determine what actions worked well and what you plan to do differently before the next exam, presentation, or project.

OUTCOME FEEDBACK TABLE
Self-Reflective Questions to Monitor Progress

Assignments	Exams
1. Did I accurately predict my grade? 2. Did my performance match the level of effort and work I did? 3. What part or parts of the assignment was I most successful with? 4. How can I use the feedback provided to improve my performance on future learning tasks? 5. Specifically, what can I do differently on the next assignment? What resources could I use to help me perform even better?	1. Did I accurately predict my exam performance? 2. Which topics did I know best? How much time did I spend studying these topics and what study strategies did I use? 3. Which topics did I struggle with? How much time did I spend studying these topics and what study strategies did I use? 4. What was the nature of any errors I made? How can I avoid these errors in the future? 5. What strategies will I use again before the next exam? What different or additional strategies might I use next time?

Self-regulation involves more than just monitoring how or how much you study. Your self-efficacy and motivation are also very important factors (Dugan, 2011; Zimmerman, 1998). If you discover that you are not performing as well as you would like, simply increasing your study time or using a new study technique may not lead to desired results if your beliefs, emotions, or motivation are the root of the problem. Success is dependent on your belief that you can successfully use these strategies and your motivation to do so. Too often we just focus on the study skill in isolation; this may not be productive. When you engage in self-reflection, you need to assess not only your use of study strategies, but also reflect on your beliefs about yourself and how much you care or value the task and outcome.

SELF-REGULATION QUICK QUIZ

1. What are the steps involved in academic self-regulation?
2. What are some self-reflective questions you can ask yourself?
3. What's the difference between cognitive and outcome feedback?

The Accuracy of Self-Assessments

Self-assessments are valuable only if they are accurate. Researchers such as Bercher (2012) have found that students who are more accurate in their self-evaluations tend to perform better. It is certainly possible for you to overestimate or underestimate your performance. If the goal of the self-reflection phase of academic self-regulation is to shape your goals and learning strategies, then both overestimates and underestimates may be more harmful than helpful. You don't want to make changes to your goals or study strategies based on faulty information.

Unfortunately, students are not typically very good at assessing their performance. In many cases, students are overconfident, having "illusions of competence" (Karpicke, Butler, & Roediger, 2009, p. 478). Cohen (2012) reports that this is particularly true for low-performing students. Dunlosky and Rawson (2012) found that students who were overconfident stopped studying too soon and did not perform as well as others on a test. They also found that students who made more accurate self-assessments performed the best. With practice, you can get better at assessing your progress and performance. Spending time and energy practicing this skill will help you improve your assessments and ultimately increase the likelihood that you will achieve your learning goals.

Why would students be overconfident? Perhaps students are using study strategies that seem effective on the surface but are not really effective (e.g., only reviewing notes). This inaccuracy problem is illustrated in a research study conducted by Karpicke and Blunt (2011). See Overconfidence Figure for a visual summary of the findings.

As you can see in the Overconfidence Figure, students were most confident (direct your attention to the third graph) when studying material more than once (repeated study). Unfortunately, students who used this approach did not perform as well as they expected (refer to the yellow bars in the first two graphs). They did not realize that repeated studying alone is not as valuable as other study approaches. In fact, reviewing the material multiple times probably led to increased familiarity, which was probably mistakenly interpreted as learning. Here's the problem: If you are overconfident, you stop studying too soon. This can minimize learning and result in lower grades and performance.

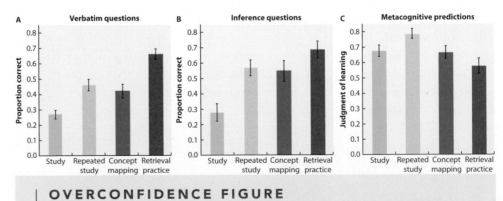

OVERCONFIDENCE FIGURE
PERFORMANCE AND METACOGNITIVE PREDICTIONS

Source: From Jeffrey D. Karpicke & Janell R. Blunt. (2011). Retrieval Practice Produces More Learning than Elaborative Studying with Concept Mapping. Science 331, 772. Published by American Association for the Advancement of Science, 1200 New York Avenue NW, Washington, DC 20005. Copyright 2011 by the American Association for the Advancement of Science; all rights reserved.

Interestingly, students in the retrieval practice group (these students had to practice recalling the information learned) underestimated how well they would perform. This group of students performed the best on both verbatim and inference questions (refer to the orange bars in the first two graphs) but predicted they would do worse than all the other groups. Perhaps these students were not fully aware of the effectiveness of retrieval practice. Increasing your knowledge of study techniques that really work can help improve your accuracy.

ACCURACY AND SELF-ASSESSMENTS

- Students who make accurate judgments about their learning progress perform better than students who are inaccurate.

- Many students are overconfident, having illusions of competence. As a result, these students may stop studying too soon, which can lead to poorer performance.

- Students may overestimate the usefulness of study strategies (e.g., reviewing notes) that are only minimally effective and undervalue techniques (e.g., testing yourself) that result in higher performance.

ACCURACY OF SELF-ASSESSMENTS QUICK QUIZ

1. Why is it important to have accurate self-assessments?

2. Are most students accurate with their self-assessments? What research supports your answer?

3. What is a negative consequence of being overconfident?

Making Mistakes: The Role of Attribution Theory

Everyone has successful experiences, and everyone makes mistakes. It's a part of life, and it will be a part of your college experience. As you reflect on your progress, it is very possible and perhaps even likely that you may not be satisfied with your current status. This may be particularly true for students in their first semester of college. As a new college student, you are learning to navigate new educational expectations and are working toward practicing all of the success strategies we've been discussing. This is a lot to manage. Students who are not on track with their goals can experience a range of emotions, including disappointment. This is natural. If this happens to you, know that you are not alone. Sometimes we even learn the most from our mistakes. The key is that you don't let yourself stay off track. Instead, you'll have to find ways to get back on the road to success. Understanding attribution theory will help you with this task.

Tyler Olson/Shutterstock.com

Attribution theory looks at how we interpret our successes and failures. For example, why do we think we were successful? Why do we think we failed? What caused the success or failure? Attributions can be internal or external and changeable or unchangeable (see Attributions Table).

ATTRIBUTIONS TABLE	
Types of Attribution	
Internal	**External**
Something within you caused the success or failure (personality, intelligence, effort).	Something outside of you caused the success or failure (situation, another person, bad luck).
Changeable	**Unchangeable**
You have the power to change the cause (effort, amount of time invested).	You do not have the power to change the cause (bad luck, snowstorm).

Your interpretation of your mistakes or failures plays a large role in whether or not you achieve success. Researchers have investigated the role of attribution in performance. For example, Grant and Dweck (2003) conducted a series of research experiments and found that students with ability-based (perceived as unchangeable) goals performed much worse than students with learning-based (perceived as changeable) goals. Based on this research, you should focus on what is within your control. A good place to start is by creating academic goals that target how much and how you will study. For example, you could decide to study for one hour each day, creating an outline or a visual concept map of the content.

Researchers have found that brief interventions can help you interpret your failures and successes more productively (Perry, Stupnisky, Hall, Chipperfield, & Weiner, 2010). In this study, college students who participated in a one-hour training on the importance of focusing on changeable, internal factors had course grades and GPAs that were almost one letter grade higher than students who did not participate in this training. This is pretty amazing—a one-hour training course and almost an entire letter grade higher! To take advantage of this research finding, you simply need to invest a little of your time to focus on the importance of attributions. If your college does not offer a training program, you can seek out an appointment with a psychologist or counselor and ask to discuss attribution theory with him or her or look for additional readings on this topic. Whether you experience success or failure, first think about how your efforts and strategies played a role in the outcome.

SHIFTING TO A PRODUCTIVE ATTRIBUTION STYLE

Ask yourself: What factors within my control might have played a role in my success or failure? For academic tasks, focus on:

- The amount of time you invested and your study schedule
- The strategies you used when reading, note-taking, and studying
- Whether or not you asked for help or support
- Overall effort

Mistakes happen. No one is perfect. Mistakes, however, do not have to be the end of the world. For some reason, many of us prefer to avoid mistakes at all costs. This is probably in part due to emotional discomfort we experience after we make a mistake. However, learning from mistakes can help you be successful. There are only two types of mistakes that should be avoided:

1. A mistake that causes harm to you or someone else

2. The same mistake (because learning didn't take place)

Developing a mistakes-are-for-learning mindset is important. If learning takes place, then the mistake was meaningful. It is true that some mistakes come with a bigger price tag (emotional, financial, time) than others, but they probably also come with a bigger opportunity to learn.

As a college student, you are not expected to perform at the level of perfection. It is very likely that your professor will give you feedback about how you can improve your performance on papers and other assignments. This is not necessarily an indicator that you are not doing well. It could simply mean that you are learning, which is, of course, the goal of attending college, but you still have more to learn. View this feedback as an opportunity to learn and grow. Embrace the mistakes that you make as learning opportunities. To reduce the price tag or cost associated with making the mistake, get involved early and seek out feedback regularly. There's no reason you can't maximize your learning opportunities when the stakes are low and it doesn't affect your grade much!

ATTRIBUTION THEORY QUICK QUIZ

1. What is attribution theory?

2. What are the two types of "bad" mistakes?

3. What is the most productive way to interpret mistakes?

Staying Motivated

Motivation, the drive that gets us to begin and complete tasks, is strongly related to success. Not surprisingly, there is extensive research showing that motivated students perform better academically (Walker, Greene, & Mansell, 2006; Waschull, 2005). This is in part due to the fact that motivated students exert more effort on tasks (Goodman et al., 2011). Getting and staying motivated increases your effort and ultimately your achievement.

Your motivation level will fluctuate—this is normal. It is therefore necessary to find ways to boost your motivation when it starts to drop. Most students typically start a semester very motivated, eager to perform well academically. This process

Maridav/Shutterstock.com

may begin with purchasing all new school supplies and feeling excited about starting a new academic journey. This is often followed by a commitment to make school a priority. New beginnings offer an opportunity for a fresh start, and this can foster high levels of motivation. A few weeks or so later, it is typical for motivation levels to drop. This is when students start to realize how much work they need to do in order to meet with success. Lower motivational levels can lead to lower effort put forth, which then results in reduced levels of achievement. It is therefore important to continually work on being motivated. Using the following theory-based motivational strategies will help you get back on track when your motivation begins to drop.

Behavioral Motivators

iQoncept/Shutterstock.com

One of the most commonly used motivational strategies is the reward. Rewards are at the heart of the behavioral approach to motivation. Behaviorism is the belief that consequences guide our actions. More specifically, behaviorists such as Skinner believe that we continue to engage in behaviors that have positive consequences or rewards, and we stop doing behaviors that have negative consequences (Myers, 2014). You can probably think of personal examples where you continued to do something because you wanted the reward that followed. Perhaps you spent a lot of time studying for an exam because you wanted a good grade. Maybe you are attending college because you want the reward of a college degree or a high salary. You may have also been motivated by wanting to avoid a negative consequence. Maybe you put time and effort into an academic task to avoid a bad grade or a negative reaction from your family.

Rewards work for two main reasons. First, they serve as a positive consequence; according to behaviorists, this reinforces our behaviors. In other words, we want to continue receiving rewards, so we continue to engage in the behavior that garners them. The second reason that rewards work is because the positive feeling of getting a reward becomes associated or connected to the task. This results in more positive feelings about the task itself, and we are more likely to engage in tasks that we feel good about doing.

REWARD STRATEGIES

- Celebrate the positive feeling of accomplishing a task.
- Reward yourself with a fun activity after working hard on a task.
- Share your accomplishments with friends and family so that they can celebrate with you.
- Be sure the reward is personally meaningful to you.
- Match the reward to the task—small rewards for small tasks and big rewards for big tasks.

BEHAVIORAL MOTIVATORS QUICK QUIZ

1. According to behaviorists, what should you do to motivate yourself?
2. Why are rewards so effective?

Cognitive Motivators

Cognitive theorists such as Beck believe that our thoughts impact our mood and behaviors, and so they aim their interventions on the thinking process (Myers, 2014). According to this approach, it is our interpretation of the events in our lives, not necessarily the event itself, that leads us to be more or less motivated. This is particularly true when we have a negative experience. Let's look at an example: Jessica and Alex both failed a midterm exam.

Anson0618/Shutterstock.com

JESSICA: Oh no! I failed the exam. I will probably fail the course, and will eventually fail out of college. I was not meant to go to college.

ALEX: Oh no! I failed the exam. I am worried about being able to pass the class. It is worth 20% of my final grade, which is a lot, but I did receive an A on the midterm project, which was also worth 20% of the final grade. I will meet with my professor to discuss study techniques so I can pass the course.

Cognitive theorists believe that this experience will be interpreted differently by different students and therefore will result in different reactions and actions. Jessica will likely be less motivated than Alex to work hard in this course even though they both had the same experience.

According to this cognitive perspective, we can increase motivation by looking at our thought patterns and reducing negative thoughts, particularly ones that are not based on accurate information. Looking at the situation from a positive yet productive viewpoint can significantly increase motivation levels. The great news here is that this entire theory is based on the power of thoughts, and thoughts are changeable! Granted, thoughts often occur automatically and it may seem like you can't control them, but you can.

Keeping the situation in perspective is an important part of the process. Failing a test is definitely not good; however, it doesn't have to mean it is the end of the world, either. As you saw in the example, Alex was able to keep this test grade in perspective, citing how much this grade counted and recalling other grades already received.

Shifting from negative to positive, productive thinking involves looking for data or evidence to support our thinking. What evidence do you have to support your thought? What evidence do you have that contradicts your thought? Using the exam example, here are some questions you can ask yourself to explore the evidence:

- What percentage of my grade is based on this one test?
- Do I have any other grades in this course? If so, how much do these assignments count?
- What is the highest grade I can now earn in the class? Grade calculator applications are great tools for this purpose.
- Have I ever passed a college-level assignment? How did I accomplish this?
- Has anyone ever failed a test but still passed the course?
- Are there college graduates who failed exams or even courses?
- What actions can I take to perform well in the future?

If you don't know the answer to one of the questions, you can ask someone else or investigate it. The main idea to this approach is that you look for data or evidence that either supports or contradicts your thinking. This keeps your thoughts in check, helping to ensure that your thinking is not exaggerated, but instead remains productive in nature (see Productive Thoughts Figure).

Stop Negative or Unrealistic Thoughts

• Say to yourself, "Wait a minute, let me check this out."

Challenge and Investigate

• How do I know my thoughts are true?
• What other possible interpretations exist?
• Create a list of questions to investigate and find out the answers.

Have Realistic (and hopefully more positive) Thoughts

• Enjoy the benefits (like higher motivation)

PRODUCTIVE THOUGHTS FIGURE
USING THE COGNITIVE APPROACH TO IMPROVE MOTIVATION

Self-efficacy.   Another important cognitive concept that relates to motivation is self-efficacy. Most people are familiar with the term *self-esteem*, which refers to how you view or feel about yourself. You may be surprised to find out that research has not always found self-esteem to be predictive of academic performance (Stupnisky et al., 2007). Self-efficacy, on the other hand, has been found to be a very powerful predictor of academic success (Chemers, Hu, & Garcia, 2001; Lynch, 2006). Bandura defines self-efficacy as your beliefs about your ability to effectively perform a task (Woolfolk, 2013). You can have different levels of self-efficacy for different tasks. For example, you might have high self-efficacy in math, but lower self-efficacy in writing.

According to cognitive psychologists, having a high self-efficacy is connected to higher levels of motivation. In fact, Lynch (2006) found that self-efficacy was the most powerful motivating factor in student success, for both first-year students and upperclassmen. It makes sense that you would be more willing and interested in doing tasks that you believe you can do successfully. Students who do not believe in their ability to perform a college-level task, however, will have low motivation. Again, this is not very shocking. Why would a person be motivated to do something that he or she does not believe he or she can successfully do? It is human nature to avoid tasks if we don't believe we will be successful. All students probably want to do well, but desire alone is not enough to get and stay motivated. Desire combined with high self-efficacy, however, can serve as a solid foundation for motivation.

Can you increase your confidence or self-efficacy levels? Yes, you can! Think about why you are confident in some areas of performance. Did someone believe in you? Positive messages from others are a good start on this road to higher self-efficacy. However, you have probably had experiences where someone said, "You can do it!" but you didn't believe it. Messages from others are not always internalized or actualized, especially if you don't agree. While positive messages from others can sometimes be useful, real confidence stems from successful experiences. To build confidence through successful experiences, start by doing the following:

1. **Have courage to take risks and try new tasks.** Whenever you attempt a new task, you don't know whether you will meet with success or failure. It therefore takes courage (sometimes lots of it!) to even try something new. The fear of failure can easily lead you to avoidance because if you don't try, you can't fail. Courage is necessary for growth.

2. **Identify action steps you can take now to move toward your goals.** Map out the steps you need to take to accomplish your goal, identifying actions you'll need to take in order to meet this goal with success. Experiencing success along the way builds your self-efficacy and confidence.

3. **Reflect on your academic experiences.** Consider keeping a journal to capture your progress and your reaction to your academic journey. When you go back and review how much your writing and other skills have increased throughout the college years, you'll be amazed!

4. **Expect mistakes to happen from time to time.** No one is perfect. Using mistakes as learning opportunities can set you up for successful experiences in the future. In fact, we often learn a lot from mistakes. The uncomfortable feeling associated with making a mistake often goes away relatively quickly, but the learning that transpired because of the mistake is likely to be long-lasting.

5. **Access help when needed.** In most cases, tasks do not need to be completed independently. Seeking help to achieve success can be an important part of this process. Because colleges want their students to be successful, they offer a variety of support from professors, counselors, and tutors.

COGNITIVE MOTIVATORS QUICK QUIZ

1. According to cognitive psychologists, what motivates us?
2. What is self-efficacy?
3. How can you increase your self-efficacy?

Humanistic Motivators

Humanists believe in a concept called self-actualization, which basically refers to your desire and ability to achieve your potential (Myers, 2014). We like to call it the "You will be all you can be" way of thinking. Humanistic psychologists believe that met or unmet needs can play an important role in motivation (Myers, 2014). More specifically, if your needs have been met, it is easier to be motivated. If, on the other hand, some of your basic needs are not met, it can be quite a challenge to motivate yourself to achieve at high levels.

Filipe Frazao/Shutterstock.com

Maslow's hierarchy of needs. Maslow, a humanistic theorist, created a pyramid to illustrate how needs impact our motivation (Myers, 2014). The most basic needs are at the bottom of the pyramid, and self-actualization is at the top. The needs he identified (starting with the most basic) are as follows: physiological, safety, love and belonging, esteem, and self-actualization. According to Maslow (1987), we all strive to reach our potential as long as our basic needs are met (see Maslow Figure).

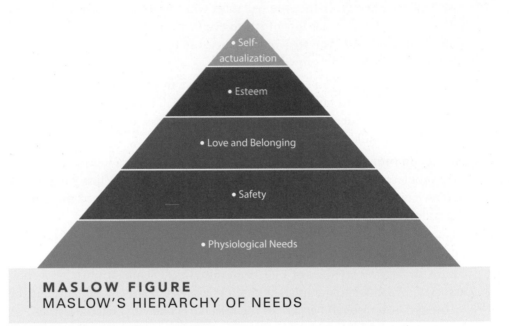

MASLOW FIGURE
MASLOW'S HIERARCHY OF NEEDS

Source: From Maslow, *Motivation and Personality*, 3rd ed. Copyright © 1987. Reproduced by permission of Pearson Learning, Upper Saddle River, NJ.

From this perspective, to increase motivation you must attend to each level of need, seeking assistance when appropriate, in order to get and stay motivated.

- **Physiological needs:** Be sure to eat a good breakfast and sleep well in order to strive toward self-actualization.

- **Safety:** College campuses emphasize safety, so this need should hopefully be easily met for the campus as a whole, but individuals may have safety concerns that need to be addressed. If this is the case for you, seek support from campus security, police, or the counseling department.

- **Belonging:** The need for belonging is strong and can be met through a variety of ways, such as a sense of community in the classroom or being a part of a sports team, club, fraternity, sorority, or other campus organization. Living in a residence hall is another great way to facilitate a sense of belonging.

- **Esteem:** Although the self-esteem need is broad in nature, we'll focus on academic self-esteem, which will likely be based on academic performance. If you are not performing as well as you had hoped, you should reach out and access help from your professor or other campus resources. Students who feel good about themselves and their accomplishments are more likely to stay motivated and move toward self-actualization.

- **Self-actualization:** Addressing all of your lower-level needs and staying motivated leads you to reach your potential and achieve your goals.

Self-determination theory. According to Ryan and Deci (2000), our psychological needs play an important role in motivation. Self-determination theory focuses on how our needs for autonomy, competence, and relatedness impact our personal growth and well-being. Autonomy refers to your ability to be self-sufficient and function independently. Competence relates to your belief in your ability to complete tasks. This is also called self-efficacy. Relatedness is the need to feel a sense of belonging and to be connected to others. As a student taking a first-year seminar course, you'll be glad to know that this course can be helpful in meeting these needs. Vaughan, Lucas, and Pote (2014), for instance, found that students taking a first-year seminar course were more likely to report having their needs for autonomy, competence, and relatedness met when compared to students who did not enroll in a first-year seminar course.

Having these needs met increases our intrinsic motivation for tasks. Intrinsic motivation refers to an internal drive to begin and continue a task. In contrast, extrinsic motivation refers to being motivated by external factors, such as rewards. Research has shown that intrinsic motivation is much more powerful and longer lasting (Ryan & Deci, 2000).

HUMANISTIC MOTIVATORS QUICK QUIZ

1. How does Maslow's hierarchy of needs relate to motivation?
2. What is self-determination theory?

Social Motivators

Social theorists such as Vygotsky believe that it does not make sense to look at individuals without looking at the systems in which they function. In other words, social theorists focus on the fact that we are social beings and believe that our relationships with others significantly impact our motivation for tasks (Myers, 2014). For example, friends and family members can provide us with words of encouragement when we are struggling and can join us with celebrating our accomplishments. Our relationships mean a lot to us, and it is therefore not surprising that others play a critical role in our motivation levels.

Syda Productions/Shutterstock.com

While our already established relationships with family, friends, and significant others play a huge role in our motivation, building new relationships with classmates, staff, and professors on campus can also be incredibly motivating. For example, when you see your roommate working in the library on a project, you may be more motivated to start working on an assigned project. Enthusiasm and positive energy can be contagious. Surrounding yourself with a social network that shares your commitment and passion for success can help you get and stay motivated.

Getting involved. By making social connections and getting involved with sports or organizations on your campus, you can increase your motivation. Students who are connected to their college are more likely to persevere and meet their academic goals than students who do not get involved on campus (Strap & Farr, 2010). As a student athlete, you would have a built-in social network of teammates and coaches who care about your success and provide you with ongoing encouragement. If you are not interested in playing a sport, you might be interested to know about a study conducted by Jones (2009). According to this study, students who attended home football games were more likely to stay in college. Students who feel a part of the campus community have higher motivation levels because members of a community care about one another. Sports are obviously not the only way to get involved and use social strategies to increase your motivation. Student clubs and organizations are also great options to make connections to faculty and students. Every college and university has numerous ways for you to get involved and increase your social motivation. Bohnert, Aikins, and Edidin (2007) found that students who join clubs or other organizations have stronger friendships and connections with others than students who do not. Being connected to others who are equally committed to being successful can be very motivating.

To summarize, there are several different motivational theories and approaches, all designed to help you get and stay motivated. Since it is natural for motivation to fluctuate, it can be helpful to use different approaches throughout college to keep you on the right track. Check out the Motivational Toolbox Table for a review of motivational techniques.

MOTIVATIONAL TOOLBOX TABLE
Motivational Theories and Approaches to Get and Stay Motivated

Motivational Theory	Motivational Techniques
Behavioral—We are motivated by consequences.	• After making progress on an assignment, reward yourself with some time on a task you enjoy (television, computer, taking a walk). • Savor the positive feeling associated with accomplishment.
Cognitive—Our thoughts and interpretations of events drive our actions.	• When you catch yourself thinking negatively, stop the thought pattern and ask yourself, "How do I know that my thought is true?" • Expect that mistakes will happen but focus on how you can learn from them.
Humanistic—We all have the potential for growth and want to do our best.	• Attend to your basic needs (get enough sleep, eat healthy meals) before you go to class or work on an assignment. • Make connections with classmates and get involved in activities. • Ask for help or support as soon as the need arises. • Fulfill your needs for autonomy, relatedness, and competence.
Social—We are motivated by our relationships.	• Spend time with family and friends who support you and understand the demands of college. • Join a sports team, club, or other organization on campus.

SOCIAL MOTIVATORS QUICK QUIZ

1. What are social motivators?
2. Why should you get involved with sports, clubs, or other organizations?

Managing Stress

Stress is a part of life. We have all experienced stress from positive events and situations (starting a new job) and negative events and situations (relationship ending). Change is stressful, so just starting a new journey, such as college, is reason enough to feel overwhelmed. A research study conducted by Pierceall and Kiem (2007) found that most college students have a moderate amount of stress; so if you are feeling stressed, you are not alone. However, high levels of stress can obviously negatively impact your performance. In fact, in a national survey conducted by the American College Health Association, college students identified "stress as the number one impediment to academic performance" (as cited in Ramler, Tennison, Lynh, & Murphy, 2016, p. 179). Students who learn about

holbox/Shutterstock.com

how to effectively manage their stress report having fewer symptoms of anxiety and stress (Iglesias et al., 2005).

Keeping your stress at a moderate level will lead to your best performance (Gaeddert & Dolphin, 1981; Rath, 2008). Some anxiety is good because it can serve as energy to help you perform well. This positive type of anxiety is referred to as facilitative anxiety. Too much anxiety, however, is not good and can hinder your performance (Raffety, Smith, & Ptacek, 1997). This is referred to as debilitating anxiety. To help you keep anxiety at a moderate and productive level, let's discuss a variety of stress management techniques that work.

Stress Management Techniques

Most of us have heard the following advice before:

- Get a good night's sleep.
- Eat nutritious meals.
- Exercise regularly.

iStock.com/udra

These are all good advice. Sleeping, eating healthily, and exercising are all connected to academic success. For example, Trockel, Barnes, and Egget (2000) found that poor sleep patterns and not eating breakfast were associated with lower academic performance. Physical activity and eating healthy meals, on the other hand, have been linked to increased school performance and higher self-esteem (Kristjánsson, Sigfúsdóttir, & Allegrante, 2010). Exercising for just 30 minutes a day (Hansen, Stevens, & Coast, 2001) and getting a good night's sleep (Hamilton, Catley, & Karlson, 2007) can significantly improve your mood and ability to cope. It has also been found that not getting enough sleep, also known as sleep deprivation, can negatively affect your ability to make good decisions (Harrison & Horne, 2000).

Although these strategies are simple in nature and do not seem to require much effort to accomplish, they are surprisingly not followed, especially among college students. In fact, many students get less sleep, skip the gym, and grab unhealthy snacks from a vending machine during stressful points of the semester such as midterm and finals week, using this time to study. Not only do these behaviors increase stress levels, research shows that cramming is not effective (Schwartz, Son, Kornell, & Finn, 2011). If you find that you are falling into this trap, stop and find ways to practice these sound stress management strategies. Going back to the basics is always a solid plan.

Another very effective stress management tool is talking with others. Leaning on your friends, family, or significant other when you are overwhelmed is a good way to cope with stress. Sharing your thoughts and concerns with someone you trust can significantly reduce your stress level. Be careful how you share your thoughts and feelings, though. With technology at your fingertips, you may be tempted to vent on Facebook, Twitter, or in a text message. This strategy can backfire on you. When you are emotional, your logic skills drop and you may make poor decisions, saying things you didn't intend to say or will regret later. The best way to vent is in person with someone you trust. Information you post online may never go away. You don't want a venting session to come back and haunt you later with future relationships or employment opportunities.

There may be times when you need to talk about your personal stressors to a professional. If this is the case, seek out a psychologist or counselor at your college for guidance. Colleges often offer confidential counseling at no cost. Referrals to outside agencies or psychologists in private practice can also be shared with you. If you are struggling with significant issues, it may be important to add a mental health professional to your support network.

Did you know that your thoughts can be your own worst enemy when it comes to anxiety? It's amazing how quickly negative thoughts can spiral, creating high levels of anxiety. Perhaps you have had the experience where you were taking a test and you didn't know the answer to a question. This situation can easily result in debilitating anxiety if you let it. The good news is that there are strategies that you

---

THOUGHTS TABLE
Negative and Positive Thought Patterns

Negative Thought Pattern	Positive, Productive Thought Pattern
I don't know this information. ↓	I don't know this information. ↓
I might fail the exam. ↓	Wait a minute—I really studied for this exam. ↓
If I fail the exam, I could fail the course. ↓	I must know some of the information on this test. ↓
Maybe I was not meant to be in college. I should think about dropping out. ↓	I'm going to skip to another question. Yes, I know this one! ↓
If I drop out of college, I will be a failure.	I do know this material fairly well. I don't have to get every question right to do well. I can do this!

can use to stop this negative spiral and shift you toward a more positive thinking pattern. See Thoughts Table for an example related to not knowing an answer to an exam question.

Challenging nonproductive thoughts is an effective stress management technique. Much of our stress is self-induced, caused by our interpretations or perceptions of events rather than the events themselves. Not everyone experiences the same level of stress following the same event. Individuals who perceive situations as being more negative tend to experience higher levels of stress. Shifting from negative interpretations to more realistic and productive ones can reduce your stress level and increase your motivation.

Because we often have physical tension in our bodies when we experience stress, muscle relaxation strategies can help reduce this tension. With this technique, you go from one muscle group to the next and shift from tensing to relaxing each muscle. The contrast between the tension and state of relaxation can be quite significant. It is amazing how much tension we can store in various muscles. Have you ever found that your hand was very tense when you were taking a test? Simply shaking out your hand and relaxing it can help quite a bit. Research has shown that learning progressive muscle relaxation techniques can help you better cope with the stressors in your life (Pluess, 2009).

STRESS MANAGEMENT QUICK QUIZ

1. What are some basic, but effective stress management techniques?

2. Where can you go if you want to talk with a professional counselor or psychologist?

Mindfulness

Mindfulness "is most commonly defined as the state of being attentive to and aware of what is taking place in the present" (Brown & Ryan, 2003, p. 822). Research has shown that first-year students benefit from engaging in mindfulness-based stress reduction training. Specifically, Ramler, Tennison, Lynch, and Murphy (2016) found that participating in mindfulness training as part of a first-year seminar course resulted in better adjustment to college and reduced stress levels as compared to students who were taking courses that did not include mindfulness training. While brief interventions or training sessions can improve psychological well-being for students with low to moderate stress levels, Bergen-Cico, Possemato, and Cheon (2013) note that students who are experiencing high levels of stress may need more extensive training or support. In addition to lower stress levels, college students who practice mindfulness are less likely to engage in negative coping strategies such as abusing alcohol (Bodenlos, Noonan, & Wells 2013). Students who practice mindfulness tend to make choices or decisions that are aligned with their goals rather than choices that are likely to have negative outcomes (Brown & Ryan, 2003).

iStock.com/francescoch

Researchers have been investigating the neuroscientific evidence behind the practice of mindfulness. Tang, Holzel, and Posner (2015) note that "there is emerging evidence that mindfulness meditation might cause neuroplastic changes in the structure and function of brain regions involved in regulation of attention, emotion and self-awareness" (p. 222). As a result, individuals who practice mindfulness are less likely to experience high levels of stress and are more likely to experience improved well-being.

Mindfulness requires you to draw your attention to what is happening at the moment and your reactions to what is happening. Many focus on their breathing when practicing mindfulness, paying close attention to breathing sensations. Focusing on your breathing brings your attention to what is happening at this particular moment, which is the primary goal. Robin, Kiken, Holt, and McClain (2013) suggest the following ways to be mindful:

1. Direct all of your attention to one task you are doing at that moment.
2. Remove distractions such as your phone when eating or working.
3. Practice taking deep breaths throughout the day.
4. Pay attention to information coming in through your senses.
5. Respond to your body, stretching and breathing when you experience tension.

MINDFULNESS QUICK QUIZ

1. What is mindfulness?
2. Who benefits from mindfulness?

Avoiding Unhealthy Behaviors: Substance Abuse

iStock.com/MelanieMaya

When you experience stress, especially high levels of stress, you may make unhealthy choices. Unfortunately, these unhealthy choices can sometimes have long-term negative consequences. Alcohol and other drugs, for example, might serve an immediate need of reducing stress but will likely take you off track from your bigger goal of academic success. This is particularly true for individuals who become addicted to a substance.

No one starts using alcohol or other substances saying, "I hope I get addicted," but this, of course, does happen to many college students. The slow progression of the addiction process can make it difficult to recognize the problem early on in the process. Think of a child that you know but only see a few times per year. Every time you see that person, you will likely notice how much the child has grown, but anyone close to the child, like a parent, does not notice it as much. Physical growth happens in such a gradual manner that it is almost impossible to notice until time has elapsed and you have an opportunity to step back and look at it. Addiction can work the same way, especially with alcohol. Amazingly, some college students are able to engage in unhealthy behaviors regarding substances and then just walk away from it. Others, however, are not so fortunate and have lifelong struggles with addiction as a result of their choices in college.

The stereotype is that all college students consume alcohol on a regular basis. While it is unfortunately true that alcohol consumption is higher during the college years than other developmental periods, you might be surprised to hear about how many college students do not drink alcohol at all or do so at minimal or moderate levels. Statistics from a national survey indicate that 60% of college students reported they were not drunk within a 30-day period (Johnston, O'Malley, Bachman, & Schulenberg, 2007).

Not surprisingly, the use of alcohol has been connected to other risky behaviors such as casual sex. Brown and Vanable (2007) found that college students were more likely to engage in casual sex if they consumed alcohol. The use of alcohol was also identified as one of the main factors by college students who looked back at their sexual experience with regret (Oswalt, Cameron, & Koob, 2005). Not surprisingly, drinking alcohol has also been found to be associated with an increase in unprotected sexual encounters (MacDonald, MacDonald, Zanna, & Fong, 2000). Deciding to consume alcohol may therefore lead you to make choices that can have long-term negative consequences. Unhealthy behaviors can quickly spiral into big problems, so you need to take action if you notice that you or others you care about are going down this negative path. Here are some suggested actions:

1. To recognize the signs that you or someone you care about needs help, go to online resources such as the National Council on Alcoholism and Drug Dependence (www.ncadd.org) or the National Institute on Alcohol Abuse and Alcoholism (www.collegedrinkingprevention.gov).

2. Express your concerns to family and friends.

3. Reach out to a psychologist or counselor at your college or a mental health professional in your community.

4. Consider attending a self-help or support group on your campus or in your community.

BASIC STRESS MANAGEMENT TOOLS

- Eat three healthy meals per day.
- Bring healthy snacks to class to avoid the vending machines!
- Exercise daily for at least 30 minutes. Check out the fitness center at the college. Leave early for class and take the scenic route.
- Establish consistent sleep patterns by going to bed around the same time every night.
- Practice mindfulness and focus on what is happening in the moment.
- Regularly take deep breaths.
- Try progressive muscle relaxation.
- Think positively and challenge nonproductive thinking.
- Talk about stressors with family, friends, significant others, or professionals.

AVOIDING UNHEALTHY BEHAVIORS QUICK QUIZ

1. What are some of the negative consequences of using and abusing alcohol?

2. If you are concerned about yourself or others, where can you go for help?

Being Resilient and Developing Grit

tomertu/Shutterstock.com

iStock.com/AntonioGuillem

Life can be challenging sometimes. However, these challenges don't have to stop us from meeting with success. In fact, many of us are able to persevere despite being faced with many adverse or challenging situations. Resilience and grit are two important concepts that explain what contributes to successful outcomes even when faced with significant challenges.

What Are Resilience and Grit?

Resilience is a person's ability to bounce back after a traumatic or tragic event. You probably know someone who has experienced tragic life circumstances (e.g., victim of a crime or abuse, loss of a loved one), yet this has not stopped that person from functioning well. Academic resilience is the ability to persevere despite negative academic experiences. Although everyone is different, most of us have had to endure some negative educational experiences. Perhaps you have experienced failure or situations where you have been embarrassed or humiliated in front of your peers. Developing skills connected to academic resilience can help ensure that these negative experiences don't act as roadblocks to your success.

Most of us are resilient and dealing with adversity can better prepare us to deal with future challenges that we may encounter (Seery, Holman, & Silver, 2010). In other words, we are often able to cope with adverse events and by doing so, we increase our ability to effectively cope with negative situations in the future. Research shows that having a positive mindset and a strong support system is critical in determining whether or not you are resilient (Carver, 1998).

Grit is related to resilience because in part it is about your ability to be resilient when faced with adversity, but it requires more than resilience. Grit also involves being deeply committed to something and sticking with it on a long-term basis (Perkins-Gough, 2013). Duckworth, Peterson, Matthews, and Kelly (2007) define grit as "perseverance and passion for long-term goals" (p. 1087), meaning individuals continue to work toward goals even when faced with failure or challenges along the way. Research shows that individuals with college degrees have higher levels of grit than individuals who did not earn a college degree and that grit predicts success better than intelligence (Duckworth, Peterson, Matthews, & Kelly, 2007). Interestingly, these researchers found that students who graduated with an associate degree had the highest level of grit (see Grit Figure).

The three key factors related to resilience and grit are perseverance, mindset, and support. Individuals who stick with tasks, have a positive and productive mindset, and a strong support system are much more likely to be resilient and gritty. Fortunately, resilience and grit can be taught (Hochanadel & Finamore, 2015).

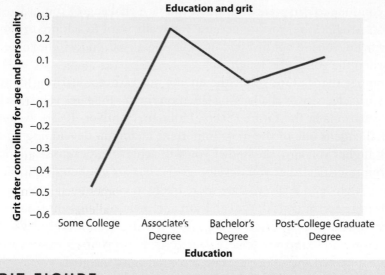

GRIT FIGURE
LEVELS OF GRIT IN STUDENTS BY DEGREE LEVEL

Source: Adapted from: Duckworth, A. L., Peterson, C., Matthews, M. D., & Kelly, D. R. (2007). Grit: Perseverance and passion for long-term goals. *Journal of Personality and Social Psychology*, 92(6), 1087–1101.

RESILIENCE AND GRIT QUICK QUIZ

1. What is resilience?
2. What is grit?

Perseverance

Most of us will encounter roadblocks at some point in our lives. Having a strong commitment to your goals (the C—care and commit element of the ABCS goal-setting framework) will increase the likelihood that you will continue to put forth effort needed to achieve your goal. Successful individuals report they work hard and don't give up even when projects require much more time and effort than expected (Duckworth, Peterson, Matthews, & Kelly, 2007). Sticking with a task is essential to being gritty.

Academic tenacity is very much related to successful outcomes. "At the most basic level, academic tenacity is about working hard, and working smart, for a long time." (Dweck, Walton, & Cohen, 2014, p. 4). Researchers have found that college students who have tenacity and are willing to keep working and exhibiting high levels of effort no matter what were more likely to achieve academic success (Hartley, 2011). As we all know, learning takes significant effort and those who are willing to invest the time and effort needed will likely be more successful. Observe how much effort successful individuals put into the work that they do and follow their lead.

To help you develop grit, use the ABCS goal-setting framework to set challenging goals that you believe you can accomplish, that you care about, and that you are committed to achieving. The importance of these goal-setting factors cannot be overstated. To be gritty, you need to be committed to your goal (Duckworth, Peterson, Matthews, & Kelly, 2007). This will make it more likely that

you will continue to persevere even when you face challenges. You realize that the short-term struggles are worth it because you really want to achieve the goal. If, on the other hand, you are not invested in achieving a goal, you will be more likely to give up when the going gets tough.

Remember that failure is not the enemy but rather a learning opportunity. Dealing with adversity or challenging situations better prepares you to tackle challenging situations in the future (Seery, Holman, & Silver, 2010). As previously noted, challenge is one of the most important factors in developing an effective goal. The higher you aim, the higher you will achieve (Locke & Latham, 2002). It is therefore critical that you develop goals that are challenging in nature. By developing high-level goals, you are more likely to encounter failure experiences, but this is not necessarily bad. We can learn a tremendous amount from our failure experiences. Challenge yourself to engage in a difficult task everyday as this will help you grow and ultimately achieve your goals. Force yourself to stick with a task until it is completed and then celebrate accomplishing the goal.

PERSEVERANCE QUICK QUIZ

1. How can you become resilient and gritty?

2. What does it mean to persevere?

Mindset

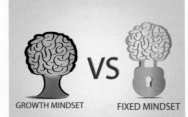

teentoinks/Shutterstock.com

Having a positive, productive mindset is one of the most powerful factors associated with being resilient. Individuals who are hopeful or optimistic about the future are more likely to persevere when faced with challenging situations. Researchers, for instance, have found that being optimistic is linked to improved academic performance (Henry, Martinko, & Pierce, 1993) and lower dropout rates among college students (Nes, 2009). Being optimistic and hopeful about the future can therefore help you meet with success in college. The good news is that hope can be learned.

Seligman's learned optimism. Individuals who are optimistic expect positive things to happen and view the world through a positive lens. Most, if not all, of us have heard the question, "Is the glass half full or half empty?" Optimists will say it is half full. Individuals who are pessimistic will say it is half empty because their tendency is to make interpretations that are more negative in nature. If you are not a "glass half full" person naturally, Forgeard and Seligman (2012) believe that you can learn to be optimistic. Seligman calls this learned optimism, believing that individuals with pessimistic thought patterns can learn to instead develop optimistic thought patterns. There is a lot of research that supports this claim that you can learn to be optimistic and illustrates the positive consequences of optimistic thinking (Duckworth, 2016). Several studies, for example, have shown that fairly simple interventions can have a long-lasting positive impact on happiness (Seligman, Steen, Park, & Peterson, 2005). In one study, people who recalled positive daily events or found ways to use a personal strength in a new way had higher rates of happiness and lower rates of depression six months later (Seligman et al., 2005). Similarly, Feldman and Dreher (2012) found that a 90-minute session on hope resulted in higher levels of hope and purpose. Research therefore provides us with evidence that we can in fact change our thinking to be more productive in nature.

There are several ways you can become more optimistic. Remember, it takes time and effort to change your thinking, but it can be done! Here are some strategies:

- Focus on the positive. For instance, keep a journal and write down three to five positive events from each day.

- Start each day with a positive thought such as, "I can and will accomplish my goals today."

- Talk about positive events with others. When you catch yourself talking about something negative, force yourself to think of a positive part of the situation, too.

- Surround yourself with optimistic people—happiness can be contagious!

Rotter's locus of control. Locus of control refers to a belief system about whether your actions contribute significantly to consequences (Rotter, 1990). Individuals have either an internal locus of control, where they believe their actions matter and play a significant role in outcomes, or an external locus of control, which is characterized by a sense of little control over what happens and the belief that luck or chance is what matters most (see Locus of Control Table). An internal locus of control facilitates a positive mindset.

LOCUS OF CONTROL TABLE Understanding Internal and External Locus of Control	
Internal Locus of Control	**External Locus of Control**
Belief that your actions significantly impact consequences.	Belief that your actions have little or no impact on consequences.
You are in control.	Others or outside factors such as luck or chance are in control.
Example: I failed the quiz because I didn't study as much as I should have.	Example: I failed the quiz because my boss wouldn't let me out of work early so that I could study.

As you would expect, students with an internal locus of control perform better than students with an external locus of control (Findley & Cooper, 1983; Stupnisky et al., 2007). Mindsets that emphasize a lack of control likely get in the way of your success, while mindsets focused on variables within your control help you achieve your goals. Not surprisingly, your view of control impacts not only your thoughts but also your behaviors. For example, individuals with an internal versus external locus of control would likely exert more effort on academic tasks. To increase your internal locus of control, think about how your effort plays a significant role in the outcome.

Dweck's growth mindset. Carol Dweck has conducted numerous, fascinating research studies on mindset about intelligence and how this plays a critical role in success. Dweck identified two different types of mindset about intelligence:

1. **A fixed mindset.** Individuals with a fixed mindset believe that intelligence is something they are born with and there's not much, if anything, that can be done to increase their intelligence. In essence, it is viewed as fixed or set in stone. If you experience failure and have a fixed mindset, it's likely that you will give up because you think you aren't smart enough to successfully complete the task, so there is no point in even trying.

2. **A growth mindset.** Individuals with a growth mindset have a very different view of intelligence. They view intelligence as something that is changeable or malleable, believing intelligence can be improved with practice, effort, and learning. If you have a growth mindset and experience failure, you will likely exert more effort or try different strategies, viewing the failure experience as a learning opportunity. Because you are engaging in productive thoughts and actions, you are more likely to experience success (Dweck, Walton, & Cohen, 2014).

The power of growth mindset was illustrated in a classic study conducted by Mueller and Dweck (1998). In this study, children were asked to do a puzzle that was of moderate difficulty. Although this puzzle was somewhat challenging, students generally were able to successfully complete the puzzle. Students were then provided feedback on their performance. They were randomly assigned to one of the following feedback conditions:

1. Wow—you did really well. You must be really smart.

2. Wow—you did really well. You must have worked hard.

3. Wow—you did really well.

After receiving this feedback, students were given another puzzle to do, but this one was very challenging and was designed to create a failure experience, so most were not able to successfully complete this puzzle. Next, students were given another puzzle that was of moderate difficulty, similar to the first puzzle they did. The researchers were interested in comparing performance on the first and last puzzle, both of moderate difficulty. The group of students who were told they did well because they worked hard performed the best. After the failure experience, the students in this group probably said to themselves, "I guess I didn't work hard enough." As a result of this thinking process, students probably exerted more effort on the last puzzle, which resulted in improved performance. The students in the group that was told they did well because they were smart not only didn't perform as well as those who were told their initial success was due to effort, but they also didn't enjoy doing the puzzles or have a desire to continue doing puzzles. It is likely that these students probably said to themselves, "I guess I'm not that smart" after their failure experience and therefore didn't try very hard on a puzzle that they could have successfully completed. Thus, how we interpret our successes and failure experiences really matter. Focusing on internal, changeable factors such as effort will increase the likelihood of success (see Dweck's Attribution Study Figure).

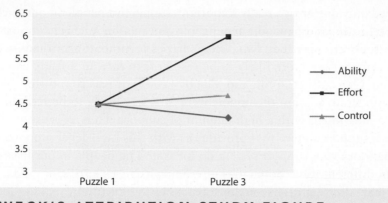

DWECK'S ATTRIBUTION STUDY FIGURE
IMPACT OF ABILITY, EFFORT, AND CONTROL ON
PERFORMANCE

MINDSET QUICK QUIZ

1. What are the similarities between Seligman's learned optimism, Rotter's locus of control, and Dweck's growth mindset?

2. Based on what you learned about mindset, what is the most important piece of advice you would give to a friend?

Support

Did you know that having others in your life who support you is one of the most important factors associated with being resilient? Look at the research on resilience, and you will discover that regardless of what type of challenging or stressful situation you encounter, being connected to others is one of the best predictors of whether or not you will be resilient (Ungar, 2013). Our social network plays a huge role in our overall well-being. Being around others who share your passion and goals and are willing to keep at it until the goals are achieved will make it more likely that you will develop grit (Duckworth, 2016). Utilizing your current support system and strengthening and expanding it can help you effectively cope with challenging situations that may arise.

Rawpixel.com/Shutterstock.com

Research has found that having a strong support system can help you stay in school and achieve academic success (Wilcox, Winn, & Fyvie-Gauld, 2005). It is also associated with better mental health. Hefner and Eisenberg (2009), for instance, found that students who had a low-quality support system, compared to students with a high-quality support system, were six times more likely to be depressed.

Quality matters more than quantity when it comes to support systems. There is no magical number of people you need supporting you. Werner (1989) found that resilient individuals had at least one person in their lives who provided a high level of support. Thus, it is not how many people you have in your support system, but rather whether you are receiving the support you need. Some of us may need only one or two really important, supportive people in our lives. Others may need to expand beyond a few people and rely on a larger support network to meet their various needs. Researchers have shown that individuals with a high level of support are more likely to be resilient. In fact, in a study conducted by Bonanno, Galea, Bucciarelli, and Vlahov (2007), it was found that individuals with a moderate amount of support were 30% less likely to be resilient as compared to individuals with a high amount of support. Thus, it is essential that we all have a support system that provides us with this high-level support.

What does your support system do for you? The people in our lives meet our needs in different ways. Some may offer knowledge, expertise, or guidance, while others may offer emotional support, listening to us without making judgments. Others provide support in more tangible ways, for instance by helping out with financial expenses or physically doing tasks that can save us time. The key is to have a support system that meets your needs. According to Duckworth (2016), every person she interviewed who was gritty "could point to someone in their life who, at the right time and in the right way, encouraged them to aim high and provided badly needed confidence and support" (p. 220).

Your support system.   Your established support system can help you adjust to college. Support systems can include friends, family, significant others, or professionals such as mental health providers. Swenson, Nordstrom, and Hiester (2008) conducted research on the value of friendships in college and found that having a close friend from high school helped students adjust to college. This connection was particularly important during the first few weeks of the semester. It is important to note that you don't have to go to the same school as your friend in order to benefit from the friendship. With today's technology and communication options, it is easy to stay connected to friends who are not physically close to us. The important people in your life before college can continue to be important to you as you start your college journey.

Family members can serve as your support system, too. Many researchers have investigated the important role of parents. College students who have good relationships with their parents are more likely to adjust well to college life (Wintre & Yaffe, 2000). Although the nature of your relationship with your parents may change significantly as you begin college, it is still important to keep the lines of communication open. Communicate by:

- Talking to your parents or family members about your thoughts and feelings
- Sharing your success stories or enjoyable experiences you've had at college
- Talking about your concerns or problems you've encountered
- Telling your family members whether you want them to just listen or to offer guidance as well

Sometimes there are important people in our life—family, friends, and significant others who distract or discourage us from pursuing our goals and may therefore not be meeting our needs. For instance, perhaps you have a friend who is not attending college and wants to spend a lot of time hanging out with you because this friend has a lot of free time and enjoys spending it with you. This pressure to spend time socializing instead of studying can get you off track. In this situation, you can tell your friend that although your friendship is important to you, you need time to study in order to achieve your academic goals. Hopefully this results in less pressure to socialize while still maintaining the relationship. There may be instances, though, when the person continues to distract you from your goals even after you've clearly communicated your needs. In this case, you will have to decide if it is a good idea for you to continue the relationship. This can be a very stressful decision, and you may want to meet with a psychologist or counselor to discuss your options.

It is particularly important to establish new relationships on campus if your friends and family don't fully understand the demands and expectations of college. This may be especially important if you are a first-generation college student because, while your family may be supportive, they may not fully understand the pressures of being a college student. Having a strong support system that appreciates the stressors of college can be incredibly powerful. Your fellow classmates know that you need to balance fun and academic work, and you won't have to explain why you are experiencing more stress toward the end of the semester. This type of support can be truly amazing. Having a new friend from college seems to be particularly helpful during the second half of your first semester (Swenson et al., 2008). Not surprisingly, this is when the college demands increase.

Campus support. College campuses are filled with supportive services. Asking for help is an important part of college and life and is something you should learn to be comfortable doing. Students sometimes think that they should be able to reach their goal without help, perhaps viewing asking for help as a weakness. This could not be further from the truth. Successful people receive help from others. For example, business professionals typically have teams of experts helping them make the best decisions. Research has shown that students who access help perform better (Raskind, Goldberg, Higgins, & Herman, 1999; Strage et al., 2002). Learning when and how to access the right type of support is a skill that will benefit you in college and beyond. Check out Campus Resources Table for an overview of campus resources.

CAMPUS RESOURCES TABLE
An Overview of Campus Support

Campus Resource	Assistance Provided
Professors	Clarification of assignments; understanding class content; advising; mentoring
Tutoring	Professional or peer support for understanding course content and completing assignments
Advisors	Academic and career planning
Librarians	Finding and evaluating information needed for assignments
Personal and career counselors	Coping with stress and personal issues; career exploration and decision-making; referrals to outside experts as needed
Disability service providers	Accessing academic accommodations in accordance with disability law (Section 504 of the Rehabilitation Act of 1973, Americans with Disabilities Act)
Resident advisor	Adjustment to college; social connections; conflict resolution related to residential issues

Sticking with tasks, developing a positive mindset, and having a strong support system will serve you well, especially if you run into academic obstacles. The truth is that most, if not all, students will experience difficulty at some point as they pursue their academic goals. Many students will have moments when they question whether getting a degree is worth the effort. According to a national survey, when students think about quitting, it is almost always a person (i.e., professor, staff member, fellow student) who is the reason they decide to continue (CCSSE, 2009). It is normal to get frustrated and overwhelmed from time to time. The trick is finding a way to get back on track. Using the motivational, stress management, and resilience and grit strategies can help you with this task!

SUPPORT QUICK QUIZ

1. What role does support play in being resilient and gritty?
2. How many people should you have in your support system?
3. What campus supports exist?

Celebrating Success

AP Images/AnnArbor.com/Melanie Maxwell

Celebrating your success is important. There are several benefits associated with celebrating success, especially when it is the result of your hard work. Celebrating can increase motivation, positively impact your overall well-being, improve your self-efficacy, and increase the likelihood of future success.

When you meet your goal with success, you feel good about it. This positive feeling serves as a powerful reward. According to behaviorists, rewards are motivating, making it more likely that we will continue to engage in similar actions in the future. Celebrating can keep us in a good mood, extending the duration of this positive feeling. Our mood can become even more positive when we celebrate with those who mean the most to us. In other words, celebrating with others makes the experience even better.

Celebrating has benefits beyond increasing motivation. Argyle (2001) found that positive mood is related to our overall well-being and happiness. Thus, celebrating with others can have a positive impact on our mood and well-being. The positive energy and feedback you receive from others can fuel your motivation and create positive emotions and experiences.

Sharing your accomplishments on professional social media sites such as LinkedIn is another way to celebrate. By posting your accomplishments such as earning Dean's list status, having your work published or highlighted, or receiving an award, others in your network will know about your successes and can join in on the celebration. There are several benefits to sharing your accomplishments online. First, you will likely receive positive feedback from others in your professional network, which positively impacts your mood and motivation. Having your accomplishments packaged in one place can also be beneficial. For instance, you may want to periodically review all that you have accomplished. It can be quite rewarding to celebrate numerous accomplishments at one time. This can be especially helpful when a challenging situation arises in the future. Reviewing evidence of your success may motivate you to keep working at the task at hand so that you can again experience the positive feeling that comes with success. Another benefit of documenting your key successes in one place is that it will be easier for you to market yourself when you are looking for employment in your field of interest.

The act of celebrating and savoring the moment can improve your self-efficacy, making it more likely that you will achieve more in the future. As you know, self-efficacy, the belief that we can successfully complete tasks, increases with successful experiences. When we have higher self-efficacy, we are more likely to believe we can be successful at future tasks. Celebrating our achievements of challenging tasks positively impacts this process. The positive mindset and increased confidence that result from accomplishing goals and celebrating those accomplishments will make it more likely that you will set challenging goals and achieve at even higher levels in the future. This is especially true when you experience success despite encountering challenges along the way. Research conducted by Maier shows that success with overcoming adversity is particularly powerful because these experiences re-wire the brain, making it more likely that you will be able to overcome adversity in the future. (as cited in Duckworth, 2016).

The bottom line is that celebrating is important. When you've worked hard to achieve a goal, take time to enjoy the rewarding feeling and share this experience with others who are important to you. Success takes effort and work; be proud of your accomplishments!

CELEBRATING SUCCESS QUICK QUIZ

1. Why is it important to celebrate our accomplishments?
2. Why is it a good idea to keep track of your accomplishments in one place?

CHAPTER 7 | Chapter Summary: Note-Taking Model

Let's summarize what you've learned in this chapter. The matrix model is used for this chapter. Remember, it is not expected that your notes will look like this right after class or reading. It takes time to organize your notes and repackage them. It is time well spent, though, because you learn the content better as you organize it and you'll have a fabulous foundation from which to study for your exams! There are several ways to use this section:

- **Preview:** Read the model before reading the chapter to familiarize yourself with the content (the S in SQ3R).

- **Compare:** Compare the notes you took on the chapter to the model provided.

- **Study:** The model along with your notes and other course materials are great resources for studying.

Matrix Notes Model

Self-Regulation Process

Set Goals	Monitor Progress	Make Changes as Needed
ABCS • Aim high • Believe in yourself • Care and commit • Specify and self-reflect	Type of feedback: • Cognitive feedback—while you are studying (i.e. practice test) • Outcome feedback—after you receive the grade (i.e. exam wrapper) Accuracy is important • Illusions of competence—students tend to be overconfident; to combat this, seek out concrete feedback	Attribution theory • View mistakes as learning opportunities • Focus on internal, changeable factors such as effort

Staying Motivated

Theory	Description	Strategies
Behavioral (Skinner)	• Consequences motivate us • Motivation increases when we are rewarded	• Reward yourself after completing tasks • Enjoy the positive feeling you experience after accomplishing a task
Cognitive (Beck)	• Thoughts and interpretations motivate us • Having higher self-efficacy (the belief in your ability to successfully achieve tasks) motivates us	• Challenge negative, unproductive thinking (look for data or evidence) • Keep the situation in perspective • Identify action steps to achieve your goal • Access help when needed to increase likelihood of success • Interpret mistakes productively

Humanistic (Maslow; Deci, and Ryan)	• Everyone will achieve his or her potential (self-actualization) if needs are met • Basic needs must be met first (physiological, safety, belonging, esteem, self-actualization) • Needs for autonomy, relatedness, and competence must also be met	• Eat nutritious meals and get enough sleep • Connect with others and become a part of the campus community • Express your ideas and thoughts to others • Accomplish tasks and learn new skills
Social (Vygotsky)	• We are social beings and our relationships with others motivate us • Interacting with others who are different from us expands our social network and increases critical thinking skills	• Maintain relationships with friends and family • Build new relationships—get involved in sports, clubs, or other organizations • Connect with faculty—find a mentor • Surround yourself with support • Go beyond your comfort zone and interact with others who are different from you

Stress Management—Coping with Stressful Events

Coping Approaches	Description
Healthy	• Sleeping enough, eating nutritious meals, and exercising regularly • Challenging negative thoughts • Talking with friends, family, or professional counselors • Practice mindfulness—being aware in the moment
Unhealthy	• While using alcohol or other drugs may temporarily distract one from stressors, there may be long-term consequences such as addiction • Using alcohol is associated with poor decision-making, such as engaging in unprotected sexual relations • For assistance with this unhealthy approach to stress management, reach out to a counselor or psychologist

Being Resilient and Developing Grit

Key Factors	Description	Strategies
Perseverance	• Sticking with a task until successful	• Care and commit to your goal and seek help when needed
Positive mindset	• Being optimistic or having a positive mindset increases resilience • Believing your actions matter builds resilience (internal locus of control)	• Focus on the positive • Talk about positive events with others • Surround yourself with optimistic people • Focus on factors within your control
Social support	• Having a high-quality support system increases resilience	• Evaluate your current support network • Expand your social support system—include campus support, such as professors, librarians, tutors, advisors, counselors, or disability providers

Celebrating Success

Key Factors	Description	Strategies
Celebrate success	• Enjoy the feeling associated with achieving the goal	• Share success experiences with others in your life

NAME:

ARTICLE: Cite the article.

INTRODUCTION: THE RESEARCH QUESTION What question did the researcher seek to answer?

METHOD: THE STUDY Who participated in the study? What did the researchers ask the participants to do?

RESULTS: THE FINDINGS What was the answer to the research question?

DISCUSSION AND SO WHAT FACTOR How can YOU use this information as a student?

Exploring the Research in Depth Appendix

Howard, H. E., & Jones, W. P. (2000). Effectiveness of a freshman seminar in an urban university: Measurement of selected indicators. *College Student Journal, 34, 509–515.*

Engage via Research Prediction

Do you think students who participated in a first-year seminar course were:

- More prepared for college?
- More committed to a college major?
- More confident as a student?
- More knowledgeable about college resources?
- More knowledgeable about studying strategies?

Read for Key Points

- What question did the researcher seek to answer? (Introduction)
- Who participated in the study and what did the participants do? (Method)
- What was the answer to the research question? (Results)

Critically Think about the Research

- Why are these findings important?
- Why do you think the course didn't seem to help students commit to a major?
- Based on these findings, what recommendations would you make to your college president about this type of course? Why?

Build Information Literacy Skills

- Are these findings consistent with other research investigating first-year seminar courses? Is there more recent research demonstrating the effectiveness of this course?
- What other benefits, if any, were found by other researchers investigating first-year seminar courses?

Research Study

Howard, H. E., & Jones, W. P. (2000). Effectiveness of a Freshman Seminar in an Urban University: Measurement of Selected Indicators

This study investigated the effectiveness of a freshman seminar in enhancing the students' overall perception of: (a) being prepared for the university experience, (b) satisfactory selection of a college major, (c) general confidence as a student, (d) knowledge of campus resources, and (e) study skills competence. One-hundred eighteen students responded to pre-and post-test questionnaires. Results indicated a significant gain on four of the five with no evident positive impact on the selection of a major. On the other four questions, positive change was evident independent of entering ability levels with the exception of study skills where the greater gain was obtained by students with low high school grade point averages.

A common concern among institutions of higher education in the United States is retention. Schaeffer (1999) reports a national attrition rate of 25 percent and notes that the costs are more than just loss of funds to the institution. There is a significant negative personal impact on many of the students.

Historically (Beal & Noel, 1980), the period between freshman and sophomore years has been the time of greatest attrition. Tinto (1987) found that of the students who leave, 75% do so during or immediately after the first semester. Liu and Liu (1999) confirm a continuing problem with freshmen retention, noting that transfer students tend to continue enrollment at a higher rate than do entering freshmen.

Students enter the college and university setting from a myriad of diverse backgrounds, including various levels of academic preparation, ages, socioeconomic backgrounds, and reasons for enrolling in college. There are, of course, many reasons for leaving, not all of which are within the scope of responsibility of the institution. It is, however, reasonable to assume that in many instances the decision to leave rests simply on the student's lack of success in the setting. This appears particularly evident for freshman who enter the setting unprepared personally and academically for the difficult transition from secondary to post-secondary education. Kendall (1999) found, for example, that in one state system, one-half of the system's entering freshmen are required to take remedial classes in math and English.

Colleges and universities often consider offering a freshman course or seminar focused on content and experiences to facilitate the transition between secondary and post-secondary education. Fidler and Hunter (1989) report that of the various interventions used to enhance freshman success, the freshman seminar is typically the most effective. With samples obtained over a period of fourteen years, they found that students at the University of South Carolina who took the freshman seminar course had a higher sophomore retention rate and found similar findings of positive relationships between retention and participation in freshman seminar courses at a variety of other institutions as well.

Shanley and Witten (1990) and Cone (1991) also report that dropout rates for freshman seminar participants were significantly lower than non-participants. Participation in such seminars results in increased knowledge about campus services and activities (Fidler & Hunter, 1989), and this may be one of the features which enhances the retention rate.

Studies also suggest a link between participation in a freshman seminar and higher eventual grade point averages. For example, Maisto and Tammi (1991) found that students enrolled in a freshman seminar course earn significantly higher grade point averages than do non participants and also report more out of class contact with faculty. In a study at a small liberal arts college, Hyers and Joslin (1998) found that grades earned in a required freshman year seminar were better predictors of academic achievement and persistence than high school rank and S.A.T. scores.

Source: Howard, H. E., & Jones, W. P. (2000). Effectiveness of a freshmen seminar in an urban university: Measurement of selected indicators. *College Student Journal, 34,* 509–515. Reprinted by permission of Project Innovation, Inc. PO Box 8508, Mobile, Alabama, 36689-8508.

Wilkie and Kuckuck (1989) report that freshman seminar courses result in many positive developments for freshmen, including development of appropriate study skills and familiarity with university resources. The importance of the latter was particularly evident in Banta and Kuh's (1998) description of several innovative approaches to increase retention rate. For example, one urban university initiated contact with all students who did not return after the freshman year. Most cited financial and personal reasons and indicated an intent to re-enroll at some point in the future. Most reported being generally satisfied with classroom instruction and advising. Of this group, however, nearly 80 percent reported that there had been no meaningful personal contact with any campus office, faculty or staff member, or student.

The national concern about retention is evident on our campus as well. In the 1997-98 academic year, data indicated a retention rate of approximately 71 percent for full-time students and 58 percent for part-time students. Almost 90 percent of our graduates needed more than four years to complete their programs with approximately ⅔ taking more than six years.

To address this concern on our campus, the Student Development Center designed and implemented a freshman seminar course. The objective of the course is to provide students with critical thinking skills, writing skills, information, and experiences that will improve their academic success rate and aid in developing realistic academic and career planning goals. This two credit seminar, offered as an elective, is taught by professional staff and Student Services' administrators with a variety of instructional methodology, including lectures, group activities, guest speakers, and videotapes.

The course is offered with an assumption that freshmen can be taught how to be successful students with belief that when students are given accurate information and ample support, they will feel more secure and therefore have a greater chance of success in this new environment. Data from other settings suggests that this assumption is reasonable, but there was no extant data to support the specific design and implementation on our campus.

This study was thus designed to gather data regarding the effectiveness of the seminar with particular attention to questions associated with the extent to which the course:

(a) increased the perception of being prepared for college, (b) assisted in developing a college major, (c) enhanced the overall level of confidence as a student, (d) enhanced knowledge about available campus resources, and (e) enhanced the perceived level of study skills competence.

Specifically, we hypothesized that all students who completed the seminar would report statistically significant growth in each of these five areas and that the extent of growth would be significantly greater among students who entered with lower high school grade point averages.

Method

Participants

A total of 154 students were enrolled in five sections of the freshman seminar course during the fall 1998 semester. Four students were absent on the day the pre-test was administered; nineteen students withdrew from the course before the end of the semester, and ten students were absent on the day the post-test was administered. High school grade point average was not available for three of the remaining students. The research sample for this study was thus comprised of a total of 118 participants, 60 female and 58 male.

Pre-test data for the students who completed the pre-test, but were dropped from the research sample because the post-test results were not available, do not suggest a selection effect in the research sample. An aggregate pre-test score (mean response on the selected survey questions) was created. The mean aggregate pre-test scores for those included and not included in the research samples were 3.20 and 3.21, respectively.

Gender distribution in the participant sample was essentially identical. Ages in the research sample ranged from 18 to 61 (mean age = 19.7). While a variety of planned academic majors were reported, approximately fifty percent had not yet selected a major area of study. The high school grade point averages in this sample ranged from 2.31 to 4.00 with a mean of 3.32, slightly higher than the mean grade point average for all entering freshmen.

To investigate the hypothesized differential impact contingent of prior ability, the sample was stratified into three groups based on high school grade point average (GPA). Categories were created with consideration of sample size and logical breakpoints.

The low group (n = 25) was comprised of participants whose high school GPA was lower than 3.0 on a four point scale. The medium group (n = 45) included participants whose high school GPA was between 3.0 and 3.49. The high group (n = 48) was comprised of participants with high school GPA at or above 3.50.

Instrumentation

Data for this study were obtained using selected questions from the pre-test and post-test in the instructor's manual for the text used in the course (Carter, Bishop, & Kravits, 1998). A copy of the instruments is available from the senior author. The pre- and post-tests from this manual included twenty questions, five of which were analyzed for this study.

On the first day of class, the complete pre-test was administered to all students in each of the five sections of the course. Then, on the last day of class, students completed the corresponding post-test. Each of the items on the pre- and post-test used a five response Likert type scale. On the scale, 1 represents a response of "not at all;" 2 represents "not much;" 3 represents "somewhat;" 4 represents "pretty well;" and 5 represents "extremely/definitely".

Five questions of particular concern were selected from the list of questions provided in the instructor's manual. The first selected pre-test question asked students how prepared they felt for college, while the corresponding post-test question evaluated whether they felt the course prepared them for the rest of college. The second pre-test question asked students if they knew what they wanted to major in; the corresponding post-test question asked if their ideas about majors developed or changed. The third question asked students if they were confident about their strengths, and later if they felt more confident as a result of the course. The fourth question surveyed their awareness of campus resources. The final question addressed development of efficient study skills.

Results

For the question regarding general improvement for all students, a null hypothesis was evaluated for each of the five areas investigated in this study using the t-test for dependent samples. Table 1 describes the results. On the question related to college preparedness, the difference between the pre-test (M = 3.43) and the post-test (M = 3.80) was statistically significant, t(117) = 3.95, p < .001. On the question related to the development of majors, the difference between pre-test (M = 3.32) and post-test (M = 3.01) was not statistically significant, t(117) = 1.93, p > .05. For the question regarding overall confidence as a student, the mean scores were 3.31 and 3.84, respectively, and the difference was statistically significant, t(117) = 4.06, p < .001. A statistically significant difference was clearly evident on the question pertaining to knowledge of campus resources, t(117) = 13.04, p < .001, with pre-test and post-test means of 2.94 and 4.54, respectively. Statistically significant gain was also evident on the question regarding perception of competence with study skills with pre-test (M = 2.98) and post-test (M = 3.61), t(117) = 5.73, p < .001.

TABLE 1 Pre-test and Post-test Responses on Selected Indicators n=118					
Legend for Chart:	A pre-test, *M*	B pre-test, s.d.	C post-test, *M*	D post-test, s.d.	E *t*
feel prepared for college	3.43	.71	3.80	.83	3.95[b]
identification/satisfaction of college major	3.32	1.20	3.01	1.27	1.93
confidence about strength as student	3.31	1.06	3.84	.92	4.06[b]
awareness of campus resources	2.94	1.15	4.54	.64	13.04[b]
efficient study skills	2.98	.93	3.61	.91	5.73[b]

bp < .001

1 = not at all; 2 = not much; 3 = somewhat; 4 = pretty well; 5 = extremely/definitely

A second set of analyses was conducted to explore the possibility that the response to the course may have been contingent on prior academic preparation operationally defined with high school grade point average classified as high (GPA 3.50 and above), medium (GPA between 3.0 and 3.49, and low (GPA below 3.0).

When the course began, the differences among the three groups were not statistically different on four of the five questions: college preparedness, $F_{(2,115)} = .033$, $p > .05$; college major development, $F_{(2,115)} = .151$, $p > .05$; student confidence levels, $F_{(2,115)} = .505$, $p > .05$, and knowledge of campus resources, $F_{(2,115)} = .234$, $p > .05$.

Differences at the beginning of the course among the three groups on the question regarding effective study skills were statistically significant, $F_{(2,115)} = 4.335$, $p < .05$. Post-hoc comparison of means using Duncan's Multiple Range test found statistically significant pre-test differences between the low high school GPA group (M = 2.52) and the middle high school GPA group (M = 3.04), $p < .05$. Statistically significant difference was also evident between the low high school GPA group (M = 2.52) and the high GPA group (M = 3.17), $p < .01$.

On the post-test the differences among the three groups were not statistically significant on any of the five questions: college preparedness, $F_{(2,115)} = .572$, $p > .05$, college major development, $F_{(2,115)} = .483$, $p > .05$; student confidence levels, $F_{(2,115)} = .562$, $p > .05$; knowledge of campus resources, $F_{(2,115)} = .397$, $p > .05$, and development of effective study skills, $F_{(2,115)} = .334$, $p > .05$.

Summary and Discussion

With the exception of the responses regarding the college major, these data suggest that the seminar was effective in enhancing the student's perceptions of efficacy related to the college experience. Statistically significant growth was evident in questions associated with college preparedness, confidence as a student, knowledge of academic and personal resources on campus, and study skills efficiency.

Although the difference was not statistically significant, the results of the question regarding development of a college major did not indicate positive gain from the course. The post-test mean score was, in fact, lower than the pre-test mean with the difference approaching statistical significance. A possible explanation for this surprising finding may be in the instructional design. Students in the course were introduced to more than 80 possible undergraduate major options, a number which may have simply overwhelmed the students, increasing, rather than reducing the degree of uncertainty.

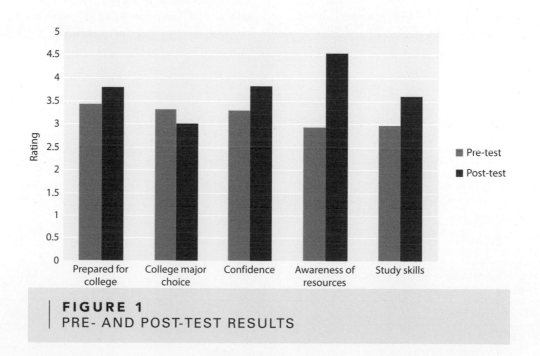

FIGURE 1
PRE- AND POST-TEST RESULTS

These data provided only limited support for our hypothesis that the seminar would be especially helpful for students whose high school grade point averages suggested less adequate preparation. On four of the five questions, neither pre-test nor post-test scores were significantly different among the low, medium, and high groups. The exception was in regard to the perceived enhanced development of study skills. Post-test scores were not significantly different, suggesting that each of the three groups attained the same level at the end of the course; pre-test scores indicated that the low group made the greater gain.

The gain in reference to study skills is consistent with the typical preconceptions of students who are considering taking the course. The overall pattern of data, however, suggests that rather than being a course for the "under-prepared", there is a pervasive positive impact of the course, regardless of prior preparation.

Further investigation is needed both to confirm these findings with other samples, and to explore the unexpected finding regarding the college majors. Investigation is also needed to determine whether the perceptions of improved skills are validated with actual performance in future classes. Especially helpful would be an investigation of the future academic performance of a matched sample of students who did and did not complete the freshman seminar, and any differential impact on retention rate. ∎

REFERENCES

Banta, T. W., & Kuh, G. D. (1998). A missing link in assessment: Collaboration between academic and student affairs professionals. *Change, 30*, 40–47.

Beal, P. E. & Noel, L. (1980). *What works in student retention*. Iowa City: American College Testing Program.

Carter, C., Bishop, J., & Kravits, S. L. (1998). *Keys to effective learning*. Upper Saddle River, NJ: Prentice-Hall.

Cone, A. L. (1991). Sophomore academic retention associated with a freshman study skills and college adjustment course. *Psychological Reports, 69*, 312–315.

Dunlosky, J., Rawson, K. A., Marsh, E. J., Nathan, M. J., & Willingham, D. T. (2013). Improving students' learning with effective learning techniques: Promising directions from cognitive and Educational Psychology. *Psychological Science in the Public Interest* (Sage Publications Inc.), *14*(1), 4–58. doi:10.1177/1529100612453266.

Fidler, P. P., & Hunter, M. S. (1989). How seminars enhance student success. In Upcraft, M. L., & Gardner, J. N. (Eds.), *The freshman year experience* (pp. 216–237). San Francisco: Jossey-Bass.

Hyers, A. D., & Joslin, M. N. (1998). The first year seminar as a predictor of academic achievement and persistence. *Journal of the Freshman Year Experience, 10*, 7–30.

Kendall, M. E. (1999). Let students do the work. *College Teaching, 47*, 84.

Liu, E., & Liu, R. (1999). An application of Tinto's model at commuter campus. *Education, 19*, 537.

Maisto, A. A., & Tammi, M. W. (1991). The effect of a content-based freshman seminar on academic and social integration. *Journal of the Freshman Year Experience, 3*, 29–47.

Schaeffer, P. (1999). Freshman orientation: College freshman receive assistance. *National Catholic Reporter, 35*, 11.

Tinto, V. (1987). *Leaving college: Rethinking the causes and cures of student attrition*. Chicago: The University of Chicago Press.

Upcraft, M. L., & Gardner, J. N. (Eds.)(1989). *The freshman year experience*. San Francisco: Jossey-Bass.

Wilkie, C., & Kuckuck, S. (1989). A longitudinal study of the effects of a freshman seminar. *Journal of the Freshman Year Experience, 1*, 7–16.

Yakovlev, P., & Leguizamon, S. (2012). Ignorance is not bliss: On the role of education in subjective well-being. *Journal of Socio-Economics., 41*(6), 806–815. doi:10.1016/j.socec.2012.08.009.

Travis, T. (2011). From the classroom to the boardroom: The impact of information literacy instruction on workplace research skills. *Education Libraries, 34(2), 19–31.*

Engage via Research Prediction

- What percentage of college graduates reported using information literacy or research skills in their current position on at least a monthly basis?
- What percentage of college graduates reported using information from empirical research in their current position on a monthly basis?
- What percentage of college graduates reported never using research skills in their current position on a daily basis?
- Where did alumni most often report learning information literacy skills?

Read for Key Points

- What question did the researcher seek to answer? (Introduction)
- Who participated in the study and what did the participants do? (Method)
- What was the answer to the research question? (Results)

Critically Think about the Research

- Why are these findings important? How can you use this research to guide your actions as a college student?
- Why do you think the students who didn't have a required information literacy requirement reported having higher confidence in their skills?
- Based on these findings, what recommendations would you make to your college president about information literacy skill development? Why?
- What future research in this area would you suggest?

Build Information Literacy Skills

- Are the beliefs of alumni consistent with the beliefs of employers?
- How do colleges and universities teach information literacy skills?
- What does the research say about the importance of information literacy skills in your personal life?

Tiffini Travis. From the Classroom to the Boardroom: The Impact of Information Literacy Instruction on Workplace Research Skills

"Many businesses are knowledge driven. Even entry level employees have to know how to identify information problems and go about solving them" ~ unidentified employer 2000.

Topsey Smalley, Workplace Quotes www.cabrillo.edu/~tsmalley/WorkplaceQuotes.html

Introduction

Since the wide-scale adoption of the ACRL *Information Literacy Standards* (2000), there have been numerous students who have graduated from universities that have formal library instruction programs. Currently there has been very little assessment of their post-graduate research skills or what role information literacy plays on workplace performance. The effect libraries have on graduates is not only of interest to librarians; the skills students gain in college have a significant impact on costs and productivity in the workplace. Within the last five years, the corporate world has acknowledged the importance of information literacy on workplace success. This has largely been linked to the growth of the knowledge management sector coinciding with the ability to access large amounts of unfiltered information on the internet.

The report, *Are they really ready to work?: Employers' perspectives on the basic knowledge and applied skills of new entrants to the 21st century U.S. workforce* (Casner-Lotto 2006) delineated 21st century skills needed by baccalaureates. While information literacy was not specifically mentioned in the report, the areas of critical thinking/problem solving, information technology application, and lifelong learning certainly correspond to the ACRL standards. The following year, information literacy was listed as an Essential Learning Outcome by the *Association of American Colleges and Universities (2007). The AACU* (2007) states these outcomes, "reflect an important emerging consensus— among educators and employers—about the kinds of learning needed for a complex and volatile world" (p. 13). Since then, variations of 21st century skills have

been increasingly adopted by universities to ensure their graduates possess the proficiencies needed to function in a knowledge-based society.

The purpose of this study is to examine various factors that may contribute to continued and sustained use of information literacy skills beyond the college experience, and specifically, what competencies students identify as essential for their work.

Literature Review
Information Literacy in the Workplace

The most significant research regarding information literacy in the workplace has been published by Christine Bruce (Bruce 1999; McMahon, C., & Bruce, C., 2002). Using her seminal seven faces framework, Bruce examined information seeking behaviors in the workplace. Seven faces of information literacy in the workplace were identified: using information technology for awareness and communication; finding information from appropriate sources; executing a process; controlling information; building a personal knowledge base in a new area of interest; working with knowledge and personal perspectives to gain novel insight; and using information wisely for the benefit of others (Bruce, 1999). What is underscored is the importance of lifelong learning and the position information literacy has in all work sectors, not solely knowledge management.

In 2002, Carmel O'Sullivan surmised that the term information literacy is "at best sporadic outside the isolation of the library and teaching professions". (p. 7) O'Sullivan also found that the corporate literature that did exist regarding information-gathering in the workplace focused on computer literacy or was framed in the context of lifelong learning. Other research laid the groundwork linking information literacy and knowledge management (Hughes, Middleton, Edwards, Bruce Mcallister, 2005; Kirton and Barham 2005; O'Farril 2008; Ferguson, 2009). Lloyd examined information literacy through the lens of sociocultural practice, specifying the ranges of information modalities involved within the context of work (Lloyd 2007). Lloyd conducted studies that examined the work of ambulance drivers and firefighters and questioned whether the information literacy skills in the traditional settings of education and in the library had the same characteristics as the workplace (Lloyd 2008).

Studies that have quantified information literacy skills in the workplace focus mainly on current practices of employees and corporate needs (Smalley, 2000; cheuk 2008). Using Bruces' seven faces framework(1999), Cheuk modeled an approach for information literacy training of employees at a large consulting firm (2008). For obvious reasons, professions that deal with the collection and creation of written product are more likely to be engaged in information gathering. However, as the importance of evidence-based practice has become a staple in medical fields and other on-the-job decision making, information literacy can conceivably be important in many other work environments.

As the body of information literacy research has expanded, several perspectives in the context of work have emerged (Halford, Lotherington, Obstefelder and Dyb 2008; Hepworth and Smith, 2008; Somerville and Howard, 2008; Klusek and Bournstein 2006). Again the focus has been on information-dependent professions. However, from the literature one key point emerges. Information seekers in the workplace require more advanced navigation and evaluation skills since often they do not have information experts to rely on nor do they always have access to vetted information sources like databases and knowledge management systems (Bruce, 1999; Lloyd , 2008; Ochs, 1991).

Assessing the transferability of information literacy Information literacy has been extensively evaluated in the K-16 settings. Standardized tests and various direct assessment tools have been developed to determine which skills students have mastered and attempt to measure the impact of information literacy skills or usage of library materials on academic success (Oakleaf and Owen 2010; de Jager 1997, Schulte, 2008; Shepherd 2011; Walsh 2011; Whitemire 2002; Wong 2011). What is lacking in the literature is a focus on what information competencies in the academic setting transfer to the workplace.

While previous research advocates collaboration between business managers and librarians to align information literacy with corporate needs, very few have tried to correlate the skills learned in college with actual use in the workplace. The most applicable methodology to use for such research is referred to as postcampus assessment (Rockman, 2002). This form of assessment measures the degree of skills students retain from their college research experience. Additionally, it helps identify which skills students and their employers' value. Ilene Rockman notes, "this post campus assessment technique can be used for gaining valuable feedback about the usefulness and applicability of course content, instructional strategies, and the campus learning environment" (p. 193). Three studies have employed this form of data collection to analyze the transferability of information seeking skills of alumni (Smalley 2000; Crawford and Irving 2006; Wu 2008). One of the earliest examples of this data collection technique was conducted by Ochs (1991). Ochs distributed surveys to both employers and alumni regarding use of information literacy and technology skills. Employers identified skill levels they expected of students while alumni rated their own skill set and where they felt they gained them. Of the most frequently identified sources of skill attainment, ""Cornell classes" or "on the job" and "on my own" often rate higher than Mann library instruction program as students' sources of information management skills" (p. 17). Ochs surmised that it was probably due to lack of librarian contact time with students. Another "postcampus" survey by Crawford and Irving (2006) was conducted after the widespread use of the internet in libraries. Alumni from Glasgow Caledonian were asked to identify which skills and to what extent research skills gained as students applied to their current workplace activities. The findings indicated that students felt the research skills they used in the university made a significant impact on their job performance.

These results raise a core issue that libraries struggle to substantiate: what impact does information literacy really have on students, especially once they no longer have to conduct research for courses?

Models of Information Literacy Instruction

While most institutions strive for the perfect combination of tiered, embedded, curricular integration at the programmatic level, the reality is usually far removed. Stephanie Sterling Brasely examined models of information literacy in academic institutions and described the landscape as "collaborations that run along a continuum from the informal and episodic or scattershot to the formal, sequential, and programmatic." (Brasley, 2008, p. 77). Sue Curzon defined various models of information literacy integration including general education; credit courses; online tutorials; faculty-led; and the most common, on-demand instruction (Curzon 2004). These models can be divided into two categories: direct and indirect information literacy instruction. Direct information literacy is curriculum-centric and either manifested as a requirement for graduation and integrated systematically at the university level. Indirect information literacy instruction is defined as library-centric and not fully diffused into the curriculum but rather intermittently throughout the university. Typically, the latter model may have an instruction plan adopted by the library; however, without curricular requirements, there is no full integration of information literacy outcomes at the university level. Very few institutions of higher education have the "perfect" model of information literacy nevertheless; several examples of direct and indirect information literacy programs exist. Perhaps one of the first examples of a systematic approach to building more direct information literacy instruction is found in the California State University System. The California State University (CSU) system has had an advantage in the area of information literacy in large part due to a centralized approach to integration. The report *Information Competence in the CSU* (1995) developed a blueprint for providing financial and institutional support at individual campuses for inclusion of information literacy into the curriculum. Rockman (2002) described a multicampus approach that focused on providing grants,

interdepartmental and cross-campus collaboration as well as faculty development opportunities. The approach was designed to take advantage of the trends in general education (GE) reform. The result was to enable many campuses in the system to create various configurations of information literacy instruction. Currently, half the libraries in the CSU System "have information literacy and competency learning outcomes as part of the institutional requirements for general education" (Travis, 2008, p. 18). The models that have been adopted at various CSU campuses can be categorized as both indirect and direct. Some examples of direct information literacy inclusion are CSU Northridge and CSU Los Angeles. Both have information literacy requirements for graduation which are fulfilled through GE courses. These are courses which are seamlessly embedded in course content, rather than a stand-alone tutorial, instruction session, or assignment. Other libraries in the system provide examples of indirect forms of information literacy integration. For example, Sonoma State has infused the first-year program with information literacy outcomes. CSU Long Beach has adopted information literacy outcomes for general education; however, there is currently no requirement in place for graduation. CSU Monterey Bay offers majors which have information literacy outcomes built into the overall departmental outcomes. Still other schools like San Diego State have established library instruction programs but no embedded information literacy curriculum. In many cases, a variety of information literacy integration can exist on the same campus. For example, CSU Long Beach has GE outcomes, some departmental outcomes, as well as faculty led information literacy instruction (Brasley, 2008). With such varying campuses and multi-pronged efforts, it is important to assess which models may have a greater or lesser impact on skills of alumni in the workplace.

Due to the variety of information literacy programs in existence, it is expected that student use of information literacy skills in the workplace will vary depending upon the method of information literacy integration. By comparing alumni from campuses with and without information literacy requirements, this study will explore the following research questions:

RQ1: Does an information literacy requirement at a campus effect research skills?

RQ2: Do alumni attribute their information literacy skills to the library or other aspects of their education?

RQ3: How much do information literacy skills learned in college impact their use in the workplace?

Background & Methodology

The model for this research study is based on the work of Crawford and Irving (2006). To modify the original survey for distribution in the United States, the language was changed from British to American English; questions were adjusted to current internet use trends; and a question about LEAP 21st century skills was added. These skills identified by *Association of American Colleges and Universities* have recently been adopted by the CSU system in the revision of the GE curriculum (CSU, 2008) and mirror similar GE curriculum revisions nationwide. Part of this study examined which of the 21st century skills participants identified as learning during college.

The purpose of this study was to:

- determine the extent to which graduates use information literacy/research skills in the workplace
- Explore any impact different models of information literacy curriculum integration has on these skills
- Compare differences between use of information sources for academic and workplace research
- Evaluate the distinction alumni make between research skills learned as college student with current research skills in the workplace.

The instrument contained forty three questions divided into five sections (figure 1):

Alumni Profile: brief demographic survey regarding school, major, and current employment.

Information Literacy/Library instruction: information regarding the mode and level of exposure to information literacy concepts as college students.

Information Sources you used at your Campus: questions about the types and names of specific resources alumni used as students.

Information Sources you use in the workplace: information sources and information needs questions.

Self-Assessment of Information Literacy/Research Skills: participants' overall judgment of their research skills before college, after college, and in the workplace.

FIGURE 1
FIVE SECTIONS OF THE INSTRUMENT.

Results: Key Findings
Demographics

In order to examine any patterns that may exist, the data was analyzed by population. Due to the low response rate, the results can only be used as a starting point of the discussion of the impact information literacy has on performance in the workplace and cannot be used to generalize all alumni experiences. This convenience sample provides descriptive data that can give insight into how information literacy has impacted respondents after they become members of the workforce.

The survey was distributed twice. The first dissemination was to graduates of the CSU system and the second was open to anyone that attended a four-year institution in the United States. There were 62 surveys started by CSU respondents with 54 usable surveys. There were 71 surveys started by the non-CSU respondents with 44 usable surveys. Eleven different CSU campuses were represented while over 24 campuses overall made up the total. Fifty-one percent of total respondents obtained master's degrees with less than one percent getting a PhD. The disciplines for undergraduates were varied with most of the students majoring in social science programs, arts & humanities, followed by business, and the sciences. The core numbers of graduates responding to the survey were psychology and library science degree holders with social sciences, education, business administration, social work and nursing respondents as well.

The majority of the respondents were female (71%). 58% of the respondents could be described as Millenials (born between the ages of 1980-2000) while next largest age group were between the ages of 31-40.

RQ1: Does an information literacy requirement at a campus make a difference in research skills?

The data was examined to determine if there were significant differences between the populations that fulfilled information literacy requirements with those that did not. From the data collected the results are mixed. Twenty-eight percent of respondents answered that they had an information literacy requirement. Forty-nine percent had no requirement while 23% couldn't remember if they had such a requirement. Of the 28% who had a requirement, a surprising 85% satisfied the requirement by completing a credit course. Six percent of those who indicated that they had information literacy (IL) requirements in college listed their most advanced degree as library science. Eleven percent of those who responded they had no information literacy requirement or didn't remember also identified their highest degree as library science.

When comparing specific questions related to research there were no major differences in their self-rating of information literacy skills (Figure 2 and Figure 3). The students who attended college without an IL requirement were more confident in their skills both

FIGURE 2

Before starting my coursework at a 4-year College/ University, my information literacy/research skills were:

Answer Options	IL Required Response Percent	IL Not Required Response Percent
Poor	19%	19%
Average	44%	41%
Good	33%	29%
Very good	3%	10%

N=95

FIGURE 3

When I completed my coursework at a 4-Year college/ University my information literacy/research skills were:

Answer Options	IL Required Response Percent	IL Not Required Response Percent
Poor	0%	0%
Average	15%	9%
Good	48%	39%
Very good	37%	52%

N=94

before and after college. This furthers the implication that students feel research skills increase as a result of attending college.

Another area of the survey where there was an expected difference was in responses to the questions regarding evaluation and application of information (Figure4).

FIGURE 4

Please mark all of the statements that best apply to you.

Answer Options	IL Required Response Percent	IL Not Required Response Percent
I use advanced search options when I search online resources.	84%	75%
I use advanced search options when I search subscription databases.	72%	69%
I use specific criteria for evaluating information I find using Internet information sources.	52%	75%
I use more than one source to verify the accuracy of information I find using Internet information sources.	76%	81%
I regularly manipulate or otherwise incorporate information I find using Internet information sources into presentations or reports for work.	40%	41%

N=89

Most respondents stated they used advanced searching features when using the internet but less in subscription databases. The criteria they list for finding websites offers insight into what criteria is used to select sites found on the internet (Figure 5).

Being familiar with a site and a referral to a site were the highest-ranking responses. Other findings regarding information-seeking behavior and undergraduates mirrors these results (Head & Eisenberg 2010). It is interesting to note that "information has been rated by other

FIGURE 5

When searching for information, how do you select which sites to use? Please mark all that apply.

Answer Options	IL Required Response Percent	IL Not Required Response Percent
I am already familiar with the site URL listed for the site.	81%	87%
Information has been rated by other users. Information is contrary to what I think.	23%	30%
See what sources the author used.	15%	19%
If the source is listed on the first page of search results.	4%	12%
Consult the credentials listed for the author(s). Information confirms my assumptions.	58%	67%
Site is well designed and easy to use.	27%	19%
I was referred to the site by a colleague or friend.	50%	48%
	4%	16%
	50%	60%
	69%	76%

N=93

users" is significantly lower than other referral-type answers due to the prevalence of user-generated rankings on sites such as *Amazon, Yahoo Answers* and *Yelp.*

Site design, while often identified in the literature as the least reliable way to evaluate site content, is still ranked by 50% or more of respondents, equal to credentials of the author. Selecting a source because it's on the first page of results is also a significant finding and should be investigated further to determine which search engines are being used and if there is any user understanding of how page rankings are calculated.

Also notable is the low number of respondents who regularly manipulate or incorporate information as part of their job (Figure 4). It begs to question what they do with the information they find in the workplace,

especially when reports and presentations were ranked highest in response to the question "for which work related projects did you perform research to complete."

RQ2: Do alumni attribute their information literacy skills to the library or other aspects of their education?

Information Literacy exposure

The results for questions relating to information literacy exposure were very revealing. Sixty-eight percent of those who had no IL requirement recall attending a library-led research session. Sixty-three percent of those with no course-related interaction with librarians stated they consulted with librarians at some point in their career. Of those that had, 97% stated they got help at the reference desk with 29% using email and 5% using instant message.

In terms of conducting research while attending university, 67% answered they used the library website to access information "often" with 18% responding "seldom" or "never". Thirty-nine percent replied they used the print collection "often" with 32% responding "seldom" or "never". All respondents affirmed using research databases in college. Seventy-six percent of respondents agreed with the statement "research databases were very important for completing my academic research." Fifteen percent disagreed or strongly disagreed with this statement.

FIGURE 6

Library's subscription research databases (e.g. Lexis Nexis, Academic Search Elite, JSTOR etc.) were very important for the completion of my academic research.

Answer Options	All Respondents
Strongly agree	53%
Agree	23%
Neutral	9.0%
Disagree	4%
Strongly disagree	11%
	N=92

When asked what respondents felt contributed most to developing information literacy skills in college the results were interesting. "Writing research papers" and "figuring it out myself' were cited most often with "using the library resources" referenced by 55% of respondents (figure 7). Librarians were ranked 8th below "professors and "general education" as resources. "Library instruction," "credit courses by the library," and "online research tutorials" ranked lowest on the list. These findings from the study are reminiscent of Ochs' (1991) finding that "Cornell courses" and "on my own" ranked higher than library instruction.

21st Century and Information Literacy Skill Areas

When asked to select LEAP 21st century skills and specific information literacy concepts they felt they current used in the workplace, the answers had interesting implications for integrating these skills into the curriculum (Figure 8).

FIGURE 7

What do you feel contributed most to developing your information literacy/research skills in college?

Task	All Respondents
Writing research papers	84%
Figuring it out myself	70%
Using library resources	55%
General education	52%
Professors	49%
Research methods course	43%
Curriculum in my major	42%
Librarians	33%
Fellow students	29%
Library instruction session(s)	27%
Online research tutorial	12%
Credit course offered by the library	0%
	N=92

FIGURE 8

As a result of attending a 4-year College/University, which skills do you think you gained from your college experience that you use most often in the workplace? (please mark all that apply)

Skill Area	All Respondents
Finding relevant information	78%
*Critical thinking	78%
Evaluating information	69%
*Problem solving	65%
*Oral communication	64%
*Writing	61%
Recognizing bias	56%
*Methods of inquiry	48%
*Quantitative reasoning	48%
*Teamwork	47%
*Intercultural competence	42%
Determining an information need	40%
*Social responsibility	40%
Using information ethically	39%
* Self-understanding	36%
*Creativity	33%
*Global awareness	28%
Information cycle	13%
	N=89

*Denotes LEAP 21st century skill

Respondents felt that college helped them gain critical thinking skills and problem solving the most, with "oral communication" and "writing" identified by more than 50% of respondents. What they felt it helped the least was "global awareness," "creativity," and "self-awareness." This isn't surprising, as these concepts are not something people typically "learn" in a classroom or through a specific assignment or course.

Of the information literacy skills, "finding relevant information" and "evaluating information" were chosen most often; the "information cycle" and "using information ethically" ranked lowest. "Determining an information need," which previous research identified as the most difficult informationseeking task, was marked by only 40% of respondents (Head 2010).

RQ3: How much do information literacy skills learned in college impact use in the workplace?

Research in the workplace

All Respondents

The transmission of information literacy skills to the workplace is also examined in this survey. One-third of all respondents use research skills to perform job daily; 30% weekly, and 19% monthly. 10% never use research skills in the workplace.

The job occupations listed by respondents who never used their research skills in the workplace included servers, sales, correctional officer, counselor, and registered nurses. Most of these respondents also indicated they spent most of their work day away from the computer. All of these respondents in this category indicated their research skills were unchanged before and after attending college.

Another indicator of the transferability of information literacy skills to the workplace setting are the responses indicating the evaluation and application of information into their work lives. Fifty-three percent believe their research skills played a role in getting hired for their current position, while 36% did not feel research skills played any role in their current employment. In the workplace, respondents were more likely to use free internet sources than subscription databases. Free sources most often cited in open- ended responses were Google, trade websites, education databases, PubMed, and blogs.

The most-cited types of information looked for at work were current news, empirical research, and

statistics while office supplies and medical information ranked lowest. The most-often cited work related projects were reports and presentations. Open-ended responses included computer fixes, lesson plans, design work, patient care, emergency preparedness, lab research, research help, engineering projects, patient diagnosis, images/graphics, and legal research (Figure 9).

FIGURE 9

What types of information do you typically search for in the workplace? (please check all that apply)

Answer Options	Response Percent
Current news	57%
Empirical research	46%
Product information	36%
Statistics	36%
Other (please specify)	30%
Information for my supervisor	27%
Law	24%
Price comparison	23%
Medical	22%
Licensing information	17%
Software	17%
Travel	14%
Human resources	12%
Office supplies	11%
Employment ads	10%

N=83

In terms of rating their current research skills, 51% of respondents reported their skills had "gotten better" while 31% responded "unchanged." Very few reported their skills as becoming worse, which corresponds with the finding that the majority of respondents were not interested in receiving continuing education to increase their informationseeking skills. Those that stated they would want more training identified "keeping up to date" as their justification.

Discussion

The results of this study offer insights for both librarians and the corporate world. When comparing results to Crawford and Irving, there are similarities. In the Crawford study, the majority of alumni also believed research skills improved as a result of attending a university and felt their research skills improved once they were employed. In related research of Millennials (individuals born between 1980-2000) at work, it was reported that 77% of respondents felt that" technology helps me improve my work". In the same study 76% felt technology made them more successful in their career (O'Dell 2010). This study found 48% felt their information literacy skills were a factor for getting hired in their current position and 77% of respondents felt "finding information is an essential part of my work." This indicates the usefulness of information literacy skills in the workplace is acknowledged as much by graduates as it is by businesses.

Another study of information-seeking behavior of college students found most turned to friends (87%) for help while only 14% asked librarians for assistance (Head & Eisenberg 2010). Likewise, the results of the present study indicate this pattern of help-seeking continues after graduation. Of note in this study was the large number of students who consulted librarians in person (97%) versus via email (27%). The increased access to instant messaging and services such as LibAnswers may impact help-seeking patterns and deserves further research due to the visibility of the products and growing usage of both library services.

The findings regarding evaluation of information can provide insight into areas that should be studied further. The number of students using "site design" to assign credibility to a website is troubling. Alison Head and Michael Eisenberg found similar results as 71% use interface design as part of their source selection (2010). There is also prevalence for alumni to use previous knowledge of a site as selection criteria. What should be examined is how individuals balance previous site content with new information needs. Research has found that students will select sites based on previous success regardless of if it appropriate for the topic. If this tendency continues after college, it may have implications, as librarians are not regularly employed in the workplace environment.

Another important aspect of the findings is the low ranking of librarians, online tutorials, and library instruction sessions as contributing to the growth of information literacy skills. What was identified most were tasks that required demonstrated use of information literacy concepts. "Writing research papers," "figuring it out myself," and "using library resources" are all active learning processes.

It appears significant that students rated doing research contributed more to gaining which skills rather than passive learning activities such as sitting through a presentation or using an online tutorial. This strengthens the argument that information literacy should be embedded in courses and assignments rather than as a stand-alone or one-shot model.

Any research conducted to see how individuals interact with information and employ information literacy skills can be used to strengthen our instruction programs. The results of this study cannot definitively determine if an information literacy requirement is the best method to approach this. However, the results indicate that students are employing research skills in the workplace; they value and use library resources; and most importantly, they value the skills they gain from engaging in the finding, evaluating and applying information. As Bruce (1999) eloquently states, librarians need to "find ways to help learners reflect on their use of information, so that they become aware of their experiences and transfer these ways of working to a wide range of situations" (p. 45). This concept of transferability not only applies to work but to contribute to a society of lifelong learners.

Limitations and Future Directions

This study had several limitations. Initially, this survey was designed to be distributed only to alumni of the California State University system. This would have allowed the research to focus on known models of information literacy, and also allow for a comparison between direct and indirect information literacy programs. The low response rate made this comparison impossible, therefore it was distributed via social media outlets (Twitter, Facebook, listservs, etc.) to a nationwide audience. The issues with distributing the survey via social media meant a disproportionate amount of respondents had library science degrees and a population that regularly uses the internet for socializing. Any future studies should be distributed to a broader, diverse population.

In addition, future research should focus on examining the different information literacy skills between students who have completed credit courses versus those who have had no formal library instruction. While it is impossible to control for other sources of information literacy skill building, longitudinal studies examining participants both in the university and workplace settings will provide greater insight. The results of this study suggest there are other sources outside of library instruction where students feel they gain research skills that should be examined further.

Additionally, comparing knowledge management professions with less information-intensive professions would further define the differences in use of information by the two groups. Using a combination of outcomes based measures and phenomenography, data can be compiled to provide a definitive assessment of the libraries role in preparing individuals for lifelong learning. ■

REFERENCES

Association of American Colleges and Universities., & National Leadership Council (U.S.). (2007). *College learning for the new global century: A report from the National Leadership Council for Liberal Education & America's Promise*. Washington, D.C: Association of American Colleges and Universities. Available: http://www.aacu.org/leap/documents/Global Century final.pdf

Association of College and Research Libraries., & American Library Association. *(2000). Information literacy competency standards for higher education. Chicago, IL: ACRL.*

Brasley, S. (2008). Effective librarian and discipline faculty collaboration models for integrating information literacy into the fabric of an academic institution. *New Directions for Teaching and Learning, 114,* 71–88.

Bruce, C. S. (1999). Workplace experiences of information literacy. *International Journal of Information Management, 19,* 33–47.

California State University. California State University retools general education courses to focus on core values of liberal Education (Press Release) Available at http://www.calstate.edu/pa/news/2008/leap.shtml

California State University. (1995). *Information competence in the CSU: A report submitted to Commission on Learning Resources and Instructional Technology Work Group on Information Competence. Sacramento, CA: California State University.*

Casner-Lotto, J., Conference Board., Partnership for 21st Century Skills., Corporate Voices for Working Families., & Society for Human Resource Management (U.S.). (2006). *Are they really ready to work?: Employers' perspectives on the basic knowledge and applied skills of new entrants to the 21st century U.S. workforce.* United States: Conference Board.

Cheuk, B. (2008). Delivering business value through information literacy in the workplace. *Libri, 58.* 137-143.

Crawford, J. (2006). The use of electronic information services and information literacy: A Glasgow Caledonian University study. *Journal of Librarianship & Information Science, 38*(1), 33–44. doi:10.1177/0961000606060958

Curzon, S. C. (2004). Developing faculty-librarian partnerships in information literacy. In Rockman, I. F. (Eds.). Integrating information literacy into the higher education curriculum: Practical models for transformation. San Francisco: Jossey-Bass.

de Jager, K. (1997). Library use and academic achievement. *South African Journal of Library & Information Science, 65,* 26–30.

Ferguson, S. (2009). Information literacy and its relationship to knowledge management. *Journal of Information Literacy, 3,* 6–24.

Halford, S., Lotherington, A. T., Obstfelder, A., & Dyb, K. (2010). Getting the whole picture? *Information, Communication & Society, 13,* 442–465.

Head A., Eisenberg M. (2010) Truth be told: How college students evaluate and use information in the digital age. Project Information Literacy Progress Report. Available http://projectinfolit.org/pdfs/PIL Fall2010 Survey FullReport1.pdf

Hepworth, M., & Smith, M. (2008). Workplace information literacy for administrative staff in higher education. *Australian Library Journal, 57,* 212–236.

Hughes, H., Middleton, M., Edwards, S., Bruce, C. and McAllister, L. (2005) Information literacy research in Australia 2000—2005, Bulletin des *Bibliothèques de France* 50, 1–23. Available http://eprints.qut.edu.au/archive/00002832/0 1/BdesB submission.pdf

Kirton, J., & Barham, L. (2005). Information literacy in the workplace. *Australian Library Journal, 54,* 365–376.

Klusek, L., & Bornstein, J. (2006). Information literacy skills for business careers: Matching skills to the workplace. *Journal of Business & Finance Librarianship, 11,* 3–21.

Lloyd, A. (2007). Recasting information literacy as sociocultural practice: Implications for library and information science researchers. *Information Research, 12,* 1–13.

Lloyd, A. (2009). Informing practice: Information experiences of ambulance officers in training and on-road practice. *Journal of Documentation, 65,* 396–419.

McMahon, C., & Bruce, C. (2002). Information literacy needs of local staff in cross-cultural development projects. *Journal of International Development, 14,* 113–127.

Oakleaf, M., & Owen, P. L. (2010). Closing the 12-13 gap together: School and college librarians supporting 21st century learners. *Teacher Librarian, 37*(4), 52-58.

Ochs, M. (1991). Assessing the value of an information literacy program. Ithaca, NY: Cornell University. ERIC EDRS340385. Available http://www.eric.ed.gov/PDFS/ED340385.pd

O'Dell, J. (February 9, 2010) How millenials use tech at work. *Read Write Web.* Available http://www.readwriteweb.com/archives/how millenials use tech at work.php

O'Farril, R. T. (2008). Information literacy and knowledge management: Preparations for an arranged marriage. *Libri: International Journal of Libraries & Information Services, 58,* 155–171.

O'Sullivan, C. (2002). Is information literacy relevant in the real world?. Reference Services Review, 30, 7–14.

Rockman, I. F. (2002). Strengthening connections between information literacy, general education, and assessment efforts. *Library Trends,* 51 185–98.

Schulte, S. J. (2008). High self-efficacy and high use of electronic information may predict improved academic performance. *Evidence Based Library & Information Practice, 3,* 35–37.

Shepherd, P. T. (2011). Journal usage factor - a promising new metric. *Serials,* 24, 64–68.

Somerville, M. M., & Howard, Z. (2008). Systems thinking: An approach for advancing workplace information literacy. *Australian Library Journal, 57,* 257–273.

Smalley, T. (2000). Investigating information age realities in the world of work. Available http://www.cabrillo.edu/~tsmalley/WorldOf Work.html

Travis, T. (2008). Librarians as agents of change: Working with curriculum committees using change agency theory. *New Directions for Teaching and Learning,* 114, 17–33.

Walsh, T. R. (2011). Evolution of an information competency requirement for undergraduates. *Journal of Web Librarianship, 5,* 3–23.

Whitmire, E. (2002). Academic library performance measures and undergraduates' library use and educational outcomes. *Library & Information Science Research, 24,* 107–128.

Wong, S. H. R., & Webb, T. D. (2011). Uncovering meaningful correlation between student academic performance and library material usage. *College & Research Libraries, 72,* 361–370.

Wu, D. (2008). Aligning information literacy with workplace expectations. 12th Biennial CARL Conference. Irvine, CA.

Tiffini A. Travis
Director of Information Literacy & Outreach Services, University Library
California State University, Long Beach
Voice: 562-985-7850
Fax: 562-985-1703
ttravis@csulb.edu

Deepa, S., & Seth, M. (2013). Do soft skills matter? Implications for educators based on recruiters' perspective. *The IUP Journal of Soft Skills, 7(1), 7–20.*

Engage via Research Prediction

- What percentage of mid-level and top-level executives believe soft skills are essential to success?
- Which soft skills are most valued by employers?

Read for Key Points

- What question did the researcher seek to answer? (Introduction)
- Who participated in the study and what did the participants do? (Method)
- What was the answer to the research question? (Results)

Critically Think about the Research

- Why do most employers report graduates coming to the world of work without having developed essential soft skills?
- How can college students put this research into practice? How are soft skills developed?
- How might the value of soft skills vary based on culture or discipline?

Build Information Literacy Skills

- Are these findings consistent with research studies conducted in different countries, including the United States, and across different disciplines?
- How do colleges and universities teach soft skills?
- What strategies or approaches work best at helping students build and strengthen soft skills?

Research Study

Deepa S* and Manisha Seth**.
Do Soft Skills Matter? - Implications for Educators Based on Recruiters' Perspective

Soft skills are very critical in the workplace today. These skills mirror the ability to communicate and interact with others. They are unique because they emphasize on action. They have become indispensable for every person in the present context. This paper deals with the significance of soft skills for getting a job and for further promotions and progress in the workplace. People who are flexible and have the zeal to understand and learn new technologies are sought after by organizations as part of their growth process. The need to provide training in soft skills is seriously being considered today. This study is an attempt to find out the importance that middle to top level executives, who are involved in recruiting employees, attach to soft skills.

Introduction

Organizations today have transformed into places where people cannot function in seclusion. Teamwork or group work is the need of the day in most industries. There are many organizations that do not necessarily design jobs on the basis of a team. Nonetheless, they require a fair amount of interaction between people within and across functional realms to successfully carry out a piece of work. The opportune discoveries made through the Hawthorne studies are now accepted as basic and universal principles of life in any organization. In this setting, soft skills have become indispensable to function competently in any interpersonal relationship.

'Soft skills' is an umbrella term covering various survival skills such as communication and interpersonal skills, emotional intelligence, leadership qualities, team skills, negotiation skills, time and stress management and business etiquettes. In recent years, the corporate world felt that soft skills are crucial at the workplace and its training must be a part of the curriculum during education. In career terms, soft skills soften the edges and provide a competitive advantage over others. However, those who ignore this critical aspect of personality learn its importance the hard way when their promotion is overlooked.

Soft skills are "attitudes and behaviors displayed in interactions among individuals that affect the outcomes of various interpersonal encounters" (Muir, 2004).

These are skills that refer to the ability to communicate and interact with other employees in a positive manner.

Soft skills are necessary in the workplace for professional success. They are vital at every level of an organization if it is to function smoothly and productively. Hard skills are technical competencies and domain knowledge, while soft skills are a combination of people skills, interpersonal skills, communication skills and emotional intelligence. Companies search for a mélange of both soft and hard skills among their employees to deliver goods and services effectively to their clients. It is rightly said that people rise in organizations because of their hard skills and fall due to a shortage of soft skills.

Kelly Pierce points out in "eSight Trend Watch: Increased Value in Soft Skills," that "There is a growing recognition that interpersonal skills are not simply helpful in business today; they are essential in today's highly focused, downsized and streamlined organizations where people tend to work in a series of small, often temporary workgroups or teams organized to accomplish short-term objectives." He lists such qualities as "attitude, initiative, cooperation, teamwork, communication, perception" among the skills that are valued in the contemporary workplace.

Soft skills deal with these behavioral aspects relevant in personal and corporate life. Today, we find employers taking hard skills as a given or as the basic requirement

* Assistant Professor, Managerial Communication, Indian Institute of Management, Kozhikode, Kerala, India; and is the corresponding author. E-mail: deepa@iimk.ac.in

** Assistant Professor, Human Resource Management, Jaipuria Institute of Management, Lucknow, Uttar Pradesh, India. E-mail: manisha.seth@jaipuria.ac.in

and the soft skills 'including communicating, relationship building, work ethic and problem solving' (Johnson, 2006), as an important consideration in deciding upon the choice of a candidate for any job.

The purpose of this paper is to understand the prospective employers' perception about importance of soft skills while hiring MBAs and provide information that may be utilized by educators to enhance the soft skills of students entering the workforce.

Literature Review

Rainsbury *et al.* (2002) categorized the competencies of superior managers identified by Spencer and Spencer (1993) as hard skills or soft skills. Only three of the 20 competencies were classified as hard skills, while the remaining 17 were organized as soft skills. The categories of soft skills, include achievement and action, impact and influence, managerial (team management and developing others), and personal effectiveness.

The last few years have witnessed a growing awareness and a need to identify the intangible factors which play a very important role in an individual's success at the workplace. Varied studies have been done in the past related to such areas. Many experts have in the past worked on and concluded that these extra skills which help to attain success at the workplace are certainly precious. Jacobs and Marshall discussed the importance of the definite class of skills that allow value additions to a person's worth. Though none of them uses the term, they actually deem it to be soft skill.

For decades, the center of management was on the so-called 'hard' skills, i.e., the emphasis centered on technical skills imperative to effectively perform within the organization. These skills tended to be more job-specific or more closely related to the actual task being performed.

Today, employers look for managers with the vital soft skills. These skills tend to be more generic in nature. In other words, these are skills strategic to effective performance across all job categories. And these soft skills have come to play an even more central role in management positions in today's setting. As the world has changed and the nature of work has changed, the skill set required for managers has also undergone a change. Studies by Stanford Research Institute and the Carnegie Mellon Foundation among Fortune 500 CEOs found that 75% of long-term job success depended on people skills and only 25% on technical skills. In fact, this stands true at other levels as well. For effective performance in the workplace, companies need their employees to not only have domain knowledge, technical and analytical skills, but also skills to deal with the external world of clients, customers, vendors, the government and public, and to work in a collaborative manner with their colleagues.

The annual rankings of MBA colleges often place communication and interpersonal skills as the most decisive skills needed for success in the corporate world.

Distinguished academician Prof. Henry Mintzberg, while speaking on the importance of soft skills for MBAs, referred to the crucial 'soft skills'—leadership, teamwork, communication and the ability to think 'outside the box' of a discipline—that separate the rest in the management world.

In a poll on Melcrum's Black Belt Training website, the skill that was voted the most vital for internal communicators to master in order to carry out their roles with utmost efficacy was building effective relationships.

Other surveys and studies also show that employers are often more concerned about soft skills or attitudes rather than technical knowledge or competencies. Empirical studies of work find that employers and workers also feel generic skills, such as problem solving, communications and the ability to work in teams, are more significant for workplace success. Another study on developing soft skills in vocation high school graduates talks about the importance of developing soft skills in students for their betterment and future career growth.

A 2007 study of recruiters found that communication skills are the most desired characteristics needed in a candidate for an ideal job.

According to a survey by Harvard University, 80% achievements in career are determined by soft skills and only 20% by hard skills. In the book, *Lesson from the Top* by Neff and Citrin, the duo talk about 10 top success tips, out of which eight are concerned with soft skills and only two criteria talk about hard skills.

Similarly, a literature review undertaken by researchers to understand best practices revealed that soft skills are given much importance by the employers worldwide. Luthans *et al.* (1985 and 1998), on the basis of their study conducted on more than 450 managers, ascertained that the average managers spend most of their time in traditional management activities, whereas in the case of managers who were successful (defined in terms of speed of promotion within their organization), networking skills made the largest contribution to their success. In the case of effective managers (defined in terms of the quantity and quality of their performance and the satisfaction and commitment of their subordinates and coworkers), communication skills made the largest contribution.

A literature review undertaken by researchers to understand best practices made known that soft skills are given much importance by the employers universally. According to them, it was found that in IT companies, projects failed not due to the lack of technical skills but due to the lack of interpersonal and communication skills. Bill (2004) showed that communication skills, self-esteem and work ethics are the main factors that determine one's achievement in his/her work. Several other works, especially on customer-focused services, have shown that customer-focused soft skills can make a big contribution to profitability even in industries regarded as highly technical. To achieve success in today's job market, employees need a combination of occupation-specific hard skills and soft skills.

According to Duncan and Dunifon (1998), "soft skills are as good a predictor of labor market success as level of formal education". Similarly, commenting on the need for high school students to develop such skills, experts have agreed on several hard skills. And over and above that, the two most important soft skills are the ability to communicate effectively and the ability to work productively with people from different backgrounds. Thus, the review of literature shows that there is a need for other types of skills than the routine hard skills to succeed in the work place, but none has completely and satisfactorily understood the skill requirements; and there is limited research done to generate specific guidance that is useful to educators and students.

According to Harvey and Knight (1996), "employers are not looking for trainees but people equipped to learn and deal with change. Employers want graduates who are adaptable and flexible, who can communicate well and relate to a wide range of people, who are aware of, but not indoctrinated into, the world of work and the culture of organizations, and who, most importantly, have inquiring minds, are willing and quick to learn, are critical, can synthesize and are innovative."

Contrary to the popular belief, soft skills do make a difference in the business world (Workforce, 1999). Even though managers still need typical techniques taught in MBA programs, they need additional tools to be effective. Today's managers need a variety of soft skills in communication, negotiation, and team building to effectively manage technological change and corporate stress resulting from downsizing and rapid growth (Deverell, 1994). Another study conducted by Caudrin (1999) revealed that while hiring MBAs, corporations seek the three most desired capabilities—communication skills, interpersonal skills and initiative—all of which are elements of emotional intelligence.

For a long time, recruitment and selection processes concentrated on finding people with the right technical or domain expertise. The focus was on the so-called hard skills. So, the requirements normally spelt out the area and the technical expertise required for a job. The person-job fit was measured typically on the basis of these qualifications. Later, employers realized that while the core skills are present, successful interpersonal relationships played a major role in achieving results. The success of a department or an organization depended on domain knowledge and also as much, if not more, on the ability of a group of individuals to work in a team and optimize their individual resources.

The 21st century workforce has experienced tremendous changes due to advances in technology; consequently, the 'old way' of doing things may be effective but not efficient (Redmann and Kotrlik, 2004). The National Business Education Association (NBEA) stated that the shortage of skills confronting today's dynamic workforce goes beyond the academic and hands-on occupational skills. Therefore, the best way to prepare potential employees for tomorrow's workforce is to develop not only technical, but also human-relation abilities (Policies Commission for Business and Economic Education (PCBEE), 2000).

Defining 'soft skills', Perreault (2004) stated that these are personal qualities, attributes, or the level of commitment of a person that set him or her apart from other individuals who may have similar skills and experience. According to James and James (2004), 'soft skills' is a new way to describe a set of abilities or talents that an individual can bring to the workplace. Soft skills characterize certain career attributes that individuals may possess such as team skills, communication skills, leadership skills, customer service skills and problem solving skills. "Employers Value Communication and Interpersonal Abilities" (2004) suggests that one who communicates effectively, gets along with others, embraces teamwork, takes initiative, and has strong work ethics is considered to have an accomplished a set of soft skills. Sutton (2002) found that soft skills are so important that employers identify them as 'the number one differentiator' for job applicants in all types of industries (p. 40). According to Sutton, soft skills have become extremely important in all types of occupations. Glenn (2008) added that hiring individuals who possess soft skills is instrumental for high-performing organizations to retain a competitive edge. Wilhelm (2004) agreed and claimed that employers rate soft skills highest in importance for entry-level success in the workplace.

Literature supports the conclusion that proficiency in soft skills is extremely important from employers' perspective. However, many employees in business are reported to be lacking in soft skills. Also, literature revealed that research is needed in the area of soft skills so that enhanced instructional methodology may be developed and applied by business educators.

The paradigm shift in the 21st century workforce has forced employees to be well armed with soft skills (Ganzel, 2001). James and James (2004) confirmed that soft skills have become extremely crucial even in technical environments. This endorses the view of Evenson (1999) who believed that equipping students with soft skills could make the difference in obtaining and retaining the jobs for which they have been prepared.

The NBEA believes that skills emphasized in the 20th century must be refocused. To ensure success, students entering the 21st century workforce must possess nontechnical soft skills along with technical competence (PCBEE, 2000). A complex labor market has been generated due to the multifaceted 21st century business world; therefore, organizations are seeking versatile individuals, who possess professional skills, even for entry-level jobs (Employers Value Communication and Interpersonal Abilities, 2004). According to Christopher (2006), employers want graduates with strong interpersonal abilities. Quite a lot of researchers (Sutton, 2002; Glenn, 2003; NBEA, 2004; and Wilhelm, 2004) substantiated that mastery of soft skills is instrumental to success for individuals entering the 21st century workforce.

With time, companies aren't just assessing their current staff and future recruits on their business skills. They are now evaluating them on a multitude of soft skills like how well they relate to and communicate with others. It is a bit shocking and somewhat disturbing when someone exhibits the old autocratic style of bullying management tactics.

Measuring these soft skills is not easy. But in the most progressive companies, managers are looking for people's ability to communicate clearly and openly, and to listen and respond empathetically. They also want them to have equally well-honed written skills so that their correspondence (including e-mails) does not undo all the good work their face-to-face communication creates.

A few companies are untouched by the ever-widening authority of other cultures and good soft skills ease better communication and people's ability to manage differences efficiently. Already everyone has some form of soft skills (probably a lot more than they realize). They just need to look at areas in their personal life where they get on with others, feel confident in the way they interact, can solve problems, are good at encouraging, can network with the best of them. All these skills are soft skills and all of them are transferable to the workplace.

It is unfortunate that people lightly esteem the significance of soft skills. In fact, the concept of soft skills is a developing ambit that people must take seriously; people have to be educated about them. Whenever a new discipline surfaces, people resist and mostly do not respect it because there is no strong research to substantiate its relevance. However, over a period of time people start accepting and respecting the discipline. For example, there were many people who initially did not take management as a discipline seriously and expressed their reservations. Today, management as a discipline is a reality, having a sacred and respectable position like many other disciplines in the world. Similarly, soft skills will evolve as a discipline during the course of time when more research is done. It is often difficult to quantify soft skills (unlike hard skills), but soft skills are both intrapersonal and interpersonal competencies that determine a person's ability to gel well with others and excel in the corporate world (Rao, 2012).

Research Methodology

Data regarding the views of employers and managers involved in interviewing and recruiting people and their expectations from new recruits was collected with the help of a questionnaire (Appendix), comprising questions on how much importance is being given to soft skills while recruiting new persons or experienced persons. The respondents were asked to rate the seven broad categories of skills included in 'soft skills' and the typical soft skills they look for when recruiting. About 160 mid-level to top level executives from about 4-5 sectors located in Delhi, Noida, Nasik, Lucknow, Indore and Mumbai were sent questionnaires. 135 responses were received, out of which 100 were found complete in all respects. Finally, the data collected through the questionnaire was analyzed and the results were compared to the previously held beliefs and theories. Telephonic discussions with some recruiters also provided insights into their perception of soft skills.

Findings and Analysis

The findings were generally on expected lines, with 86% respondents agreeing that soft skills are indeed very important to succeed at the work place (Figure 1).

But when asked about the quality of new entrants entering the workforce today, 60% said that the new entrants do not possess the necessary soft skills to succeed at the workplace. And an overwhelming majority, that is 82% respondents, agreed that there were gaps between the industry requirements and the products churned out by the colleges and universities of today. On the question whether they thought that the new entrants can acquire soft skills on joining a good organization, 50% felt that they would. And 85% strongly felt that adding soft skills in college curricula will improve the quality of the workforce.

When asked what ratio they would offer to soft skills and work experience while recruiting, 68% of the respondents stated 60:40 if it is an entry level job, 50:50 if it is a mid level management position and 60:40 in case of a higher management position.

The respondents were also asked to divide a percentage score of 100 among the six must-have soft skills to succeed at the workplace. The results showed that communication skills received the maximum weightage of 22%, while interpersonal skills followed a close second with 20%, teamwork and leadership qualities

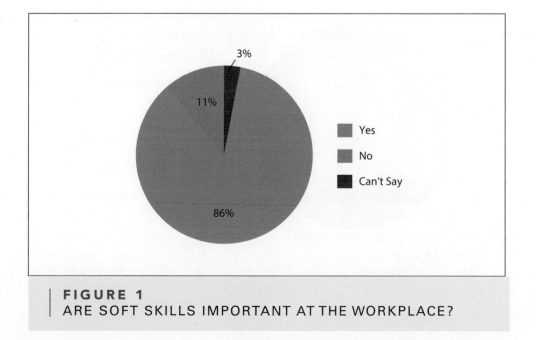

FIGURE 1
ARE SOFT SKILLS IMPORTANT AT THE WORKPLACE?

received 16% and 15%, respectively, time management got 13%, while conflict management received 14% weightage (Figure 2).

While expressing his thoughts on how much importance is attached to soft skills while recruiting candidates for entry level jobs in Management, Himojyoti Sengupta, Human Resources - North, Reliance General Insurance Company Ltd., opines, "The said skill set is very much important for an entry level position but it is hard to find. The same gives an edge over other candidates." When asked whether the organization got the candidates with required soft skills, he stated that they needed to provide the necessary training.

In this regard, Khyati Seth, Assistant Manager - HR, Abhitech IT Solutions Private Limited states, "Soft skills are a very important aspect considered while selecting a candidate, especially for the freshers. As observed, the quality of the candidates is deteriorating day by day, they lack basic skills like communication and social behavior". She further says, "We do not get candidates with the required set of soft skills. Also, the time and resources involved in the training of the candidates are very high".

Mohit Kumar, AVP - HR, Aditya Birla Group said, "We hire candidates from management institutes under Young Leaders' program. We have a competency framework in our organization. We believe that soft skills like communication, influencing, teamwork, getting things done, developing self and others are very important for people to successfully perform and excel in the various roles in the organization. Proficiency levels for these competencies for various roles in job hierarchy are very much defined, including that for entry level roles. We look forward to people demonstrating these competencies appropriately while we make a hiring decision." He added, "We get the candidates with required soft skills. Training is a continuous process and it is equally important for people having these competencies to further hone their skills to the next level."

Tanmay Panda, Head HR, National Payment Corporation of India, said that soft skills are indeed very important while recruiting candidates for entry level jobs in management. He added that they are generally required to train the employees in the crucial soft skills.

Nidhi Bhatnagar, Human Resources, Fidelity Info Services, while expressing her views on the importance of soft skills in recruiting stated, "It is always important to be really good at soft skills. However, the weightage of this parameter actually depends on the role that one is appearing for. For instance if one has appeared for a HR job, soft skills will be given high weightage along with the other prerequisites, lack of soft skills might even result in elimination/rejection, since a HR professional

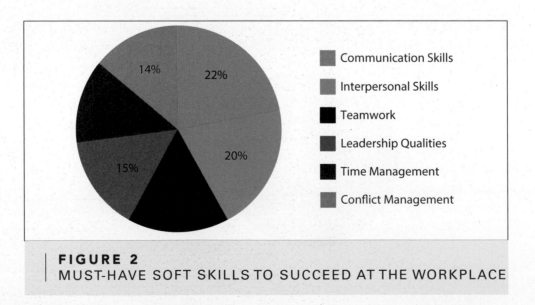

FIGURE 2
MUST-HAVE SOFT SKILLS TO SUCCEED AT THE WORKPLACE

needs to cater to the aspirations and emotions of human capital, it is important that one has excellent soft skills. On the other hand, if one applies for a sales job, soft skills need to be modified in a way where the person is able to crack a deal, the conviction required over there will be slightly different, the weightage of soft skills parameter might differ/might be less as well, however it will carry its due importance".

On probing whether they got candidates with the required soft skills or they needed to train them, Nidhi Bhatnagar said, "We cannot expect excellent soft skills in candidates applying for entry level jobs, as it will be quite unfair to them since they do not hold a practical exposure to the corporate world. We certainly believe in training the candidate in case we feel that he/she has all the prerequisites for the role and needs slight polishing on soft skills. We too would not want to lose such good resources, yes; they need to have that aptitude and attitude to learn which paves way for us to make them shine as any other seasoned employees. Training them on soft skills is something which is always an option as that is a very softer aspect which can be evolved in a person to bring about that desired change in one's personality, both professionally and personally."

Conclusion

Recruitment managers respect and expect technical expertise. Results show that they do prefer people with experience, but at the same time, they also look for certain other qualities in them. However, technical or the so-called hard skills soon become outdated when there is no motivation to keep learning new ones. So, they also look for people who are flexible and have the passion to appreciate and learn new technologies as part of their growth process. And as Beck and Yaeger pointed out, "The ability to effectively communicate with the managers, superiors, bosses and coworkers plays a definite role in workplace success." Furthermore, "the interpersonal skills, alignment with the corporate culture, the ability to work as an effective and contributing team member and the political savvy to know how to get things done in the organization" also determine a person's long-term success in an organization. Therefore, our results have shown that in generic terms,

hiring managers are not happy with the new workforce coming out of the colleges and they do think that they should be much better equipped with soft skills in addition to hard skills. On the basis of these results, we have made an attempt to provide to the educators a guideline to design the soft skills course curriculum in such a way so as to bridge the gap that exists between the existing one and the industry expectations. The results also pointed out that the basic skills should include good communication style along with the ability to work in teams and ability to get things done on time as well as manage conflicts tactfully.

This study may be quite useful to business educators because the findings reported help to recognize the most important workforce skills. In addition, this information may allow educators to more effectively include employability skills in their courses.

Scope for Further Research

This study was basically a preliminary (probing) research to tap into the minds of recruiters across Indian companies and find out the importance of soft skills in their scheme of things, particularly the recruitment process. Although an attempt was made to take samples from across India from the banking, insurance, automobile, real estate and retail sectors, there is a lot of scope for further research. All these companies have a more urgent need for employees having better soft skills. Research can be extended to these as well as other sectors like hospitality and aviation, to further look into the difference these skills would make to their career graph. Besides, it would be interesting to know how the educators feel about the industry requirement of teaching soft skills at the college/b-school level. The desire to raise academic performance and, at the same time, provide opportunities for students to be successful at the workplace creates sizeable challenges for educators. And expanding the curriculum to meet the new skill demands raises several questions such as: What should be the college and university curriculum that can inculcate problem solving, teamwork, interpersonal and communication skills in students? Further research in this area could provide exciting ideas to bridge the existing gap between education curricula and industry demands. ∎

BIBLIOGRAPHY

Buhler P M (2001), "The Growing Importance of Soft Skills in the Workplace", *Supervision,* Vol. 62, No. 6, p. 13, available at http://connection.ebscohost.com/c7 articles/4514272/growing-importance-soft-skills-workplace

Caudrin S (1999), "The Hard Case for Soft Skills", *Workforce,* Vol. 78, No. 7, pp. 60–64.

Christopher D A (2006), "Building Better Communicators: Integrating Writing into Business Communications Courses", *Business Education Forum,* Vol. 61, No. 2, pp. 40–43.

Coplin B (2004), "For New Graduates, "Soft-Skills'' Are The Secret Weapon in Job Hunt", June 9, available at http://usatoday30.usatodaycom/news/opinion/editorials/ 2004-06-09-coplin_x.htm

Deverell J (1994), "The Most Valuable Quality in a Manager", *Fortune,* Vol. 136, No. 12, pp. 279–280.

Duncan G J and Dunifon R (1998), "Soft Skills and Long-Run Labor Market Success", *Research in Labor Economics,* Vol. 17, pp. 123–150, JAI Press, London.

"Employers Value Communication and Interpersonal Abilities" (2004), *Keying In,* Vol. 14, No. 3, pp.1–6.

Evenson R (1999), "Soft Skills, Hard Sell. Techniques: Making Education and Career Connections", Vol. 74, No. 3, pp. 29–31.

Ganzel R (2001), "Hard Training for Soft Skills", *Training,* Vol. 38, No. 6, pp. 56–60.

Glenn J L (2003), "Business Success Often Depends on Mastering the 'Sixth R' Relationship Literacy", *Business Education Forum,* Vol. 58, No. 1, pp. 9–13.

Glenn J L (2008), "The 'New' Customer Service Model: Customer Advocate, Company Ambassador", *Business Education Forum,* Vol. 62, No. 4, pp. 7–13.

Harvey L and Knight P T (1996), *Transforming Higher Education,* Open University Press, SRHE.

http://www.melcrum.com/products/training_courses/bbinternational/index. html?mxmroi=23962826/24254731/false

http://wwwsoftskillsindia.com/why develop softskills/importanceofsoftskills.html

Huba M E and Freed J E (2000), *Learner Centered Assessment on College Campuses,* Allyn and Bacon, MA.

Information Technology Association of America (2004), 'Adding Value... Growing Careers: The Employment Outlook in Today's Increasingly Competitive IT Job Market", Annual Workforce Development Survey, September.

Jacobs J (1969), *The Economy of Cities,* Vintage, New York.

James R F and James M L (2004), "Teaching Career and Technical Skills in a 'Mini' Business World", *Business Education Forum,* Vol. 59, No. 2, pp. 39–41.

Johnson J (2006), "More Employers are Focusing on Soft Skills When Seeking out New Employees", *Colorado Springs Business Journal (CO),* September 29. Retrieved on November 25, 2008, from Regional Business News database.

Kane T E (2009), "Soft Skills are Hard and Critical to Career Success", available at http://wwwchartresource.com/featurekane.htm.

Kennedy and Kathy (2005), "Integrating Technical Skills and Soft Skills to Ensure Student Success", *Best Practices,* Summer, pp. 1–3.

Luthans F (1988), "Successful vs Effective Real Managers", *The Academy of Management Executive,* Vol. 11, No. 2, pp. 127–132.

Luthans F, Rosenkrantz S A and Hennessey H W (1985), "What do Successful Managers Really Do? An Observation Study of Managerial Activities", *Journal of Applied Behavioral Science,* Vol. 21, No. 3, pp. 255–270.

Marshall A (1890), *Principles of Economics,* MacMillan, London.

Meenakshi S (2009), "How Important are Soft Skills from the Recruiter's Perspective", *The IUP Journal of Soft Skills,* Vol. III, No. 2.

Muir C (2004), "Learning Soft Skills at Work", *Business Communication Quarterly,* Vol. 67, No. 1, pp. 95–101.

Perreault H (2004), "Business Educators Can Take a Leadership Role in Character Education", *Business Education Forum,* Vol. 59, No. 1, pp. 23–24.

Polack-Wahl J A (2000), "It is Time to Stand up and Communicate", Proc. 30th ASEE/ IEEE Frontiers in Educ. Conf., pp. F1G-16-F1G-21, Kansas City, USA.

Policies Commission for Business and Economic Education (2000), "This we Believe About Teaching Soft Skills: Human Relations, Self-Management, and Workplace Enhancement", Statement No. 67.

Rainsbury E, Hodges D, Burchell N and Lay M (2002), "Ranking Workplace Competencies: Student and Graduate Perceptions", *Asia-Pacific Journal of Cooperative Education,* Vol. 3, No. 2, pp. 8–18.

Rao M S (2012), "Soft Versus Hard Skills", *T+D;* Vol. 66, No. 5, pp. 48–51.

Redmann D H and Kotrlik J W (2004), "Technology Integration into the TeachingLearning Process by Business Education Teachers", *The Delta Pi Epsilon Journal,* Vol. 46, No. 2, pp. 76–91.

Sireesha M (2009), "Use of Portfolios in a Soft Skills Course", *The IUP Journal of Soft Skills,* Vol. III, No. 1, pp. 7–18.

Stasz C, Ramsey K, Eden R *et al.* (1996), *Workplace Skills in Practice: Case Studies of Technical Work* (MDS-773), National Center for Research in Vocational Education, University of California, Berkeley.

Sutton N (2002), "Why Can't We All Just Get Along?", *Computing Canada,* Vol. 28, No. 16, p. 20.

Thomas Neff J and Citrin James M (1999), *Lessons from the Top: The Search for America's Best Business Leaders,* p. 448, Doubleday, New York.

Timm J A (2005), "Preparing Students for the Next Employment Revolution", *Business Education Forum,* Vol. 60, No. 2, pp. 55–59.

Wilhelm W J (2004), "Determinants of Moral Reasoning: Academic Factors, Gender, Richness of Life Experiences and Religious Preferences", *The Delta Pi Epsilon Journal,* Vol. XLVI, No. 2, pp. 105–121.

Appendix

Questionnaire

Name (Optional): Mr./Ms.: _____

Designation: _____

Organization: _____

Location:- _____

Gender: _____

Age Group (Years):　20-30 ☐　　30-40 ☐　　　　40-50 ☐　　　　　>50 ☐

Mark your perception on the following statements where 1 - Strongly Agree, 3 - Neutral and 5 - Strongly Disagree

S. No.	Statements	1	2	3	4	5
1.	Soft skills are crucial to achieve success at the workplace.					
2.	Soft skills are important criteria when interviewing job applicants.					
3.	Soft skills are more important than experience in similar position.					
4.	New entrants/joiners possess the required soft skills to be successful at the workplace.					
5.	There is a gap between the industry requirements and the products of the colleges today.					
6.	Recruiters are satisfied with the current workforce available for their industry/sector.					
7.	Soft skills can be acquired even after joining a good company or an organization.					
8.	Adding soft skills in the college curricula will provide better equipped personnel.					

What ratio would you offer to Soft skills and work experience?

S. No.	Statements	40:60	50:50	60:40
1.	For considering lower level management positions			
2.	For considering middle level management positions			
3.	For considering higher management positions			

Rate the following soft skills in order of their importance (1-6) with 1 being the topmost essential skill and 6 the least essential that a new job applicant/fresher must possess to join an organization:

S. No.	Soft Skill	Order					
		1	2	3	4	5	6
1.	Team Work						
2.	Conflict Management						
3.	Communication Skills						
4.	Time Management						
5.	Interpersonal Skills						
6.	Leadership Qualities						

Reference # 50J-2013-03-01-01

Oliver, J., & Kowalczyk, C. (2013). Improving student group marketing presentations: A modified Pecha Kucha approach. *Marketing Education Review*, 23(1), 55–58.

Engage via Research Prediction

- Does the Pecha Kucha presentation approach work better than traditional PowerPoint presentations?

Read for Key Points

- What question did the researcher seek to answer? (Introduction)
- Who participated in the study and what did the participants do? (Method)
- What was the answer to the research question? (Results)

Critically Think about the Research

- Why do you think the Pecha Kucha approach resulted in better performance? What are the most important elements of the Pecha Kucha approach?
- Would the results be different for different disciplines or different purposes?
- How does this research finding connect to Mayer's (2009) multimedia principles?

Build Information Literacy Skills

- What additional evidence exists for Pecha Kucha? What does the research say about effective PowerPoint presentations?
- What type of presentation works best in the world of work?

Research Study

Jason Oliver* and Christine Kowalczyk**. Improving student group marketing presentations: a modified pecha kucha approach

Student presentations can often seem like a formality rather than a lesson in representing oneself or group in a professional manner. To improve the quality of group presentations, the authors modified the popular presentation style of Pecha Kucha (20 slides, 20 seconds per slide) for marketing courses to help students prepare and deliver professional business presentations. Data were collected and analyzed from marketing student presentations that used two different presentation styles: the proposed modified Pecha Kucha and traditional PowerPoint presentations. The authors' modified version of Pecha Kucha resulted in higher individual and group assessments along with other key findings relevant to marketing courses.

Students can often view project presentations as a formality, something that they just have to do as a requirement of a course. This can lead to behaviors such as reading from PowerPoint slides, including too much text on the slides, presenting for more than the allotted time or not enough time, and not knowing who should be presenting next. These are only a few of the challenging issues professors are confronted with when marketing students make group presentations.

As marketing graduates enter the business world, employers are seeking more than just marketing knowledge and skills, but also effective communication, presentation, and teamwork skills (Taylor 2003; Young and Murphy 2003). Team selling has become a popular approach, and the importance of effective public speaking, both individually and as a group, has never been more crucial. Marketing students may need to present or sell ideas to clients, customers, as well as internal and external stakeholders. However, many students are not natural presenters; for some, it is a skill that must be learned (Anderson and Anderson 2010).

In order to better prepare marketing students for their careers, recommendations have been made to enhance the effectiveness of student oral presentations through a comprehensive and systematic approach (Bonnici and Luthar 1996; Calcich and Weilbaker 1992; Haley 1993; Martin 1990). These recommendations included discussions with the instructor, the number of presentations per semester, as well as dress rehearsals. In addition, research has suggested how student presentations should be evaluated by instructors and their peers (Carroll 2006). To our knowledge, no marketing article addresses the modified Pecha Kucha presentation style in undergraduate marketing courses.

Pecha Kucha (which means "chitchat" in Japanese) was created in 2003 in Tokyo by Astrid Klein and Mark Dytham of Klein-Dytham Architecture, who hoped to attract people to their special events venue. The Pecha Kucha Night events allowed young designers an opportunity to show their work in a concise and fast-paced environment. Each presenter was only allowed 20 PowerPoint slides to be shown for 20 seconds each on a timer, limiting the presentation time to 6 minutes and 40 seconds. Ideas were explained visually with graphics and little text. Since 2003, Pecha Kucha Nights have become a worldwide phenomenon in more than 460 cities worldwide because of its fast-paced and powerful imagery, which often yields entertaining, energetic presentations (www.pechakucha.org). We wanted to bring that energy into the classroom and address the other presentation challenges. Therefore, we decided to adapt and utilize this unique presentation style in three different marketing courses.

***Jason Oliver** (Ph.D., University of Rhode Island), Assistant Professor, Department of Marketing and Supply Chain Management, College of Business, East Carolina University, Greenville, NC, oliverj@ecu.edu.

Christine Kowalczyk (Ph.D., University of Memphis), Assistant Professor, Department of Marketing and Supply Chain Management, College of Business, East Carolina University, Greenville, NC, kowalczykc@ecu.edu.

The Need to Innovate Student Presentations

In the business world, presentation skills are imperative. This innovation of using Pecha Kucha is one way to address the need to improve the quality of student marketing presentations. The Pecha Kucha format requires students to practice presenting so they can more effectively and efficiently address their projects' main points. In the past, we observed students frequently spending too much time talking about their background information and not enough time talking about critical facts, key takeaways, and their analyses.

Further, we noted that students were not as well prepared as they should be for professional presentations in class. Students frequently used PowerPoint slides as note cards, turning their backs to the audience as they read from the slides, or relied heavily on actual note cards. They also stumbled over transitions, often filling the awkward moment, where they were unsure who was supposed to go next, with laughter that changed the professional tone of the presentation. Therefore, Pecha Kucha was introduced as a group presentation style to strengthen presentation skills and encourage more extensive preparation.

As mentioned, the traditional Pecha Kucha presentation style utilizes 20 PowerPoint slides in 6 minutes and

TABLE 1 **Original and Author-Modified Pecha Kucha**

	Original Pecha Kucha	Modified Pecha Kucha
Number of Presenters	1	3-5
Time per Slide	20 seconds	Variable
PowerPoint Setup	Timed slides	Use of remote to advance slides
Total Time	6 minutes, 40 seconds	6 minutes, 40 seconds

Marketing Education Review, vol. 23, no. 1 (spring 2013), pp. 55–58.
© 2013 Society for Marketing Advances. All rights reserved.
Permissions: www.copyright.com
ISSN 1052-8008 (print) / ISSN 2153-9987 (online)
DOI: 10.2753/MER1052-8008230109

40 seconds with each slide only being presented for 20 seconds. In addition, Pecha Kucha was intended for individual presentations. We hypothesized the Pecha Kucha approach would increase student preparation and force them to focus more on the key arguments and the solutions instead of background information that was less critical to the presentation. We also hypothesized that students would spend more time preparing for the Pecha Kucha presentations since this format took them out of their comfort zone, where they used slides as note cards or used note cards as a crutch.

The Teaching Innovation: Modifying Pecha Kucha

The innovation is a modified version of the presentation style Pecha Kucha. The basic rules of Pecha Kucha are 20 slides to be presented in 6 minutes and 40 seconds, resulting in 20 seconds per slide. Traditionally, Pecha Kucha was completed as an individual presentation via timed PowerPoint slides that are automatically advanced.

We modified the traditional rules of Pecha Kucha to be used in group presentations. We wanted to make sure the presentations were engaging, concise, and visual. Twenty slides were still the requirement. However, based on previous research that suggested the time limitation was too restrictive and had a negative impact on communication effectiveness (e.g., Lehtonen 2011), we modified the rules by allowing the time allotted per slide to vary as long as it did not affect the total presentation length of 6 minutes 40 seconds. In other words, the students could "borrow" time from one slide to focus more time on other important points. The students were also given the option to use a remote to advance the slides.

The students were encouraged to focus on the visual aspect of each slide, instead of text and bullet points, and to spend time on the main points rather than background information. For example, if a group project involved a new product or service, the slides would incorporate pictures that represented the new product or service. Sometimes the pictures were accompanied with a few bullet points to emphasize the most important parts of the project's presentation. Further, the students were encouraged to spend time together as a team to practice their Pecha Kucha presentations. Practicing their presentations built confidence and allowed the students to feel like experts on the marketing project. The specific adaptations to the original Pecha Kucha presentation style are summarized in Table 1.

The modification of the original Pecha Kucha format allowed for more flexibility in a classroom setting. It still kept the fast-paced presentation environment, but it did not force the students to structure the presentations at 20 seconds per slide. Although some students used the timing feature in PowerPoint, we observed that the more structured timing would often lead to students getting ahead or behind the slides, which distracted from the overall presentation, so using the remote was more effective than using the PowerPoint timing feature. The presentation remote allowed for more flexibility for possible interruptions, which may take place in the business environment. We also used the format for group presentations instead of individual presentations, which is where Pecha Kucha is more commonly used.

The course assignment required a paper along with a presentation. The paper provided an outlet for more in-depth background and analysis of the course-specific marketing project so the presentation could focus on key takeaways.The students presented the big idea(s), which allowed for more time for elaboration during the question-and-answer session. This process mimics professional presentations where the presenter may want the energy level to be high while presenting the key ideas, but also allow ample time for more detail to address client/colleague inquiries.

Because the Pecha Kucha presentation format is unique and new to many students, it was important to provide students with additional training and support prior to the final presentations. Guidelines were provided to each team, including the specific number of slides (20) and the time range for presenting the topic. Moreover, sample presentations via YouTube examples allowed students to view Pecha Kucha. Also, students were referred to the Pecha Kucha Web site (www.pechakucha.org), which provides more examples on a variety of topics as well as a listing of local Pecha Kucha nights, enabling students see live examples of this presentation style. A review of this information was completed several times throughout the semester. References were made throughout the semester to the development of the Pecha Kucha group presentations, reminding the students to capture favorite images and outline the main points of the presentation.

Assessment: Modified Pecha Kucha Contributes to Student Presentation Success

The modified Pecha Kucha presentation style was utilized in three different marketing courses: customer relationship management, sustainability marketing, and cultural environments in international business. Feedback on the modified Pecha Kucha was compared to feedback on more traditional group presentations in three other marketing courses: advertising and promotion management, marketing strategy, and consumer behavior. All the courses had a required group project and presentation.

After the group presentations, the students were provided with a questionnaire to evaluate their marketing presentations, including questions about their presentation work as individuals and as a group as well as their anticipated grade and practice time. There were also questions designed to measure respondent anxiety and vanity (physical concern, achievement concern). Finally, there were basic demographics (age, gender, class standing), and a few open-ended questions were included in the survey.

A total of 132 students responded to the survey. There were some responses from students who were assigned to a group project but did not actually participate in the presentation their responses were not included in our analysis. In addition, incomplete surveys were removed, resulting in a total of 114 usable responses (68 Pecha Kucha presentations and 46 traditional presentation).

The results were analyzed using ANCOVA (analysis of covariance). The students were asked to rate their performance based on their group presentation style (Pecha Kucha versus traditional PowerPoint presentations) compared to other group presentations that semester. The students responded to a seven-point Likert scale ranging from "much weaker" to "much stronger." Those assigned to the modified Pecha Kucha presentation style rated their individual performance to be significantly stronger ($M = 4.96$, $N = 68$) as compared to the traditional presentation group ($M = 4.01$, $N = 46$; $F = 6.47$, $p < 0.01$). The same was found when students were asked to evaluate their group's performance. The Pecha Kucha groups had stronger ratings ($M = 5.10$, $N = 68$) of relative group performance than the traditional presentation style ($M = 4.26$, $N = 46$; $F = 4.76$, $p < 0.01$). None of the covariates (anxiety, vanity/physical concern, vanity/achievement concern) were found to be significant in either model.

We also evaluated student's confidence by comparing their anticipated grades across presentation styles. Presentation style was a significant predictor of anticipated grade ($F = 3.810$, $p < 0.05$). Those who presented with the Pecha Kucha style anticipated a higher grade than those in the traditional presentation groups. The covariate vanity/physical concern was a significant predictor in this model ($p < 0.01$), which seemed to make sense given that the dependent variable was the student's confidence in anticipated grade.

Lastly, we compared the amount of presentation practice across presentations styles. When considering the number of hours students practiced for their presentations, the Pecha Kucha presentation style was found to be significantly different from the traditional presentation style ($F = 3.69$, $p < 0.05$). Students who presented with the Pecha Kucha style, on average, practiced more than two hours, whereas the traditional presentation groups practiced, on average, an hour or less. None of the covariates (anxiety, vanity/ physical concern, vanity/achievement concern) were found to be significant in the model.

The survey also allowed students to provide written comments about their presentation experiences. The following are highlighted comments:

I like the presentation method because it really forces you to prepare for presentations. You really have to know what you are going to say without having to rely on the slides.

I thought it went very well because I felt that everyone in the group was prepared.

Loved this new way of doing a presentation. I felt very prepared.

I thought the presentation ran a lot smoother and asked for more preparation time due to the necessary preparedness of the presentation style.

Instructor Perspective: Challenges to Adopting Pecha Kucha

Implementing Pecha Kucha into marketing courses came with some challenges. Utilizing the traditional Pecha Kucha was too restrictive for students; however, we found that adapting the guidelines for the students based on the courses and project needs made for more successful and engaging presentations. Even so, getting students to properly apply the principles of Pecha Kucha was challenging. Many times students are not provided with guidelines for marketing project presentations, and they prefer the flexibility, perhaps they feel they can "wing it." The modified Pecha Kucha format forced students to collaborate with their teams and spend more time practicing as a group. Further, the student audiences were more engaged in the presentations, asking questions and providing insight to the project presentations.

Challenges were not limited to the students. As professors, we were challenged with properly communicating the Pecha Kucha style to the students. At the time, there was a lack of student examples of Pecha Kucha in a classroom setting. We recorded outstanding examples to show in future semesters on a voluntary basis. In addition, we dedicated time throughout the semester to reiterate the guidelines of the Pecha Kucha style and meet with teams to review and practice their presentations. It should be noted that the resulting improvement in student presentations indicates that adapting this presentation style and spending the time during class to go over the structure was worth the effort.

Conclusion: Future Adaptation of Pecha Kucha For Marketing Courses

Utilizing a modified Pecha Kucha presentation style increased students' evaluations of their marketing project presentations. Pecha Kucha challenges students to focus on developing visually entertaining presentations.

It allows students to more critically think about the information they are presenting and focus on the main takeaways in the time frame they have to present. Any marketing course with business-related presentations could utilize this unique presentation format. It also develops a good work ethic for public speaking and presentations. The students who used our modified Pecha Kucha presentation style took time to prepare and work together. The students' hard work was evident in the quality level of their presentations as observed by their professors and in their own self-assessments.

This adaptation of the popular Pecha Kucha presentation style resolves concerns about Pecha Kucha restrictions hindering communication and should help bring marketing students' presentation skills to the next level. The students came across as experts who knew their subject matter inside and out, which was evident, even in 6 minutes and 40 seconds. ■

REFERENCES

Anderson, Randy J., and Lydia E. Anderson (2010), "Professorial Presentations: The Link Between the Lecture and Student Success in the Workplace," *Academy of Educational Leadership Journal*, 14 (1), 55–62.

Bonnici, Joseph, and Harsh K. Luthar (1996), "Peer Evaluated Debates: Developing Oral Communication Skills Through Marketing Case Studies," *Marketing Education Review*, 6 (2), 73–81.

Calcich, Stephen E., and Dan C. Weilbaker (1992), "Selecting the Optimum Number of In-Class Sales Presentations," *Marketing Education Review*, 2 (1), 31–33.

Carroll, Conor (2006), "Enhancing Reflective Learning Through Role-Plays: The Use of an Effective Sales Presentation Evaluation Form in Student Role-Plays," *Marketing Education Review*, 16 (1), 9–13.

Haley, Debra A. (1993), "Optimizing the Graduate Sales Management Seminar: Enhancing Presentation Skills and Expanding Knowledge," *Marketing Education Review*, 3 (2), 40–43.

Lehtonen, Miikka (2011), "Communicating Competence Through Pechakucha Presentations," *Journal of Business Communication*, 48 (4), 464–481.

Martin, Charles L. (1990), "Enhancing the Effectiveness of Student Oral Presentations," *Marketing Education Review*, 1 (November), 56–60.

Taylor, Kimberly A. (2003), "Marketing Yourself in the Competitive Job Market: An Innovative Course Preparing Undergraduates for Marketing Careers," *Journal of Marketing Education*, 25 (2), 97–107.

Young, Mark R., and J. William Murphy (2003), "Integrating Communications Skill into the Marketing Curriculum: A Case Study," *Journal of Marketing Education*, 25 (1), 57–70.

Coulter-Kern, R. G., Coulter-Kern, P. E., Schenkel, A. A., Walker, D. R., & Fogle, K. L. (2013). Improving student's understanding of career decision-making through service learning. *College Student Journal,* 47(2), 306–311.

Engage via Research Prediction

- Do college students who teach high school students about the career decision-making process through a service learning project have higher levels of career knowledge?

Read for Key Points

- What question did the researcher seek to answer? (Introduction)
- Who participated in the study and what did the participants do? (Method)
- What was the answer to the research question? (Results)

Critically Think about the Research

- How can you put these research findings into action?
- Do you think the results would be the same if the students who were not in the service learning project had to do an independent project on careers? Why or why not?
- Why do you think the students in the service learning group learned so much more than the other students?

Build Information Literacy Skills

- What are some of the other benefits of participating in service learning?
- What other strategies can college students use to help them make good career decisions?

Research Study

Coulter-Kern, R. G., Coulter-Kern, P. E., Schenkel, A. A., Walker, D. R., & Fogle, K. L. (2013). Improving Student's Understanding of Career Decision-Making Through Service Learning

This study examines the impact of an experiential service-learning project designed to help high school students begin to choose a career path and increase college students' understanding about how to make career decisions. In the study, two groups of college students attended information sessions on career advising. The first group then helped provide career information to high school students as part of a service project in a college class. The second group did not help provide career information to high school students. Posttest comparisons of the two groups of college students indicated that college students who participated in the service project showed significantly more understanding of career decision-making than students who had not participated in the service project.

As technology and globalization progress, job opportunities are continually changing, and for college students, deciding on a career in this rapidly changing environment is a daunting task. As challenging as this task might be, it is one of the most influential decisions we make in our lives. Hackett and Betz (1995) noted, "There are few other decisions that exert as profound an influence on people's lives as the choice of a field of work or career" (p. 249). However, career decision-making skills needed to make informed career choices are not always self-evident to students, and students need to learn these skills in order to successfully choose career paths and transition between school and the work force (Kraus & Hughey, 1999).

One way that career service programs at colleges and universities help students make career decisions is through the use of career interest inventories. A popular, empirically supported inventory is the Self-Directed Search (SDS) developed by John Holland and based on his theory of vocational personality and work environments (Spokane & Holland, 1995; Holland, Powell, & Fritzsche, 1997; Reardon & Lenz, 1998; Gottfredson & Johnstun, 2009). According to Holland's theory, people prefer work environments that are congruent with their personality types (Gottfredson & Johnstun, 2009). Holland's SDS is based on the RIASEC model, where RIASEC stands for Realistic, Investigative, Artistic, Social, Enterprising, Conventional personalities and work environments. A person's responses on the SDS yield a personality code type that can be used to determine the type of work environment the person may prefer (Gottfredson & Johnstun, 2009). Each personality combination can be matched with different types of occupations and interests (Reardon & Lenz, 1998).

Some colleges and universities incorporate career support into their curriculum. Heffner, Macera, and Cohen (2006) described a one-credit course for psychology majors offered at West Virginia University developed to help students understand psychology-related careers and develop the knowledge needed to meet their career goals. Fouad, Cotter, and Kantamneni (2009) described the benefits of a college career course designed to help students choose a college major and future career path. Students participated in class discussions and completed trainings and career assessments as part of the course. Overall, results indicated that students in the class reported fewer career decision-making difficulties and greater career decision-making self-efficacy. However, their perception of barriers to career decision-making did not change.

Experiential learning experiences like internships, cooperative education, practica, and service learning are another valuable way for students to learn more about potential careers (Aldas et al., 2010; Eyler, 2009). Eyler (2009) suggested that experiential learning is a practical avenue for students to "transform inert knowledge into knowledge-in-use" that will help them transition seamlessly from college to career (p. 24). She also noted that experiential learning is associated with academic achievements, such as deeper understanding of course material and greater ability to think critically and apply classroom knowledge in new contexts (Eyler, 2009).

Service learning is a type of experiential learning that combines community service and academic learning, providing academic benefits and practical experience while also introducing students to the importance of civic engagement (Eyler, 2009; Rhoads, 1998; Vogelgesang & Astin, 2000). Students who participate in service-learning experiences in courses indicated these classes were more academically challenging, and that they understood course material better (Gallini and Moely, 2003; McCluskey-Fawcett & Green, 1992; Vogelgesang & Astin, 2000) by applying what they learned to practical situations. McCluskey-Fawcett and Green (1992) also reported that a majority of their students viewed service-learning experiences as positive experiences, and many planned to continue volunteering in the future. McClam et al. (2008) found that after completing a service-learning experience, students reported that they learned more by applying classroom learning to actual experience and they felt more confident in their choice of profession.

Although some career assistance is available to college students in the form of access to career guidance, courses tailored to specific majors, and experiential service-learning experiences, additional assistance is valuable in helping students develop an understanding of career decision-making and how their career interests lead to career choices. This study utilizes a service-learning experience related to career decision-making to help college students better understand career theory and gain confidence in their career choices.

In the current study, college students participated in a service-learning experience in which they met with high school students who were undecided about their future college majors and career paths. In light of the literature reviewed, we expected that by applying knowledge about career decision-making in a practical setting, college students who received instruction in career decision-making and participated in a related service project would gain significantly greater knowledge about the SDS and RIASEC theory and greater confidence in their own potential career choices than students who received instruction in career decision-making but did not participate in a service-learning experience.

Method
Overview

We used a quasi-experimental design to examine the impact of an experiential service-learning project designed to increase college students' understanding about how to make career decisions. Two upper-division psychology classes were selected, and students in both classes attended information sessions on career advising. Students in one of the two classes then helped provide career information to high school students as part of a class service-learning project.

Participants

Fourteen college students from two different upper division psychology courses at a small Midwestern college participated in this study. Students' ages ranged from 20 to 23 years with an average age of 21. All but one were female. There were eight seniors, three juniors, and three sophomores, and all of the students were psychology majors. All of the participants received career information in the classroom, but only the students in the experimental group participated in a service-learning experience with high school students.

Materials

The participants completed a packet of materials that included an informed consent form, the SDS (Holland, 1994); a values inventory, and a demographic questionnaire. At the conclusion of the service-learning project, the college students completed a posttest assessing career knowledge and confidence in career decision-making.

Procedure

The instructor of the two upper division psychology classes devoted two 90-minute class periods to instruction about the role of career instruments in making career decisions. He introduced them to the Self-Directed Search and RIASEC theory and the usefulness of these tools in selecting a college major or potential career. Also during these two class periods, all participants completed an informed consent, a demographic questionnaire, the SDS, and a values inventory. At the end of the instruction, they learned how to score the SDS.

A week later, half of these college students participated in a class project, a service-learning experience in which they met with high school students who were attending a college visit day. The high school students who attended were undecided about a college major, so, as part of their college visit itinerary, high school students completed the same SDS and values inventory that the college students completed. The participating college students then scored the high school students' tests, which were double-checked by a psychology professor or the career center director. Later in the day, high school students met for a 90-minute to two-hour feedback session with the college students in a large meeting room set up with small tables. Each high school student was paired with one or two college students to discuss the results of the career interest inventory. They also discussed issues related to selecting a major, what it is like to be a college student, and potential careers. A psychology professor and the college's career center director were present and available for consultation and to answer questions from either high school or college students. A posttest was administered to all college students two weeks after the career advising session.

Posttest

Two weeks after visit day, all college students who were present for the initial in-class career instruction completed a two-part posttest. The students were never reminded that they would be tested over the material, and it was mentioned only once in class at the beginning of the study more than a month earlier.

Posttest-1, the Career Knowledge Questionnaire, had 10 questions designed to assess college students' understanding of college majors and career options as well as assess their confidence in making decisions about careers. It was created by the researchers and used a Likert Scale (see Table 1). We conducted a Cronbach's Alpha Reliability test on the questionnaire and obtained an Alpha co-efficient of .826, which is in the acceptable range. We then summed all ten items into a single score in order to compare the groups.

Posttest-2 was a recall task assessing college students' recall and understanding of RIASEC theory, the

TABLE 1 **College Students' Understanding of Career Advising Measure**

Statement	Treatment		Control	
	M	SD	M	SD
I understand how my interests may help me make career choices.	4.714	.490	4.143	.900
I understand how my values may help me make career choices.	4.714	.490	4.143	.690
I have a good idea about potential college majors.	4.714	.490	4.286	.756
I have a good idea about some potential career options.	4.143	.900	3.857	1.069
I feel confident in my ability to make a good career choice.	4.000	.577	3.571	.976
I feel confident in my ability to make a good choice about a major.	4.429	.535	4.000	1.155
I understand how people choose careers.	4.286	.488	3.571	.787
I understand how people choose college majors.	4.429	.534	4.143	.900
I would recommend career advising to my friends.	4.714	.756	4.000	.817
Career testing is an interesting experience.	4.714	.488	3.571	.976

Note. N = 14 total, p < .05.

career theory used in the SDS. Researchers gave each student a half sheet of paper with the letters R, I, A, S, E, and C printed down the left side. Students were asked to describe potential skills, jobs, or traits associated with each letter of the RI-ASEC theory. All posttests were numerically coded by student researchers and graded by the first author, who was unaware which posttests came from students in the experimental group and which posttests came from the control group. Each letter of the RIASEC theory was worth three points for a total of 18 points possible, and students were given partial credit for incomplete responses.

Results

Our goal was to compare the learning achieved by college students participating in the service-learning project with that of students who received career instruction only. First, we examined college students' understanding and confidence in making decisions about careers on posttest-1. Then, we compared the students' recall of RIASEC theory on posttest-2.

We performed an independent-samples t-test to compare the scores on the Career Knowledge Questionnaire of college students who participated in the service-learning project to the scores of those college students who did not participate in the service-learning experience. The scores of students who participated ($M = 44.86$) were significantly higher than those who did not participate in the service-learning project ($M = 39.29$), $t(12) = 2.41$, $p = .02$ (see Table 1).

We also performed t-tests to compare the college students' knowledge of RIASEC theory from the Self-Directed Search. We found that students who participated in the service-learning experience had significantly greater knowledge of RIASEC theory ($M = 5.50$) than students who did not participate in the service project ($M = 0.14$), $t(12) = 3.57$, $p = .01$.

Discussion

Both hypotheses in this study were supported. As indicated by previous research, service-learning is a useful means of encouraging college students to learn about career decision-making. Students who participated in the service-learning experience performed well on the posttest,

even though it was unannounced and given two weeks after the college visit day. Those who participated in the visit day had significantly greater knowledge of the SDS and RIASEC theory than the students who were present for the in-class career theory instruction but did not participate in the service-learning experience. In addition, all of the college students in the study were upper division psychology students who were already on their way to making career choices. With this in mind, the fact that they still showed significant improvement in their understanding of career theory shows the strength of the service-learning experience in increasing career knowledge.

Informally, a number of students in the service-learning group also reported that they enjoyed the experience. Following their experiences, several students remarked that they felt they were doing something important and using knowledge they learned about in class in practical ways. One student went on to complete a field placement experience in the college career center. She has since been accepted to a graduate program in counseling psychology with the intention of becoming being a career counselor. Others have expressed similar interests in career counseling or guidance counseling.

There could be many reasons the service-learning project helped the students better recall career decision-making material. One possible explanation for this is that students who participated in the service-learning experience took additional time to reflect on the material and viewed the material as more important by the time they were finished with the project.

In retrospect, a good addition to the study would have been a pretest measuring students' knowledge of the SDS and RIASEC model prior to participation. However, there is no reason to suspect that either group of psychology majors had more exposure to the SDS or RIASEC theory than the other one. We also could have randomly assigned students to be in the service-learning and control groups. In the current study, students who participated in the service-learning experience were recruited from one upper-division class, and a matching control was obtained from another upper-division psychology class.

Overall, our findings were consistent with previous research noting benefits related to service learning (Gallini & Moely, 2003; McCluskey-Fawcett and Green, 1992; Vogelgesang & Astin, 2000). In the current study, psychology majors were able to share what they learned about their own career interests with others, and they also reported that they were glad to have an opportunity to apply information from the classroom in a practical way. As more students attend college and more career options are available to them, it is important to equip them with the skills to make effective career decisions.

Self-efficacy is also an important part of making career decisions. Luzzo (1993) found that career decision-making self-efficacy is an important predictor of career decision-making attitudes and skills in college students. He suggested that future research should further examine career decision-making self-efficacy and whether implementing interventions focused on career decision-making self-efficacy may improve students' attitudes towards making career decisions and give them the confidence needed to make more informed career choices.

Future research on career decision-making in the context of a service-learning experience could examine career decision self-efficacy in addition to understanding of career decision theory. A service-learning experience similar to the one described in the present study may be an especially useful way increase students' confidence and help them understand career decisions, something they consider both important and personal. ∎

REFERENCES

Aldas, T., Crispo, V., Johnson, N., & Price, T. A. (2010). Learning by doing: The Wagner plan from classroom to career. *Peer Review, 12(4)*, 24–28.

Eyler, J. (2009). The power of experiential education. *Liberal Education, 95(4)*, 24–31.

Fouad, N., Cotter, E. W., & Kantamneni, N. (2009). The effectiveness of a career decision-making course. *Journal of Career Assessment, 17(3)*, 338–347.

Gallini, S. M. & Moely, B. E. (2003). Service-learning and engagement, academic challenge, and retention. *Michigan Journal of Community Service Learning, 10(1)*, 5–14.

Gottfredson, G. D., & Johnstun, M. L. (2009). John Holland's contributions: A theory-ridden approach to career assistance. *The career Development Quarterly* (December, 2009), 99–107.

Hackett, G., & Betz, N. E. (1995). Self-efficacy and career choice and development. In J. E. Maddux (Ed.), *Self-efficacy, adaption, and adjustment: Theory, research, and application* (pp. 249–280). New York: Plenum.

Heffner Macera, M. & Cohen, S. H. (2006). Psychology as a profession: An effective career exploration and orientation course for undergraduate psychology majors. *The Career Development Quarterly, 54*, 367–371.

Holland, J. L. (1994). *The Self-Directed Search*. (1994 ed.) Odessa, FL: Psychological Assessment Resources.

Holland, J. L., Powell, A. B., & Fritzsche, B. A. (1994). *Self-Directed Search: Professional User's Guide*. Odessa, FL: Psychological Assessment Resources.

Kraus, L., & Hughey, K. (1999, June). The impact of an intervention on career decision-making self-efficacy and career indecision. *Professional School Counseling, 2*, 384.

Lee, Y., & Choi, J. (2011). A review of online course dropout research: Implications for practice and future research. *Educational Technology Research and Development, 59*(5), 593–618.

Lincoln, S., & Holmes, E. K. (2010). The psychology of making ethical decisions: What affects the decision?. *Psychological Services, 7*(2), 57–64. doi:10.1037/a0018710

Luzzo, D. A. (1993). Value of career-decision-making self-efficacy in predicting career-decision-making attitudes and skills. *Journal of Counseling Psychology, 40(2)*, 194–199.

McClam, T., Diambra, J. F., Burton, B., Fuss, A., & Fudge, D. (2008). An analysis of a service-learning project: Students expectations, concerns, and reflections. *Journal of Experiential Education, 30(3)*, 236–249.

McCluskey-Faweett, K., & Grooen, P. (1992, October). Using community service to teach developmental psychology. *Teaching of Psychology, 19(3)*, 150–152.

Poirier, C. R., & Feldman, R. S. (2004). Teaching in cyberspace: Online versus traditional instruction using a waiting-list experimental design. *Teaching of Psychology, 31*(1), 59–62.

Reardon, C. R., & Lenz, J. G. (1998). *The self-directed search and related Holland career materials: A practitioner's guide*. Lutz: Psychological Assessment Resources, Inc.

Rhoads, R. A. (1998). In the service of citizenship. The *Journal of Higher Education, 69(3)*, 278.

Spokane, A. R., & Holland J. L. (1995). The Self-Directed Search: A family of self-guided career interventions. *Journal of Career Assessment, 3*, 373–345.

Vogelgesang, L., & Astin, A. (2000). Comparing the effects of community service and service-learning. *Michigan Journal of Community Service Learning*, 725–34. Retrieved from ERIC database.

Fritson, K. K. (2008). Impact of journaling on students' self-efficacy and locus of control. *InSight: A Journal of Scholarly Teaching*, 3, 375–383.

Engage via Research Prediction

- Do you think journaling increased self-efficacy (a student's belief in his or her ability to be successful at a task)?
- Which type of journaling (cognitive-behavioral-challenging thoughts or using visual imagery or reflective thinking about performance) was most beneficial?

Read for Key Points

- What question did the researcher seek to answer? (Introduction)
- Who participated in the study and what did the participants do? (Method)
- What was the answer to the research question? (Results)

Critically Think about the Research

- How can you apply these findings to your daily actions as a college student?
- What explanation might you offer for why there were no differences found between cognitive-behavioral and reflective journaling?
- What other factors (in addition to journaling) could have led to increased self-efficacy?
- Do you think the findings might have been different if students from other disciplines (not just psychology) participated in the study? Why or why not?

Build Information Literacy Skills

- What does the research say about how to build self-efficacy?
- What are some additional benefits of journaling?

Research Study

Fritson, K. K. (2008). Impact of Journaling on Students' Self-Efficacy and Locus of Control

While considerable research has examined the academic and cognitive value of journaling, little has examined the psychological impact of journaling on the personal development of college students. Research on cognitive-behavioral therapy indicates that journaling can have a positive impact on individuals' self-growth and intrapersonal characteristics. The purpose of this study is to examine the impact of classroom-based journaling on students' self-efficacy and locus of control. Students in two undergraduate courses were required to complete weekly journal assignments; one class received targeted information on cognitive-behavioral therapy (CBT) and one class did not. Students completed pre-, mid-, and post-course assessments on self-efficacy, locus of control, and learning. Results revealed that self-efficacy scores for both groups significantly improved after the early journaling assignments; however, there were no differences between those who received direct CBT instruction and those who did not. These findings indicate that journaling may have important psychological benefits above and beyond its expected academic and cognitive outcomes.

While post-secondary educators frequently implement new teaching strategies to improve their students' academic development, less attention has been devoted to understanding how academic activities influence students intrapersonally. Research in cognitive-behavioral therapy (CBT) reveals a variety of strategies and techniques that positively impact self-efficacy, locus of control and other psychological characteristics, although little information exists on the value of CBT strategies for non-clinical populations. This study seeks to apply the empirical findings from psychological research to examine the value of journaling, a popular CBT technique, on students' self-efficacy and locus of control.

Traditional post-secondary education is designed to enhance student engagement, promote content learning, encourage critical thinking, and increase students' intellectual growth. Many instructors aim to achieve these academic goals while simultaneously attempting to foster students' intrapersonal growth, self-reflection and personal insight. However, it is particularly challenging to design course assignments and activities that effectively address both the academic and psychological goals. Borrowing from research in clinical psychology, CBT strategies may provide a means of simultaneously encouraging advanced content knowledge and increased self-reflection. While there are a variety of effective CBT techniques, the current study focuses on the value of journaling due to the widespread use of journaling as an accepted academic strategy.

In clinical studies, journaling is often used to promote self-introspection, reflection, and change in the client's perceptions, behaviors and cognitions. Similarly, journaling is seen as a viable tool in academia to promote reflection on and articulation of students' thinking and problem-solving strategies (Fogarty & McTighe, 1993), to support students in effectively acquiring and transferring cognitive and metacognitive skills (Perkins, Simmons, & Tishman, 1990), and to assist students in identifying and analyzing their deficits while improving problem-solving skill strategies (Clarke, Waywood, & Stephens, 1993). Academic journaling typically takes the form of dialogue or reflective narrative. Reflective journaling requires students to reflect on course information and their perceptions of the information, critically analyze information, and/or share how practical or field experiences relate to course information of life applications. Proponents of academic journaling believe that it is a non-traditional way for students to ground their

Source: Fritson, K. K. (2008). Impact of journaling on students' self-efficacy and locus of control. *InSight: A Journal of Scholarly Teaching*, 375–383. All inquiries should be directed to: PRIMARY CONTACT: Lolly Ockerstrom, PhD, Managing Editor, *InSight: A Journal of Scholarly Teaching*, Associate Professor of English, Park University, lolly.ockerstrom@park.edu.

personal experiences such as those in field or practicum experiences into course information, allows students to improve their writing skills, and promotes critical thinking for students (O'Connell & Dyment, 2006). Current research by Dunlap (2006) also supports guided reflective journaling as a means to recognize students' changing perceptions as information is learned.

The specific nature of journaling assignments varies, depending on the academic setting. Journaling can be unstructured, allowing students to reflect on self-identified information from a course or experience. Conversely, journaling may be very structured with the instructor identifying specific topics and objectives related to students' journals. Regardless of the style of journaling, the primary aim is to have students contemplate and integrate information from courses to real-life experiences, promote critical thinking, and communicate their perceptions/experiences in a written manner.

In CBT, journaling may take many forms and is used as a means to assist clients in becoming more aware of their harmful behavior, establishing healthier coping skills, and incorporating change into their lives. Clients may be required to identify specific thoughts, their resultant feelings and behaviors, and journal about the impact of altering their thoughts. By using such strategies, individuals actively alter their behavior in attempt to improve their personal perspectives, mood, and daily functioning (Beck & Beck, 1995). Significant research suggests cognitive strategies such as journaling improve mood and functioning of depressed and anxious individuals (Nicholas, 2006). Journaling has been shown to improve clients' self-awareness, promote active reflection on clients' selves and make changes in clients' thoughts, perceptions, behaviors, and mood.

Self-efficacy and locus of control are two constructs associated with CBT strategies that may be involved in changing individuals' thoughts, behaviors, and emotions. Self-efficacy refers to individuals' personal beliefs about their ability to initiate, persist in, and be successful in behavior (Bandura, 1977, 1982, 1997). Self-efficacy has been shown to be an accurate predictor of success in a range of behaviors from smoking cessation to athletic endeavors to academic performance (Manstead & Van-Eekelen, 1998; Sadri & Robertson, 1993; Stajkovic & Luthans, 1998). There is an established correlation

between individuals' self-efficacy and their willingness to engage in and be successful in differing areas of life functioning (Bandura, 1997). Bandura recognized individuals' self-esteem, as well as how they attribute blame or credit, impacted their self-efficacy and engaging behaviors. Since self-esteem and attribution of events are also associated with mood and anxiety, it follows that they could be involved in changes that might occur in thoughts, behavior, and moods of students as a result of cognitive-behavioral information and activities.

Locus of control refers to individuals' perceptions about the underlying main causes of events in their lives (Rotter, 1966). Rotter believes locus of control is an important component to individuals' personality and largely predicts whether they attribute success and failure to things within their control or to external entities. According to Rotter, individuals typically fall on a continuum in their beliefs about what causes their actions. Individuals with a primarily internal locus of control believe that their own behavior drives their destiny; conversely, individuals with a primarily external locus of control believe that external forces are largely responsible for one's fate. As with self-efficacy, cognitive-behavioral strategies are believed to correlate with potential changes in individuals' locus of control.

Self-efficacy and locus of control are essential components for student success in an academic setting. Improving students' self-efficacy enhances their ability to initiate, persist, and succeed with classroom activities; likewise, encouraging an internal locus of control helps to ensure that students take active responsibility for their learning. Thus, anything that faculty can do to facilitate learners' personal growth on these dimensions should translate into improved classroom performance and content-mastery.

Current Investigation

The aim of the present study is to investigate the impact of journaling on students' self-efficacy and locus of control. In addition, due to the academic context of the assignments, the study will also examine the impact of journaling on student learning and students' perceptions of the instructor and course. Because the existing literature on the psychological impact of journaling stems from research in CBT, it is important to examine whether any psychological benefits of journaling are due to the simple

Fritson, 2008   277

process of self-reflection inherent in journaling activities or if there is something unique about CBT approaches to the journaling process. As such, the current study will compare the impact of journaling assignments where students were given explicit instruction in CBT versus journaling assignments where students had no explicit CBT instructions. It is hypothesized that participants who apply cognitive-behavioral strategies via journaling assignments will show enhanced self-efficacy, internal locus of control, academic success, and perceptions of the instructor and course when compared to the students who journal without cognitive-behavioral directions.

Method

Participants

The participants are 41 psychology student volunteers ranging in age from 19 to 44 years (29 females, 12 males, Age $M = 21.3$, $SD = 4.11$) from a public, mid-western university. Participants are all enrolled in one of two introductory level *Abnormal Behavior and Society* classes taught by the same instructor.

Each class was randomly assigned to either the CBT journaling or non-CBT journaling condition. The CBT journaling condition included 25 students (17 females, 8 males, mean age = 20.9) who completed weekly written journals applying targeted cognitive-behavioral strategies to their personal experiences. One new cognitive-behavioral strategy was introduced and discussed for approximately 10 minutes each week throughout the semester. The non-CBT journaling condition included 16 students (12 females, 4 males, mean age = 21.8) who completed weekly journals pertaining to any topic from the course textbook or class discussions. No cognitive-behavioral strategies were introduced or discussed beyond what is normally in the course.

Materials

All participants independently completed the following measures at the beginning of the course, midterm, and end of the semester:

- *Demographics Form.* The demographic form included information on age, gender, academic year and GPA, college major, and estimated times they planned to study or studied for quizzes and exams for the course.

- *Self-Efficacy Questionnaire (SEQ).* The SEQ is a 23-question measure used to assess individuals' self-efficacy regarding their personal belief about their ability to initiate and persist in behavior (Sherer et al., 1982). This scale was established to measure individuals' General Self-Efficacy and individuals' Social Self-Efficacy. The 23 questions are answered on a 14-point Likert Scale.

- *Locus of Control Scale.* The Locus of Control Scale is a 10-item questionnaire used to measure whether individuals perceive themselves as having a more external or internal locus of control. It was developed by Rotter (1971) to assess individuals' beliefs that their destiny is controlled by themselves (internal) or factors outside of themselves (external).

- *Grades.* Participants/students final percentage grade for the course was used as the measure of academic outcome.

- *Perception of Professor Form.* This questionnaire included 10 questions on a 5-point Likert Scale to assess individuals' perception of their professor. This form was administered at midterm and the end of the semester.

- *Course/Professor Evaluation Form.* This questionnaire included 15 questions on a 5-point Likert Scale to assess individuals' evaluation of the course and professor's performance. This form was administered at mid-term and the end of the semester.

- *Cognitive-Behavioral Education/Discussion.* Each week, the CBT journaling students were introduced to one new cognitive-behavioral strategy and given an assignment to journal regarding that concept and explain at least two real life examples of its use during their lives. Refer to Appendix A for examples of the cognitive-behavioral strategies introduced in the course. Students were encouraged to apply the concept to their current life situation, though they had the freedom to conceptualize regarding any life experiences. The length of the journal assignment was at least three quarters of a page. The journal assignments were due the following week when the instructor would reiterate the concept, then teach a new cognitive-behavioral strategy. Each assignment was included in the students' grade; credit was awarded on a completion-only basis. Refer to Appendix B for an example of the journal assignments for the CBT journaling group. The non-CBT journal students were asked to write an equivalent journal entry regarding any class or text topic for the week. These assignments were assigned and submitted in the same fashion as the CBT journaling condition. Refer to Appendix C for an example of the journal assignments for the non-CBT journal group.

Procedure

A brief description of the study was given at the beginning of the class. All participants from both conditions then completed the packet of questionnaires including the above-described measures minus the *Perception of Professor Form* and the *Course/Professor Evaluation Form* (since the participants had not had adequate time to evaluate those factors). The two classes were then taught using the same text, syllabus, curriculum, and lecture-discussion format. The only difference between the two classes was in the nature of the journal activities; the CBT journaling class received the 10 minute weekly discussion on cognitive-behavioral strategies along with the journal assignment, while the non-CBT journaling class received only the journal assignment. At midterm and the end of the semester, all participants completed the packet of questionnaires again, now including the *Perception of Professor Form* and the *Course/Professor Evaluation Form*. The students were then debriefed regarding the research project.

Results

A 2 × 3 mixed-design ANOVA was calculated to examine the effects of journaling (CBT or non-CBT) and time (beginning of course, midterm, and end of course) on Self-Efficacy. The main effect for time was significant $(F_{(1,39)} = 82.89, p < .001)$, but the main effect for type of journaling was not significant $(F_{(1, 39)} = .006, n.s.)$. The interaction between type of journaling and timing was not significant $(F_{(1, 39)} = 2.51, n.s.)$. For the main effect of time, a repeated measures ANOVA indicated that the significant change occurred from the beginning of the semester to the midterm test regarding

Self-Efficacy $F_{(1, 39)} = 104.65, p < .01$. The results of the ANOVA indicated no significant differences between the midterm and end-of-semester measures $F_{(1, 39)} = 3.18, n.s.$ These results indicate that there was significant positive change in self-efficacy in all participants in the study, regardless of the type of journaling. Further, the results show the change was most significant at midterm, and there was not a significant change in self-efficacy between the midterm and end of the semester.

Additional ANOVAs examining the impact of journaling (CBT or non-CBT) by timing (beginning, midterm, and end of the semester) on locus of control, perception of the instructor, course evaluation, and grades did not show any significant differences between groups or time.

Discussion

The results indicate that all students showed significant improvement in self-efficacy, regardless of the type of journaling they engaged in. Specifically, the data suggest that all students' self-efficacy improved from the beginning of the course to the midterm, regardless of whether or not they received additional information on cognitive-behavioral techniques. These results do not support the hypothesis that students completing cognitive-behavioral instruction and journaling would show improvements in self-efficacy over journaling without specific CBT information.

These findings suggest that journaling, regardless of the nature of the journal, may have positively impacted students' self-efficacy. Given that previous research indicates reflective journaling is an effective way to impact students' problem-solving, thought articulation, and exploration of metacognition (Dunlap, 2006), this study suggests journaling may play a significant role in affecting students' self-efficacy. However, as is the nature of classroom-based research, the relationship between journaling and self-efficacy may be clouded by other instructional variables such as instructor style or course content.

Other results exploring students' locus of control, grades, perception of the instructor, attendance, and course evaluation did not support the hypotheses that individuals receiving the cognitive-behavioral education and journaling would demonstrate significantly better scores than the students not receiving the CBT assignments. In contrast, the journaling implemented in this course did not have an impact on any of these factors. It is important to note that the current study did not implement a pure control condition (in which there was no journaling), so it is still unclear on the overall impact of journaling on these dimensions.

It is important to note that the findings from this pilot study should serve as a basis for ongoing research into the psychological impact of academic journaling rather than a conclusive finding on the role of journaling in college classrooms. Because this study was conducted within the constraints of a live classroom, the study balanced experimental control with the demands of the classroom. Future research should isolate variables such as instructor, course content, and journaling in an attempt to replicate the findings and/or identify which variables may have accounted for the change in students' self-efficacy. Exploration of the timeline in which the change in self-efficacy occurred could also be included in future studies.

Self-efficacy research strongly indicates that self-efficacy is a good predictor of successful task completion, correlates with levels of performance, and is related to self-esteem (Manstead & Van-Eekelen, 1998; Sadri & Robertson, 1993; Stajkovic & Luthans, 1998). Given the potential positive ramifications of improving students' self-esteem, the incorporation of journaling in the college classroom may provide students with far-reaching benefits beyond simple mastery of course content. The psychological value of journaling mandates further study regarding how journaling and teaching variables impact students' intrapersonal characteristics.

Though this pilot study is based in psychology, the value of the findings is relevant to all disciplines. While all faculty actively promote content mastery, it can be argued that we should also focus on the intrapersonal and psychological growth of our students. As indicated by this study, academic journaling may be one means of simultaneously fostering the academic and psychological growth of students. Virtually all disciplines can incorporate journaling into the curriculum to improve academic variables as well as positively impact self-efficacy. To effectively utilize journaling to encourage students' intrapersonal growth, students' journal assignments should include the following aspects:

1. Identify a life experience/situation which exemplifies a concept from their text/course material

2. Reflect on various perspectives when a new concept or idea is introduced

3. Consider a perspective opposite of what they truly believe regarding a particular concept or matter

Instructors should allow students flexibility while still providing structure to promote critical thinking and self-exploration. This study's findings provide an opportunity for a range of disciplines within higher education to positively impact students' academic needs, critical thinking skills, and intrapersonal attitudes/beliefs that promote success in life functioning. ■

REFERENCES

Bandura, A. (1977). Self-efficacy: Toward a unifying theory of behavioral change. *Psychological Review, 84*, 191–215.

Bandura, A. (1982). Self-efficacy mechanisms in human agency. *American Psychologist, 37*, 122–147.

Bandura, A. (1997). *Self-efficacy: The exercise of control*. New York: W. H. Freeman.

Beck, J. & Beck, A. T. (1995). *Cognitive therapy: Basics and beyond*. New York: Guilford Press.

Clarke, D., Waywood, A., & Stephens, M. (1993). Probing the structure of mathematical writing. *Educational Studies in Mathematics, 25*, 235–250.

Dunlap, J. C. (2006). Using guided reflective journaling activities to capture students' changing perceptions. *TechTrends, 50*(6), 20–26.

Fogarty, R. & McTighe, J. (1993). Educating teachers for higher order thinking: The three-story intellect. *Theory into Practice, 32*(3), 161–169.

Manstead, A. S. R. & Van-Eekelen, S. A. M. (1998). Distinguishing between perceived behavioral control and self-efficacy in the domain of academic intentions and behaviors. *Journal of Applied Social Psychology, 28*, 1375–1392.

Nicholas, A. B. (2006). *An introduction to the psychotherapies*. New York: Oxford University Press.

O'Connel, T. & Dyment, J. (2006). Reflections on using journals in higher education: a focus group discussion with faculty. *Assessment and Evaluation in Higher Education, 31*(6), 671–691.

Perkins, D., Simmons, R., & Tishman, S. (1990). Teaching cognitive and metacognitive strategies. *Journal of Structured Learning, 10*(4), 285–303.

Rotter, J. (1966). Generalized expectancies for internal versus external control of reinforcements. *Psychological Monographs, 80*, 609.

Rotter, J. (1971, June). Locus of control scale. *Psychology Today, 42*.

Sadri, G. & Robertson, I. T. (1993). Self-efficacy and work-related behavior: A review and meta-analysis. *Applied Psychology, 42*, 139–152.

Sherer, M., Maddux, J. E., Mercadante, B., Prentice-Dunn, S., Jacobs, B. & Rogers, R.W. (1982). The self-efficacy scale: Construction and validation. *Psychological Reports, 51*, 663–671.

Stajkovic, A. D. & Luthans, F. (1998). Self-efficacy and work-related performance: A meta-analysis. *Psychological Bulletin, 124*, 240–261.

Appendix A: Sample Cognitive Behavioral Strategies

1. Cognitive Distortions (Aaron Beck)

   Description: For each of the cognitive distortions, the participants were given a definition and examples of its use, they then identified times in which they use the distortion at least twice that week and journal about it. Students were required to journal about two distortions as assigned by the instructor. The cognitive distortions included the following:

   - All or Nothing: The tendency to see situations as either black or white.
   - Overgeneralizations: Drawing a conclusion based on a single event or small piece of evidence.
   - Filters: We only see what we want to see in a situation.
   - Magnification: The propensity to make mountains out of molehills.
   - Labeling: Putting tags on people or situations that are one dimensional.
   - Jumping to Conclusions: Making snap judgments or assumptions.
   - Shoulds: Following an inflexible list of rules regarding how the world at large "should" behave.
   - Blaming: Constantly pointing the finger of blame at others or yourself.
   - Disqualifying: A person reverses a compliment so that it really becomes a put down.
   - Mistake of Control: Thoughts of feeling totally helpless or that you must be in complete control of a given situation.

2. Assertiveness Skills

   Description: The four communication styles of Passive, Aggressive, Assertive, and Passive-Aggressive were discussed in class. The students described two incidents of these styles in their journals.

3. Progressive Relaxation

   Description: Progressive relaxation strategies were described and briefly demonstrated. The students described two incidents of using this strategy during the week in their journals.

4. Thought-Stopping/Self-Talk Training

   Description: Thought stopping/self-talk strategies were described and demonstrated in class. The students described two incidents of using these strategies during the week in their journals.

5. Visual Imagery

   Description: Visual imagery strategies were described and demonstrated in class. The students described two incidents of using these strategies during the week in their journals.

Appendix B: Sample Cognitive-Behavioral Journal Assignment

List two examples in which you have caught yourself doing "all or nothing" thinking. Fill in the situation, thoughts/feelings section, new thought, and changes according to directions below (do this for 2 examples). Write 4-8 sentences (at least 3/4 page) about your thoughts about all or nothing thinking and how it impacts you and/or others.

All or Nothing: The tendency to see situations as either black or white.

Thought Distortion	Situation	Thoughts/ Feelings	New thought	Changes
All or nothing thinking	Write description of situation	Write your thoughts/feelings about situation	Alter your thought from all or nothing to different type of thinking	What do you think and feel now....?

Appendix C: Sample Journal Assignment for Non-Cognitive-Behavioral Journaling

Journal about your impressions, beliefs, ideas regarding chapters 1 and 2, possibly chapter 3, of your text.

Describe in about 6-8 sentences (at least ¾ page). Be sure it is related to topics we have discussed and that are in your text. ∎

Answer Key Appendix

INTRODUCTION: GETTING STARTED

Student Success Myths or Facts

1. Myth. While it is true that the world continues to change and information is at our fingertips, the more you know, the easier it will be for you to learn more. Thus, memorizing general information is still important. It will be easier for you to engage in higher-level tasks such as critical thinking when you have a strong background knowledge in the subject matter (Anderson & Krathwohl, 2001).

2. Myth. Highlighting is a strategy that many college students use, but unfortunately, most do not highlight well. In many cases, students highlight too much. This is probably because it is difficult for new learners to differentiate the important from the unimportant. When used ineffectively, such as highlighting too much, the learning becomes more difficult (Dunlosky et al., 2013). When done well, highlighting can be helpful, but there is no evidence that highlighting is the best strategy.

3. Myth. Reading skills are important but research has shown that one of the best predictors of reading comprehension is how much you know about the subject matter (Recht & Leslie, 1988). In other words, prior knowledge is one of the best predictors of how well you will understand what you read.

4. Myth. We are social beings and learning is most likely to happen in the social context. Research has shown that students who study in study groups outperform students who study alone (Schmidt & Moust, 1998). It is obviously important for the study group to function effectively.

5. Myth. Reviewing and rereading notes is one of the most widely used study techniques used by students, but it is also unfortunately one of the least effective study strategies (Karpicke & Blunt, 2011). It is a good idea to use your notes as a study tool, but reorganizing or repackaging notes will lead to higher levels of learning as compared to reviewing. Reviewing is a pretty passive task that results in students becoming overconfident with the material because it looks more and more familiar every time you review it, but familiarity is not the same as learning. There are many other more effective techniques such as testing yourself and teaching someone else the content.

6. Myth. Students do believe they are good multitaskers, probably because they engage in multitasking often. However, research shows that this is not the case. Multitasking is not effective (Bowman et al., 2010; Junco, 2012). It is much better to single-task it.

7. Myth. Students have often heard the phrase "go with your gut" when it comes to taking multiple-choice tests, which implies that it is a bad idea to change an answer on a test. Research has not supported this belief. In fact, research shows that you are more likely to change a wrong answer to a right answer, especially if you have a good reason for doing so (Di Milia, 2007; Shatz & Best, 1987).

8. Myth. Professors will expect you to use scholarly sources when creating academic products; however, professors are much more interested in you reading and paraphrasing ideas rather than using a lot of quotes. Using too many quotes may communicate that you don't fully understand the material. Use quotes sparingly. You will of course need to cite your sources even when paraphrasing.

9. Myth. Unfortunately, students often overestimate their performance, displaying what Karpicke, Butler, and Roediger (2009) call illusions of competence. In order to be more accurate in your assessment of your performance, seek out feedback and data about how well you are learning the content or skill.

10. Myth. While grades do matter, research has shown that students who focus on learning as opposed to grades are more likely to achieve at high levels (Grant & Dweck, 2003). This is because you may do just enough to earn a certain grade if you are focused on grades as the goal, but if learning is your goal, you will likely put forth higher levels of effort and this will result in higher levels of learning.

CHAPTER 1

Value of a College Education Quick Quiz

1. There are many societal benefits associated with you getting a college education. For example, you are more likely to be engaged in the community and vote. You are also more likely to engage in productive parenting behaviors that can positively impact society. In addition, you will likely be earning a higher salary so can contribute more taxes that can be used to benefit your community.

2. As a college graduate, you are more likely to engage in healthy behaviors such as exercising and less likely to engage in unhealthy behaviors such as smoking. College graduates are more likely to be healthy, both physically and mentally. It is also more likely that you will have access to healthcare and benefits such as vacation time.

3. College graduates, on average, earn more than those without a college degree. A person with a bachelor's degree, as compared to a person with a high school diploma, earns approximately $23,000 more per year.

Decision-Making Quick Quiz

1. The six steps of the decision-making process are as follows: keeping your goal visible, gathering relevant information, creatively identifying and exploring options, evaluating options, deciding and taking action, and evaluating whether your decision worked.

2. Others play a huge role in our decisions. Our friends and family can help us make good decisions. It is also important to remember that our decisions impact others.

Information Literacy Quick Quiz

1. Information literacy is the ability to determine what information you need, find that information, and evaluate the credibility and usefulness of the information.

2. In order to make good decisions, we will need to be able to sort through the endless amount of information that is available. Information literacy is a skill desired by employers as many positions will require you to find, evaluate, and use information.

Websites and Evaluating Sources Quick Quiz

1. Anyone can post information on most websites, so it is important to determine if the information posted is credible and useful.

2. To determine if a source is credible, you will need to determine if the author was qualified, the reason or purpose of the information, how related and useful the information is to the task at hand, whether the information is consistent with other sources, and whether the information is current.

Peer-Reviewed Journal Articles Quick Quiz

1. A peer-reviewed research article is an article published in a professional journal, which has been reviewed and approved by experts in the field of study for that topic.

2. The abstract is a summary of the article. The introduction provides us with the research question and purpose of the study, the method tells us who participated and what they had to do, and the answer to the research question can be found in the results section. The discussion explains the results again, emphasizing the value of the findings.

3. Read the abstract first, then the introduction and discussion sections. Then go back and read the entire article in order.

Critical Thinking Quick Quiz

1. Critical thinking involves taking in and evaluating information, viewing the information from multiple perspectives, and drawing conclusions.

2. According to Perry, there are four stages of intellectual development: absolute (believing there is a right and wrong), personal (focus is on opinions), rules-based (judgments based on rules), and evaluative (can describe process and defend conclusion).

Bloom's Taxonomy Quick Quiz

1. According to Bloom's taxonomy, there are different levels of knowing. Each level builds on the other. In order to engage in higher-level thinking such as analyzing or evaluating, you will first need to be able to remember and understand the concept.

2. The six levels from lowest to highest are remembering, understanding, applying, analyzing, evaluating, and creating.

3. Remembering typically refers to memorizing content. Creating, on the other hand, is a high-level task where you need to take the information you've learned and create a new idea or product based on this knowledge.

Process of Becoming a Critical Thinker Quick Quiz

1. The three foundational conditions are having a strong knowledge base, high self-efficacy, and desire and drive.

2. The two learning conditions are challenging tasks and opportunities and learning strategies and support.

CHAPTER 2

Importance of Goal Setting Quick Quiz

1. If you aim for a B, you are most likely going to earn a B.

2. Students with high goals are more likely to stay in school, achieve higher grades than students with low goals, and have improved overall well-being.

3. Short-term goals are valuable because they pave the way for long-term goal achievement. In essence, they are the steps that need to be taken in order to achieve the long-term goal. Motivation is often higher for short-term goals, making them even more valuable.

ABCS of Goal Setting Quick Quiz

1. The ABCS of effective goal setting refers to aiming high, believing in yourself, caring and committing to your goals, and specifying and self-reflecting.

2. According to the research conducted by Reynold and Baird (2011), there is no emotional cost associated with high goals. In fact, individuals with higher goals had lower levels of depression later on (regardless of whether or not they achieved their goal).

3. "Do your best" goals do not work. Because these goals are not specific enough, they result in less effort being put forth, which in turn leads to lower achievement levels.

Making Career Decisions Quick Quiz

1. According to the social cognitive theory, the people we care about play an important role in our decisions. Others can encourage and motivate us to pursue a particular career path.

2. According to the happenstance theory, planned and unplanned events play an important role in how we make career decisions. By taking action steps, you'll never know what doors may open.

3. Holland's theory focuses on how individuals who choose careers that match their interests and personality will be more satisfied.

Career Indecision Quick Quiz

1. The three main reasons for career decision-making difficulties are not being ready to make a decision, not having enough information, and having inconsistent information.

2. Career specialists will help you explore your options and make a decision that matches your interests and values. Students who work with a career counselor are less likely to change majors, which can save them time and money.

Self-Assessment Quick Quiz

1. Values are what matters most to you. It is important to choose a career path that is aligned to your core values. This will be more likely to lead to higher levels of career satisfaction.

2. Technical skills are skills that are specific to a certain career. An example would be that a nurse will need to know how to take someone's blood pressure. Soft skills are more general skills that are needed in almost every career. Examples include communication skills and the ability to work well as part of a team.

3. The Big Five personality factors are openness, conscientiousness, extraversion, agreeableness, and neuroticism. Finding a career that matches your personality style will lead to higher levels of career satisfaction.

Career Information Quick Quiz

1. The Occupational Outlook Handbook and Career One Stop are examples of credible websites. Information about the job tasks, educational requirements, and salary will be found on these websites.

2. The informational interview is when you interview a person who works in a career that you are interested in learning more about. The purpose of the interview is to learn about the career from that person's perspective. This information can help you learn about careers and will ultimately help you make an informed career decision.

CHAPTER 3

Memory Process Quick Quiz

1. We used to think that the memory process was one-directional but we now know that it is much more complex and interactive in nature. For example, our long-term memory influences what information we attend to and encode and can help us learn new content.

2. Paying attention to important content and using a multisensory approach will increase the likelihood that information is encoded.

3. According to research conducted by Miller, we can only hold onto approximately seven pieces of information at a time.

Memory Strategies Quick Quiz

1. Rehearsal is a good beginning strategy, but it needs to be combined with another strategy in order to be effective.

2. There are several strategies that work really well. Elaboration, chunking, mnemonics, and retrieval practice all have good research support.

Prior Knowledge Quick Quiz

1. According to this research, prior knowledge is more important than reading skills when it comes to reading comprehension. If you know a lot about the subject, it will be easier for you to read.

2. You can build knowledge by reading the chapter summary, reviewing the table of contents, and searching for a video or more basic-level reading on the topic before reading the chapter.

3R and SQ3R Quick Quiz

1. Both methods have the 3R component, which means read, recite, and review.

2. The SQ3R adds two additional steps: survey and question.

3. During the second R, you should close your book and recall what you just read. Writing down this summary works best.

Highlighting Quick Quiz

1. If you highlight important points, then it is an effective strategy. However, ineffective highlighting can be distracting and not helpful. It may even lower your reading comprehension and achievement.

2. Don't highlight until the third R in the 3R or SQ3R reading methods. Only highlight one or two sentences in each paragraph or section.

Preparing for and Participating in Class Quick Quiz

1. Reading the chapter before class gives you the necessary background that makes note-taking easier and more productive. You'll know what information is in the text and that you therefore do not need to write down.

2. You can maintain good eye contact, nod, engage in note-taking, and ask questions to show your professor you are invested in the learning process.

Note-Taking Methods Quick Quiz

1. The matrix has been found to be the most effective note-taking model.

2. Linear notes are not effective because there is little to no organization.

3. The concept map and matrix require significant cognitive effort, so these options usually work best when you repackage your notes after class.

Note-Taking Tips Quick Quiz

1. Spending a lot of time on the topic, repeating the information, providing several examples, talking in a louder voice or with more passion, or writing on the board or presenting information on a PowerPoint slide suggest the content is important.

2. Use the PowerPoint slides as an organizational tool, but you'll still need to take notes next to the slides or in your notebook because the slides won't have all of the information you need.

Multisensory Learners Quick Quiz

1. There is no research support for learning styles. We all are much more similar than different when it comes to learning.

2. We are more likely to remember pictures versus words. When we look at images related to the content, we will learn the material better.

Testing Your Knowledge Quick Quiz

1. Researchers have found that testing is a powerful memory tool. We learn the most when we test ourselves and try to recall information.

2. Take practice tests online or create your own quizzes or flashcards to put the testing effect research into practice.

Teaching to Learn and Study Groups Quick Quiz

1. When you have to teach someone else, you will need to do a lot of preparation, really learning the content. You will also need to be prepared to answer questions. This too results in you spending more time and energy preparing and learning.

2. Research shows that studying in a group leads to higher achievement.

3. Be sure to select members for the study group who share your goals and passion for learning. Develop rules and consider assigning roles to different members.

Organizing Quick Quiz

1. High and low performers spent about the same amount of time reading and reviewing, but the high performers spent more time organizing and studied longer.

2. Dickinson and O'Connell (1990) defined organizing as putting information into your own words, finding connections between concepts, and creating examples.

CHAPTER 4

Soft Skills Quick Quiz

1. Soft skills are skills needed in life and in most, if not all, careers.

2. Some of the most valued soft skills include professionalism, communication, interpersonal skills, planning, and problem-solving skills.

Professionalism Quick Quiz

1. Professionalism refers to engaging in behaviors that are honest, respectful, and aligned to the mission of the organization.

2. Professionals complete tasks on time and produce high-level products. In other words, others can count on those with high levels of professionalism to do what it takes to successfully complete a project or assignment. Professionals are also respectful and honest.

Time and Project Management Quick Quiz

1. Tracking your time will make it easy to see if you are spending your time in a way that is consistent with your values and goals.

2. Time traps are activities that take up a lot of your time. For example, watching television, playing games, and socializing are time traps.

Work–School–Life Balance Quick Quiz

1. Working too much can take your time away from school, making it less likely for you to achieve your goals. However, some researchers have found that working part-time is beneficial. In addition to financial benefits, working also helps you develop important skills.

2. First, determine if it is necessary for you to continue doing all of the tasks you are currently involved in. Planning a schedule can help you accomplish all of the tasks.

Meeting Deadlines Quick Quiz

1. To-do lists allow you to keep track of your progress, and it is rewarding to cross items off the list. Research has found that students who use to-do lists are more likely to complete tasks ahead of schedule (Cavanaugh, Lumkin, & Hu, 2012).

2. The most important factor when deciding what to do first should be your goals. Tasks that assist you in meeting your goals should be completed first.

3. The best way to combat procrastination is to break large tasks up into smaller, more manageable ones.

Multitasking Quick Quiz

1. The two types of multitasking are task switching and dual-tasking.

2. Multitasking doesn't work. In fact, it often results in both tasks taking longer and can also increase your stress.

3. Multitasking during class negatively impacts your academic performance. It also negatively impacts the performance of other students sitting near you (Sana, Westin, & Cepeda, 2013).

Communication and Conflict Management Quick Quiz

1. Active listening involves giving the other person our undivided attention, asking clarifying questions as needed, and paraphrasing what the person said to be sure you are accurately understanding.

2. Nonverbal communication plays a large role in communication. Our facial expression and body language send powerful messages. Research has found that we can accurately make judgments based on nonverbal messages.

3. The five styles for managing conflict are integrating, obliging, dominating, avoiding, and compromising.

Emotional Intelligence Quick Quiz

1. Emotional intelligence is the ability to manage one's own emotions and the emotions of others.

2. Yes, research has shown that you can learn the competencies associated with being emotionally intelligent.

Teamwork and Collaboration Quick Quiz

1. The 5R approach includes establishing rapport, determining rules, identifying roles, getting ready to work, and remembering to evaluate.

2. Some examples of group rules are attend meetings on time, come prepared to meetings, respond to e-mails within 24 hours, and respect one another.

3. Some examples of group roles are group leader, notetaker, visual aid leader, finishing touch specialist, questioner, rehearsal director, and timekeeper.

Leadership Quick Quiz

1. Research has shown that leadership skills are learned.

2. Transformational leaders are charismatic, inspire and motivate others, promote intellectual stimulation, and are respectful of others.

CHAPTER 5

Purpose of Academic Tasks Quick Quiz

1. Program learning outcomes are what graduates will be able to know, think, or do upon graduation. Course learning outcomes are what students will be able to know, think, or do by the end of the course. Assignments are designed to help students achieve course and program learning outcomes.

2. Research shows that having a learning goal will increase motivation and performance. Students with learning goals are more likely to put forth high levels of effort and persevere when faced with challenges.

3. To find out the purpose of an assignment, start by looking at the syllabus. Some faculty will explicitly share how the assignments are linked to the outcomes. If this is not the case, you can look for the link yourself and ask your professor to clarify the purpose if it is not clear.

What Is Academic Integrity? Quick Quiz

1. Academic integrity refers to engaging in honest actions. It means that you have done your own work independently and have given credit to those who shaped or guided your work.

2. Academic integrity benefits everyone. Community partners are more likely to provide internships and other experiential learning experiences to students at colleges and universities with good reputations. You will also learn more when you engage in honest actions. Your character matters much more than your grade.

Citing Sources and Paraphrasing Quick Quiz

1. You always need to cite the source. The only two situations where a source is not needed is when an idea is entirely your own or the information is general knowledge.

2. Paraphrasing involves summarizing someone else's work into your own words. It requires more than changing a few words and should relate to the big ideas presented, not sentences.

Developing a Plan Quick Quiz

1. The first step when developing a plan is to find out the purpose and the specific expectations of the assignment.

2. The most common mistake that students make when selecting a topic is to choose a topic that is too broad. This can result in a very general presentation or paper.

Writing Process Quick Quiz

1. The writing process begins with planning, followed by writing a draft and then engaging in revising and proofreading. It takes several drafts to create a good final product.

2. When you begin the revision process, start with the big picture. In other words, focus on purpose, audience, and the overall organization.

Presentations Quick Quiz

1. The best way to combat performance anxiety is to practice. The more you know your material and feel prepared, the more confidence and less anxiety you will have.

2. You can begin with a hook such as an interesting story or statistic. During the presentation, you can take very brief active learning breaks using techniques such as polling or asking audience members to briefly discuss what they learned with a partner.

3. According to Mayer's (2009) research, use images, put only essential information on the slide, draw attention to what is most important, use conversational language, and allow audience members the opportunity to read slides if there is a need for a lot of words.

Multiple-Choice Tests Quick Quiz

1. High-performing students anticipate the answer, read all answer choices, skip difficult questions, eliminate wrong choices, write on their exams, and change their answer if they have a good reason for doing so.

2. It is a good idea to change your answer on a test if you have a good reason for doing so. A good reason might be that you initially misread the question or you came across information later in the test that reminded you of the correct response.

Short-Answer and Essay Exams Quick Quiz

1. The three steps involved with writing a good essay response are planning, writing, and proofreading.

2. Spend about one-fifth of the time on the first and last steps, planning and proofreading, and spend the other three-fifth of the time writing the response.

Take-Home and Online Exams Quick Quiz

1. Take-home and online exams can be more challenging and time-consuming. While you may be less anxious, it is still important to prepare well. There may be no time limit, which means you may have to devote more time to this type of assessment.

2. You will need to find out from your professor if you are allowed to use materials and resources when taking an online exam. Some professors will not allow the use of materials while others may treat it as an open-book exam.

CHAPTER 6

Connecting with Your Advisor or Academic and Career Mentor Quick Quiz

1. Students who meet with their advisors are more likely to be successful.

2. Advisors can help you determine your academic and career goals and develop a plan to achieve these goals. Advisors can also provide support when you encounter challenges.

Understanding Curriculum Requirements Quick Quiz

1. Most bachelor's degrees consist of general education courses, courses required for your selected major and elective credits, which can be used for a double major or minor.

2. If you double major, you need to complete all of the requirements for both majors. If you select a minor instead of a double major, you complete approximately half of the courses that would be required for a major to complete the minor in addition to the courses for your major.

3. Online courses promote critical thinking skills and are more convenient. Some students find it more difficult to determine what is most important in an online class and miss the in-person opportunities to connect with the professor and other students.

Exploring Experiential Learning Opportunities Quick Quiz

1. Structured learning experiences such as internships or co-ops will give you valuable work experience that employers desire and will also give you the opportunity to learn skills and network.

2. Students who study abroad report long-lasting benefits such as being independent and open-minded.

3. Service learning is when you engage in a service project related to the course learning outcomes. In essence, you are meeting the needs of a community while also learning valuable course-related information and skills.

Importance of Network Quick Quiz

1. Networking is establishing and nurturing relationships that are beneficial to both parties.

2. There are many benefits associated with having a strong network. For example, members of your network can provide you with support and encouragement as well as access to information about potential career opportunities.

Creating a Professional Presence Quick Quiz

1. Employers often view social media sites before making hiring decisions. Employees can also be fired for using social media in a way that is not consistent with company policies.

2. Review current social media posts and delete posts that may be viewed negatively by employers. Create a LinkedIn account, sharing positive work, volunteer, or other professional activities.

3. An elevator speech is very brief overview of your goals and skills. It is brief enough that you could share it on a quick elevator ride. To develop an elevator speech, identify just one or two key goals and skills. Keep it simple and stay focused on what is most important. Package the information in a creative way that is meaningful to the audience.

Expanding and Strengthening Your Network Quick Quiz

1. Joining clubs or organizations is a great way to expand your network. You can also attend professional workshops or conferences.

2. Mentors can help you develop skills, can support you when needed, and can provide you with access to professional opportunities.

3. To maintain and strengthen your relationships within your network, take time to stay in touch. A brief call or e-mail to inquire about how someone in your network is doing or to share exciting news can keep relationships strong.

Job Search Tips Quick Quiz

1. Although many people spend countless hours using online job search tools, most jobs are found through networking.

2. Customizing your cover letter and resume to the specific position you are interested in will make your resume stand out. Clearly communicate the skills and experiences you have that are directly related to the position.

3. Preparation is key before an interview. Research the company to find out about its mission and values and practice discussing how you can support this mission. Go to career services to see if there are opportunities to engage in mock interviews.

Financing Your Education Quick Quiz

1. Need-based aid is based on financial situation. You typically do not need to repay most need-based aid, with loans being the primary exception. Merit-based aid is given to high-achieving students, often in the form of a scholarship. You will often need to meet certain academic requirements in order to continue receiving the merit aid.

2. If you have a subsidized loan, interest doesn't accrue while you are in school. Thus, the loan amount stays the same from the time you take it out to the time you graduate. Unsubsidized loans start accruing interest as soon as you take them out; so by the time you graduate, you will already owe more than you initially borrowed.

3. In this case, your monthly payments would be approximately $300 for the $30,000 loan and $1,000 for the $100,000 loan.

Return on Investment Quick Quiz

1. Return on investment refers to whether there is a financial benefit associated with an investment. For example, if you put your money in the stock market, how much do you expect to gain? If you invest in your education, is this a wise financial choice? Education has one of the highest returns at approximately 14%–15%.

2. Direct costs refer to the actual cost (e.g., tuition). Opportunity costs refer to income lost because you are engaging in a certain activity such as college. The opportunity cost would be that you wouldn't be earning a full-time salary if you are attending college full time.

Establishing Good Credit Quick Quiz

1. A good credit score will make it more likely for you to get loans in the future and lower interest rates.

2. To establish good credit, only charge up to 25% of the maximum allowed, and pay your bill on time.

Financial Planning and Budgeting Quick Quiz

1. Financial decisions you make today can have long-lasting consequences.

2. As your emotions go up, logic goes down, so it is often a good idea to wait before making a big financial decision.

3. To help you stay within your budget, investigate whether you have the best deals on current expenses such as on your cell phone. It's also a good idea to determine where you can reduce expenses such as not paying a gym membership and instead using the fitness center on campus.

CHAPTER 7

Self-Regulation Quick Quiz

1. Academic self-regulation involves goal setting, identifying learning strategies, and then monitoring progress and making changes as needed.

2. Some questions are as follows: Am I spending enough time studying? What learning strategies are working well? What changes might I need to make? Who might be able to assist me?

3. Cognitive feedback is when you use feedback while studying or completing an assignment. For example, your performance on a practice test can help you determine how well you are learning the content. Outcome feedback is when you reflect on your performance after you receive a grade from your professor. For example, an exam or assignment wrapper is when you ask yourself self-reflective questions about your performance after the assignment was completed and graded.

Accuracy of Self-Assessments Quick Quiz

1. Good decisions are based on accurate information. Dunlosky and Rawson (2012) found that students who were more accurate with their self-assessments performed better than those who were inaccurate.

2. Most students are not accurate with self-assessments. Karpicke and Blunt (2011) found that those who engaged in repeated study thought they performed well but did not.

3. Students who are overconfident may stop studying too soon. This can minimize learning and lead to lower grades.

Attribution Theory Quick Quiz

1. Attribution theory refers to how we interpret our successes and mistakes.

2. The two types of "bad" mistakes are mistakes where someone is hurt and mistakes that are repeated; in the latter case, no learning occurred.

3. The most productive way to interpret a mistake is to attribute it to something that is internal and changeable, such as effort.

Behavioral Motivators Quick Quiz

1. Behaviorists suggest giving yourself a reward when you successfully accomplish a task or reach a goal.

2. Rewards give you a positive feeling and positive consequences make it more likely for us to engage in this action again. The positive feeling also becomes connected or associated to the task, which increases our enjoyment for the task, again making it more likely that we will continue to engage in this behavior.

Cognitive Motivators Quick Quiz

1. Cognitive psychologists believe our thoughts play a powerful role in motivation. How we interpret experiences will have a positive or negative impact on motivation.

2. Self-efficacy refers to whether we believe we can successfully complete a task.

3. To build self-efficacy, you need to have the courage to try new tasks and be successful at these tasks. By mapping out a plan, monitoring your progress, and seeking help when needed, you will increase the likelihood of meeting with success.

Humanistic Motivators Quick Quiz

1. According to Maslow, everyone strives for self-actualization, being the best one can be, and can achieve this when basic needs are met. The basic needs that need to be met, in hierarchical order from most basic, are physiological needs such as hunger, safety, love and belonging, esteem, and self-actualization.

2. According to the self-determination theory, we will grow and develop when core needs are met. The core needs are our need for autonomy, competence, and relatedness.

Social Motivators Quick Quiz

1. The people in our lives play an important role in motivation and are our social motivators. They can encourage and support us as we strive to accomplish our goals.

2. Getting involved in a club, sport, or other organization increases motivation. Students who are involved are more likely to achieve their goals.

Stress Management Quick Quiz

1. Getting a good night's sleep, eating healthy, exercising, and talking to others are all very effective stress management techniques.

2. Your college or university should have a counseling center where you may be able to speak confidentially to a counselor or be able to refer you a psychologist or counselor in the community.

Mindfulness Quick Quiz

1. Mindfulness is being aware of what is happening in the moment, noticing your breathing and other reactions to the environment.

2. We all can benefit from practicing mindfulness regularly but it is most helpful to those who have low to moderate levels of stress. Students with high levels of stress can benefit from mindfulness but may also need to use additional stress management techniques. Counselors or psychologists can help you learn to cope effectively with stress.

Avoiding Unhealthy Behaviors Quick Quiz

1. Alcohol and other drugs can have long-term negative consequences. One consequence is the possibility of becoming addicted to the substance. In addition to addiction, individuals under the influence of alcohol make poorer choices, such as engaging in unprotected sexual relations.

2. If you or someone you know needs professional help, visit the college counseling center or find a local mental health provider. There are of course also many online resources for you to learn about addiction.

Resilience and Grit Quick Quiz

1. Resilience is the ability to bounce back and be successful after facing a traumatic or very challenging situation.

2. Grit refers to your passion and commitment to a goal and your willingness to do whatever it takes to accomplish the goal.

Perseverance Quick Quiz

1. Invest in the tasks you take on, being passionate and committed to finishing the task successfully. Engage in positive and productive thinking, focusing on factors you can control, and be sure to have a strong support system.

2. Perseverance means you stick with a task until you have successfully completed it.

Mindset Quick Quiz

1. All three theories focus on the importance of mindset. More specifically, learned optimism, locus of control, and growth mindset all encourage us to engage in positive and productive thinking and focus on factors within our control such as effort. Having a positive mindset plays a critical role in being more resilient and gritty.

2. It is very important to have a positive mindset and to focus on what is within your control such as how much effort you put into a task.

Support Quick Quiz

1. Support is a key factor in being resilient and gritty. Those with a high level of support are more likely to be resilient and achieve goals.

2. Quality matters more than quantity when it comes to support. The key is that your needs are being met by your support system. Sometimes having just one important person in your life can be all you need.

3. Every college or university has a wide array of supports for their students. Some examples include professors, counselors, advisors, tutors, and librarians.

Celebrating Success Quick Quiz

1. Celebrating increases our motivation and self-efficacy, both of which play an important role in future experiences.

2. Having your accomplishments in one place will help you in a couple of ways. First, if you are feeling discouraged, reviewing your accomplishments can boost your mood and motivate you to persevere. It can also be very helpful when you engage in a job search.

References Index

Page numbers provided in blue refer to where the referenced material appears within the text.

AACC, Association of Community Colleges (2014). 2014 Fact Sheet. Retrieved from: www.aacc.nche.edu. 194

Abel, J. R., & Deitz, R. (2014). Do the benefits of college still outweigh the costs? *Current Issues in Economics & Finance, 20*(3), 1-12. Retrieved from Academic Search Premier. 25, 193

Albion, M. J., & Fogarty, G. J. (2002). Factors influencing career decision making in adolescents and adults. *Journal of Career Assessment, 10*(1), 91-126. 60

Albitz, R. S. (2007). The what and who of information literacy and critical thinking in higher education. *Portal: Libraries and the Academy, 7*(1), 97–109. Retrieved from Academic Search Premier database. 145

Ambrose, S. A., Bridgers, M. W., DiPietro, M., Lovett, M. C., & Norman, M. K. (2010). *How learning works: Seven research-based principles for smart teaching.* San Francisco: Jossey-Bass. 205

American Psychological Association. (2008). Summary report of journal operations, 2007. *American Psychologist, 63*(5), 490–491. doi:10.1037/0003-066X.63.5.490 33

Anderson, L., & Krathwohl, D. A. (2001). *Taxonomy for learning, teaching and assessing: A revision of Bloom's taxonomy of educational objectives.* New York: Longman. 40, 42, 282

Appelbaum, S. H., Marchionni, A., & Fernandez, A. (2008). The multi-tasking paradox: Perceptions, problems and strategies. *Management Decision, 46*(9), 1313–1325. doi:10.1108/00251740810911966 118, 119

Archer, W., & Davison, J. (2008). Graduate employability: What do employers think and want? *The Council for Industry and Higher Education,* 1-20. 109

Argyle, M. (2001). *The psychology of happiness 2nd edition.* New York: Routledge. 230

Armstrong, J. L. (2004). Seven keys for small groups success. *Adult Learning, 15*(1–2), 34–35. Retrieved from ERIC database. 127

Arnold, K. A. (2017). Transformational Leadership and Employee Psychological Well-Being: A Review and Directions for Future Research. Journal of Occupational Health Psychology. Advance online publication. http://dx.doi.org/10.1037/ocp0000062 132

Artis, A. B. (2008). Improving marketing students' reading comprehension with the SQ3R method. *Journal of Marketing Education, 30*(2), 130–137. Retrieved from Business Source Elite. 85

Association of American Colleges & Universities (2010). New research on internships and experiential learning programs. (2010). Peer Review, 12(4), 29-30. 176

Association of College and Research Librarian (ACRL) (2016). Framework for information literacy for higher education. Retrieved from: http://www.ala.org/acrl/standards/ilframework 28, 30, 242

Ashford, K. (2014, August 29). 5 steps to calculating your college R.O.I. Forbes. Retrieved from: http://www.forbes.com/sites/learnvest/2014/08/29/5-steps-to-calculating-your-college-r-o-i/#72fa55b144c9 191

Atkinson, R. C., & Shiffrin, R. M. (1968). Human memory: A proposed system and its control processes. In K. W. Spence, &

J. T. Spence, The Psychology of Learning and Motivation (Vol. 2, pp. 89–195). New York, NY: Academic Press. 78

Balsch, W. (2007). Effects of test expectation on multiple-choice performance and subjective ratings. *Teaching of Psychology, 34*(4), 219–225. doi:10.1080/00986280701700094 156

Balsamo, M., Lauriola, M., & Saggino, A. (2013). Work values and college major choice. Learning and Individual Differences, 24, 110-116. 62

Bandura, A., & Walters, R. H. (1963). Social learning and personality development. New York: Holt, Rinehart & Winston. 57

Barnett, K. (2012). Student interns' socially constructed work realities: Narrowing the work expectation-reality gap. *Business Communication Quarterly, 75*(3), 271–290. Retrieved from ERIC database. 177

Barrington, L., Wright, M., Casner-Lotto, J. (2006). Are they really ready to work? Employers' perspectives on the basic knowledge and applied skills of new entrants to the 21st century U.S. workforce. The Conference Board. 109

Baum, S., Ma, J., & Payea, K. (2010). Education pays 2010: The benefits of higher education for individuals and society. *College Board Advocacy and Policy.* Retrieved from http://advocacy.collegeboard.org/sites/default/files/Education_Pays_2010.pdf 22, 23

Belter, R. W., & du Pré, A. (2009). A strategy to reduce plagiarism in an undergraduate course. *Teaching of Psychology, 36*, 257–261. doi:10.1080/00986280903173165 142

Bercher, D. A. (2012). Self-monitoring tools and student academic success: When perception matches reality. *Journal of College Science Teaching, 41*(5), 26–32. 204, 205, 206

Bergen-Cico, D., Possemato, K., & Cheon, S. (2013). Examining the efficacy of a brief mindfulness-based stress reduction (brief MBSR) program on psychological health. Journal of American College Health, 61(6), 348-360. doi:10.1080/07448481.2013.813853 219

Beyer, A. M. (2011). Improving student presentations: Pecha Kucha and just plain PowerPoint. Teaching of Psychology, 38(2), 122-126. 155

Bidwell, A. (2014). Average student loan debt approaches $30,0000. US News. Retrieved from: https://www.usnews.com/news/articles/2014/11/13/average-student-loan-debt-hits-30-000 191

Blair, B. F., & Millea, M. (2004). Student Academic Performance and Compensation: The Impact of Cooperative Education. College Student Journal, 38(4), 643-743. 176

Bodenlos, J. S., Noonan, M., & Wells, S. Y. (2013). Mindfulness and alcohol problems in college students: The mediating effects of stress. Journal of American College Health, 61(6), 371-378. doi:10.1080/07448481.2013.805714 219

Bohnert, A. M., Aikins, J., & Edidin, J. (2007). The role of organized activities in facilitating social adaptation across the transition to college. *Journal of Adolescent Research, 22*(2), 189–208. doi:10.1177/0743558406297940 216

Bohnert, D., & Ross, W. H. (2010). The influence of social networking web sites on the evaluation of job candidates. *Cyberpsychology,*

Behavior, and Social Networking, 13(3), 341–347. doi:10.1089/cyber.2009.0193 181

Bonaccio, S., O'Reilly, J., O'Sullivan, S. L., & Chiocchio, F. (2016). Nonverbal Behavior and Communication in the Workplace. Journal of Management, 42(5), 1044-1074. doi:10.1177/0149206315621146 122

Bonanno, G. A., Galea, S., Bucciarelli, A., & Vlahov, D. (2007). What predicts psychological resilience after disaster? The role of demographics, resources, and life stress. Journal of Consulting And Clinical Psychology, 75(5), 671-682. doi:10.1037/0022-006X.75.5.671 228

Boudreau, C. A., & Kromrey, J. D. (1994). A longitudinal study of the retention and academic performance of participants in freshman orientation course. *Journal of College Student Development, 35*, 444–449. Retrieved from PsycINFO database. 7

Bowles, B., Gintis, H., & Osborne, M. (2001). The determinants of earnings: A behavioral approach. Journal of Economic Literature, 39, 1137-1176. 108

Bowman, L. L., Levine, L. E., Waite, B. M., & Gendron, M. (2010). Can students really multitask? An experimental study of instant messaging while reading. *Computers & Education, 54*(4), 927–931. doi:10.1016/j.compedu.2009.09.024 119, 282

Breivik, P. (2005). 21st century learning and information literacy. *Change, 37*(2), 20–27. Retrieved from ERIC database. 145

Brown, M. (2011). Effects of graphic organizers on student achievement in the writing process. *Online Submission*. Retrieved from ERIC database. 147

Brown, J., & Vanable, P. (2007). Alcohol use, partner type, and risky sexual behavior among college students: Findings from an event-level study. *Addictive Behaviors, 32*(12), 2940–2952. doi:10.1016/j.addbeh.2007.06.011 221

Bruce, C. S. (1999). Workplace experiences of information literacy. International Journal of Information Management, 19, 33-47. 30, 242, 250

Bruss, O. E., & Hill, J. M. (2010). Tell me more: Online versus face-to-face communication and self-disclosure. *Psi Chi Journal of Undergraduate Research, 15*(1), 3–7. Retrieved from Academic Search Premier database. 174

Brusso, R. C., Orvis, K. A., Bauer, K. N., & Tekleab, A. G. (2012). Interaction among self-efficacy, goal orientation, and unrealistic goal-setting on videogame-based training performance. *Military Psychology (Taylor & Francis Ltd), 24*(1), 1–18. doi:10.1080/08995605.2012.639669 52

Bureau of Labor Statistics (2015). Number of jobs held, labor market activity, and earnings growth among the youngest baby boomers: Results from a longitudinal study. US Department of Labor. Retrieved from: https://www.bls.gov/news.release/pdf/nlsoy.pdf 55

Bureau of Labor Statistics, U.S. Department of Labor. Kindergarten and elementary school teachers. *Occupational outlook handbook*, (2014–15 Ed.). Retrieved from http://www.bls.gov/ooh/education-training-and-library/kindergarten-and-elementary-school-teachers.htm 68

Burton, V. T., & Chadwick, S. A. (2000). Investigating the practices of student researchers: Patterns of use and criteria for use of internet and library sources. *Computers and Composition, 17*(3), 309–328. doi:10.1016/S8755-4615(00)00037-2 32

Caligiuri, P., & Tarique, I. (2012). Dynamic cross-cultural competencies and global leadership effectiveness. Journal of World Business, 47(4), 612-622. doi:10.1016/j.jwb.2012.01.014 130, 131

Callanan, G., & Benzing, C. (2004). Assessing the role of internships in the career-oriented employment of graduating

college students. Education and Training, 46(2), 82-89. Doi: 10.1108.00400910410525261 177

Cameron, J., Pierce, W., Banko, K. M., & Gear, A. (2005). Achievement-based rewards and intrinsic motivation: A test of cognitive mediators. *Journal of Educational Psychology, 97*(4), 641–655. Retrieved from ERIC database. 118

Carlston, D. L. (2011). Benefits of student-generated note packets: A preliminary investigation of SQ3R implementation. *Teaching of Psychology, 38*(3), 142–146. Retrieved from ERIC database. 85

Carrier, L. M., Cheever, N. A., Rosen, L. D., Benitez, S., & Chang, J. (2009). Multitasking across generations: Multitasking choices and difficulty ratings in three generations of Americans. *Computers in Human Behavior, 25*(2), 483–489. doi:10.1016/j.chb.2008.10.012 118

Carter, J., & Van Matre, N. (1975). Note taking versus note having. *Journal of Educational Psychology, 67*(6), 900–904. doi:10.1037/0022-0663.67.6.900 94

Carver, C. S. (1998). Resilience and thriving: Issues, models, and linkages. *Journal of Social Issues, 54*(2), 245–266. Retrieved from Academic Search Premier database. 222

Casad, B. J., & Bryant, W. J. (2016). Addressing stereotype threat is critical to diversity and inclusion in organizational psychology. Frontiers in Psychology, 7(8), 1-18. 130

Cavanaugh, T., Lamkin, M. L., & Hu, H. (2012). Using a generalized checklist to improve student assignment submission times in an online course. *Journal of Asynchronous Learning Networks, 16*(4), 39–44. 116, 285

Celio, C. I., Durlak, J., & Dymnicki, A. (2011). A meta-analysis of the impact of service-learning on students. *Journal of Experiential Education, 34*(2), 164–181. Retrieved from ERIC database. 168

Chemers, M., Hu, L., & Garcia, B. (2001). Academic self-efficacy and first year college student performance and adjustment. *Journal of Educational Psychology, 93*(1), 55–64. doi:10.1037/0022-0663.93.1.55 212

Chen, P. (2011). Guiding college students to develop academic self-regulatory skills. *Journal of College Teaching & Learning, 8*(9), 29–34. 204

Cheng and Cheou Pi-Yueh, C., & Wen-Bin, C. (2010). Achievement, attributions, self-efficacy, and goal setting by accounting undergraduates. *Psychological Reports, 106*(1), 54–64. doi:10.2466/PR0.106.1.54-64 53

Cheung, C., & Kwok, S. (1998). Activities and academic achievement among college students. *Journal of Genetic Psychology, 159*(2), 147–163. Retrieved from Academic Search Premier database. 81

Chiou, C. C. (2008). The effect of concept mapping on students' learning achievements and interests. Innovations in Education and Teaching International, 45(4), 375–387. 92

Chope, R. C. (2002). Family matters: Influences of the family in career decision making. *International Career Development Conference*, 175–182. Retrieved from ERIC database. 56

Christian, T. Y., & Sprinkle, J. E. (2013). College student perceptions and ideals of advising: An exploratory analysis. College Student Journal, 47(2), 271-291. 170

Clark, D., Tanner-Smith, E., Killingsworth, S., Bellamy, S. (2013). *Digital games for learning: A systematic review and meta-analysis (executive summary)*. Menlo Park, CA: SRI International. 96

Clark, G., Marsden, R., Whyatt, J. D., Thompson, L., & Walker, M. (2015). 'It's everything else you do…': Alumni views on extracurricular activities and employability. Active Learning in Higher Education, 16(2), 133-147. Doi: 10.1177/1469787415574050. 106, 109

Claxton, G., Costa, A. L., & Kallick, B. (2016). Hard thinking about soft skills. Educational Leadership, 73(6), 60-64. 109

Clayson, D. E. (2013). Initial impressions and the student evaluation of teaching. Journal of Education For Business, 88(1), 26-35. 180

Cohen, M. (2012). The importance of self-regulation for college student learning. College Student Journal, 46(4), 892-902. 203, 206

Cohen, M. T. (2012). The importance of self-regulation for college student learning. *College Student Journal, 46*(4), 892–902. 203, 206

Cole, M. S., Rubin, R. S., Field, H. S., & Giles, W. F. (2007). Recruiters' perceptions and use of applicant resume information: Screening the recent graduate. Applied Psychology: An International Review, 56(2), 319-343. 188

Community College Survey of Student Engagement (2009). Making Connections: Dimensions of Student Engagement (2009 CCSSE Findings). Austin, TX: The University of Texas at Austin, Community College Leadership Program. 230

Cottringer, W. (2015). Setting the standards. Supervision, 76(7), 25-26. 110

Coulter-Kern, R. G., Coulter-Kern, P. E., Schenkel, A. A., Walker, D. R., & Fogle, K. L. (2013). Improving students understanding of career decision-making through service learning. *College Student Journal, 47*(2), 306–311. 268, 269

Council of Writing Program Administrators, National Council of Teachers of English, & National Writing Project. (2011). Framework for success in postsecondary writing. *National Writing Project*. Retrieved from ERIC database. 149

Cranney, J., Morris, S., Spehar, B., & Scoufis, M. (2008). Helping first year students think like psychologists: Supporting information literacy and teamwork skill development. Psychology Learning & Teaching, 7(1), 28-36. doi:10.2304/plat.2008.7.1.28 125

Crittenden, V. & Woodside, A. G. (2007). Building skills in thinking: Toward a pedagogy in metathinking. *Journal of Education for Business, 83*(1), 37–43. 27

Crosby, O. (2010). Informational interviewing: Get the inside scoop on careers. *Occupational Outlook Quarterly, 54*(2), 22–29. Retrieved from ERIC database. 69

Davis, M., & Hult, R. (1997). Effects of writing summaries as a generative learning activity during note taking. *Teaching of Psychology, 24*(1), 47. Retrieved from Academic Search Premier database. 94

Day, T., & Tosey, P. (2011). Beyond SMART? A new framework for goal setting. *Curriculum Journal, 22*(4), 515–534. 51

DeBerard, M., Spielmans, G., & Julka, D. (2004). Predictors of academic achievement and retention among college freshmen: A longitudinal study. *College Student Journal, 38*(1), 66–80. Retrieved from PsycINFO database. 9

Deci, E. L., & Ryan, R. M. (1985). *Intrinsic motivation and self-determination in human behavior.* New York: Plenum. 53

Deepa, S., & Seth, M. (2013). Do soft skills matter? Implications for educators based on recruiters' perspective. The IUP Journal of Soft Skills, 7(1), 7-20. 108, 252

deCarvalho, M., & Junior, R. (2015). Impact of risk management on project performance: the importance of soft skills. International Journal of Production Research, 53(2), 321-340. doi:10.1080/00207543.2014.919423 108

de Janasz, S. C., & Forret, M. L. (2008). Learning the art of networking: A critical skill for enhancing social capital and career success. Journal of Management Education, 32(5), 629-650. doi: 10.1177/1052562907307637 183, 189

DeLaune, L. D., Rakow, J. S., & Rakow, K. C. (2010). Teaching financial literacy in a co-curricular service-learning model. *Journal of Accounting Education, 28*(2), 103–113. doi:10.1016/j.jaccedu.2011.03.002 178

Dennick, R. (2012). Twelve tips for incorporating educational theory into teaching practices. *Medical Teacher, 34*(8), 618–624. doi:10.3109/0142159X.2012.668244 39

Derby, D. C., & Smith, T. (2004). An orientation course and community college retention. *Community College Journal of Research and Practice, 28*, 763–773. doi:10.1080/10668920390254771 7

De Vet, E., Nelissen, R. A., Zeelenberg, M., & De Ridder, D. D. (2013). Ain't no mountain high enough? Setting high weight loss goals predict effort and short-term weight loss. Journal of Health Psychology, 18(5), 638-647. doi:10.1177/1359105312454038 51

DeVos, A., DeClippeleer, I., & Dewilde, T. (2009). Proactive career behaviours and career success during the early career. Journal of Occupational and Organizational Psychology, 82, 761-777. 179

DeVry University (2015, June 29). Successful job seekers reveal job search strategies. Regional Business News. Retrieved from: http://www.businesswire.com/news/home/20150629005016/en/ 185

Dickinson, D. J., & O'Connell, D. Q. (1990). Effect of quality and quantity of study on student grades. *Journal of Educational Research, 83*(4), 227–231. Retrieved from the Academic Search Premier database. 84, 100, 101, 284

Di Milia, L. (2007). Benefiting from multiple-choice exams: The positive impact of answer switching. *Educational Psychology, 27*(5), 607–615. doi:10.1080/01443410701309142 157, 158, 282

Doyle, A. (2016). Top 10 communication skills for workplace success. The Balance. Retrieved from: https://www.thebalance.com/communication-skills-list-2063779 120, 121

Driscoll, A., Jicha, K., Hunt, A. N., Tichavsky, L., & Thompson, G. (2012). Can online courses deliver in-class results?: A comparison of student performance and satisfaction in an online versus a face-to-face Introductory Sociology Course. *Teaching Sociology, 40*(4), 312-331. Retrieved from ERIC database. 174

Duckworth, A. (2016). Grit: The power of passion and perseverance. New York: Scribner. 53, 224, 227, 228, 231

Duckworth, A. L., Peterson, C., Matthews, M. D., & Kelly, D. R. (2007). Grit: Perseverance and passion for long-term goals. Journal of Personality and Social Psychology, 92(6), 1087-1101. 222, 223

Dugan, R.F. (2011). Exploring the construct validity of academic self-regulation using a new self-report questionnaire—The survey of academic self-regulation (SASR). *The International Journal of Educational and Psychological Assessment, 7*(1), 45–63. 205

Dundes, L., & Marx, J. (2006). Balancing work and academics in college: Why do students working 10–19 hours per week excel? *Journal of College Student Retention: Research, Theory, and Practice, 8*(1), 107–120. doi:10.2190/7UCU-8F9M-94QG-5WWQ 115

Dunlosky, J., & Rawson, K. A. (2012). Overconfidence produces underachievement: Inaccurate self evaluations undermine students' learning and retention. *Learning and Instruction, 22*(4), 271–280. doi:10.1016/j.learninstruc.2011.08.003 206, 287

Dunlosky, J., Rawson, K. A., Marsh, E. J., Nathan, M. J., & Willingham, D. T. (2013). Improving students' learning with effective learning techniques: Promising directions from cognitive and Educational Psychology. *Psychological Science in the Public Interest (Sage Publications Inc.), 14*(1), 4–58. doi:10.1177/1529100612453266 85, 282

Dunn, D. Halonen, J. S & Smith, R. A. (Eds.), *Teaching Critical Thinking in Psychology: A Handbook of Best Practices*, 11–22. Chichester, West Sussex: Wiley-Blackwell. 39

Dweck, C., Walton, G., & Cohen, G. (2014). Academic Tenacity: Mindsets and Skills that Promote Long-Term Learning. Bill & Melinda Gates Foundation. 223, 226

Earnest, D. R., Rosenbusch, K., Wallace-Williams, D., & Keim, A. C. (2016). Study abroad in psychology: Increasing cultural competencies through experiential learning. Teaching of Psychology, 43(1), 75-79. doi:10.1177/0098628315620889 178

Edmondson, M. (2016). Major in happiness: Debunking the college major myth. NACE Journal. 1-8. 60

Edmunds, S., & Brown, G. (2010). Effective small group learning: AMEE Guide No. 48. Medical Teacher, 32(9), 715–726. doi:10.3109/0142159X.2010.505454 127

Einstein, G. O., Mullet, H. G., & Harrison, T. L. (2012). The testing effect: Illustrating a fundamental concept and changing study strategies. Teaching of Psychology, 38(3), 142–146. doi:10.1177/0098628312450432 96, 97, 154

El-Ghoroury, N. H., Galper, D. I., Sawaqdeh, A., & Bufka, L. F. (2012). Stress, coping, and barriers to wellness among psychology graduate students. Training and Education In Professional Psychology, 6(2), 122-134. doi:10.1037/a0028768 114

End, C. M., Worthman, S., Mathews, M. B., & Wetterau, K. (2010). Costly cell phones: The impact of cell phone rings on academic performance. Teaching of Psychology, 37(1), 55–57. doi:10.1080/00986280903425912 111, 119

Ericsson, K. A., Prietula, M. J., & Cokely, E. T. (2007). The making of an expert. Harvard Business Review, 85(7-8), 114. 108, 132, 186

Feldman, D. B., & Dreher, D. E. (2011). Can hope be changed in 90 minutes? Testing the efficacy of a single-session goal-pursuit intervention for college students. Journal of Happiness Studies, 13, 745-759. doi: 0.1007/s10902-011-9292-4. 224

FICO (2011). Understanding your FICO score. Retrieved from http://www.myfico.com/Downloads/Files/myFICO_UYFS_Booklet.pdf 194

Findley, M. J., & Cooper, H. M. (1983). Locus of control and academic achievement: A literature review. Journal of Personality and Social Psychology, 44(2), 419–427. doi:10.1037/0022-3514.44.2.419 225

Flaming, L., Agacer, G., & Uddin, N. (2010). Ethical decision-making differences between Philippines and United States students. Ethics & Behavior, 20(1), 65–79. doi:10.1080/10508420903482624 110

Foos, P. W., & Goolkasian, P. (2008). Presentation format effects in a levels-of-processing task. Experimental Psychology, 55(4), 215–227. doi:10.1027/1618-3169.55.4.215 95

Foret, M. L., & Dougherty, T. W. (2001). Correlates of networking behavior for managerial and professional employees. Group & Organizational Management, 26(3), 283-311. 187

Forgeard, M. C., & Seligman, M. P. (2012). Seeing the glass half full: A review of the causes and consequences of optimism. Pratiques Psychologiques, 18(2), 107–120. doi:10.1016/j.prps.2012.02.002 224

Fox, A. B., Rosen, J., & Crawford, M. (2009). Distractions, distractions: Does instant messaging affect college students' performance on a concurrent reading comprehension task? Cyberpsychology and Behavior, 12(1), 51–53. doi:10.1089/cpb.2008.0107 119

Fritson, K. K. (2008). Impact of journaling on students' self-efficacy and locus of control. InSight: A Journal of Scholarly Teaching, 3, 75–83. 274, 275

Gadzella, B., & Baloglu, M. (2003). High and low achieving education students on processing, retaining, and retrieval of

information. Journal of Instructional Psychology, 30(2), 99. Retrieved from Academic Search Premier database. 81, 100

Gaeddert, W., & Dolphin, W. (1981). Effects of facilitating and debilitating anxiety on performance and study effort in mastery-based and traditional courses. Psychological Reports, 48(3), 827–833. Retrieved from PsycINFO database. 217

Galbraith, J., & Winterbottom, M. (2011). Peer-tutoring: What's in it for the tutor? Educational Studies, 37(3), 321-332. 98

Gardner, H. (1983). Frames of mind: The theory of multiple intelligences. New York: Basic Books. 63, 64

Gardner, M. P. (1985). Mood states and consumer behavior: A critical review. Journal of Consumer Research, 12(3), 281–300. doi:10.1086/208516 197

Garrison, D. R., Anderson, T., & Archer, W. (2000). Critical inquiry in a text-based environment: Computer conferencing in higher education. The Internet and Higher Education, 2(2-3), 87–105. 98

Gati, I. (1986). Making career decisions- a sequential elimination approach. Journal of Counseling Psychology, 33(4), 408-417. 67

Gati, I., Krausz, M., & Osipow, S. H. (1996). A taxonomy of difficulties in career decision making. Journal of Counseling Psychology, 43(4), 510-526. 61

Gati, I., Tikotzki, Y. (1989). Strategies for collection and processing of occupational information in making career decisions. Journal of Counseling Psychology, 3(3), 430-439. Retrieved from PscyInfo. 67

Gault, J., Leach, E., & Duey, M. (2010). Effects of business internships on job marketability: The employers' perspective. Education and Training, 52 (1), 76-88. doi: 10.1.108/00400911011017690 176

Gerard, J. G. (2012). Linking in with LinkedIn: Three exercises that enhance professional social networking and career building. Journal of Management Education, 36(6), 866-897. doi: 0.1177/1052562911413464 183

George, D., Dixon, S., Stansal, E., Gelb, S. L., & Pheri, T. (2008). Time diary and questionnaire assessment of factors associated with academic and personal success among university undergraduates. Journal of American College Health, 56(6), 706–715. Retrieved from Academic Search Premier database. 113

Gettinger, M., & Seibert, J. (2002). Contributions of study skills to academic competence. School Psychology Review, 31(3), 350. Retrieved from Academic Search Premier database. 81

Gier, V., Kreiner, D. S., & Natz-Gonzalez, A. (2009). Harmful effects of preexisting inappropriate highlighting on reading comprehension and metacognitive accuracy. Journal of General Psychology, 136(3), 287–300. doi:10.3200/GENP.136.3.287-302 85

Goesling, B. (2007). The rising significance of education for health? Social Forces, 85(4), 1621–1644. 23

Gollwitzer, P. M., Sheeran, P., Michalski, V., & Seifert, A. E. (2009). When intentions go public: Does social reality widen the intention-behavior gap?. Psychological Science, 20(5), 612-618. doi:10.1111/j.1467-9280.2009.02336.x 54

Goodman, S., Keresztesi, M., Mamdani, F., Mokgatle, D., Musariri, M., Pires, J., & Schlechter, A. (2011). An investigation of the relationship between students' motivation and academic performance as mediated by effort. South African Journal of Psychology, 41(3), 373–385, 93. 209

Goswami, U (2008). Principles of learning, implications for teaching: A cognitive neuroscience perspective. Journal of Philosophy of Education, 42(3–4), 381–399. 42, 44, 95, 100

Grant, A. (2013). Give and take: A revolutionary approach to success. New York: Penguin Group. 186

Grant, H., & Dweck, C. (2003). Clarifying achievement goals and their impact. Journal of Personality & Social Psychology, 85(3), 541–553. doi:10.13514.85.3.541 140

Grasz, J. (2009). Forty-five percent of employers use social networking sites to research job candidates, CareerBuilder survey finds. *CareerBuilder press releases*. Retrieved February 21, 2010, from http://www.careerbuilder.com/share/aboutus/pressreleasesdetail.aspx?id=pr519&sd=8%2f19%2f2009&ed=12%2f31%2f2009&siteid=cbpr&scmp1=cb_pr519_ 181

Greenbank, P. (2011). Improving the process of career decision making: An action research approach. *Education & Training, 53*(4), 252–266. Retrieved from ERIC database. 56

Guiller, J., Durndell, A., & Ross, A. (2008). Peer interaction and critical thinking: Face-to-face or online discussion? *Learning and Instruction*, 18(2),187–200. 173, 174

Gurung, R. A. R. (2005). How do students really study (and does it matter?). *Teaching of Psychology, 32*(4), 239–241. Retrieved from Academic Search Premier database. 81, 95, 100

Hadis, B. F. (2005). Why are they better students when they come back? Determinants of academic focusing gains in the study abroad experience. *Frontiers: The Interdisciplinary Journal of Study Abroad, 11*, 57–70. Retrieved from ERIC database. 177

Hall, N., Hladkyj, S., Perry, R., & Ruthig, J. (2004). The role of attributional retraining and elaborative learning in college students' academic development. *Journal of Social Psychology, 144*(6), 591–612. Retrieved from Academic Search Premier database. 62, 81, 100

Hamilton, N. A., Catley, D., & Karlson, C. (2007). Sleep and the affective response to stress and pain. *Health Psychology, 26*, 288–295. doi:10.1037/0278-6133.26.3.288 217

Hamilton, R. J. (1997). Effects of three types of elaboration on learning concepts from text. Contemporary Educational Psychology, 22, 299–318. doi:10.1006/ceps.1997.0935 101

Hansen, C. J., Stevens, L. C., & Coast, J. R. (2001). Exercise duration and mood state: How much is enough to feel better? *Health Psychology, 20*, 267–275. doi:10.1037/0278-6133.20.4.267 217

Hansen, R. S. (2006). Benefits and problems with student teams: Suggestions for improving team projects. Journal of Education For Business, 82(1), 11-19. 125, 126

Harrison, Y., & Horne, J. (2000). The impact of sleep deprivation on decision making: A review. *Journal of Experimental Psychology: Applied, 6*(3), 236–249. doi:10.1037/1076-898X.6.3.236 217

Hartle, R., Baviskar, S., & Smith, R. (2012). A field guide to constructivism in the college science classroom: Four essential criteria and a guide to their usage. *Bioscene: Journal of College Biology Teaching, 38*(2), 31–35. 39

Hartley, M. T., (2011). Examining the relationships between resilience, mental health, and academic persistence in undergraduate college students. Journal of American College Health, 59(7), 596-604. 223

Hayati, A., & Shariatifar, S. (2009). Mapping strategies. *Journal of College Reading and Learning, 39*(2), 53–67. Retrieved from ERIC database. 85

Hayes-Bohanan, P., & Spievak, E. (2008). You can lead students to sources, but can you make them think? College and Undergraduate Libraries, 15(1-2), 173- 210. doi: 10.1080/10691310802177200 33

Head, A. J., & Eisenberg, M. B. (2009). What today's college students say about conducting research in the digital age. *Project Information Literacy Report*. Retrieved from http://projectinfolit.org/pdfs/PIL_ProgressReport_2_2009.pdf 146

Hefner, J., & Eisenberg, D. (2009). Social support and mental health among college students. *American Journal of Orthopsychiatry, 79*(4), 491–499. doi:10.1037/a0016918 227

Heikkilä, A., & Lonka, K. (2006). Studying in higher education: Students' approaches to learning, self-regulation, and cognitive strategies. *Studies in Higher Education, 31*(1), 99–117. doi:10.1080/03075070500392433 50

Henderson, F., Nunez-Rodriguez, N., & Casari, W. (2011). Enhancing research skills and information literacy in community college science students. *The American Biology Teacher, 73*(5), 270-275. 33

Hendry, G. D., Hyde, S. J., & Davy, P. (2005). Independent student study groups. *Medical Education, 39*(7), 672–679. doi:10.1111/j.1365-2929.2005.02199.x 98

Henry, J., Martinko, M., & Pierce, M. (1993). Attributional style as a predictor of success in a first computer course. *Computers in Human Behavior, 9*(4), 341–352. doi:10.1016/0747-5632(93)90027-P 224

Hill, P. L., Jackson, J. J., Roberts, B. W., Lapsley, D. K., & Brandenberger, J. W. (2011). Change you can believe in: Changes in goal setting during emerging and young adulthood predict later adult well-being. *Social Psychological and Personality Science, 2*(2), 123–131. doi:10.1177/1948550610384510 49, 50

Hochanadel, A., & Finamore, D. (2015). Fixed and growth mindset in education and how grit helps students persist in the face of adversity. *Journal of International Education Research, 11*(1), 47-50. 222

Holland, J. L. (1997). *Making vocational choices: Theory of vocational personalities and work environments*. Odessa, FL: Psychological Assessment Resources. 59, 65

Hopkins, M. M., & Yonker, R. D. (2015). Managing conflict with emotional intelligence: Abilities that make a difference. *Journal of Management Development, 34*(2), 226-244. doi:10.1108/JMD-04-2013-0051 124

Howard, H. E., & Jones, W. P. (2000). Effectiveness of a freshmen seminar in an urban university: Measurement of selected indicators. *College Student Journal, 34*, 509–515. Retrieved from Professional Development Collection database. 235, 236

Howard, R. M., Serviss, T., & Rodrigue, T. K. (2010). Writing from sources, writing from sentences. *Writing and Pedagogy, 2*(2), 177-192. Doi: 10.1558/wap.v2i2.177 143, 145

Hughes, A. (2010). 8 rules for perfecting your pitch. *Black Enterprise, 41*(1), 100. 184

Hughes, C., Toohey, S., & Velan, G. (2008). eMed Teamwork: A self-moderating system to gather peer feedback for developing and assessing teamwork skills. *Medical Teacher, 30*(1), 5-9. doi:10.1080/01421590701758632 128

Iglesias, S. L., Azzara, S., Squillace, M., Jeifetz, M., Lores Arnais, M. R., Desimone, M. F., & Diaz, L. E. (2005). A study on the effectiveness of a stress management programme for college students. *Pharmacy Education, 5*(1), 27–31. doi:10.1080/15602210400028614 202, 217

The Institute for College Access and Success (2013). *College debt and the class of 2012*. Retrieved from http://projectonstudentdebt.org/files/pub/classof2012.pdf 190

Ishitani, T. T., & Association for Institutional, R. (2009). The effects of academic programs and institutional characteristics on post-graduate social benefit behavior. *Association for Institutional Research*. Retrieved from ERIC database. 22

Issa, N., Schuller, M., Santacaterina, S., Shapiro, M., Wang, E., Mayer, R., & DaRosa, D. (2011). Applying multimedia design principles enhances learning in medical education. *Medical Education, 45*(8), 818–826. doi:10.1111/j.1365-2923.2011.03988.x 138

Jagger, L., Neukrug, E., & McAuliffe, G. (1992). Congruence between personality traits and chosen occupation as a predictor of job satisfaction for people with disabilities. *Rehabilitation Counseling Bulletin, 36*(1), 53–60. Retrieved from Academic Search Premier database. 59

Jaijairam, P. (2016). First-year seminar-The advantages that this course offers. *Journal of Education and Learning, 5*(2), 15-23. doi: 10.5539/jel.v5n2p15 7

Jobvite. (2014), Available at: http://www.jobvite.com/wpcontent/uploads/2014/10/Jobvite_SocialRecruiting_Survey2014.pdf 181

Johnson, E. C., Robbins, B. A., & Loui, M. C. (2015). What do students experience as peer leaders of learning teams? Advances in Engineering Education, 4(4), 1-22. 98

Johnson, J. (1997). Commuter college students: What factors determine who will persist and who will drop out? *College Student Journal, 31*(3), 323–332. Retrieved from PsycINFO database. 9

Johnson, M. & Ashton, B. (2015). Money matters on campus: Driving student success through financial literacy. *University Business, 18*(2), 22-23. 190

Johnston, L. D., O'Malley, P. M., Bachman, J. G., & Schulenberg, J. E. (2007). *Monitoring the future national survey results on drug use, 1975–2006: Volume 2, college students and adults ages 19–45* (NIH Publication No. 07–6206). Bethesda, MD: National Institute on Drug Abuse. 221

Jones, C. (1984). Interaction of absences and grades in a college course. *Journal of Psychology, 116*(1), 133. Retrieved from Academic Search Premier database. 86

Jones, M., Baldi, C., Phillips, C., & Waikar, A. (2016). The hard truth about soft skills: What recruiters look for in business graduates. *College Student Journal, 50*(3), 422-428. 108

Jones, S., Johnson-Yale, C., Millermaier, S., & Perez, F. S. (2008). Academic work, the Internet, and U.S. college students. *The Internet and Higher Education, 11*(3-4), 165–177. doi:10.1016/j.iheduc.2008.07.001 31

Jones, W. A. (2009). Football and freshmen retention: Examining the impact of college football on institutional retention rates. *Journal of College Student Retention: Research, Theory and Practice, 11*(4), 551–564. doi:10.2190/CS.11.4.f 216

Judge, T. A., Hurst, C., & Simon, L. S. (2009). Does it pay to be smart, attractive, or confident (or all three)? Relationships among general mental ability, physical attractiveness, core self-evaluations, and income. *Journal of Applied Psychology, 94*(3), 742–755. doi:10.1037/a0015497 63

Julian, T. A. and Kominski, R. A. (2011). Education and synthetic work–life earnings estimates. *American Community Survey Reports*, ACS-14. U.S. Census Bureau, Washington, DC. 24, 193

Junco, R. (2012). In-class multitasking and academic performance. *Computers in Human Behavior, 28*, 2236–2243. 119, 282

Karp, M. M., Raufman, J., Efhimiou, C., & Ritze, N. (2015). Redesigning a student success course for sustained impact: Early outcomes findings. CCRC Working Paper No. 81. 7

Karpicke, J. D., & Blunt, J. R. (2011). Retrieval practice produces more learning than elaborative studying with concept maps. *Science, 331*, 772–772. doi: 0.1126/science.1199327 80, 206, 282, 287

Karpicke, J. D., Butler, A. C., & Roediger, H. (2009). Metacognitive strategies in student learning: Do students practise retrieval when they study on their own?. *Memory, 17*(4), 471–479. doi:10.1080/09658210802647009 97, 206, 282

Karpicke, J. D., & Roediger, H. L. (2006). Repeated retrieval during learning is the key to long-term retention. *Journal of Memory and Language, 57*, 151–162. 82, 95, 96

Kennedy, R., & Kennedy, D. (2004). Using the Myers-Briggs Type Indicator" in career counseling. *Journal of Employment Counseling, 41*(1), 38–44. Retrieved from Academic Search Premier database. 66

Ketonen, E. E., Haarala-Muhonen, A., Hirsto, L., Hanninen, J. J., Wahala, K., & Lonka, K. (2016). Am I in the right place? Academic engagement and study success during the first years at university. Learning and Individual Differences, 51, 141-148. 203

Kiewra, K., DuBois, N., Christian, D., & McShane, A. (1988). Providing study notes: Comparison of three types of notes for review. *Journal of Educational Psychology, 80*(4), 595–597. doi:10.1037/0022-0663.80.4.595 91, 92

Kiewra, K., DuBois, N., Christian, D., McShane, A., Meyerhoffer, M., & Roskelley, D. (1991). Note-taking functions and techniques. *Journal of Educational Psychology, 83*(2), 240–245. doi:10.1037/0022-0663.83.2.240 91, 92

Kim, C., Tamborini, C. R., & Sakamoto, A. (2015). Field of study in college and lifetime earnings in the United States. *Sociology of Education, 88*(4), 320-339. doi: 10.1177/0038040715602232 25

Kitsantas, A., Winsler, A., & Huie, F. (2008). Self-regulation and ability predictors of academic success during college: A predictive validity study. *Journal of Advanced Academics, 20*(1), 42–68. Retrieved from Academic Search Premier database. 50

Kluemper, D. H., & Rosen, P. A. (2009). Future employment selection methods: Evaluating social networking web sites. Journal of Managerial Psychology, 24(6), 567-580. doi: 10.1108/02683940910974134 182

Komarraju, M., & Nadler, D. (2013). Self-efficacy and academic achievement: Why do implicit beliefs, goals, and effort regulation matter? *Learning and Individual Differences, 2567–2572. 53

Kornell, N., & Bjork, R. A. (2008). Optimising self-regulated study: The benefits—and costs—of dropping flashcards. *Memory, 16*(2), 125–136. doi:10.1080/09658210701763899 97

Kot, F. C. (2014). The impact of centralized advising on first-year academic performance and second-year enrollment behavior. *Research in Higher Education, 55*(6), 527-563. doi:10.1007/s11162-013-9325-4 169

Knight, L., & McKelvie, S. (1986). Effects of attendance, note-taking, and review on memory for a lecture: Encoding vs. external storage functions of notes. *Canadian Journal of Behavioural Science, 18*(1), 52–61. doi:10.1037/h0079957 88, 94

Knight, L. J., & McKelvie, S. J. (1986). Effects of attendance, note-taking, and review on memory for a lecture: Encoding vs. external storage functions of notes. *Canadian Journal of Behavioral Science, 18*(1), p. 52-61. 88, 94

Krätzig, G. P., & Arbuthnott, K. D. (2006). Perceptual learning style and learning proficiency: A test of the hypothesis. *Journal of Educational Psychology, 98*(1), 238–246. doi:10.1037/0022-0663.98.1.238 95

Kristjánsson, Á., Sigfúsdóttir, I., & Allegrante, J. (2010). Health behavior and academic achievement among adolescents: The relative contribution of dietary habits, physical activity, body mass index, and self-esteem. *Health Education & Behavior, 37*(1), 51–64. doi:10.1177/1090198107313481 217

Krumboltz, J., & Levin, A. (2004). *Luck is no accident: Making the most of happenstance in your life and career.* Atascadero, CA: Impact. 59

Krumboltz, J. D. (2009). The happenstance learning theory. Journal of Career Assessment, 17(2), 135-154. 59, 60

Krumrei-Mancuso, E. J., Newton, F. B., Kim, E., & Wilcox, D. (2013). Psychosocial factors predicting first-year college student success. *Journal of College Student Development, 54*(3), 247–266. Retrieved from ERIC database. 116

Kulm, T. L., & Cramer, S. (2006). The relationship of student employment to student role, family relationships, social interactions and persistence. *College Student Journal, 40*(4), 927–938. Retrieved from Academic Search Premier database. 115

Kuksov, D., & Villas-Boas, J. M. (2010). When more alternatives lead to less choice. *Marketing Science, 29*(3), 507-524. doi:10.1287/mksc.1090.0535 27

Kulik, C. T., & Roberson, L. (2008). Common goals and golden opportunities: Evaluations of diversity education in academic and organizational settings. *Academy of Management Learning & Education, 7*(3), 309-331. doi:10.5465/AMLE.2008.34251670 130

Lammers, W. J., Onwuegbuzie, A., & Slate, J. R. (2001). Academic success as a function of the gender, class, age, study habits, and employment of college students. *Research in the Schools, 8*(2), 71–81. Retrieved from PsycINFO database. 9, 81, 115

Larkin, J. E., LaPort, K. A., & Pines, H. A. (2007). Job choice and career relevance for today's college students. *Journal of Employment Counseling, 44*, 86-94. 115

Lee, Y., & Choi, J. (2011). A review of online course dropout research: Implications for practice and future research. *Educational Technology Research and Development, 59*(5), 593–618. 174

Lent, R. W., Brown, S. D., & Hackett, G. (1994). Toward a unifying social cognitive theory of career and academic interest, choice, and performance. *Journal of Vocational Behavior, 45*, 79-122. 57, 58

Lent, R. W., Brown, S. D., Talleyrand, R., McParthland, E. B., Davis, T., Chopra, S. B., Alexander, M. S., Leung, S. A. (2008). The big five career theories. In J. A. Athanasou and R. Van Esbroeck (Eds.) *International Handbook of Career Guidance*, Hong Kong, Spring Science and Business Media. 57

Levin, M. (2016, May 12). The most important rule of networking no one talks about. Inc. Retrieved from: http://www.inc.com/marissa-levin/the-most-important-rule-of-networking-no-one-talks-about.html 179

Lincoln, S., & Holmes, E. K. (2010). The psychology of ethical decisions: What affects the decision? *Psychological Services, 7*(2), 57–64. doi:10.1037/a0018710 110

Linde, J. A., Jeffery, R. W., Finch, E.A., Ng, D. M., & Rothman, A. J. (2004). Are unrealistic weight loss goals associated with outcomes for overweight women? *Obesity Research, 12*(2), 569–576. doi:10.1038/oby.2004.65 51, 52

Linderholm, T. (2002). Predictive inference generation as a function of working memory capacity and causal text constraints. *Discourse Process, 34*(3), 259–280. Retrieved from PsycINFO database. 84

Locke, E. A., & Latham, G. P. (2002). Building a practically useful theory of goal setting and task motivation: A 35-year odyssey. *American Psychologist, 57*(9), 705–717. doi:10.1037/0003066X.57.9.705 49, 51, 52, 54, 224

Latham, G. P., & Locke, E. A. (2006). Enhancing the benefits and overcoming the pitfalls of goal setting. *Organizational Dynamics, 35*(4), 332–340. Retrieved from Business Source Elite Database. 54

Loes, C., Pascarella, E., & Umbach, P. (2012). Effects of diversity experiences on critical thinking skills: Who benefits? *Journal of Higher Education, 83*(1), 1–25. Retrieved from Academic Search Premier. 44

Lopes, P. N. (2016). Emotional intelligence in organizations: Bridging research and practice. *Emotion Review, 8*(4), 316-321. doi:10.1177/1754073916650496 125

LoSchiavo, F., & Shatz, M. (2002). Students' reasons for writing on multiple-choice examinations. *Teaching of Psychology, 29*(2), 138–140. Retrieved from Academic Search Premier database. 156, 157

Lynch, D. J. (2006). Motivational strategies, learning strategies, and resource management as predictors of course grades. *College Student Journal, 40*(2), 423–428. Retrieved from Academic Search Premier database. 212

Lynch, D. (2007). "I've studied so hard for this course, but don't get it!" Differences between student and faculty perceptions. *College Student Journal, 41*(1), 22–24. Retrieved from Academic Search Premier database. 95

Macan, T. F., Shahani, C., Dipboye, R. L., & Phillips, A. P. (1990). College students' time management: Correlations with academic performance and stress. *Journal of Educational Psychology, 82*(4), 760–768. Retrieved from PsycINFO database. 112

MacDonald, T., MacDonald, G., Zanna, M., & Fong, G. (2000). Alcohol, sexual arousal, and intentions to use condoms in young men: Applying alcohol myopia theory to risky sexual behavior. *Health Psychology, 19*(3), 290–298. doi:10.1037/0278-6133.19.3.290 221

Mangels, J. A., Good, C., Whiteman, R. C., Maniscalco, B., & Dweck, C. S. (2012). Emotion blocks the path to learning under stereotype threat. *Social Cognitive and Affective Neuroscience, 7*(2), 230-241. doi:10.1093/scan/nsq100 130

Maslow, A. H. (1987). *Motivation and personality*. London: Harper & Row. 214

Mayer, R. E. (2009). *Multimedia learning* (2nd ed.). New York: Cambridge University Press. 87, 95, 139, 153, 154

McArther, J. (2011). Reconsidering the social and economic purposes of higher education. *Higher Education Research & Development, 30*(6), 737-749. doi: 10.1080/07294360.2010.539596. 21

McBride, D. M., & Dosher, B. (2002). A comparison of conscious and automatic memory processes for picture and word stimuli: A process dissociation analysis. *Consciousness and Cognition: An International Journal, 11*(3), 423–460. doi:10.1016/S1053-8100(02)00007-7 96

McCabe, D. L., Butterfield, K. D., & Trevino, L. K. (2012). *Cheating in college: Why students do it and what educators can do about it*. Baltimore: The John Hopkins University Press. 141

McCallum, S., & O'Connell, D. (2009). Social capital and leadership development." *Leadership & Organization Development Journal, 30*(2), 152-166. doi: 10.1108/01437730910935756. 131

McClain, L. (1983). Behavior during examinations: A comparison of 'A', 'C', and 'F' students. *Teaching of Psychology, 10*(2), 69. Retrieved from Academic Search Premier database. 156

McCorkle, D. E., Alexander, J. F., Reardon, J., & Kling, N. D. (2003). Developing self-marketing skills: Are marketing students prepared for the job search? *Journal of Marketing Education, 25*(3), 196-207. 180

McCrae, R. R., & Costa, P. T., Jr. (1990). *Personality in adulthood*. New York: Guildford. 64, 65

McDaniel, M., Howard, D., & Einstein, G. (2009). The read-recite-review study strategy: Effective and portable. *Psychological Science, 20*(4), 516–522. doi:10.1111/j.1467-9280.2009.02325.x 76, 84

Menzel, K., & Carrell, L. (1994). The relationship between preparation and performance in public speaking. *Communication Education, 43*(1), 17–26. doi:10.1080/0363452 9409378958 151

Meriam Library at California State University (2010). *Evaluating information: Applying the CRAAP test*. Retrieved from http://www.csuchico.edu/lins/handouts/eval_websites.pdf 31

Miller, G. A. (1956). The magical number seven, plus or minus two: Some limits on our capacity for processing information. *Psychological Review, 63*, 81–97. Retrieved from Academic Search Premier database. 10, 79

Miller, A., Shoptaugh, C., & Wooldridge, J. (2011). Reasons not to cheat, academic-integrity responsibility, and frequency of cheating. *Journal of Experimental Education, 79*(2), 169–184. doi:10.1080/00220970903567830 142

Miller, J. W., Janz, J. C., & Chen, C. (2007). The retention impact of a first-year seminar with varying pre-college academic performance. *Journal of the First-Year Experience and Students in Transition, 19*(1), 47-62. 7

Millis, B. J. (2002). Enhancing learning—and more!—through cooperative learning. *IDEA Paper #38*. Retrieved from http://www.theideacenter.org/sites/default/files/IDEA_Paper_38.pdf 99

Moeller, A. J., Theiler, J. M., & Wu, C. (2012). Goal setting and student achievement: A longitudinal Study. *Modern Language Journal, 96*(2), 153–169. Retrieved from Academic Search Premier. 49

Morisano, D., Hirsh, J. B., Peterson, J. B., Pihl, R. O., & Shore, B. M. (2010). Setting, elaborating, and reflecting on personal goals improves academic performance. *Journal of Applied Psychology, 95*(2), 255–264. doi:10.1037/a0018478 49

Mueller, C. M., & Dweck, C. S. (1998). Praise for intelligence can undermine children's motivation and performance. *Journal of Personality and Social Psychology, 75*(1), 33-52. Retrieved from PsycInfo database. 226

Murray, C., & Wren, C. T. (2003). Cognitive, academic, and attitudinal predictors of the grade point averages of college students with learning disabilities. *Journal of Learning Disabilities, 36*(5), 407–415. Retrieved from HealthSource: Nursing/Academic Edition database. 9

Myers, D. G. (2014). *Exploring psychology* (8th ed.). New York: Worth. 55, 78, 81, 88, 152, 210, 211, 213, 214, 215

National Service-Learning Clearinghouse (2013). *What is service learning?* Retrieved from http://www.servicelearning.org/what-service-learning 178

Nauta, M. M. (2010). The development, evolution, and status of Holland's theory of vocational personalities: Reflections and future directions for counseling psychology. *Journal of Counseling Psychology, 57*(1), 11–22. doi:10.1037/a0018213 59

Nauta, M. M., & Kokaly, M. L. (2011). Assessing role model influences on students' academic and vocational decisions. *Journal of Career Assessment, 9*(1), 81-99. 56

Nelson, D.W., and Knight, A.E. (2010). The power of positive recollections: Reducing test anxiety and enhancing college student efficacy and performance. *Journal of Applied Social Psychology, 40*(3), 732–745. doi:10.1111/j.1559-1816.2010.00595.x 156

Nes, L., Evans, D. R., & Segerstrom, S. C. (2009). Optimism and college retention: Mediation by motivation, performance, and adjustment. *Journal of Applied Social Psychology, 39*(8), 1887–1912. doi:10.1111/j.1559-1816.2009.00508.x 224

New, J. (2016, December 13). Looking for career help. Inside Higher Ed. Retrieved from: https://www.insidehighered.com/news/2016/12/13/only-17-percent-recent-graduates-say-career-centers-are-very-helpful?utm_source=Inside+Higher+Ed&utm_campaign=b9ab9667e8-DNU20161213&utm_medium=email&utm_term=0_1fcbc04421-b9ab9667e8-199685953&goal=0_1fcbc04421-b9ab9667e8-199685953&mc_cid=b9ab9667e8&mc_eid=1bd4cf0705 180

Nonis, S. A., & Hudson, G. I. (2006). Academic performance of college students: Influence of time spent studying and working. *Journal of Education for Business, 81*(3), 151–159. Retrieved from ERIC database. 115

Nonis, S. A., Philhours, M. J., & Hudson, G. I. (2006). Where does the time go? A diary approach to business and marketing students' time use. *Journal of Marketing Education, 28*(2), 121–134. Retrieved from ERIC database. 113

Oley, N. (1992). Extra credit and peer tutoring: Impact on the quality of writing in Introductory Psychology in an open admissions college. *Teaching of Psychology, 19*(2), 78. Retrieved from Academic Search Premier database. 151

Oreopoulos, P., & Petronijevic, U. (2013). Making college worth it: A review of the returns to higher education. The *Future of Children, 23*(1), 41-65. 25

Oswalt, S., Cameron, K., & Koob, J. (2005). Sexual regret in college students. *Archives of Sexual Behavior, 34*(6), 663–669. doi:10.1007/s10508-005-7920-y 221

Oviedo, V., Tornquist, M., Cameron, T., & Chiappe, D. (2015). Effects of media multi-tasking with Facebook on the enjoyment and encoding of TV episodes. *Computers in Human Behavior, 51*(Pt A), 407-417. doi:10.1016/j.chb.2015.05.022 119

Palumbo, M. V., & Steele-Johnson, D. (2014). Do test perceptions influence test performance? Exploring stereotype threat theory. *North American Journal of Psychology, 16*(1), 1-12. 130

Parsons, F. (1909). *Choosing a vocation.* Boston: Houghton Mifflin. 56

Pashler, H., McDaniel, M., Rohrer, D., & Bjork, R. (2008). Learning styles: Concepts and evidence. *Psychological Science in the Public Interest, 9*(3), 105–119. doi:10.1111/j.1539.6053.2009.01038 95

Pauk, W., & Ross, J. Q. O. (2008). *How to study in college* (9th ed.). Boston: Houghton Mifflin. 92

Perlman, B., McCann, L. I., & Prust, A. (2007). Students' grades and ratings of perceived effectiveness of behaviors influencing academic performance. *Teaching of Psychology, 34*(4), 236–240. doi:10.1080/00986280701700284 49

Perry, W. G. (1970). *Forms of intellectual and ethical development in the college years.* New York: Holt, Rinehart and Winston. 39

Perry, R. P., Stupnisky, R. H., Hall, N. C., Chipperfield, J. G., & Weiner, B. (2010). Bad starts and better finishes: Attributional retraining and initial performance in competitive achievement settings. *Journal of Social and Clinical Psychology, 29*(6), 668–700. Retrieved from Academic Search Premier database. 208

Peterson, R. M., & Dover, H. F. (2014). Building student networks with LinkedIn: The potential for connections, internships, and jobs. *Marketing Education Review, 24*(1), 15-20. doi: 10.2753/MER1052-8008240102 183

Peverly, S. T., Brobst, K. E., Graham, M., & Shaw, R. (2003). College adults are not good at self-regulation: A study on the relationship of self-regulation, note taking, and test taking. *Journal of Educational Psychology, 95*(2), 335-346. doi: 10.1037/0022-0663.95.2.335 88

Phillips, S. D., Christopher-Sisk, E. K., & Gravino, K. L. (2001). Making career decisions in a relational context. *The Counseling Psychologist, 29*(2), 193-213. 57

Pierceall, E. A., & Keim, M. C. (2007). Stress and coping strategies among community college students. *Community College Journal of Research and Practice, 31*(9), 703–712. doi:10.1080/10668920600866579 217

Plecha, M. (1998). Influence of study group attendance and students' perceived helpfulness on expected grade. Retrieved from ERIC database. 98

Pluess, M., Conrad, A., & Wilhelm, F. (2009). Muscle tension in generalized anxiety disorder: A critical review of the literature. *Journal of Anxiety Disorders, 23*(1), 1–11. doi:10.1016/j.janxdis.2008.03.016 219

Poirier, C. R., & Feldman, R. S. (2004). Teaching in cyberspace: Online versus traditional instruction using a waiting-list experimental design. *Teaching of Psychology, 31*(1), 59–62. 174

Poppick, S. (2015). Here's what the average grad makes out of college. Retrieved from: http://time.com/money/collection-post/3829776/heres-what-the-average-grad-makes-right-out-of-college/ 191

Potts, G., & Schultz, B. (2008). The freshman seminar and academic success of at-risk students. *College Student Journal, 42*(2), 647–658. Retrieved from PsycINFO database. 7

PRNewswire (2013, April 25). It's who you know: Survey:-Quality trumps quantity for IT professionals when networking. *PR Newswire US.* Retrieved from Regional Business News database. 201304250807PR.NEWS.USPR.SF01372 180

Prater, C. (2010). *A Guide to the Credit Card Act of 2009.* Retrieved from http://www.creditcards.com/credit-card-news/credit-card-law-interactive-1282.php 195

Prince, M. (2004). Does active learning work? A review of the research. *Journal of Engineering Education, 93*(3), 223–231. 98

Quimby, J. L., & DeSantis, A. M., (2006). The influence of role models on women's career choices. The *Career Development Quarterly, 54*, 297-306. 57

Raffety, B., Smith, R., & Ptacek, J. (1997). Facilitating and debilitating trait anxiety, situational anxiety, and coping with an anticipated stressor: A process analysis. *Journal of Personality and Social Psychology, 72*(4), 892–906. doi:10.1037/0022-3514.72.4.892 151, 217

Raimes, A., & Jerskey, M. (2011). *Keys for writers* (6th ed.). Boston: Wadsworth. 34, 143

Ramler, T. R., Tennison, L. R., Lynch, J., & Murphy, P. (2016). Mindfulness and the college transition: The efficacy of an adapted mindfulness-based stress reduction intervention in fostering adjustment among first-year students. *Mindfulness, 7*(1), 179-188. doi:10.1007/s12671-015-0398-3 217, 219

Raskind, M. H., Goldberg, R. J., Higgins, E. L., & Herman, K. L. (1999). Patterns of change and predictors of success in individuals with learning disabilities: Results from a twenty-year longitudinal study. *Learning Disabilities Research and Practice, 14*, 35–49. doi:10.1207/sldrp1401_4 229

Rath, S. (2008). Converting distress into stress. *Social Science International, 24*(1), 98–103. Retrieved from PsycINFO database. 217

Rawes, E. (2014). 5 common unprofessional workplace behaviors. USA Today. Retrieved from: http://www.usatoday.com/story/money/business/2014/08/02/unprofessional-workplace-behaviors/13420381/ 111

Rawson, K. A., Dunlosky, J., & Thiede, K. W. (2000). The rereading effect: Absolute monitoring accuracy improves across reading trials. *Memory & Cognition, 28*, 1004–1010. Retrieved from Academic Search Premier database. 82, 84

Recht, D. R., & Leslie, L. (1988). Effect of prior knowledge on good and poor readers' memory of text. *Journal Of Educational Psychology, 80*, 16–20. doi:10.1037/00220663.80.1.16 83, 282

Reio, T. R., & Crim, S. J. (2006). The emergence of social presence as an overlooked factor in asynchronous online learning. Retrieved from ERIC database. 174

Reynolds, J. R., & Baird, C. L. (2010). Is there a downside to shooting for the stars? Unrealized educational expectations and symptoms of depression. *American Sociological Review, 75*(1), 151–172. 52

Robb, C. A., Moody, B., & Abdel-Ghany, M. (2012). College student persistence to degree: The burden of debt. *Journal of College Student Retention: Research, Theory & Practice, 13*(4), 431–456. 190

Robins, J. W., Kiken, L., Holt, M., & McCain, N. L. (2014). Mindfulness: An effective coaching tool for improving physical and mental health. *Journal of The American Association Of Nurse Practitioners, 26*(9), 511-518. doi:10.1002/2327-6924.12086 220

Robles, M. M. (2012). Executive perceptions of the top 10 soft skills needed in today's workplace. *Business Communication Quarterly, 75*(4), 453–465. Retrieved from ERIC database. 64, 109, 145

Rode, J. C., Arthaud-Day, M. L., Mooney, C. H., Near, J. P., & Baldwin, T. T. (2008). Ability and personality predictors of salary, perceived job success, and perceived career success in the initial career stage. *International Journal of Selection & Assessment, 16*(3), 292–299. doi:10.1111/j.1468-2389.2008.00435.x 64

Rohrer, D., & Pashler, H. (2012). Learning styles: Where's the evidence? *Medical Education, 46*(7), 634–635. doi:10.1111/j.1365-2923.2012.04273.x 95

Roney, C. R., & O'Connor, M. C. (2008). The interplay between achievement goals and specific target goals in determining performance. *Journal of Research in Personality, 42*(2), 482–489. doi:10.1016/j.jrp.2007.07.001 54

Rotter, J. B. (1990). Internal versus external control of reinforcement: A case history of a variable. *American Psychologist, 45*(4), 489–493. doi:10.1037/0003-066X.45.4.489 225

Rubin, L., & Hebert, C. (1998). Model for active learning: Collaborative peer teaching. *College Teaching, 46*(1), 26–30. 98

Russo, K. (2015). Hard skills vs. soft skills: What they mean to your job search and the weight they carry with HR. Huffington Post. Retrieved from: http://www.huffingtonpost.com/kristi-russo/hard-skills-vs-soft-skill_b_8341566.html 108

Ryan, M. (2013). Improving retention and academic achievement for first-time students at a two-year college. *Community College Journal of Research & Practice, 37*(2), 130–134. doi:10.1080/106689 26.2012.715266 169

Ryan, R. M., & Deci, E. L. (2000). Self-determination theory and the facilitation of intrinsic motivation, social development, and well-being. *American Psychologist, 55*(1), 68–78. doi:10.1037/0003-066X.55.1.68 215

Salary.com (2014). *Teacher elementary school, New York City and San Antonio.* Retrieved from http://swz.salary.com/SalaryWizard/Teacher-Elementary-School-Salary-Details-San-Antonio-TX.aspx 68

Salisbury, F., & Karasmans, S. (2011). Are they ready? Exploring student information literacy skills in the transition from secondary to tertiary education. *Australian Academic and Research Libraries, 42*(1), 43-58. 31, 32

Samson, S. (2010). Information literacy learning outcomes and student success. *The Journal of Academic Librarianship, 36*(3), 202-210. 28, 32

Sana, F., Weston, T., & Cepeda, N. J. (2013). Laptop multitasking hinders classroom learning for both users and nearby peers. *Computers and Education, 62*, 24–31. 119, 285

Sánchez Abril, P., Levin, A., & Del Riego, A. (2012). Blurred boundaries: Social media privacy and the twenty-first-century employee. *American Business Law Journal, 49*(1), 63–124. doi:10.1111/j.1744-1714.2011.01127.x 181, 183

Sanders, M. L. (2012). *Becoming a learner: Realizing the opportunity of education.* Institute for Communication and Leadership. 22, 140, 142

Sarfo, F., & Elen, J. (2011). Investigating the impact of positive resource interdependence and individual accountability on students' academic performance in cooperative learning. *Electronic Journal of Research in Educational Psychology, 9*(1), 73–94. Retrieved from ERIC database. 99, 128

Sargent, L. D., & Domberger, S. R. (2007). Exploring the development of a protean career orientation: Values and image violations. *Career Development International, 12*(6), 545–564. doi:10.1108/13620430710822010 62

Schloemer, P., & Brenan, K. (2006). From students to learners: Developing self-regulated learning. *Journal of Education for Business, 82*(2), 81–87. 55, 203

Schmidt, H. G., & Moust, J. C. (1998). *Processes that shape small-group tutorial learning: A review of research.* Retrieved from ERIC database. 98, 282

Schreiber, L. M., & Valle, B. (2013). Social constructivist teaching strategies in the small group classroom. *Small Group Research, 44*(4), 395–411. doi:10.1177/1046496413488422. 131

Schunk, D. H. (1990). Goal setting and self-efficacy during self-regulated learning. *Educational Psychologist, 25*(1), 71–86. 50

Schutte, N. S., & Loi, N. M. (2014). Connections between emotional intelligence and workplace flourishing. *Personality and Individual Differences, 66*134-139. doi:10.1016/j.paid.2014.03.031 124

Schwartz, B. L., Son, L. K., Kornell, N., & Finn, B. (2011). Four principles of memory improvement: A guide to improving learning efficiency. *The International Journal of Creativity and Problem Solving, 21*(1), 7–15. 101, 128, 218

Seery, M. D., Holman, E., & Silver, R. (2010). Whatever does not kill us: Cumulative lifetime adversity, vulnerability, and resilience. *Journal of Personality and Social Psychology, 99*(6), 1025–1041. doi:10.1037/a0021344 222, 224

Seifert, L. S. (1997). Activating representations in permanent memory: Different benefits for pictures and words. *Journal of Experimental Psychology: Learning, Memory, and Cognition, 23*(5), 1106–1121. doi:10.1037/0278-7393.23.5.1106 95

Seifert, T., Goodman, K., Lindsay, N., Jorgensen, J., Wolniak, G., Pascarella, E., & Blaich, C. (2008). The effects of liberal arts experiences on liberal arts outcomes. *Research in Higher Education, 49*(2), 107–125. doi:10.1007/s11162-007-9070-7 171

Seijts, G. H., & Latham, G. P. (2011). The effect of commitment to a learning goal, self-efficacy, and the interaction between learning goal difficulty and commitment on performance in a business simulation. *Human Performance, 24*(3), 189–204. doi:10.1080/08959285.2011.580807 54, 133

Seijts, G. H., & Latham, G. P. (2012). Knowing when to set learning versus performance goals. *Organizational Dynamics, 41*(1), 1-6. doi:10.1016/j.orgdyn.2011.12.001 54, 133

Seligman, M., Steen, T., Park, N., & Peterson, C. (2005). Positive psychology progress: Empirical validation of interventions. *American Psychologist, 60*(5), 410–421. doi:10.1037/0003-066X.60.5.410 224

Sellnow, D. D. (2005). *Confident public speaking* (2nd ed.). Belmont, CA: Wadsworth. 152

Shatz, M., & Best, J. (1987). Students' reasons for changing answers on objective tests. *Teaching of Psychology, 14*(4), 241. Retrieved from Academic Search Premier database. 158

Shellenbarger, T. (2009). Time and project management tips for educators. *The Journal of Continuing Education In Nursing, 40*(7), 292-293. doi:10.3928/00220124-20090623-08 115, 116, 117, 120

Shen, Z. (2015). Cultural competence models and cultural competence assessment instruments in nursing: A literature review. *Journal of Transcultural Nursing, 26*(3), 308-321. doi:10.1177/1043659614524790 129

Shimazoe, J., & Aldrich, H. (2010). Group work can be gratifying: Understanding and overcoming resistance to cooperative learning. *College Teaching, 58*(2), 52–57. doi:10.1080/87567550903418594 98

Sironi, M. (2012). Education and mental health in Europe: School attainment as a means to fight depression. *International Journal of Mental Health, 41*(3), 79–105. Retrieved from PsycINFO database. 23

Skinner, N. (2009). Academic folk wisdom: Fact, fiction, and falderal. *Psychology Learning & Teaching, 8*(1), 46–50. Retrieved from PsycINFO database. 158

Smart, J. C., Feldman, K. A., & Ethington, C. A., (2006). Holland's theory and patterns of college student success. *National Postsecondary Education Cooperative.* 1-44. 59

Smetana, L., & Bell, R. L. (2012). Computer simulations to support science instruction and learning: A critical review of the literature. *International Journal of Science Education, 34*(9), 1337–1370. 96

So, J. Y., & Chan, A. S. (2009). Validity of highlighting on text comprehension. *AIP Conference Proceedings, 1177*(1), 217–224. doi:10.1063/1.3256250 85

Sommer, R., & Sommer, B. (2009). The dreaded essay exam. *Teaching of Psychology, 36*(3), 197–199. doi:10.1080/00986280902959820 158

Son, L. K., & Metcalfe, J. (2000). Metacognitive and control strategies in study-time allocation. *Journal of Experimental Psychology: Learning, Memory, and Cognition, 26*(1), 204–221. doi:10.1037/0278-7393.26.1.204 117

Sparkman, L. A., Maulding, W. S., & Roberts, J. G. (2012). Non-cognitive predictors of student success in college. *College Student Journal, 46*(3), 642-652. 124

Spieker, C. J., & Hinsz, V. B. (2004). Repeated success and failure influences on self-efficacy and personal goals. *Social Behavior & Personality: An International Journal, 32*(2), 191–197. 53

Srivastava, T. K., Waghmare, L. S., Mishra, V. P., Rawekar, A. T., Quazi, N., & Jagzape, A. T. (2015). Peer teaching to foster learning in physiology. *Journal of Clinical and Diagnostic Research, 9*(8), 1-6. doi: 10.7860/JCDR/2015/15018.6323 98

Sterling, E., Bravo, A., Porzecanski, A. L., Burks, R. L., Linder, J., Langen, T., Fernandez, D., Ruby, D., & Bynum, N. (2016). Think before (and after) you speak: Practice and self-reflection bolster oral communication skills. Journal of College Science Teaching, 45 (6), 87- 99. Doi: 10.2505/4/jcst16_045_06_87 155

Stewart, J. (2006). Transformational leadership: An evolving concept examined through the works of Burns, Bass, Avolio, and Leithwood. *Canadian Journal of Educational Administration and Policy, 54*, 1-29. 132

Stinebrickner, R., & Stinebrickner, T. R. (2004). Time-use and college outcomes. *Journal of Econometrics, 121*(1/2), 243–269. doi:10.1016/j.jeconom.2003.10.013 115

Stone, M. J., & Petrick, J. F. (2013). The educational benefits of travel experiences: A literature review. *Journal of Travel Research, 52*(6), 731–744. 176, 178

Stowell, J., & Bennett, D. (2010). Effects of online testing on student exam performance and test anxiety. *Journal of Educational Computing Research, 42*(2), 161–171. doi:10.2190/EC.42.2.b 160

Strage, A., Baba, Y., Millner, S., Scharberg, M., Walker, E., Williamson, R., & Yoder, M. (2002). What every student affairs professional should know: Student study activities and beliefs associated with academic success. *Journal of College Student Development, 43*(2), 246–266. Retrieved from PsycINFO database. 87, 229

Strang, K. (2011). How can discussion forum questions be effective in online MBA courses? *Campus-Wide Information Systems, 28*(2), 80–92. Retrieved from ERIC database. 43

Strap, C. M., & Farr, R. J. (2010). To get involved or not: The relation among extracurricular involvement, satisfaction, and academic achievement. *Teaching of Psychology, 37*(1), 50–54. doi:10.1080/00986280903425870 215

Strehlke, C. (2010). Social network sites: A starting point for career development practitioners. *Journal of Employment Counseling, 47*, 38-48. 183

Stupnisky, R., Renaud, R., Perry, R., Ruthig, J., Haynes, T., & Clifton, R. (2007). Comparing self-esteem and perceived control as predictors of first-year college students' academic achievement. *Social Psychology of Education, 10*(3), 303–330. doi:10.1007/s11218-007-9020-4 212, 225

Sukkon, B. Z. (2016, June 20). Higher education's public purpose. Association of American Colleges & Universities. Retrieved from: https://www.aacu.org/leap/liberal-education-nation-blog/higher-educations-public-purpose 22

Sulastri, A., Handoko, M., & Janssens, J. M. A. M. (2015). Grade point average and biographical data in personal resumes: Predictors of finding employment. *International Journal of Adolescence and Youth, 20*(3), 306-316. doi: 10.1080/02673843.2014.996236 177, 180, 185

Sundheim, K. (2011, July 27). Networking: It's not about who you know, it's about who knows you. Business Finder. Retrieved from: http://www.businessinsider.com/networking-its-not-about-who-you-know-its-about-who-knows-you-2011-5 179

Swenson, L., Nordstrom, A., & Hiester, M. (2008). The role of peer relationships in adjustment to college. *Journal of College Student Development, 49*(6), 551–567. doi:10.1353/csd.0.0038 228

Tang, Y., Hölzel, B. K., & Posner, M. I. (2015). The neuroscience of mindfulness meditation. *Nature Reviews Neuroscience, 16*(4), 213-225. doi:10.1038/nrn3916 219

Tham, C., & Werner, J. M. (2005). Designing and evaluating e-learning in higher education: A review and recommendations. *Journal of Leadership & Organizational Studies, 11*(2), 15–25. doi:10.1177/107179190501100203 174

Thatcher, A., Fridjhon, P., & Cockcroft, K. (2007). The relationship between lecture attendance and academic performance in an undergraduate psychology class. *South African Journal of Psychology, 37*(3), 656–660. Retrieved from Academic Search Premier database. 86

Thompson, D. E., Orr, B., Thompson, C., & Grover, K. (2007). Examining students' perceptions of their first semester experience at a major land-grant institution. *College Student Journal, 41*(3), 640–648. Retrieved from Academic Search Premier database. 112

Timberlake, S. (2005). Social capital and gender in the workplace. *The Journal of Management Development, 24*(1), 34-44. 179

Tozoglu, D., Tozoglu, M. D., Gurses, A., & Dogar, C. (2004). The students' perceptions: Essay versus multiple-choice type exams. *Journal of Baltic Science Education,* (6), 52–59. Retrieved from Academic Search Premier database. 156

Trail-Ross, M. (2012). Linking classroom learning to the community through service learning. *Journal of Community Health Nursing, 29*(1), 53–60. doi:10.1080/07370016.2012.6457 46 178

Travis, T., (2011). From the classroom to the boardroom: The impact of information literacy instruction on workplace research skills. *Education Libraries, 34*(2), 19-31. 29, 31, 241

Triandis, H. C., & Suh, E. M. (2002). Cultural influences on personality. *Annual Review of Psychology, 53*(1), 133–160. doi:10.1146/annurev.psych.53.100901.135200 25

Trockel, M., Barnes, M., & Egget, D. (2000). Health-related variables and academic performance among first-year college students: Implications for sleep and other behaviors. *Journal of American College Health, 49*(3), 125. Retrieved from Academic Search Premier database. 217

Trostel, P. A. (2010). The Fiscal Impacts of College Attainment. *Research In Higher Education, 51*(3), 220-247. doi:10.1007/s11162-009-9156-5 25

Turner, J. E., & Husman, J. (2008). Emotional and cognitive self-regulation following academic shame. *Journal of Advanced Academics, 20*(1), 138–173. 54

Ungar, M. (2013). Resilience, trauma, context, and culture. *Trauma, Violence, & Abuse, 14*(3), 255–266. Retrieved from PsycINFO database. 227

Valentine, B. (2001). The legitimate effort in research papers: Student commitment versus faculty expectations. *The Journal of Academic Librarianship, 27*(2), 107–115. doi:10.1016/S0099-1333(00)00182-8 31

Valle, A., Cabanach, R. G., Nunez, J. C., Gonzalez-Pienda, J., Rodriguez, S., & Pineiro, I. (2003). Multiple goals, motivation and academic learning. *British Journal of Educational Psychology, 73*(1), 71. 140

Van Hoye, G., van Hooft, E. A. J., & Lievens, F. (2009). Networking as a job search behavior: A social network perspective. *Journal of Occupational and Organizational Psychology, 82*, 661-682. Doi: 10.1348/096317908X360675 180, 184

Vaughan, A. L., Lucas, K., Pote, S. (February, 2014). The role of a first year seminar course on student self-determination. Paper presented at the annual meeting on the First Year Experience, San Diego, CA 215

Velez, G. S., & Giner, G. R. (2015). Effects of business internships on students, employers, and higher education institutions: A systematic review. *Journal of Employment Counseling, 52*, 121- 130. 176

Vertsberger, D., & Gati, I. (2015). The effectiveness of sources of support in career decision-making: A two-year follow up. Journal of Vocational Behavior, 89, 151-161. Doi: 10.1016/j.jvb.2015.06.004 61, 62

Villar, E., Juan, J., Corominas, E., & Capell, D. (2000). What kind of networking strategy advice should career counsellors offer university graduates searching for a job? *British Journal of Guidance and Counselling, 28*(3), 389-409. 180, 184

Vilorio, D. (2011). Focused jobseeking: A measured approach for looking for work. *Occupational Outlook Quarterly,* 2-11. 189

Wade, C. (2008). Critical thinking: Needed now more than ever. In D. Dunn, J. S. Halonen, & R. A. Smith (Eds.), *Teaching critical thinking in psychology: A handbook of best practices,* 11–22 Chichester, West Sussex: Wiley-Blackwell. 39

Walker, C. O., Greene, B. A., & Mansell, R. A. (2006). Identification with academics, intrinsic/extrinsic motivation, and self-efficacy as predictors of cognitive engagement. *Learning and Individual Differences, 16*(1), 1–12. doi:10.1016/j.lindif.2005.06.004 209

Walker, I., & Crogan, M. (1998). Academic performance, prejudice, and the Jigsaw classroom: New pieces to the puzzle. *Journal of Community & Applied Social Psychology, 8*(6), 381-393. doi:10.1002/(SICI)1099-1298(199811/12)8:6<381::AID-CASP457>3.0.CO;2-6 131

Wallace, D. L., Hayes, J. R., Center for the Study of Writing, B. A., & Center for the Study of Writing, P. A. (1990). Redefining revision for freshmen. *Occasional paper no. 21.* Retrieved from ERIC database. 149

Warr, P., & Pearce, A. (2004). Preferences for careers and organisational cultures as a function of logically related personality traits. *Applied Psychology: An International Review, 53*(3), 423–435. doi:10.1111/j.1464-0597.2004.00178.x 64

Waschull, S. B. (2005). Predicting success in online psychology courses: Self-discipline and motivation. *Teaching of Psychology, 32*(3), 190–192. doi:10.1207/s15328023top3203_11 174, 209

Washington Higher Education Coordinating, B. (2012). Key Facts about Higher Education in Washington. 2012. *Washington Higher Education Coordinating Board.* Retrieved from ERIC. 23–24, 25

Weible, R. (2009). Are universities reaping the available benefits internship programs offer? *Journal of Education for Business, 85*(2), 59–63. Retrieved from Business Source Elite database. 177

Werner, E. E. (1989). High-risk children in young adulthood: A longitudinal study from birth to 32 years. *American Journal of Orthopsychiatry, 59*(1), 72-81. doi:10.1111/j.1939-0025.1989.tb01636.x 227

West, E. J. (2004). Perry's legacy: Models of epistemological development. *Journal of Adult Development, 11*(2), 61–70. doi:10.1023/B:JADE.0000024540.12150.69 39

Wilcox, P., Winn, S., & Fyvie-Gauld, M. (2005). "It was nothing to do with the university, it was just the people": The role of social support in the first-year experience of higher education. *Studies in Higher Education, 30*(6), 707–722. doi:10.1080/03075070500340036 227

Williamson, G. L. (2008). A text readability continuum for postsecondary readiness. *Journal of Advanced Academics, 19*(4), 602–632. Retrieved from PsycINFO database. 82

Willingham, D. T. (2009). *Why don't students like school? A cognitive scientist answers questions about how the mind works and what it means for the classroom.* San Francisco: Jossey-Bass. 42, 78, 95

Winston, M. D., & Bahnaman, S. (2008). Preparation for ethical decision-making: An analysis of research in professional education. *Library & Information Science Research (07408188), 30*(3), 222–230. doi:10.1016/j.lisr.2008.02.007 110

Wintre, M., & Yaffe, M. (2000). First-year students' adjustment to university life as a function of relationships with parents. *Journal of Adolescent Research, 15*(1), 9–37. doi:10.1177/0743558400151002 228

Wise, A., Saghafian, M., & Padmanabhan, P. (2012). Towards more precise design guidance: specifying and testing the functions of assigned student roles in online discussions. *Educational Technology Research & Development, 60*(1), 55–82. doi:10.1007/s11423-011-9212-7 127, 128

Wolfe, C. T., & Spencer, S. J. (1996). Stereotypes and prejudice: Their overt and subtle influence in the classroom. American Behavioral Scientist, 40(2), 176-185. doi:10.1177/0002764296040002008 130, 131

Wolff, H., & Moser, K. (2009). Effects of networking on career success: A longitudinal study. Journal of Applied Psychology, 94(1), 196-206. 180, 184

Wood, E., Zivcakavoa, L, Gentile, P, Archer, K., De Pasquale, D., & Nosko, A. (2012). Examining the impact of off-task multi-tasking with technology on real-time classroom learning. *Computers and Education, 58*(1), 365–374. doi: 10/1016/ j.compedu.2011.08.029 119

Woolfolk, A. (2013). *Educational psychology* (12th edition). Boston: Pearson Education. 55, 79, 212

Workman, J. L. (2015). Parental influence on exploratory students' college choice, major, and career decision making. College Student Journal, 49(1), 23-30. 56

Yakovlev, P., & Leguizamon, S. (2012). Ignorance is not bliss: On the role of education in subjective well-being. *Journal of Socio-Economics, 41*(6), 806–815. doi:10.1016/j.socec.2012.08.009 23

Young, D. G., & Hopp, J. M. (2014). 2012-2013 *National Survey of First-Year Seminars: Exploring high-impact practices in the first college year* (Research Report No. 4). Columbia, SC: University of South Carolina, National Resource Center for the First-Year Experience & Students in Transition. 8

Zhang, W., Chen, Q., McCubbin, H., McCubbin, L., & Foley, S. (2011). Predictors of mental and physical health: Individual and neighborhood levels of education, social well-being, and ethnicity. *Health & Place, 17*(1), 238–247. doi:10.1016/j.healthplace.2010.10.0085884.2008.00370. 23

Zimmerman, B. J. (1998). Academic studying and the development of personal skill: A self-regulatory perspective. *Educational Psychologist, 33*(2/3), 73. 205

Zimmerman, B. J. (2002). Becoming a self-regulated learner: An overview. *Theory into Practice, 41*(2), 64–72. Retrieved from ERIC database. New York: Free Press. 51, 53, 55

Subject Index